NO MAN'S LAND

NO MAN'S LAND

Globalization, Territory, and
Clandestine Groups in Southeast Asia

Justin V. Hastings

CORNELL UNIVERSITY PRESS, ITHACA AND LONDON

First published 2010 by Cornell University Press
First printing, Cornell Paperbacks, 2010
Printed in the United States of America

Library of Congress Cataloging-in-Publication Data

Hastings, Justin V. (Justin VanOverloop)
    No man's land : globalization, territory, and clandestine groups in Southeast Asia / Justin V. Hastings.
        p. cm.
    Includes bibliographical references and index.
    ISBN 978-0-8014-4889-8 (cloth : alk. paper)
    ISBN 978-0-8014-7679-2 (pbk.)
    1. Terrorism—Southeast Asia.   2. Secret societies—Southeast Asia.
3. Transnational crime—Southeast Asia.   4. Human territoriality—Southeast Asia.   5. Jemaah Islamiyah (Organization)   6. Gerakan Aceh Merdeka.   I. Title.
    HV6433.A785H37 2010
    363.3250959—dc22   2010017130

Cornell University Press strives to use environmentally responsible suppliers and materials to the fullest extent possible in the publishing of its books. Such materials include vegetable-based, low-VOC inks and acid-free papers that are recycled, totally chlorine-free, or partly composed of nonwood fibers. For further information, visit our website at www.cornellpress.cornell.edu.

Cloth printing   10 9 8 7 6 5 4 3 2 1
Paperback printing   10 9 8 7 6 5 4 3 2 1

Contents

Tables, Figures, and Maps

TABLES

FIGURES

MAPS

Preface and Acknowledgments

I came to study Southeast Asia in general, and Indonesia more specifically, almost by accident. As an undergraduate, I spent four years studying Chinese, but when it came time to choose a senior thesis topic, I decided that staying focused on one country was too confining—particularly if my university was going to pay for me to spend a summer wandering around doing field research. Thailand seemed as good a place as any—great food, tropical weather, and safely exotic. As a result, I spent a month in Chiang Mai doing research that compared how Thailand and China's view of their ethnic minorities as national security problems affected the policies the governments adopted toward them. My experience in Thailand ignited a genuine interest in Southeast Asia's people and culture.

Several years later, during my first week of graduate school, I was looking for another region to study that had problems with political violence and weak states. Less than a year after 9/11, the Middle East seemed for obvious reasons like the best place to start, so I signed up for an introductory course in Arabic. On the first day of class, the teacher went through the alphabet and asked all the students to explain why they were studying Arabic. After I gave a boilerplate response, the sociology graduate student next to me raised her fist in solidarity with some imaginary comrade and shouted, "I'm taking Arabic because I want to help free Palestine!"

It was at that moment that I began thinking about returning to the study of Southeast Asia, a region with political violence and weak states but not quite as fraught with political tension as the Middle East. I began taking Indonesian-language classes, discovered that Indonesia too has great food and tropical weather, and never looked back. I don't remember your name, sociology graduate student, but your inappropriate outburst changed my life for the better.

Figuring out the ideas about territory held by illicit groups may be straightforward (at least for those groups that broadcast their goals), and determining the political conditions they face may be as simple as picking up the newspaper, but uncovering the ins and outs of how terrorists, insurgents, and criminals do what they do is considerably more difficult. Sources on clandestine groups are scant and often biased or simply wrong, and wherever possible I have attempted to corroborate any particular source.

The book as a whole is based mostly on documentary sources. Much of my data on Jemaah Islamiyah (JI) come from recently published books and reports in both English and Indonesian, and to a large extent the chapters on JI in this book are a reinterpretation of the conclusions of earlier researchers. To complement these sources, I also use Indonesian-language newspaper articles, police interrogation reports, and prosecutors' dossiers on captured JI suspects. I treated the interrogation reports and dossiers critically, because they may have been extracted under duress. However, because I was more interested in extracting operational details than assessing the detainees' state of mind or the reasons given for their alleged involvement in terrorist activities, I hope I have avoided some of the pitfalls of such sources. With that said, most of the reports are from the trials of the first Bali bombers and afterward, trials that were generally seen as fair and above board by impartial observers, so I am generally confident of the contents of those reports.[1] Documentary information on Gerakan Aceh Merdeka (GAM) comes from newspaper articles, some police interrogation reports of captured GAM operatives, and the numerous books written in Indonesian both supporting and attacking GAM over the years. Finally, my data on maritime pirates and smugglers come from local newspaper articles, and government and think tank reports, particularly International Maritime Organization datasets.

Interviews provided supplemental information for the cases. Because much of what is known about illicit groups in Southeast Asia remains unwritten or unavailable from English-language sources, I conducted interviews in English, Indonesian, and intermittently Chinese in 2004, 2005, and 2006 in Singapore, Malaysia, Indonesia, the Philippines, Thailand, Taiwan, and Hong Kong with a variety of informants who could be divided into roughly three groups. The first group consisted of academics, businessmen, and non-governmental organization workers, who were peripherally involved with or studied illicit groups and provided context. The second group was a relatively small number of smugglers, insurgents, and "retired" terrorists who were involved in the illicit groups I was studying. The third group included regional police, military, customs, and intelligence officials whose job was to track down and stop the illicit groups' operations. For information on JI, I talked with people who study, track down, or have been involved with the group in some way. For GAM, I conducted interviews with both Indonesian government officials and GAM leaders. For pirates and smugglers, to a greater degree than either of the other two cases given the paucity of good written sources, I conducted interviews with people involved in stopping or aiding and abetting piracy and smuggling in Southeast Asia.

The agendas behind official sources are certainly an issue, but I have no reason to believe that the terrorists, insurgents, and criminals to whom I was able to talk were inherently less (or more) biased than officials.[2] There is a credibility problem for both state and non-state informants. Thus, where possible, I attempted to interview people on opposite sides of an issue, and corroborate interviews with written sources. I did, for instance, talk to both police and smugglers in Batam. For the most part, dueling sources agreed on the general shape of a given topic, and often even on details, although I also note where they disagreed. I granted all interviewees anonymity unless they specifically asked to be named, but recognizing that credibility is an issue, I have tried to provide enough information about sources to show that they know what they are talking about without compromising their identities.

In large part because of the nature of the research, I cannot name many people to whom I am indebted. Of those that I can name, however, Lynn T. White III at Princeton guided me through the undergraduate senior thesis process, a process that I enjoyed enough to replicate on a larger scale at Berkeley.

Kevin O'Brien agreed to be my adviser even after I left the safe confines of Chinese politics, and provided incisive comments during the many drafts of my dissertation. Ron Hassner encouraged me to keep an inherently interesting subject actually interesting. T. J. Pempel supported my research and introduced me to the Pacific Forum Young Leaders Program. Tom Gold leaped into the breach at a critical time. All of them were willing to take on what is a rather unusual topic within political science. Scott Sagan, Lynn Eden, and Don Emmerson at Stanford University's Center for International Security and Cooperation provided much needed comments on an earlier draft of this work.

During my fieldwork, the Institute of Defence and Strategic Studies at Nanyang Technological University in Singapore gave me an office, an affiliation, and a dorm room to call my own. The Centre for Strategic and International Studies provided me with an office, lunch partners, and absurdly cheap photocopying assistance whenever I was in Jakarta. Jean Hung of the Universities Service Centre at the Chinese University of Hong Kong was also a gracious host. Carolina Hernandez and the Institute for Strategic and Development Studies in Manila helped arrange interviews in the Philippines.

The National Security Education Program's Boren Graduate Fellowship program funded the main part of the fieldwork. Susan Shirk's Public Policy and Nuclear Threats program of the University of California's Institute on Global Conflict and Cooperation also funded some of the research for this book, and has provided friends and collaborators ever since the summer of 2004. Ralph Cossa and Brad Glosserman at the Pacific Forum Young Leaders Program provided an opportunity to meet fascinating people in Asia and beyond, and have provocative discussions on Asian security issues. They were also instrumental in arranging some of the interviews in this book.

In this book, several pages, one table (2.1), and two figures (5.1, and 5.2) from my article, "Geography, Globalization, and Terrorism: The Plots of Jemaah Islamiyah," *Security Studies* 17, no. 3 (2008): 505–30, are reprinted in chapters 1, 2, and 5 with the permission of Taylor & Francis. Several pages from my chapter, "Corruption's Corrosive Effect on Counterinsurgency: The Free Aceh Movement in Southeast Asia," in *State of Corruption, State of Chaos: The Terror of Political Malfeasance*, ed. Michaelene Cox (Lanham, MD: Lexington Books, 2008), 127–42, are reprinted in chapter 6 with the permission of Rowman & Littlefield. The table (9.1) in the Conclusion is taken from my article, "Geographies of State Failure and Sophistication in Maritime Piracy Hijackings," *Political Geography* 28, no. 4 (2009): 213–23, with the permission of Elsevier.

Thanks also to Roger Haydon and Cornell University Press, who saw something of value in this book and saw it through to a successful conclusion.

Finally, this book is dedicated to Tiffany, my *cewek cantik,* my Indonesian conversation partner and my wife, who, in her total, eyes-glazed-over lack of interest in what this book is about, puts everything into perspective.

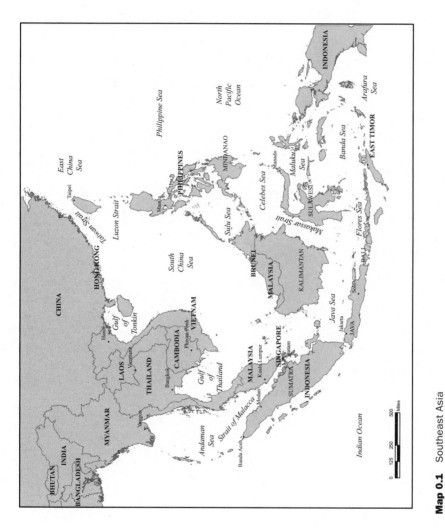

Map 0.1 Southeast Asia

Credit: Ramachandra Sivakumar, Center for Geographic Information Systems, Georgia Institute of Technology

NO MAN'S LAND

INTRODUCTION

It should not be hidden from you that the people of Islam had suffered from aggression, iniquity and injustice imposed on them by the Zionist-Crusaders alliance and their collaborators; to the extent that the Muslims' blood became the cheapest and their wealth as loot in the hands of the enemies. Their blood was spilled in Palestine and Iraq. The horrifying pictures of the massacre of Qana, in Lebanon are still fresh in our memory. Massacres in [Tajikistan], Burma, [Kashmir], Assam, [the] Philippines, [Pattani], [Ogaden], Somalia, [Eritrea], [Chechnya] and in Bosnia-Herzegovina took place, massacres that send shivers in the body and shake the conscience.

—Osama bin Laden, August 1996

Osama bin Laden and the terrorist group al-Qaeda considered themselves at war with the United States in August 1996, a full five years before the United States reciprocated. In his declaration of war, bin Laden lists fifteen countries or regions where the infidels, in various guises, have either oppressed Muslims, or where Muslims are fighting or have fought back.[1] Of those, only Palestine, Lebanon, Saudi Arabia (the Land of the Two Holy Places), and Iraq are solidly in the Middle East. The rest span Eastern Europe, Central Asia, South Asia, Southeast Asia, and the Horn of Africa. Al-Qaeda clearly has a global view of perceived aggression against Muslims. Bin Laden makes clear that Muslims have fought back across the world, in Afghanistan, Bosnia-Herzegovina, Chechnya, and Tajikistan. At least in the 1990s, what al-Qaeda perceived as its realistic area of operations stretched over a large swath of territory. The September 11, 2001 terrorist attacks in New York and Washington, DC, reinforced this perception, as al-Qaeda showed that it could reach from Afghanistan (and Germany) and strike hard against the United States. It seemed as if a "new terrorism" had finally arrived, one that was organized in a superior form—the network—that took advantage of the technologies and processes of globalization, and had finally shaken loose of the constraints of time and space.[2]

After the fall of the Berlin Wall, it was fashionable to say that, as globalization progressed, borders were ceasing to exist, that states would become increasingly meaningless, that geography was irrelevant.[3] Certainly this mode of thinking has shaped the public debate on security issues, leading to concerns that globalization has allowed terrorists to slip the bounds of the state, making it that much more difficult to stop them as they dance around the world just out of the grasp of obsolete nation-states.[4] Violence has become diffused and internationalized— al-Qaeda can be conceived as a "malevolent NGO" that operates *between* states rather than within them. After all, didn't al-Qaeda's leadership just retreat to lawless northwestern Pakistan upon the fall of Afghanistan?[5]

With every proclamation of a brave new world inevitably come those who demur: the world is never as brave as idealists claim, nor is it particularly new. Transnational organizations—mercantile companies, maritime piracy syndicates, mercenaries—have existed for hundreds of years, and have occasionally become powerful enough to match the global scope of the empires of nation-states.[6] States have never had perfect control over movements across their borders, but have nonetheless remained sovereign entities.[7] Even with that imperfect border control, states have incentives to continue to try to police their borders against illicit groups like terrorists, and modern technology might actually allow them to do this more effectively than in the past.[8] Moreover, the movement of goods and people around the world is not necessarily on a larger scale than it has been in the past, such as during the mass migrations of the nineteenth century. Although modern transportation and communications technology make possible the quick and cheap movement of people, goods, and information, it is not necessarily a given that states will allow globalization to spread indefinitely, especially when their economic well-being or political security is threatened.[9] Even weak states retain an important advantage over transnational organizations— states alone have "the right to grant legitimate access" to their territory.[10]

These technologies cannot force economic globalization to continue apace or states to give up sovereign authority, but to a certain extent they exist separately from both issues. Raising tariffs to put a damper on trade or refusing to ratify a new global governance treaty will not make the Internet or cheap plane flights disappear. And it is these technologies that are most interesting when we consider the primary weapons in the September 11, 2001 attacks: the planes. Some took this to be a bitter irony and a sign of new vulnerabilities—the very tools of globalization had been turned against the West. I suggest instead that it reveals a weakness in al-Qaeda.[11]

Al-Qaeda was a global terrorist network, with global ambitions and global operations, that was able to use the technologies and processes associated with globalization to reach out and strike the United States over vast distances. At the same time, it was dependent on those very technologies and processes—regular and cheap commercial air travel, satellite phones, and relatively lax attitudes to cross-border movement—in ways that territorially and operationally constrained and shaped its plots. Flying into the United States from Germany and using knives (or some other sharp object) to hijack passenger planes and fly them into buildings was tactically creative, but depended on a number of pieces falling into place. If the hijackers were to fly into the United States on passenger planes, there was a large but limited number of cities into which they could have flown. If they were to drive, there were only two countries from which they could have driven. If they wanted to attack buildings in New York and Washington using planes full of fuel (that is, planes about to make transcontinental flights), there was again a limited (large but not infinite) number of flights they could have taken from a few particular East Coast cities. Finally, they managed to hijack the planes and turn them into missiles, but it was essentially a one-off operation. After September 11th, the United States (and many other countries) adopted such draconian security procedures over what was already a closely regulated environment that that avenue of attack was essentially cut off, short of further tactical innovation (such as Richard Reid, the shoe bomber). Al-Qaeda had a global vision, and it carried out the 9/11 attacks on a global scale. Before the United States retaliated, the latent geographical weaknesses in al-Qaeda's dependence on the technologies of globalization remained, unfortunately, latent.

This book is not about al-Qaeda. Instead, it is about the travails of a different terrorist organization—Jemaah Islamiyah (JI)—and to a lesser extent insurgent and criminal groups, in Southeast Asia. In Southeast Asia, at least, al-Qaeda's notional geographical weaknesses became real for these groups, and constrained and shaped their behavior in interesting ways. Their adventures and misadventures lead to questions about what this seeming weakness in the face of the unprecedented availability of technology means for how we think about terrorists, insurgents, criminals, and other exemplars of the dark side of globalization.

Nasir Abas, a Malaysian, describes how he went to Afghanistan during the Soviet-Afghan War in the late 1980s for military training as part of what would become the al-Qaeda-allied terrorist group Jemaah Islamiyah. The Indonesians who were to join him had snuck out of Indonesia by boat, and then traveled in secret up the Malayan peninsula, all in order to avoid the attention of Indonesian government spies. But upon reaching Kuala Lumpur, the group openly booked flights to Pakistan on Soviet airline Aeroflot. When Nasir asked whether it made sense to fly on the state airline of the country they were going to fight, he was informed that they were flying Aeroflot because "it was the cheapest."[12] The Indonesian recruits may not have enjoyed the fruits of modern transportation in leaving Indonesia, but they flew from Kuala Lumpur to Pakistan with reckless openness. Why did the Indonesians take a boat from Indonesia to Malaysia, and then a bus to Kuala Lumpur? Why didn't the recruits simply fly from Indonesia to Pakistan, or even from Indonesia to Malaysia?

Elsewhere in Indonesia, the Free Aceh Movement (Gerakan Aceh Merdeka [GAM] in Indonesian), a separatist insurgency on the northwest tip of Sumatra, fought the Indonesian government for control of the province of Aceh over nearly thirty years. GAM managed to build an extensive transnational support network: from its headquarters in Sweden, GAM directed the insurgency in Aceh, set up advocacy units across the West, assassinated enemies in Malaysia, and brought weapons to Aceh from as far away as Thailand and Cambodia. Yet when, in the wake of the 2004 Asian tsunami, GAM made peace with the Indonesian government, it had trouble scrounging up the 840 weapons it was required to hand over.[13] It had a globalized structure and an excellent grasp of modern communications and transportation, both of which allowed it to survive for thirty years, so why did GAM have such difficulty solving the problem of the final mile—the ability to get weapons into Aceh so that it could fight the Indonesian army?

On the Indonesian island of Batam immediately south of Singapore, a smuggler named "Edi" made a good living selling stolen cars that he obtained from a contact in Malaysia. He was successful in other ventures as well, having become one of Batam's biggest suppliers of pirated video compact discs through an in-depth knowledge of local conditions and a reliable supply route from his factory in Jakarta.[14] Yet when the contact in Malaysia felt heat from the police and could no longer guarantee supply, Edi did not find a way to continue to take advantage of relatively easy transport between Indonesia and Malaysia, and the weak government in Indonesia. Instead, he pulled out of the car business entirely.[15] Why?

All three groups showed themselves quite capable of using cheap and fast communications and transportation to create transnational networks that moved people and goods secretly across international borders. But their ingenuity had limits: the torturous route of the recruits who joined Nasir Abas by taking a boat across the Malacca Strait stands in contrast to the high-flying routes of the 9/11 plotters—apparently the waters of the Strait offered a route for evading Indonesian spies, which was more important than getting to Pakistan quickly. Likewise, GAM's extensive transnational support network was of limited use when it came to supplying fighters in Aceh. Even Edi, who presumably had few ideological hang-ups tying him to a specific piece of territory, was unable to bounce back from his setback in Malaysia. Criminal organizations, it appears, are not always more flexible than other types of illicit groups, or any more capable of using the technologies of globalization to their advantage in difficult times.

This book explains the puzzling mixed record of clandestine transnational organizations that use modern technology to their advantage. Clearly the role of technology in illicit groups' movements is more complicated than simply saying that globalization has granted such groups an advantage vis-à-vis states. But it would also be too simple to conclude that globalization is overrated, that territory and borders continue to matter, and leave it at that. It *is* easier than it used to be for people, goods, and information to cross borders, and illicit groups are no exception. But for states that are trying to figure out how to stop transnational terrorists, insurgents, and criminals, neither conclusion is particularly useful. The examples above suggest that the ability of the tools of globalization to help clandestine transnational organizations varies by what the groups are trying to do, where they are trying to do it, and what conditions they face. It is not enough simply to ask whether territory matters in a globalizing world. We must find out *how* and *when*—under what kinds of political conditions—territory matters to the movements and ideas of illicit transnational groups such as criminals, Jemaah Islamiyah, GAM, and al-Qaeda.

The Trials and Tribulations of Clandestine Transnational Organizations

This book explains the paradoxically strong roles that territory, ideas about territory, and local political conditions play in the lives of clandestine transnational organizations (CTOs) in Southeast Asia. Even if we accept that such organizations are not in fact liberated from territory, clearly they find some activities easier than others at certain times and in certain places. The very technologies of globalization that allow us to talk about how time, distance, and cost are no longer related—air travel, telecommunications, and the Internet—are also the technologies that are, loosely speaking, the most dependent on state encouragement and investment, and thus state control. In effect, the farther and faster any nonstate actor wants to move around the world, the more dependent it becomes on chokepoints—international airports, massive transshipment ports—that have been set up by states to encourage global commerce. For those moving legally, or at least in favorable political conditions, this is a good thing. But for terrorists, insurgents, and criminals, many of whom are moving illegally, this is problematic.[16] Moving through these international chokepoints renders illicit groups subject to interdiction. Avoiding them means that the groups are denied the ability to move very far or very fast for very cheaply. They must move along routes with less state scrutiny, such as highways, that are not conducive to the feats made possible by new technology. Or, in the case of severe state hostility, they must create their own illicit infrastructure in areas with topography that makes them difficult for states to control. The costs of doing this are high, not only in terms of money, but also in terms of time and effort.

Moreover, the groups' movements are territorially constrained—people moving through mountain passes do not have the option of skipping over several countries as those in planes do. In some cases—when a group is diffusing ideas, for example—the world is indeed flat, in the words of Thomas Friedman.[17] Time and space have become less obviously important. But at the most basic level, many illicit groups do not only want to spread their ideas. They also want to stage violent attacks, a more logistically intensive enterprise, and for this, given political conditions, the world is not flat at all. Even moving information can be logistically difficult under harsh political conditions, as groups have to resort to messengers and couriers in lieu of cell phones and e-mail, both of which can be tracked by determined states with sufficient resources. Given how the technologies of globalization work, there is little reason to think this will change.

Although territory is at the center of this book, neither physical territory nor modern transportation infrastructure should be taken as the sole cause of anything. We cannot understand what role territory plays in the activities of violent non-state actors without bringing in non-territorial factors. Physical territory and infrastructure might be considered part of the "activity space" of illicit groups, the space where they operate and draw resources. Conversely, Alexander Murphy argues that terrorists (in this case) also operate in a "policy space"—the political environment created by government actions, and a "perceptual space"—the ideas that the terrorists have about the territory in which they are operating.[18] Situating illicit groups in space means more than simply mapping their presence or absence on a given piece of land.

Building on Murphy's insights, I suggest there is an iterative interplay of the ideas of a CTO, its transnational activities, political conditions, and territory. All CTOs have ideas about where they want to accomplish their goals, and what they want to do with the territory that is the focus of their aspirations. As a CTO tries to carry out illicit transnational activities by moving people, weapons, and information across international borders, state hostility and the level of logistical sophistication required for those activities determine how the group depends on physical topography and transportation infrastructure of the borders it is trying to cross. In situations with extreme political hostility and the absence of advantageous geography on which the CTO would otherwise depend, failure is a very real possibility. Aside from the consequences for the potential victims of its plots, when we take into account the scope of its territorial ambitions, and its intentions toward that territory, success or failure in a CTO's illicit activities provides the backdrop for a reconfiguration in the group's transnational aspirations.

These changing ideas matter a great deal in explaining the territorial and ideational trajectories of certain illicit groups in Southeast Asia. Jemaah Islamiyah started in the late 1970s as a branch of the group Darul Islam, and like the rest of Darul Islam initially cared only about building an Islamic state in Indonesia. After its experiences in Afghanistan, which included Nasir Abas's travels on

Aeroflot, JI emerged in 1993 as a transnational organization with cells in Singapore, Malaysia, Indonesia, and the Philippines. What happened? By contrast, the organization GAM built to fight against the Indonesian government was never used to do anything but move people and weapons into and out of Aceh, and Edi the smuggler preferred to pursue other business interests rather than pick up and move shop in the face of repression. What didn't happen?

The answer lies in the conceptual relationship that CTOs have with territory, and the difficulty of setting up networks to support illicit transnational activities. More expansive territorial ambitions are likely to make a group amenable to change, while a desire to control and govern its targeted territory is likely to hold it to one place. If the group's territorial ideas are amenable to change, the support structures that it must set up to carry out its illicit activities can make expansion of its ambitions realistic, thus creating security problems for affected states. Conversely, failure can remove a country from a CTO's purview as those support structures are crushed. Thus, territory has a role not only in how illicit groups' activities are constrained, but also in how their ideas are shaped by those activities.

Clandestine Transnational Organizations across Southeast Asia

To explore the argument, I closely follow the trials and tribulations of Jemaah Islamiyah, and then in somewhat less detail compare them to GAM, as well as organized crime networks, with a specific focus on maritime piracy hijacking syndicates and smuggling rings. All of these groups are clandestine transnational organizations in Southeast Asia, and as such are especially good cases with which to examine how the ability of illicit groups to use globalizing technology is shaped by territory and changing political conditions.

Because they are concentrated in one part of the world, the groups are facing the same governments (generally Indonesia, Singapore, Malaysia, Thailand, and the Philippines) at approximately the same time (from the mid-1970s to the present), though exact dates and countries may vary. Although this book has applications outside of the region, Southeast Asia is an especially interesting region on which to focus. Like Europe, Southeast Asia has an unusual combination of physical and virtual interconnectedness, with well-traveled intra-regional routes serviced by buses, planes, and ships. Like Africa, it has highly variable concentrations of state capacity and difficult geographies—mountains, jungles, and archipelagos. Singapore, for instance, is one of the more capable governments in the world, while Indonesia and the Philippines are much weaker. In essence, Southeast Asia is like the Wild West with Internet access.

Jemaah Islamiyah and the other groups all share four characteristics that speak to certain aspects of the argument, and follow closely Peter Andreas's definition of clandestine transnational actors as "nonstate actors who operate across national borders in violation of state laws and who attempt to evade law enforcement efforts."[19] First, they are clandestine. The groups all have (or had at some point in their history) a hostile relationship with at least one state in whose territory they are trying to operate, because of either what they believe or what they are trying to do. Even if the governments in Southeast Asia did not care what JI, GAM, or criminals believed, what the groups try to do makes states hostile. All of the groups discussed in this book have engaged or attempted to engage in violent or otherwise illegal physical activities, such as bombings, assassinations, armed offensives, hijackings, smuggling operations, or simple theft. Although JI, GAM, and pirates are all armed groups, smugglers of mundane goods are generally not.[20] However, their activities also occur in the face of hostility from the state.

Second, they are transnational. At some point in their life cycles, all of these groups have moved people, goods, or information across an international border in a substantial enough way that they have built support structures in more than one country. This does not mean they actually want to be in more than one country, just that political necessity required them to relocate part of their operations outside of the country.

Third, these groups are organizations—they have a recognizable, day-to-day command and control structure. This does not necessarily mean they have a top-down, hierarchical organization (although both Jemaah Islamiyah and GAM did), but indicates that there is a set of people who make decisions on a regular basis about where to operate and what to do there. Modern communications technologies allow networks to coalesce and swarm in new ways, but when someone in the network decides to stage a violent attack, some form of command and control, whether flat or top-down, has to come together.[21] A leader who only makes ideological pronouncements and sporadically communicates with his followers is running a movement, not a coherent clandestine transnational organization. Thus, arguably, the late Abu Musab al-Zarqawi's al-Qaeda affiliate in Iraq, is a coherent network; post–9/11 al-Qaeda is more of a social movement composed of many related, but semi-autonomous or fully autonomous networks with common goals and ideologies.[22]

Fourth, and this is key, all three cases—Jemaah Islamiyah as a terrorist organization, GAM as a separatist insurgency, and transnational criminals—are non-state actors. At issue is not whether the group has any state-like features (it would be surprising if long-term insurgencies did *not*), but whether the CTO has acquired sufficient uncontested territory or state-like properties to have control over physical infrastructure such as major airports, seaports, highways, or railroads, or over virtual infrastructure, such as telecommunications networks. If state power over illicit groups in a globalized world comes from states' control over the chokepoints through which groups move people, goods, and information, then a CTO that is able to control those chokepoints or has sufficient support from a state to bypass them entirely—such as Hezbollah and the assistance it gets from Iran and Syria—should be treated less as a non-state actor, and more as a state, in which case it passes from the purview of this book. This does not mean I am limiting myself to groups that are either incompetent or immature—JI, GAM, and many criminal organizations are neither. In fact, control over chokepoints was always less the issue for those proclaiming the ascendancy of globalized illicit groups than their flexibility and stateless freedom.

Acquisition by what were formerly non-state actors of the combination of military strength, uncontested control of territory, and access to transportation infrastructure necessary to reach the state actor threshold is not unheard of. Arguably the Tamil Tigers, al-Qaeda in Afghanistan from 1996 to 2001, and some of the pirate-sponsoring warlords of Somalia, are examples of clandestine transnational organizations that have approached or cross the threshold.[23] A number of groups, such as Hezbollah, Hamas, and the Kurds (whose envisioned state stretches through Turkey, Syria, Iraq, and Iran), have also established more institutionalized quasi-states, although some of them would not necessarily be considered either clandestine or transnational. It is safe to assume, however, that most clandestine transnational organizations do not have control over transportation or communications chokepoints.

Status as a non-state actor also does not necessarily mean that the CTO does not look like a state at all. Many CTOs acquire state-like properties over time, either because they need to in order to carry out their mission or because their intention is to set up a state. For example, in al-Qaeda's early 1990s operation to fight for an Islamic state in Somalia, it experienced the greatest headway with local warring clans when it adjudicated disputes and provided security, that is, services that the state would have provided in Somalia at one time.[24] Likewise, the Free Aceh Movement was formed in 1976 with structures already in place to administer any territory they captured in the future. Even criminal groups have at times attained some trappings of statehood, such as when early nineteenth-century pirate fleets in southern China established a confederation that stymied Qing Dynasty control of the coast and eventually amassed seventy thousand sailors.[25]

Terrorists, Insurgents, and Criminals

As a large, long-lived, and fairly coherent transnational terrorist group, Jemaah Islamiyah is an ideal case to study with regard to how territory and political conditions affect a group's activities over time. That not only Jemaah Islamiyah, but also the Free Aceh Movement, and transnational criminals, in the form of pirates and smugglers, should all be in the same book is not obvious. While doing field-work in Southeast Asia, on a number of occasions I had conversations with local analysts who would ask about the topic of my research. "Terrorists, insurgents, and criminals," I would respond. To this they would retort that comparing such a wide variety of groups was difficult. "After all," they usually said, "terrorists have political or religious goals, and criminals just want money." Alan Dupont echoes this sentiment, when he notes that "the essential difference between [transna-tional crime and terrorism] is that criminals are primarily driven by money while terrorists are politically motivated."[26]

This is in fact why I chose them, as a way to move beyond this intellectual logjam. Categorizing groups based on presumed overarching motivations has led to large literatures on terrorist groups, particularly al-Qaeda, or particular in-surgent groups, or maritime piracy, but only rarely about all of them together.[27] Moreover, much of the research on Islamic terrorist groups looks at their ori-gins, behavior, and goals through the lens of political Islam, which is understand-able, but does not provide much basis for comparing them with non-Islamic groups, particularly those without political or religious goals.[28]

The organizations discussed in this book have radically different ideas about why they exist and what they want to accomplish, but they all have ideas about territory and what they want to do with it, and they all move people, goods, and information across borders and over territory. Jemaah Islamiyah has religious and political motivations, with the end goal of creating a pan-Islamic caliphate in Southeast Asia; GAM's primarily political agenda was to establish an indepen-dent state in Aceh, and the maritime pirates and smugglers want to make money, and care little about whether they control territory or not. The cases discussed in this book are diverse and are "representative in the minimal sense of representing the full variation of the population."[29]

This is not to say that Jemaah Islamiyah is identical to other terrorist groups, merely that it is a transnational terrorist group that on its face is not atypical. Likewise, GAM inevitably has characteristics that differentiate it from other separatist insurgencies, but its transnational network, though extensive, is not uniquely so—the Tamil Tigers arguably had a larger international presence, and a number of other separatist groups, such as the Provisional Irish Republican Army and the Palestinian Liberation Organization, have had to deal with issues related to operating across international borders. I could have chosen any of many different kinds of transnational criminal networks, but small-scale smug-glers of mundane goods and large-scale maritime piracy syndicates have several advantages. They are both fairly well-entrenched and well-documented phe-nomena in Southeast Asia, and share some characteristics with many other kinds of criminal networks—like drug trafficking and human smugglers, they move goods and people secretly across international borders. Because they are engaged in physical illicit activities, unlike money laundering rings, their operations can be compared with terrorists and insurgents.

What is interesting here is that while GAM, which sought to govern Aceh, remained focused on that one province, and JI's predecessor organization Darul Islam (DI) has been a group dedicated solely to establishing an Islamic state in Indonesia, Jemaah Islamiyah transformed itself into a pan-Southeast Asian organization. Like GAM and DI, some criminal organizations such as small-time smugglers do not change the location or scope of their efforts; unlike the other two groups, they often disappear under pressure. Conversely, large-scale maritime syndicates have shown an ability to adapt to crackdowns by shifting their operations around a region to avoid hostile governments. Jemaah Islamiyah's post-1993 flexibility in this respect was similar to the transnational behavior of large-scale maritime pirate syndicates, with whom they certainly do not share common goals. Some groups that appear different when we consider only the broad nature of their objectives had similar outcomes in the fluidity of the scope and location of their ambitions and transnational operations, while others that are on their face quite similar to each other had more variation in their outcomes.

Outline of the Book

The book is organized into three sections. The first section introduces the main elements of the argument. In chapter 1, I compare the ideas that JI, GAM, pirates and smugglers have about territory, specifically their intentions and the scope of their territorial ambitions at the beginning of their respective histories. The advantage of focusing on groups' ideas about territory is that we can understand the common process by which the technologies of globalization, territory, and political conditions determine the success or failure of illicit groups' plots. It is possible to imagine a terrorist group with ambitions that encompass a large number of countries but with no desire to control territory—merely a desire to cause havoc. I would expect it to behave similarly to the maritime pirate syndicates discussed here. Likewise, it is possible (though difficult) to imagine a pirate group that seeks to administer a province of some country, in which case it would act similar to GAM. Territory and ideas about territory can thus be used as a basis for the systematic comparison of clandestine transnational organizations that have wildly differing goals. Acknowledging the existence of a complicated relationship between territory and globalization, in chapter 2 I situate CTOs in space, and suggest specifically how and when CTOs' transnational activities are constrained by a combination of territorial factors, political conditions, and the nature of those activities.

The second section builds the argument in detail by outlining the territorial constraints faced by Jemaah Islamiyah, the central case in the book, as it tried to use globalizing technology to move around within and outside of Southeast Asia under often adverse political conditions. Given its extensive history, expansive transnational infrastructure, and well-documented activities, JI is an ideal case for examining the ins and outs of territorial constraints on every aspect of a CTO's operations. Specifically, I look at how JI has carried out command and control, training, and logistical activities in successive time periods defined by a particular level of state hostility. Chapters 3 and 4 trace Jemaah Islamiyah's operations from when it became a transnational terrorist group fighting for an Islamic caliphate across Southeast Asia until it came under pressure in different countries following 9/11 and its own violent missteps. Chapter 5 details the process by which Jemaah Islamiyah carried out (or tried to carry out) four bombings from 2000 to 2003 under increasing state hostility, using different routes and methods.

In the final section, I use somewhat less detailed comparative case studies to see how the argument travels beyond Jemaah Islamiyah, both within and beyond Southeast Asia, and discuss the implications of the argument for changes in CTOs' ideas and structure.

Chapter 6 explains how GAM was able to run an insurgency from outside of Indonesia for almost thirty years, and recover from near defeat on two occasions, but was unable to seal the deal, and ultimately accepted autonomy rather than independence. Chapter 7 looks at transnational criminals, in the form of maritime pirates and smugglers in Southeast Asia, and shows how and when they are subject to considerations of territory and state power as they smuggle goods and hijack ships. Because I replicate the structure of my examination of JI with those of GAM and criminals, I can show that the processes by which they are constrained as they move across borders, by which they succeed or fail, and by which they do or do not adapt their territorial ambitions are the same across cases.

Chapter 8 moves beyond my main argument about territorial and political constraints and compares JI and the other groups to explore the role that the outcomes of their transnational activities and ideas about territory play in the fluidity or rigidity of individual CTOs' transnational configurations and territorial aspirations. Some groups, such as Jemaah Islamiyah and large-scale maritime piracy hijacking syndicates, are fluid in their ideas and movements. Others, such as GAM and small-time mundane smugglers, are not, even in a globalized world.

In the conclusion, I extend the argument beyond Southeast Asia to look at the fortunes of clandestine transnational organizations in other parts of the world, notably the Tamil Tigers, al-Qaeda, and Somali maritime piracy hijacking syndicates. In some cases the argument works quite well. In others, more research, as ever, is needed.

Part I

GRAPPLING WITH TERRITORY IN A GLOBALIZING WORLD

TERRITORY AND THE IDEAS OF CLANDESTINE TRANSNATIONAL ORGANIZATIONS

What do they want? This is the question often asked of terrorist groups such as Jemaah Islamiyah. Goals are often used to categorize different types of terrorist organizations, either for analytical clarity or to tailor counterterrorism strategies.[1] Barbara Walter and Andrew Kydd, for example, list five main goals of political terrorism—social control, territorial change, policy change, regime change, and maintenance of the status quo.[2] If we want to include other types of illicit groups, ethnic separatism (and insurgency in general) can be subsumed into the goal of territorial change, but criminal organizations are not so straightforward. Although criminals may have political interests, such as in maintaining a corrupt status quo, not all criminals have easily identifiable political goals, and not all criminals actually resort to terrorism, or even violence.

However, other problems exist. There is a tradeoff between clarity and complexity when we take the top level of groups' motivations as the basis for comparison. The complexity of any illicit group's ideas means that it is often difficult to make categorical assumptions about what actually motivates the group. Are all terrorists motivated solely by political or religious beliefs? Are criminals somehow free of ideology? Abu Sayyaf Group in the southern Philippines, for instance, is less notorious for its purportedly radical Islamic beliefs than its practice of kidnapping for ransom, while many European and Asian pirate gangs of the seventeenth to nineteenth centuries may have been guided by a somewhat anti-authoritarian, libertarian ideology.[3]

Criminals can use terroristic activities to shape their political and economic environment favorably by assassinating political officials trying to pass anti-crime legislation, or by attacking competing businesses. Likewise, terrorist organizations can engage in criminal activities to raise money for their plots. Al-Qaeda and the Taliban have been implicated in drug trafficking in Afghanistan, for instance, and many Southeast Asian terrorist groups (including Jemaah Islamiyah) have taken to petty robbery for financial support.[4] Sufficient blurring of lines can lead to "convergence," where terrorist organizations and criminals each augment their capabilities by adopting the tactics, and more important, the supporting networks and structures (such as semi-autonomous cells typical of terrorists) of the other. In some cases groups move toward a situation where they are motivated by a combination of political and criminal goals.[5] Over the course of its existence, for example, the Irish Republican Army acted as a standard cell-based terrorist organization, a classical insurgency with guerrilla units, a police agency, mercenaries, rioters, a militia, and a criminal organization.[6] Categories can thus overlap despite initially varying motivations, or because groups have multiple goals. Putting terrorism and criminality on a continuous spectrum recognizes the complexity of the project, but sacrifices some clarity.

There has been a proliferation of other categorizations of terrorist groups, usually related to the terrorists' violent and non-violent activities, their organizational structure, or the environments in which they operate.[7] Categorizing groups' non-violent activities, especially propaganda and organizing over the Internet, is a good way to show that terrorism, or even violence in general, is only one tool in clandestine transnational organizations' (CTOs) repertoire. It also shows that CTOs exist apart from their more infamous acts.[8] Even the most violent groups cannot be focused full-time on blowing things up, for the simple reason that they have to plan the attacks and recruit members. If we want to compare groups with different kinds of goals, the key is to find activities pursued by all types of CTOs—a pirate syndicate does not usually have a propaganda branch, but both terrorist groups and criminals struggle with identifying and integrating new members.

Looking at CTOs' organizational structures, be they hierarchical or diffuse and networked, works well if we want to compare the behavior of terrorists, insurgents, and criminals. Regardless of their disparate goals, clandestine organizations that are operating with enough communications technology might adopt similar structures to survive and even thrive as they fight states.[9] But if the main reason a group organizes itself in a certain way is for political and technological expediency, this says little about how its ideas provide the context for its behavior. One way out of this is to see maintaining organizational coherence as the engine for the group's violent behavior, regardless of the political consequences.[10] The result, however, is that the goals a group might espouse are taken as superficial, and could change depending on what the group needs to justify its existence.

Approaches that focus on a group's operational environment come much closer to the geographical tenor of this book, but ignore the group's ideas. Boaz Ganor, for instance, describes how organizations that control territory can use that territory to launch attacks and train recruits, but are then vulnerable to counterattacks by security forces, and have to provide for the people under their control.[11] But whether or not the group controls territory is surely determined in part by whether the group *wants* to control (and administer) territory. Such a categorization deals more with facts on the ground than with the group's actual beliefs.

This chapter is not an attempt to come up with yet another typology of terrorist groups, or any other type of illicit group. Instead, I lay out how to use territory to think about clandestine transnational organizations' ideas, and thus create a conceptual basis for separating out the commensurable components of very different groups' goals, be they political, economic, or religious, or even some combination of all three. Conceptions about territory—where a group wants to be, what it wants to do there, and the magnitude of its ambitions—provide much of the context for a CTO's activities. I am less concerned with the overarching nature of the goals than subsets of those goals that inform both violent and non-violent (but still clandestine) transnational activities, and provide a backdrop for how the group arrays itself over the physical landscape. Territorial ideas also have an advantage in that CTOs can change their structure, even the nature of their day-to-day activities without changing the nature of their territorial ideas or their territorial ambitions. The IRA for example, through all its permutations, always remained focused on establishing a state in all of Ireland.[12]

Conceptions of Territory

All CTOs have goals—what they want to accomplish—and all goals have a territorial component.[13] This is true regardless of how globalized a group is. Modern telecommunications and global media can actually strengthen local communities by enabling them to maintain an ongoing connection to a specific piece of territory, no matter where they are in the world.[14] Unlike the anti-colonial wars of the nineteenth and early twentieth centuries, terrorists and their victims are now physically and perceptually closer together, allowing attacks far from the terrorists' home ground.[15] Furthermore, far from bringing people together, globalization can exacerbate differences and make territory more important. Observe, for example, how diasporic communities remain fixated on a specific piece of disputed territory, and often fund and supply local insurgencies, such as the IRA or the Tamil Tigers, at levels disproportionate to their physical experience of the conflict.[16]

In looking at this territorial component, I ask four questions. Where does the CTO want to accomplish its goals? The target area is the territorial focus of the CTO's goals, the geographic area in which the CTO seeks to achieve those goals. How extensive is this target area? The target area can be part of one country (as in the case of GAM's focus on Aceh), an entire country (as in the case of the predecessor of Jemaah Islamiyah, Darul Islam, which wanted to establish an Islamic state in Indonesia), or two or more countries (as in the case of some of the pirate syndicates in this study).[17] The countries, or parts of countries, that are within the CTO's target area are by definition where the CTO would most like to be, where analysts would "look first" in tracking it. Yet, as we will see, the CTO does not always (or even usually) get its first choice about where to operate.

Does the CTO want to control the target area? Has it made concrete plans to govern the territory if it does want to control it? I divide CTOs into three general categories, according to their territorial intentions. The first two types of CTOs usually have political or religious goals, and are the violent non-state actors typically studied by political scientists: separatist movements, insurgencies, and terrorist groups. Here, however, I look at how each group relates to the territory within its target area.

Groups in the first category, of which many separatist movements are prime examples, seek to control that territory, and have in place plans, and even administrative structures, to govern the target area. Groups of all stripes could in theory provide state-like goods. However, a distinct difference exists between state-like services related to governing (such as creating a taxation system) and state-like services designed to garner support from the population (such as providing social services). As this study shows, governance structures are often anchored in a specific territory, and are not designed to be replicable.

Groups in the second category also seek to control territory in the target area, but they have no governance structures in place, nor plans about how they will govern, either because they anticipate some other organization taking over upon completion of their mission, or because they assume that success is so far off that such concerns are premature. Without concerns about governance, these groups' command and control structures are often replicable, and not necessarily tied to any particular territory (although they would still prefer to be within the target area). Many (but not all) terrorist groups would fall into this category.

The third category consists of networks that have no desire to control the territory in which they operate, and certainly do not have plans to govern it. Such groups are usually motivated primarily by economic gain, notably crime syndicates. Unlike many political and religious organizations, networks with economic goals do not see violent and/or illicit activities (that is, much of logistics) as a means to an end, but as the end in themselves. This is *not* to imply that criminal syndicates will necessarily have no desire to control territory (or do not have political goals), or that it is political or religious groups that will try to control territory, although that is generally the case. Although most organizations fall into the categories we would expect them to, my categories compare groups with different territorial ideas, rather than terrorists with criminals per se. A drug producer, for instance, might seek to control territory so that it can protect its plantations, even though most other criminals groups would not have any desire to follow its lead.

Together, territorial intentions and the size of the target area cover what are generally the territorial ideas of the three commonsense types of clandestine transnational organizations. Both GAM and Darul Islam started out intending to take over and govern territory, while the criminals discussed in this book have no such desires. Both GAM and small-time smugglers have limited territorial ambitions, while post-expansion JI and large-scale maritime pirate syndicates are spread out over several countries.

An interesting pattern emerges. Groups that appear to have similar political or religious goals might actually behave differently based on their relationship to territory: a violent group, for example, that wants to take over an entire country but has made no plans to govern it versus a related group that has exactly the same goal but has set up preliminary administrative structures. Conversely, groups that appear to have different goals—terrorist groups with political agendas and criminal organizations with economic motivations—might behave in similar ways if they have territorial aspirations of a similar size. The next section discusses the territorial ideas of Jemaah Islamiyah, Gerakan Aceh Merdeka, and maritime pirates and smugglers at their respective beginnings. These ideas will have important consequences both for where they operate (and thus the conditions and challenges they face), and how they respond to changes in their political environments.

Table 1.1   Clandestine organizations and their ideas about territory

	SIZE OF TERRITORIAL AMBITIONS		
TERRITORIAL INTENTIONS	PART OF ONE COUNTRY	ONE COUNTRY	TWO OR MORE COUNTRIES
Control/Plans to govern	GAM	Darul Islam (1947–2009)	
Control/No plans to govern		Jemaah Islamiyah (1979–1993)	Jemaah Islamiyah (1993–2009)
No control	Mundane smugglers		Maritime piracy hijacking syndicates

Jemaah Islamiyah's Origins

The story of Jemaah Islamiyah's origins is largely the story of its predecessor Darul Islam. Darul Islam began as an organization dedicated to controlling and governing at first only certain sections of Indonesia, and later the entire country. Their territorial administrative structures were not replicable, or easily transferred to other areas. By contrast, the branch of Darul Islam that would become Jemaah Islamiyah was initially structured in proselytization (*dakwah*) cells that had no ambition to govern territory over the short term, were successful in replicating themselves across a large area, and were open to change when the opportunity (forcibly) presented itself.

Sekarmadji Maridjan Kartosuwirjo started a militia in West Java in the mid-1940s in alliance with independence leaders Sukarno and Mohammed Hatta. After the proclaimed (but not yet officially independent) Indonesian republic was forced to withdraw its forces from parts of Java under an agreement with the Dutch in January 1948, Kartosuwirjo proceeded to fight the Dutch with his new Tentara Islam Indonesia (TII) (Indonesian Islamic Army). He moved on to fighting the avowedly secular Indonesian republican forces, and on 7 August 1949 proclaimed the Negara Islam Indonesia (NII) (Indonesian Islamic State). Negara Islam Indonesia was not limited to West Java—there were also rebellions in Aceh, South Sulawesi, Central Java, and throughout Sumatra—but Kartosuwirjo's component in West Java was called Darul Islam (DI). The name eventually spread to include all NII components throughout Indonesia, such that DI became synonymous with NII. Interestingly, "Darul Islam" means "Abode of Islam," and what concerns us here is its view of territory.[18]

From 1949 until the Sukarno government captured Kartosuwirjo in 1962, NII/DI was an odd mixture of multiple insurgencies within a larger movement. From 1953 NII was (formally) a unified movement with a command and control structure divided geographically. The leaders set up commands for South Sulawesi, Sumatra, Kalimantan, East Java, Central Java, and two for West Java, and installed Kartosuwirjo as the imam. The extent to which he actually exercised control over the commands outside of West Java is unclear. The South Sulawesi component, for example, proclaimed its own Islamic Republic of Sulawesi outside of NII in 1962.[19] The split was later "blamed on poor communication," but it still shows the extent to which command and control even within Indonesia was difficult for the DI leadership.[20]

Darul Islam was simultaneously a religious, political, and territorial insurgency. It actively sought to take over and *administer* small, secure areas (labeled D1) where it could apply shari'a law, and shelter refugees. It intended to use those areas as bases from which to expand, both by force of arms into areas fully under the control of the Republic of Indonesia (D3) and, by *dakwah* into areas (D2) that were wavering between NII and the Republic of Indonesia. Until 1962, NII had several such safe areas in West Java, Aceh, and South Sulawesi and administered them accordingly. This was a lasting theme. When in 1974 DI reconstituted, it returned to an administrative structure centered around territory. Sumatra, Java, and Sulawesi became the centers of commands that covered most of the densely populated parts of Indonesia, while various leaders became regional military commanders or obtained portfolios as minister of foreign affairs or minister for home affairs.[21]

In theory, NII was (and is) a nationwide movement, but DI's emphasis on territorial entrenchment and creating a functional administrative structure encouraged a parochialism that limited the flexibility of the different territorial commands. Although crossover between different branches of DI occasionally did occur, interaction generally only seemed to occur at the very top, among the leaders who met to choose the imam, and who maintained their own strongholds in Sumatra, Java, and Sulawesi. They did not range freely throughout Indonesia. Thus, DI's target area consisted of a strange mixture of extremely small pieces of territory that it tried to govern combined with a much larger, more abstract goal of an Indonesia-wide NII. So how did the pan-Southeast Asian Jemaah Islamiyah emerge from such a parochial movement?

In 1976, two DI leaders—Gaos Taufik from Sumatra and Danu Mohamed Hassan from Java—met to form a new militant organization by the name of Komando Jihad for two reasons. First, they would fight communist infiltration with the support of BAKIN—the Indonesian intelligence service, which funded the early meetings of Komando Jihad and riddled the organization with moles. Second, they would start their own Islamic revolution throughout Indonesia. BAKIN's support allowed DI alumni from all over Indonesia to come together and interact.[22] In essence, it became even more reasonable for branches of Darul Islam to have territorial aspirations that encompassed all of Indonesia. In May 1976, Komando Jihad started blowing things up throughout Sumatra, and tried to instigate a revolution in West Java.[23] The same year, Abdullah Sungkar and Abu Bakar Ba'asyir joined DI in Central Java. Shortly thereafter, the Indonesian government, realizing that things had gotten slightly out of control and that their goal of drawing the jihadis out into the open had been realized, cracked down on Komando Jihad, and began arresting members, including Sungkar and Ba'asyir in December 1978. They were tried in 1982, and on appeal sentenced to time served. Both were freed while the government's appeal worked its way through the system.[24]

They returned to the school they had run pre-crackdown near Solo, Pesantren al-Mukmin, in the village of Pondok Ngruki, and began building a *dakwah* structure. This was an innovation that separated their cells from the rest of DI; they had no immediate ambitions to govern territory, and did not establish structures for that purpose. Nor were their aspirations limited to their home base. Although it was initially based in Central and East Java, the structure began to spread to Jakarta. The structure adopted by Sungkar and Ba'asyir had an advantage in that it was cellular. The cells were *usroh*, groups of "ten to fifteen people prepared to live according to Islamic principles and Islamic law."[25] But the cellularity meant flexibility, scalability, and most important, detachment from territorial bases. Upon his return to Pondok Ngruki, Sungkar gathered former Komando Jihad fighters, and Ba'asyir taught them how to form their own *usroh* as the basis for NII, meaning the *usroh* network was to a certain extent self-replicating and free of territorial considerations: the secure areas became functional groupings rather than actual territory. *Usroh* members swore an oath of loyalty to Abdullah Sungkar and the concept of NII, and Sungkar and Ba'asyir seem to have managed the cells somewhat openly and quite actively. They were in effect building a scalable, *dakwah* network throughout Indonesia that was *not* structured to govern territory.[26]

As chapter 8 shows, these differences between mainstream Darul Islam and the founders of Jemaah Islamiyah in terms of how they related to territory had important consequences not only for the future territorial scope of Jemaah Islamiyah, which would grow to include all of Muslim Southeast Asia within its ambit, but also for its flexibility when confronted with crackdowns or when presented with political openings.

GAM's Origins

GAM's origins were somewhat similar to Jemaah Islamiyah's. The Acehnese were among the fiercest fighters during the Indonesian war for independence, and one of Darul Islam's strongholds was Aceh, which was a separate command in NII's structure in the 1950s. Existing uncomfortably with Aceh's contributions to Indonesian independence was the hope among many Acehnese that an Indonesian state (secular or Islamic) would provide a significant degree of regional autonomy. Confronted with attempts by the Indonesian government to impose a highly centralized government on the country, Aceh, like a number of other provinces in the 1950s, rose in revolt. Teungku Daud Beureueh announced that Aceh was joining the Islamic State of Indonesia in 1953, but nonetheless his branch of Darul Islam moved away from the main NII in 1955 to become a "federal state" within NII. Although Daud Beureueh maintained notional solidarity with other Islamist regional movements in Indonesia, he (and his followers) also thought of Aceh as somehow different from the other breakaway regions.[27] Thus the idea for a Free Aceh Movement was not unprecedented. There was historical precedent for two of GAM's defining characteristics: its rigid focus on Aceh, and Aceh alone, and its intention to establish a functional government over the territory as soon as it could. Although it did not have exactly the same territorial doctrine as Darul Islam, GAM's strategy was virtually identical inasmuch as it committed GAM to controlling and governing the territory of Aceh.

The pre-history of GAM is interesting not so much for what was going on in Aceh as what was going on outside of it. The founder of GAM, Hasan Di Tiro, worked on the staff of the Indonesian embassy to the United Nations in New York in the early 1950s. On 1 September 1954, a year after Daud Beureueh proclaimed Darul Islam in Aceh, Di Tiro wrote an ultimatum to the Indonesian prime minister demanding that the government stop its "genocide" in Aceh, or else he would open an embassy for Darul Islam at the UN and in the United States. In a rage, the prime minister demanded that Di Tiro return to Indonesia. Instead, Di Tiro requested asylum in the United States. He became a representative in the United States and at the UN for the "republic" established by Darul Islam and a loosely allied Revolutionary Government of the Republic of Indonesia (Pemerintahan Revolusioner Republik Indonesia [PRRI]) until the leaders of DI and PRRI gave in to the Indonesian government in the early 1960s. Hasan Di Tiro remained in the United States, married an American, and became a successful businessman.[28]

Over the next fifteen years living as an expatriate, he developed the territorial concept of Aceh to which GAM has adhered since its establishment. Aceh, according to Di Tiro, was an independent sultanate through the nineteenth century, and although the Dutch tried to take it over beginning in 1873, the Acehnese fought back fiercely, in a war that lasted, in fits and starts, until 1911. It was the longest colonial war the Dutch fought, and they still did not have tight control over some parts of Aceh when the Japanese arrived in 1941. The Dutch conquered the Javanese fairly easily, and upon Indonesia's independence, the new government reinvaded Aceh to make sure it was part of Indonesia even though there was no particular reason why Aceh would be part of the same country as Java.[29] The official name of GAM in English is the Aceh-Sumatra National Liberation Front. According to Di Tiro's formulation, the Acehnese sultanate once exercised control over all of Sumatra, and as such not only is GAM the vanguard of an eventual Sumatra-wide movement for independence (with the result being a loose confederation of states free of Java), but Aceh is the rightful leading territory of the island.[30] The association of Aceh with the rest of Sumatra waxed and waned throughout GAM's life. In the independence proclamation, the eventual goal appears to be the establishment of an independent state over all of Sumatra.[31] But the 2005 peace agreement, the Memorandum of Understanding, refers solely to "GAM" without mention of the rest of Sumatra, suggesting that GAM was focused entirely on Aceh.[32] In addition, in 1971, years after Darul Islam in Aceh had fallen, Daud Beureueh visited Di Tiro in the United States, where the latter discussed his ideas for Acehnese independence, and apparently received Beureueh's blessing. Beureueh's approval of GAM suggests that Di Tiro was trying to carry on the legacy of the Acehnese Darul Islam, including its limited target area.[33]

Hasan Di Tiro, as president of GAM, declared Acehnese independence on 4 December 1976, in a statement released in English and Acehnese. Because it was explicitly designed to be the government-in-waiting for Aceh, GAM had a hierarchical, formal structure with a cabinet containing typical government positions— ministers of education, social services, commerce, finance, and so on. Di Tiro served simultaneously as head of state, foreign minister, and defense minister.[34] Angkatan Gerakan Aceh Merdeka (AGAM), the armed wing of GAM, came into existence at the same time, and was led by Teungku Fauzi Hasbi Geudong (who later had a falling out with GAM), although it is not clear how organized the military was. There were also governors of Aceh's provinces, although at its inception, GAM only had governors for Pase, Batee Ulik, Perlak, Teming, and Linge. The other provinces were slated to be added once GAM had more than imaginary control over at least some of their territory, although in practice from 1976 to 1979 GAM never had any influence outside of Pidie, Aceh Utara (North Aceh), and Aceh Timur (East Aceh), not coincidentally Darul Islam's base areas from the 1950s.[35] It is important that GAM's initial structure was wedded to controlling and governing territory—the elements of GAM that were within Aceh itself were not designed to be replicable outside of the province. Much as the government of Poland is not set up to govern the Central African Republic, GAM was setting itself up from the start to be the government of Aceh and nothing else.

Maritime Pirates and Smugglers

Ferreting out the territorial ideas of pirates and smugglers is less straightforward than for separatists or terrorists. Criminals, after all, do not usually release press statements on their ideology, or write manifestos, and for specific criminal organizations it is difficult to figure out when they first started. Consequently I try to piece together pirates and smugglers' relationships to territory by thinking about how expansive the spread of their networks would have to be to accomplish their main goals, and calling this their target area. In the case of smugglers, this would mean a network designed to move goods across a border that they neither control nor govern. In the case of the pirates, this network would encompass a great deal more.

Categorizing the types of goods is critical, for the means by which smugglers and pirates make money is determined by what they are smuggling or attacking. Making money by evading tariffs and smuggling everyday items that are not otherwise illegal across a single border requires a significantly smaller network than, say, heroin or cocaine trafficking. These types of drugs have only a few sources in the world—mostly Central Asia, Colombia, and the Golden Triangle in Southeast Asia—and thus often have to be transported long distances across hostile territory to reach their prospective markets.[36] Smugglers who specialize in mundane goods are unlikely to have large networks. If they were to move into drug trafficking, they would have much bigger networks (and aspirations). Likewise, pirates who want to hijack and sell off ships (and their cargo) are likely to have wider territorial aspirations (and networks) than those who merely steal money and supplies from ships at sea.

Why do people smuggle goods at all? Because there is a limited number of collection points and a relatively straightforward means of taxation, tariffs on imports are popular in developing countries with low levels of state capacity. High tariffs can lead to a difference in the price of goods between two adjacent countries, which creates conditions in which smugglers can make profits by buying goods in one country, moving them illicitly into the neighboring country, and selling them.[37] Profit margins for smuggling, at least in Indonesia, are high. If smugglers are caught even once in every three trips, they can still make a profit, according to practitioners.[38] For mobile phones, for example, the price difference between phones in Indonesia and those outside is about 30 percent.[39] Likewise, cigarettes are smuggled from both Indonesia and Malaysia into Singapore due to the high price of cigarettes in Singapore relative to those in the other two countries.[40] High levels of corruption and poor enforcement mechanisms are also symptomatic of countries with low state capacity.

As for the motivations of the smugglers, let us assume that these smugglers' primary motivation is economic: to make a profit. If there is no money to be made, there will be no smuggling—unlike JI or GAM, small-time smuggling syndicates cannot withdraw from all operations whiling away their time until political conditions improve. By design, the smuggling syndicates have humble territorial aspirations: their goals are focused on only a part of one country, and they seek neither to control nor to govern territory. A commonsense expectation is that, with no political goals, smugglers are extremely flexible in where they operate. In fact, they often do not adapt well to changes in the political environment (see chapter 8). Crackdowns lead either to different smuggling methods along similar routes or to cessation of smuggling.

Given the high cost in time and effort of crossing borders surreptitiously, small-time smugglers' territorial aspirations are only large enough to encompass a transnational structure needed to transport and dispose of goods. For those with limited territorial ambitions, this means essentially obtaining goods (even legally) in one country, finding a means of transportation (generally ship or truck), and finding a buyer in the second country. At times, customs and police officials, generally in the receiving country, must also be paid off. Compared to the networks for other operations, such as hijacking ships, or Jemaah Islamiyah's bombings, this is quite a small network. Smugglers in Batam often operate in groups of five to ten, with no discernible leader.[41] What is more, the smuggling syndicates are often broken down into even smaller components with truly small territorial aspirations, components whose only job is to receive goods, bribe an official or two, and send the goods on their way. If the link is broken, or a route is cut off for smuggling a particular good, the nodes do not have access to a larger network with other nodes that have not been compromised. Consequently they either stop operating or move into another business.

As for the territorial conceptions of maritime pirates, it is useful to think of two types of pirate syndicates: those with names and those without. Those with names most closely approximate what the general public thinks of as pirates: coherent gangs that exist over the long term, have an identifiable leader (who often lends his name to the group), maintain a hideout on some tropical island, and sally forth in boats occasionally to attack passing ships. In the late 1990s, Indonesian intelligence estimated that there were four or five coherent, long-lived pirate syndicates in Indonesia, each with their own theater of operations corresponding to four hotspots in western and central Indonesia.[42] The Philippines seems to have a large number of these types of syndicates, over and above any piracy activities that might be undertaken by the ongoing separatist insurgencies in the area. The Ambak Pare pirate gang, for example, is the best-known gang in southern Mindanao, and robs fishing boats of motors, gasoline, and diesel fuel. The Philippines has a number of small pirate gangs with names like Villamor, Alinso-ot, Sumayan, and the Tirzo Arnaiz groups, with four to twenty pirates moving about in one to three boats. They generally engage in sea robbery (stealing money and engines on boats within the waters of one country) rather than hijack ships.[43] Pirates that strip everything off a ship are generally local because they want to bring it back to their *kampung* (village) to use or sell.[44] These small-time syndicates, with limited target areas and humble monetary ambitions, do exist, and are quite similar to small-time smuggling gangs, but by way of providing contrast within the range of transnational organized crime, I focus on maritime piratical hijacking syndicates with expansive territorial ambitions.

The larger, loose-knit networks generally do not have names. International hijacking in Southeast Asia appears to be a part-time calling, with a partly ad hoc organization coming together around each operation, and disbanding after its successful completion. This is not to say that there are not habitual offenders—some syndicates carry out a number of attacks. In fact, hijacking is often a side business of shady ship owners, bankers, or businessmen, a lucrative operation that dovetails with their legitimate trading networks.[45] A syndicate generally consists of a financier (who could be considered the leader of the syndicate), middlemen and pirate brokers (who may be the same people), and the pirates. When we take into account all of the people who might be involved in a single hijacking operation, we can see why some pirate syndicates have such large target areas. The financier goes through middlemen and pirate brokers, who may be in a different country than the pirates who are hired to take the ship, while the ship could be owned by a company from across the globe and flagged in yet another country. The actual attack can occur in international waters or a country's territorial waters. The ship and the cargo are then taken to one port (possibly in another country) where the cargo might be offloaded, and possibly to another port where the ship is repainted and recertified. Both the ship and the cargo might then be sold to a buyer from somewhere else. To maintain secrecy and increase the difficulty that concerned states have in coordinating with each other, a syndicate might want to spread itself over as large an area, and as many countries, as possible. The ability (indeed necessity) to operate over such large distances has implications for how pirate syndicates can adapt themselves in response to crackdowns, but also reveals weaknesses in the physical and virtual links that syndicates use to keep themselves together.

Jemaah Islamiyah, GAM, and criminals have a shifting combination of religious, political, and economic motivations that at first glance appear incommensurable. Although various categorizations of terrorist groups can generally be applied to insurgent movements, they often fail when extended to criminal organizations, and in any case often make unnecessary distinctions among groups. But if we break down their motivations into how they relate to territory, we can see that groups as disparate as GAM and Darul Islam share a desire to control and govern territory, even though, as its ambitions covered all of Indonesia, Darul Islam would have opposed any independence for GAM. Mundane smugglers and GAM also share similarly sized target areas, even though their goals could not be more different, and as a result set up networks designed to move into small swathes of territory. Likewise, the Jemaah Islamiyah of the 1990s and 2000s shares widespread territorial ambitions with large-scale pirate syndicates. A territorial approach to the ideas of CTO places us on firm ground when later in the book we look at their common territorial constraints, and the cross-cutting differences and similarities in how their territorial ideas affect their response to success and failure in the context of political openness and state crackdowns.

TERRITORY, POLITICS, AND THE
TECHNOLOGIES OF GLOBALIZATION

No matter what their beliefs about territory, most of the clandestine transnational organizations that most concern policymakers want to blow things up, and all engage in illegal activities. Certainly Jemaah Islamiyah and two of the comparative cases (GAM and maritime pirates) stage violent attacks, while smugglers undermine the formal economies of a number of countries in Southeast Asia. Ideas about territory provide the context for CTOs' actions, and are essential for analysts to understand, if for no other reason than to give us a rough understanding of where a group wants to be, and what it wants to accomplish there. But once a group has decided to attempt something, be it a violent attack, issuing orders, or training its recruits, we have to answer less abstract questions. Given all the space- and time-compressing technology they have at their disposal, how and when are terrorists, insurgents, and criminals constrained by territory? What determines the routes and methods the groups use in their activities? What role do territory and political conditions play in the success or failure of those activities?

After considering the importance of territory both in the history of Southeast Asian illicit groups and in the face of modern technology, I suggest that mapping CTOs' activities onto territory is a useful way to understand how both territory and state power constrain illicit groups. This can be done by thinking of CTOs as agglomerations of transnational activities, and of transnational activities as flows moving across borders between nodes. I argue that the technologies of globalization do not inevitably lead to greater CTO flexibility vis-à-vis states. The methods that CTOs use to move people, goods, and information, and the

legitimate and illegitimate routes over which they move, are shaped and channeled by the political conditions they face and the topographical features and
infrastructure available to them. Modern communications and transportation
infrastructure are instrumental to the success or failure of CTOs' activities. When
a CTO enjoys political openness, it moves along the routes and through territorially grounded chokepoints made possible by the state. When it is facing hostility, it loses easy access to those routes, and must use advantageous geographical
features to avoid state power, thus limiting its options, and possibly leading to
failure. Even in a world with globalizing technologies, territory can constrain
how CTOs cross borders in pursuit of their goals, although *how* it constrains
them depends on other factors.

Situating CTOs in Space

How does territory in general matter in a globalizing world? The argument that
territory, and by extension territorially based states, have become irrelevant in the
face of globalization is only one view. Globalization might simply be a process
that will broaden and deepen current trends. Brynjar Lia, for example, argues
that globalization probably means that terrorists will make increasing use of sophisticated technology, that non-state armed groups will become more numerous, and the political economies of conflicts will become more globalized, thus
expanding the international reach of terrorist groups.[1] This argument does not
dismiss states and territory out of hand, but does not aim to produce any specific
ideas about how transnational terrorist groups (and other clandestine organizations) might be constrained by territory and state-centric political conditions.

Globalization does not monotonically lead to a decrease in the importance of
territory or state power, but is a complex process of deterritorialization and reter-
ritorialization. More specific, Neil Brenner suggests thinking of globalization as a
process by which political economic forces push global capitalism ever outward
and deemphasize territory, borders, and the power of states, and at the same time
depend on territorially grounded states' cities, regulations and infrastructure
(such as airports, seaports, and telecoms) for transportation, communication,
production, and sales.[2] Thus, in Brenner's view, the sub- and supra-national
scales for production and interaction across boundaries are becoming more important relative to the state, but only because of the tools the state provides. That
is, even when we see a phenomenon that seems to have transcended territory, it
may have achieved that transcendence through means for which both territory
and the state still matter. It is states that decide what authority should be de-
volved or given up, to either lower-level entities or multilateral institutions. For

threats that are inherently transnational (as much of terrorism and organized crime is), the multilateral agreements and institutions that are arguably the most effective means of fighting them are the products of states' resources and political will, not of irresistible abstract forces.[3]

Thus a complicated relationship emerges among territory, globalizing technologies, state power, and illicit groups. We can make analysis easier by looking at CTOs' activities, and using the concepts of nodes and flows to map clandestine organizations' transnational activities onto territory and situate them in space.[4] Gerard O'Tuathail suggests conceiving of the world not only as made up of changing state-centric maps, but also as maps of flows, with "centralized routing stations, interconnected nodes, dense concentrations of flows, and sharp digital divides."[5] Colin Flint agrees, but adds that the nodes of the networks are just as important as flows.[6] These are good ideas.

I conceive of CTOs as the sum of their transnational activities, which involve flows of people, materials, or information between nodes separated by international borders, borders that continue to be "pervasive and problematic."[7] The nodes in this study are countries or cities, rather than individuals, and the flows are activities of the groups rather than personal ties. The flows consist of *what* is being moved, and *how* it is being moved, across borders and over virtual and physical landscapes, which are characterized by physical terrain, and transportation and communications infrastructure. Any given transnational activity is thus a series of linked nodes and flows across international borders. This way of thinking has the added benefit of showing what groups with drastically different organizational structures have in common. No matter how hierarchical or diffuse an illicit organization is, it still has to find a way to get weapons, explosives, or smuggled goods to its target.

Historians have long used the concepts of nodes and flows, if not necessarily the language, to situate illicit transnational movements in the political and economic geography of Southeast Asia. With seventeen thousand islands in Indonesia, seven thousand in the Philippines, and nearly impenetrable interiors accessible largely by riverboat, before the Europeans arrived in the sixteenth century Southeast Asia was a region of small coastal states that were intimately involved in and prospered from shipping-based commercial flows. Economic power came from controlling labor (in the form of slaves), shipping routes, or access to precious commodities, not from controlling land.[8] The idea of relatively fixed, formal territorial borders would have seemed bizarre to Southeast Asians of the period—both legitimate and illegitimate transnational movements were the order of the day. In some sense, from a historical Southeast Asian perspective, what is surprising is not so much that illicit transnational movement occurs or occurred, but that there was a period of time when they were not considered the norm.

The end of the Age of Commerce in Southeast Asia coincided with the destruction or cooptation of many of the local coastal states by European powers in the seventeenth century.[9] Although many of the states themselves fell away, traders, brigands, and others who moved transnationally adapted to the changed political conditions. Eric Tagliacozzo argues in his book on historical smuggling in Southeast Asia that the late nineteenth and early twentieth centuries saw a hardening and formalizing of the region's borders, particularly the lines separating the United Kingdom's territories in the Malayan Peninsula and Borneo from the Dutch East Indies as the European powers moved to clamp down on goods that they deemed illegal—narcotics, guns, slaves, and even mundane goods like rice—because they threatened revenue or security, or both. The encroachment of European ideas about territory, and more concretely, naval patrols, forts, checkpoints, and border guards into parts of Southeast Asia that had previously only been considered ungoverned frontiers was connected with a rise in the smuggling of illicit goods across these same borders. The smugglers adapted their routes and methods to resist encroachment of state power, or at the very least to continue to live as they did before, moving freely by sea (and to a lesser extent land) among the islands and peninsulas of Southeast Asia. The picture Tagliacozzo paints is of borders that, no matter how hard the governing states tried to clamp down, were porous and difficult to control.[10] If one of the unfortunate traits of globalization is the ease of illicit movement across international borders, then perhaps globalization has existed in Southeast Asia for hundreds of years.

This was also true of other types of transnational phenomena that were considered harmful to some states or people, notably maritime raiders. The pirates of the late eighteenth and early nineteenth centuries in Southeast Asia, the Iranun and the Balangingi ethnic groups in what would become the southern Philippines who terrorized indigenous people of the Indonesian archipelago and European trading ships alike, were in some sense a reaction to the globalization of their time.[11] As James Warren chronicles, as the British, Dutch, and Spanish built colonies that became wealthy enough to be plundered, and especially as the so-called Sulu Zone—the islands stretching from Sulawesi to Mindanao—was thrust into the global economy, the Iranun found it paid off to go forth and capture slaves from settlements as far away as the Malacca Strait. The slaves would then be used to collect and process exotic goods (notably fish and forest delicacies) that could be traded to European traders, who would in turn trade with the Chinese for tea.[12]

Just as European powers had found it useful to give letters of marque to privateers as a means of augmenting their state power on the cheap, so the Sulu Sultanate viewed the Iranun maritime raiders as a way to extend its reach, economically and to a lesser extent politically, throughout Southeast Asia. The result was that it was often unclear, both to the indigenous inhabitants being attacked and the European colonial rulers, whether the raiders were state or non-state actors. Whatever their technical status, the Iranun maritime raiders had a great deal of firepower at their disposal, and as they accrued wealth through slaving, pushed farther away from the Sulu, until they had established forward bases in Sumatra to attack settlements in the Malay Peninsula.[13] Here, in Warren's formulation, we can see the eighteenth-century equivalent of globalization, inasmuch as global forces affected people's lives in a local (violent) way: raiders from the Sulu Zone took captives in the Malacca Strait to produce goods for the faraway Chinese market, which was producing goods for the even more distant European market. Given the fluidity of illicit groups in Southeast Asia, territorial constraints would not seem to be a very powerful inhibitor of their success in the pre-modern era, let alone now with all that modern technology has to offer.

Yet aspects of pre-modern smugglers and pirates that prefigure the argument here already existed. The Iranun raiders reached their height as extensions of the Sulu state. Shorn of that support, and at the mercy of Spanish, Dutch, and British naval power by the 1840s, they were destroyed relatively quickly. Both smugglers and pirates used the political, economic, and natural terrain to their advantage, although this also had the effect of constraining their movements. Strategically located port cities, especially Singapore, were popular with smugglers, who could hide in the teeming, multinational throngs and piggyback on legitimate transnational commerce. But inasmuch as these same port cities were also often at the center of colonial power, they were vulnerable to being cut off, and obviously centralized and limited smugglers' routes. Smugglers also used frontier areas far from the locus of colonial power, and chokepoints created by geography, such as the Malacca Straits and valleys and rivers in Borneo.[14] In all cases, however, illicit groups had the option of depending on the infrastructure and terrain controlled by states, and simultaneously increasing the speed at which they could operate and the risk to their enterprise; avoiding the state entirely in frontier areas; or creating their own illicit infrastructure, as the Iranun raiders did in building forward bases.

The political and territorial logic of CTOs' operations in Southeast Asia remains the same today, with the added layer of telecommunications, quick and efficient road networks, and jet airplanes. In some situations, modern technology does allow CTOs to operate in ways that are qualitatively different from pre-modern era. In others, CTOs must fall back on the same tools used by illicit groups of old. To this is added the fact that borders have indeed hardened, CTOs in Southeast Asia no longer enjoy quasi-state status (as the Iranun did), states too have new technology and resources at their disposal, and there are no longer political frontier areas, even if they continue to exist in practice on the periphery of weak states. The next section discusses how and when territorial and political constraints determine the shape and success (or failure) of CTOs' transnational activities—when the technologies of globalization work to their advantage, and when circumstances force CTOs to abandon technology and depend on the ways of their forebears.

Success and Failure amid Territorial and Political Constraints

At the heart of an illicit group's transnational activities are what it is the group is moving, and how it is moving it. The routes the group chooses are influenced by the level of hostility it faces from the states that make up the nodes, if by hostility we mean that the states have come out against the group (or one of its activities), and have mobilized law enforcement or military resources against it. Within and around its target area, the CTO encounters different levels of state hostility. Because transnational activities are of primary concern, I look at the levels of hostility faced by the CTO as it crosses between two countries, whether in a generally non-hostile environment (if the CTO is moving between two non-hostile countries) or in a generally hostile environment (if the CTO is attempting to enter a hostile country, whether from another hostile country, or a non-hostile one). It is true that state capacity and political pressure that a group feels cannot be separated entirely—a strong, hostile state might be able to make life for CTO much more difficult than a state that has little control over its territory. But, as was the case with JI in the Philippines, even weak states can raise the costs of illicitly crossing borders to high enough levels that many CTOs would prefer to take their chances with legitimate routes rather than bypass the state entirely and create an illicit infrastructure.

I suggest a spectrum of different transnational activities. For each activity, the CTO can choose several methods: moving not at all (via telecommunications), moving people, or moving materials (weapons, explosives, or contraband). Criminals, insurgents, and terrorists at some point in their operational lives all have command and control structures, and logistics networks, although arguably only insurgents and terrorists go to the trouble of training their members.

The command and control structure, that aspect of the network through which the leaders direct their subordinates and plan their activities, is the least tied to territory. Time and space are no longer significant barriers, and a leader can in principle lead a group from anywhere in the world using modern telecommunications. But telecommunications are not the only means, or even the primary means for the terrorist leaders to hold their networks together. The plotters in Jemaah Islamiyah traveled around and held face-to-face meetings quite a bit as they planned their attacks.

Training requires physical transportation. When terrorist and insurgent groups in particular want to carry out paramilitary training for their members, they must find a way to get their members to the training camp. Although they incur costs in time and money, the weapons they use, if any, are pre-positioned for them, and the groups themselves do not have to figure out how to smuggle guns or explosives.

Logistics, the efforts that go into actually bombing or shooting something, or moving illicit materials, can be considered the activity most tied to the landscape, inasmuch as the network must move both people and material. The network has to figure out how to find a supply of guns or explosives, how to get those materials into the target country (and to the target location), and how to make sure that both the bombers and other plotters, as well as the bombs, are in the right places at the right times.

Given varying levels of state hostility, a CTO can choose to move in three different ways through each leg of its journey. It can make legitimate use of legitimate routes, it can make illicit use of those same legitimate routes, or it can create its own illicit routes that bypass state authority entirely. Routes can either be virtual (in the case of communications) or physical (when the network moves people and material). Physical routes are transportation links, by road, by rail, by sea, or by air. The network is likely to make legitimate use of legitimate routes in non-hostile conditions, and will only use illicit routes in more hostile environments. In a friendly environment, the network has no incentive to incur the extra cost, time, and trouble of creating its own illicit routes when it can use the legitimate routes in and around states that, in a globalizing world, are largely designed to encourage rapid communication and movement. In a hostile environment, the group might have to resort to bypassing state authority entirely, using additional time and effort. Smuggling people and material through legitimate routes (such as through a government-run checkpoint) is a bit more complicated, and is something the group could conceivably do either in a non-hostile or a hostile environment. Although the CTO faces little pressure in a non-hostile environment, it could choose to make illicit use of a legitimate route in order to maintain operational security, or to avoid angering the state that up to this point has been ignoring it. In a hostile environment, illicitly using regular routes might be preferable to using illicit routes, particularly if the network wants to save time or money. Table 2.1 shows the routes available for different transnational activities under different levels of hostility.

When a CTO uses telecommunications along virtual routes, little meaningful distinction is made between legitimate and illicit use of what are for the most

Table 2.1 Relationships between methods and routes

CTO'S GOALS AND TERRITORIAL IDEAS		

↓

METHODS GIVEN TRANSNATIONAL ACTIVITIES		
COMMAND AND CONTROL	**TRAINING**	**LOGISTICS**
Communications		
Movement of people	Movement of people	Movement of people
		Movement of material

→

RELEVANT COUNTRIES GIVEN CTO'S TARGET AREA		

↓

ROUTES GIVEN STATE HOSTILITY		
ROUTES UNDER NON-HOSTILE CONDITIONS		**ROUTES UNDER HOSTILE CONDITIONS**
Legitimate use of legitimate routes	Illicit use of legitimate routes	
Legitimate use of legitimate routes	Illicit use of legitimate routes	Use of illicit routes
	Illicit use of legitimate routes	Use of illicit routes

part lines of communication set up and encouraged by the state. However, in a hostile environment, where the state is attempting to monitor and crack down on a group's communications, the group might take illicit measures to avoid detection, such as frequently changing cell phone SIM cards, using e-mail inboxes as virtual dead drops, and the like. This is in fact what Jemaah Islamiyah did in its Singapore plot.[15]

Moving people around the world can be a part of any of the network's transnational activities, and can use any route, legitimate or illicit. In an open political environment, the network might behave in a way similar to a multinational corporation, with its leaders flying around the world on high-powered business trips. Under extremely hostile conditions, couriers and messengers allow the group to maintain its command and control network where telecommunications have been shut off or compromised, but this limits the network's behavior in other ways.

Moving material goods is where CTOs probably differ the most from typical legitimate multinational corporations. Because CTOs are trying to stage violent attacks or smuggle contraband, even in a non-hostile environment, they cannot simply ship their needed materials without any subterfuge, be they weapons, explosives, or machine parts. No matter how hospitable the environment, CTOs must make illicit use of legitimate routes or, faced with more hostility, use illicit routes.[16] As CTOs' most constrained activity, logistics and the movement of material will become useful in helping us see the difficulties that CTOs have to overcome to operate.

Given a CTO's desired transnational activity, and the level of hostility in the relevant states, I suggest that the CTO will try a small range of movements along certain kinds of routes. This tells us little about the success of those attempts or where those routes are. For our purposes, success is simply whether the CTO succeeds in carrying out the transnational activity that it set out to do. Whether this actually helps the CTO accomplish its overall goals, or whether it is counterproductive is beyond the scope of this study. Jemaah Islamiyah carried out the 2002 Bali bombing successfully, inasmuch as it managed to build several bombs, transport them to Bali, and explode them, but the backlash that the attack created arguably worked against JI's long-terms goals.

What then determines success? In non-hostile conditions the CTO will probably succeed in what it is trying to do, but it would not be a clandestine organization if it did not face some level of state hostility. Under hostile conditions, the story becomes more complicated. The CTO's success depends on the infrastructure and topographic features of the region in which it is operating.

Think back to the example of al-Qaeda at the beginning of the book. Before 2001, al-Qaeda faced what was probably its friendliest political environment as the West and certainly the United States were not paying much attention to what was going on in Afghanistan. Consequently al-Qaeda was able to use what we generally think of as the tools of globalization, airplanes and modern telecommunications, to organize and carry out the 9/11 plot. But al-Qaeda depended on those tools to strike against the United States from across the world. Was al-Qaeda free from considerations of geography? It was certainly not free of communications and transport infrastructure. We can think of the virtual and physical infrastructure that CTOs use to move from country to country as being on a continuum from air travel and telecommunications—the tools of globalization that allow people, goods, and information to move across the globe with little consideration for time and space—to transportation infrastructure that follows the contours of the physical landscape, such as sea travel, highways, and railroads, and finally to natural terrain. Chains of many small (and often uninhabited) islands, treacherous mountain passes, nearly impenetrable jungle, and blistering deserts are all difficult for states to police. It is through these topographical features that CTOs create their illicit routes in order to bypass hostile state power.

Even in a globalized world, a CTO is always constrained in some way because of one of the seeming paradoxes of globalization. The technologies, methods of transportation, and processes that are most liberated from territory are also the ones that move through global chokepoints, that have received the most aid from states, and thus, are the ones most subject to curtailment by state power, sometimes even nominal state power. Air travel allows travelers to move around the world most quickly, but airports and airplanes are also subject to concentrations of state scrutiny. The logistical miracles of modern shipping have greatly decreased the costs of moving goods, but for extremely long distances, the ships tend to go through a few major transshipment ports, which are often in countries, such as Singapore and Hong Kong, with high levels of state capacity.[17] As groups move over large (or even small) distances, we can see where these chokepoints are, and how they use them. We will see that Malaysia, for instance, became even more important to the Free Aceh Movement after it globalized its operations, and that Jemaah Islamiyah used certain airports frequently as it plotted its attacks, even in a politically open environment.

With an increase in state hostility, organizations must go to ground, so to speak, and increasingly rely on methods and routes that are dissociated from the state, and hence more dependent on difficult natural terrain. Although they might thus be able to escape the state, because they must follow the contours of the land, their options are limited, and they are prone to being cut off. If there are only two valleys along a mountainous border, the CTO will likely have to go through one of them. Conversely, it is possible that a border the CTO wants to cross contains no natural terrain amenable to avoiding the state. In this case, it is likely to fail. Clandestine organizations can choose the middle way, and try to sneak along legitimate routes, but because these routes follow the contours of the landscape, unless they can successfully string together a series of routes across a number of different countries, they are limited in the sheer distance they can travel, and in the speed at which they can move.

When CTOs must choose between sneaking across borders along legitimate routes or using illicit routes, the problems they face are analogous to the quandaries they face in general in weak and failed states.[18] Conversely, chokepoints at international borders encourage CTOs to bypass state power, as borders are often the areas in which state power is most evident. For weak states in particular, borders are one of the most visible manifestations of their (sometimes otherwise nonexistent) sovereignty, inasmuch as internationally recognized boundaries prevent other states from interfering.[19] This is especially true when we make the distinction between weak and failed (or worse, collapsed) states.[20] Although collapsed states, such as Somalia, would not be expected to have any border controls, weak states might put a disproportionate amount of their coercive apparatus on borders to show their continuing relevance. As a result, according to Colin Flint, "terrorists are wary of crossing them, and the most likely settings for control nodes are areas that allow movement with minimal state observation—frontier areas where the level of state control is weak."[21]

Bypassing state power along illicit routes creates a situation analogous to operating in an area of state failure. In both situations, the CTO loses access to the public goods that even weak states provide, in the form of general security from criminal predation and maintenance of transportation infrastructure such as roads and airports. This is why, while some analysts worry that failed states provide ideal safe havens for terrorists and other illicit groups, inasmuch as the costs of evading the state are low and there is a body of willing, impoverished recruits,[22] there are good reasons for terrorists not to like them any more than the countries they are opposing.[23] States often broadcast their political power, and encourage economic development, by building roads and other transportation infrastructure over a given piece of territory.[24] Logically, CTOs that want to avoid the state might operate in areas where the state has not been able to broadcast power, but these areas are also out of reach of the public security and transportation goods provided by the state. In weak states, these areas would likely be those with impenetrable terrain. In failed or collapsed states, they might be most of the country's territory. From an analyst's perspective, the outcome is the same: CTOs have difficulty engaging in transnational activities that require fast and cheap transportation and communication. Moving across difficult terrain is a second choice for CTOs and states alike.

For CTOs, this tradeoff between dealing with a weak (or worse, a strong) state and getting to use its globalizing infrastructure (with some amount of risk) or bypassing the state completely and moving slowly and painfully through difficult terrain (or moving through areas of state failure) is exhibited by the problem of the final mile. In the southern Philippines and eastern Indonesia (the so-called Mindanao-Sulawesi Axis), there is a number of terrorist and insurgent groups, including Abu Sayyaf Group, the Moro Islamic Liberation Front, and Jemaah Islamiyah, all of whom have operatives hiding in central Mindanao in the southern Philippines. The infrastructure for getting into Mindanao is quite good—there are daily flights and ferries—but the roads to the mountainous, jungle-covered interior are poor, and even impassable in the rainy season. Furthermore, if terrorists want to move illicitly from Mindanao to Sulawesi in Indonesia, their only option is by boat, which hampers their mobility.[25] The ability of illicit groups to do much more than seek refuge in the center of Mindanao is thus limited, even though Philippine state power is almost completely absent. Central Mindanao is a failed state, but this has led to a poor operating environment for illicit groups.

Al-Qaeda encountered similar problems when it attempted to infiltrate Somalia in the early 1990s to train local Islamist militants. Transportation links to and within Kenya are widely available, but when al-Qaeda wanted to continue on to Somalia from Kenya, it essentially had to create its own transportation options (in this case, chartering a plane and buying a boat) and defend its operatives from ambushes, which obviously took up a major chunk of its budget.[26] Once in Somalia, al-Qaeda found that the more remote areas, away from state scrutiny (such as it was), were indeed better in theory for training camps, but it had to find ways to get recruits to those camps and feed them while they were there. The difficulty of doing this became a source of tension within the group.[27]

Al-Qaeda found a situation in Somalia where the time and costs associated with moving people and goods around were increased greatly because of the lack of infrastructure and the need to provide its own security for its activities.[28] As a result, it was Kenya, a weak state that nonetheless had passable air and road connections, and provided some level of security to its citizens, not Somalia, a collapsed state that provided none of these things, that afforded greater opportunities for al-Qaeda penetration.[29] Globalizing technologies are only useful if they are available, and they are generally most available in states that also have some ability to control borders and the infrastructure on which CTOs depend. Clandestine transnational organizations can overcome this problem by creating their own illicit infrastructure, or by taking on some of the qualities of the state, such as provision of public security goods, but both of these solutions are costly and time-consuming, and beyond the means of the vast majority of CTOs. They also require a rigorous knowledge of local terrain, language, customs, and power structures.[30]

Weak and failed states bring another factor into the puzzle of CTO success and failure amid territorial and political constraints—what happens when the state is divided against itself. Up until now it has been useful to take the state as a single entity with a single position vis-à-vis the CTO. In developed countries, this is arguably true most of the time—there is no faction within the U.S. government, for instance, that is not hostile to al-Qaeda, although certain groups might have differing views on how to fight terrorism. In less developed countries, however, central state weakness can hinder the government's efforts. In such a country, the government is often at odds with itself, or unable to implement its policies fully. Even in a situation where the state is generally hostile to a CTO's activities, significant and/or well-placed factions within the government might be more favorably inclined to the CTO, or even aid it in some way in ways that rise above petty corruption. In Indonesia, for instance, during the Maluku and Poso ethno-religious conflicts from 1999 to 2002 (and continuing with less intensity even today), the central government condemned the violence, and eventually brokered peace deals, but elements within the Indonesian military incited Muslims and Christians to attack each other, and made sure that the combatants got weapons to continue fighting.[31]

In a non-hostile environment, a state faction favorably inclined to the CTO would most likely be superfluous. But once the state has turned against the CTO, the CTO's routes and methods become more complicated. Assuming we can identify any friendly factions, we would need to know what the factions' goals are vis-à-vis the CTO, and what tools the factions have at their disposal to help the CTO. The goals and characteristics of the friendly state faction would further shape the CTO's routes and methods. Depending on their role within the government, they could arrange for operatives to escape from prison, supply the CTO with weapons, conveniently fail to track the CTO after a bombing, send money to the CTO, or adopt any number of other tactics as the CTO moves along roads and through seaports. Even in weak states, however, help from within the government is rarely enough to create a friendly overall political environment over the objections of the central state, meaning that the group needs to continue to use some level of subterfuge. Whatever help militias received from the military in Poso and Ambon before the 2002 Bali bombing, in the aftermath of the bombing the military became largely unsympathetic to JI's operations. Rather, friendly factions within state improve the probability that CTOs move successfully through legitimate routes using illicit means. This is how, as chapter 6 shows, GAM was able to obtain weapons from Indonesia's arms supplier in Bandung and from soldiers in Aceh itself, but struggled to break the Indonesian naval blockade once the Indonesian military clamped down on imports from Thailand and Malaysia.

Using the technologies of globalization subjects CTOs to concentrated state power at certain chokepoints. Avoiding state power limits access to those same technologies, and thus constrains CTOs' options. Even for an organization with relatively expansive territorial ambitions, the sheer number of routes that it can use to accomplish its logistical, command and control, or training goals is not infinite. What is more, the inevitable hostility of various states and the probability that the network will not be able to be completely open with its logistical activities mean that the number of routes and topographic features that we would realistically have to analyze when tracking a CTO is quite limited. In effect, if we know enough about the network's goals and ideas about territory, and we have a firm grasp of the geography and infrastructure of a region, the success or failure of specific routes and methods becomes somewhat predictable.

Next, I examine the territorial constraints faced by Jemaah Islamiyah's transnational activities as it rose from its origins as a breakaway branch of Darul Islam to become the most widespread terrorist group in Southeast Asia, and then largely collapsed under the crackdowns that followed 9/11 and the first Bali bombings. Again and again, Jemaah Islamiyah's operatives either did their utmost not to be clandestine at all, moved across borders surreptitiously in ways that were successful but nonetheless showed weaknesses that states could later exploit, or, in the absence of advantageous geography or any ability to get through chokepoints, failed.

Part II
TERRITORY AND TRANSNATIONAL TERRORISM

THE RISE OF JEMAAH ISLAMIYAH, 1985–1999

This chapter explains how Jemaah Islamiyah's command and control, training, and smuggling activities were shaped and channeled by territory and political conditions during its time in exile, from Abdullah Sungkar and Abu Bakar Ba'asyir's flight from Indonesia to Malaysia in 1985 until Suharto fell in 1998 and Jemaah Islamiyah spread back into Indonesia. Aside from its proscription in Indonesia, the late 1980s and early 1990s were a period of relative ease for Jemaah Islamiyah. It built training camps in the Philippines and Afghanistan, set up cells in Malaysia and Singapore, and organized itself into a formal organization, all with little hostility from its host nations. Even as it became one of the most sophisticated globalized terrorist groups in the world, and certainly in Southeast Asia, tracing how exactly JI built its empire reveals vulnerabilities in its transnational routes and methods that would come back to haunt it once governments started paying attention.

In the aftermath of 9/11, and amid increased U.S. government concern about Southeast Asian terrorism, Jemaah Islamiyah has attracted its own small literature, most of which seeks to answer three related questions: Where did JI come from? Why does it engage in terrorism? What kind of threat does JI pose? Nearly every study that examines Jemaah Islamiyah's origins and goals places it within the milieu of radical Islam, or of political Islam more generally.[1] What this means for Jemaah Islamiyah's activities or the threat it poses is debatable. Many of the authors who have written on Jemaah Islamiyah are concerned with the ideological, strategic, and tactical links the group might have with al-Qaeda at the global level, as well as with the Abu Sayyaf Group, the Moro Islamic Liberation Front, and other Southeast Asian militant groups closer to home. The implication is that JI is either the Southeast Asian branch of al-Qaeda or of a piece with other militant groups in the region.[2] By this logic, JI is just one manifestation of a more general phenomenon of militant Islamist organizations in Southeast Asia, alongside not only the separatist groups in the Philippines, but also other Islamic groups in Malaysia and Thailand, as well as the militias that fought Christians in Maluku and Central Sulawesi in the late 1990s and early 2000s.[3] The conclusion is that given the rich stew from which Jemaah Islamiyah has emerged, it and its allied organizations will continue to be a threat unless strong action is taken.

Such views have come in for criticism from some quarters on several points, although even in critics' work the emphasis on JI's beliefs and links with outside groups (or not) largely remains.[4] Natasha Hamilton-Hart divides the literature on the Southeast Asian terrorist motivations into political grievances—the terrorists have goals that cannot be achieved through peaceful means in the present political system[5]—and religious grievances, where terrorists have been radicalized by the preaching of extremist imams.[6] She then proceeds to criticize both explanations as pathologizing terrorists, leading to analyses that do not take their grievances, or more generally their ideas, seriously.[7] Critics also caution against viewing Islam as a religion divided between moderates and radicals or drawing too close a connection with political Islam in Indonesia. They argue that political Islam, especially as practiced in Indonesia, is not simply a precursor for terrorism. Even some Muslims with radical views tend to look at Jemaah Islamiyah's behavior as reprehensible.[8] Moreover, one of the main differences between mainstream Islamic groups and JI is that the latter has specifically rejected participation in the political process.[9] In addition, the grievances of many militant Islamic groups, JI included, are rooted in domestic causes that are both unrelated to and predate al-Qaeda's presence in the region.[10] The connection to al-Qaeda, in this reading, is more feared than real, and serves mainly to obfuscate and sensationalize the threat posed by terrorism in the region.

The following three chapters are not a comprehensive account of Jemaah Islamiyah, but can be taken as a companion to works that focus on JI's ideological underpinnings and links with other terrorist groups. A book on the political geography of illicit groups necessarily has different focuses from a standard political science text. I am unconcerned with JI's outside links except when they support or limit JI's flows of people, goods, and information in concrete ways. As for ideology, to the extent this book is about ideas, it is about very specific ideas—those related to groups' political ambitions for given pieces of territory. Islam, political or not, is relevant to my analysis only inasmuch as terrorists motivated by political grievances, religious beliefs, or both, often have goals that are more concerned with controlling (and possibly governing) territory than are those with economic goals. If anything, a focus on transnational activities downplays the importance of Islam (or any overarching ideology) in Jemaah Islamiyah's day-to-day behavior. The starting point for my analysis is thus the fact that Jemaah Islamiyah wanted to blow things up, not why it wanted to do so.

Before Jemaah Islamiyah, 1985–1993

Command and Control: The *Hijrah* to Malaysia

In February 1985, as it became more apparent that the Indonesian Supreme Court was going to rule in favor of the prosecution in Sungkar and Ba'asyir's case, and order them rearrested, the clerics had three choices. They could allow themselves to be taken back into custody, they could go into hiding inside Indonesia, which, given Suharto's tight control of security in Indonesia, was not a winning proposition, or they could flee the country. They chose to call their flight a *hijrah*, after Muhammad's flight from Mecca to Medina, as they repaired to Malaysia in April 1985.[11] Under political pressure, Sungkar and Ba'asyir made the decision to go transnational. This had advantages, as they were no longer under threat from the Indonesian government, but presented problems for maintaining control of their cells.

Fortunately for Sungkar, Ba'asyir, and the followers who fled with them, the Indonesian government has traditionally had a problem convincing other countries to take action against groups or people it opposes, and the leaders of the network faced a world that at the time was fairly indifferent to their presence. If they had been completely indifferent to distance, Sungkar and Ba'asyir could have gone to Pakistan, near the mujahidin battles with the Soviets, or to Saudi Arabia, home of Wahhabism and a number of other Islamist refugees from Southeast Asia. Instead, they chose Malaysia. This is not because they were particularly interested in Malaysia, but because they were still focused on Indonesia. In theory, the pair could have gone almost anywhere in the world and used phones and faxes to communicate with their followers, as the leadership of GAM had done several years earlier. Moreover, if Sungkar and Ba'asyir's relationship with their followers was simply one of spiritual leadership, continual two-way communication was unnecessary, and the two clerics could have moved farther away than Malaysia. In 1985 Jemaah Islamiyah was not yet an operational terrorist network, but the level of control that Sungkar in particular sought to maintain in Indonesia required more frequent contact than simply sending a few sermon tapes every year or so. Maintaining operational control of a network of covert cells through a system of couriers who fly or sail back and forth between one's place of exile and Indonesia would seem to dictate a location fairly close to Indonesia, and in fact Sungkar and Ba'asyir lived in a small coastal town with a ferry connection to Sumatra.[12]

Indonesian government hostility not only kept Sungkar from entering Indonesia, but also forced him to have his operatives sneak over the border, through both legitimate and illegitimate routes. Because the only way to get into western Indonesia without flying is by boat, Sungkar's couriers would have had to come from Singapore, Malaysia, or Thailand across the Malacca or Singapore Straits.

Sungkar used at least one courier, Muzahar Muhtar, to shuttle back and forth with letters between Malaysia and Jakarta for over a year in an attempt to keep the *usroh* network afloat. Typically, in his trips between Indonesia and Malaysia, Muzahar went overland or by air from Jakarta to Medan (or some other port city in northeastern Sumatra), from which he took a ferry to Selangor, Malaysia.[13] Occasionally some people involved in Sungkar's group flew to Malaysia, but most seem to have taken the ferry from Sumatra. Such a travel-intensive means of command and control would have been unthinkable if Sungkar and the exiles had been any farther from Indonesia than an adjacent country, and unnecessary if the Indonesian government were not so watchful.

Sungkar did intend to remain in control. The structure of the Jemaah NII network that Muzahar outlines in his September 1986 interrogation is hierarchical, and divided into informal territorial and functional groupings. Sungkar and Ba'asyir are described as heads of the Malaysia section, while a certain Muchliansyah was the *ketua* (head) of the Jakarta section, overseeing sections for *hijrah, dakwah,* and various financial functions.[14] Muzahar's documents also list a *fa'i* section, wherein the members commit crimes against infidels to raise money, although Abdullah Sungkar apparently did not approve of *fa'i,* and was quite angry when people connected to his network began killing infidels and each other.[15] Thus, it is possible that the *fa'i* section described by Muzahar was more de facto than approved by Sungkar. Elsewhere Muzahar describes the purpose of the network almost entirely in terms of *dakwah,* with the only mention of physical or military training in reference to going to fight the Soviets in Afghanistan.[16] Given the number of crackdowns in Indonesia, there was no place for anything but *dakwah* at this stage if the network wanted to survive.

Although the bulk of the Sungkar *usroh* network had been concentrated in Central and East Java, many of the members fled to Jakarta to escape the crackdown, and tried to establish some semblance of an organization there. The *usroh* structure was useful in its portability from the traditional Sungkar stronghold of Central Java to Jakarta. But maintaining any coherent organization under pressure from the Indonesian government—which set about destroying the *usroh* around the time Sungkar and Ba'asyir fled—proved difficult. International Crisis Group describes the Jakarta rings of Darul Islam in the mid-1980s as more havens for those wanted by the police in other parts of Indonesia than as coherent groups. Some of the Jakarta people simply left Indonesia and went to join Sungkar in Malaysia. In any event, the political pressure on the Jakarta group was such that the costs of going operational solely in Indonesia were too high, and the costs of trying to run such a network from Malaysia higher still. Sungkar apparently told Muzahar in August 1985 to return to Indonesia to have one of the leaders still in the country restart the Central Java *usroh*, but nothing seemed to come of the trip. Essentially, the Abdullah Sungkar branch of Darul Islam was less than fully operational in Indonesia from the time Muzahar and the others were arrested until Jemaah Islamiyah expanded back into Java in the late 1990s.[17]

Abdullah Sungkar and Abu Bakar Ba'asyir's experience in Malaysia comports well with the argument up to this point. Having been forced out of Indonesia, the pair sought a country from which they could establish transnational links along both legitimate and illicit routes that avoided the power of the Indonesian state. As one of the nearest countries, Malaysia was ideal.

Training in Afghanistan

Abdullah Sungkar and his merry band of exiles began sending Indonesian recruits to Afghanistan almost as soon as they got to Malaysia. Going to train and fight in Afghanistan was not a new idea, even in 1985. Southeast Asians had appeared in the theater in the early 1980s and Darul Islam saw sending fighters to Afghanistan as a natural extension of their fight for Negara Islam Indonesia, both to help other Muslims, and to train future leaders of NII. Sungkar's goal by December 1985 was thirty people, but according to Muzahar, by that time they had only reached six, all Indonesians.[18] They also needed a network to facilitate this. There seem to have been DI recruiters in Indonesia who would find willing recruits, and then send them to Malaysia.

The ways in which the recruits moved from Java to Afghanistan illustrate what exactly the network was afraid of vis-à-vis the Indonesian government, and what steps they took to avoid another crackdown. Going overland from Jakarta through Sumatra to Medan, then by ferry to Malaysia (either Johor or Selangor) seems to have been the route followed by many recruits, in part because of government scrutiny. Darul Islam remained a banned organization, and recruits flying directly between Jakarta and Karachi could be subject to more intense government scrutiny than usual. Nasir Abas describes how he became part of the third class of DI recruits to go to Afghanistan. His teacher asked him one day in 1987, "Do you want to go to Afghanistan or to Perlis [a state in Malaysia]?"[19] After several years of being steeped in stories of the depredations suffered by Muslims in Afghanistan, Nasir decided he wanted to go there to engage in jihad.

His teacher assured him that all of his expenses would be paid for by Abdul Halim (Abdullah Sungkar's pseudonym); he only had to bring a willing heart and body. After getting permission from his father, Nasir went to a house in Kuala Pilah, Negeri Sembilan state, and found himself with fourteen other recruits: thirteen Indonesians and one other Malaysian (Mat Beduh). He says no indication existed of where the Indonesians came from (aside from Indonesia, obviously), how they had gotten into Malaysia, or whether they were there for work or had come specifically for jihad. They were warned to tell no one of their plans to go to Afghanistan, and were ordered to adopt aliases, which they were to use from then on (Nasir became Sulaiman). The night before the group was to leave through Subang airport (Kuala Lumpur's old international airport), they assembled in the house of Pak Ristan, also known as Natsir, in Serting, Negeri Sembilan. Abdullah Sungkar, Abu Bakar Ba'asyir and other leaders were there (operating under their Malaysian aliases), and after some words of encouragement, the recruits pledged an oath of loyalty known as *bayat*.[20]

Several observations are relevant. First, it was Nasir's teacher, not Abdullah Sungkar or Abu Bakar Ba'asyir, who recruited him for jihad. Sungkar knew Malaysians even before he left Indonesia. He had also built a network in Malaysia sufficient to begin recruiting Malaysians through third parties by the end of 1987, and had sufficient funds (presumably from non-DI sources) to pay for non-Indonesian jihadis who were not devoted to NII. Second, NII was never mentioned; Nasir joined because he wanted to go fight the Soviets and protect Muslims. Whether he was part of a larger cause or organization did not seem to occur to him, and at first he was reluctant to pledge *bayat* because he had not done such a thing with his own teacher.[21] In fact, Nasir claims he heard no mention of NII until he actually arrived in Pakistan and began talking with Indonesians. Third, Nasir was consternated by the secrecy of the Indonesians: they concealed their names, intentions, and movements. It was not illegal in Malaysia to go for jihad to Afghanistan, and if he had been in a solely Malaysian organization, he would have had little reason to hide his movements at all. The difference in political climates between Indonesia and Malaysia suggests the extent to which the states' policies affected the behavior of the jihadis. In moving within Indonesia, and from Indonesia to Malaysia, the network took great care to be secretive, and consequently was forced to rely on routes that elicited less scrutiny from the Indonesian government (i.e., taking the ferry from Sumatra rather than flying). By contrast, in moving from Malaysia to Pakistan, aside from the residual aliases, very few precautions were taken. Nasir's class of fifteen recruits drove to Kuala Lumpur, then flew from there to Karachi on an Aeroflot flight. Abas wondered whether it was wise to fly the Soviet national airline when they were going to Afghanistan to wage jihad on the Red Army, but he was told that the organizers chose Aeroflot only because it was "the cheapest."[22] With the increased distance from Indonesia, security was becoming less of a concern, and the recruits were free to use more modern, faster modes of transportation.

Upon their arrival in Karachi, Nasir's class took a bus over the course of two nights to Pabbi, a small town near Peshawar, where they were placed in a school that doubled as a clearing center for mujahidin before they were moved to Akademi Militer Mujahidin Afghanistan (Afghanistan Mujahidin Military Academy), also known as Harbiy Pohantun or Camp Saddah. It was only in Pabbi that Nasir and Mat Beduh were told that rather than going directly to the front to fight the Soviets they would be training at Camp Saddah for three years. Both Malaysians were initially put off by the news (and noticed that the Indonesians apparently already knew about the long training). They had been under the impression that they were going to begin fighting right away, but were told that it was necessary to study war before they could engage in it.[23] If Sungkar had shifted to the goal of a pan-Southeast Asian caliphate by this time, he kept it secret from the non-Indonesians that he sent to Afghanistan. Rather, Abdullah Sungkar's network seems to have been undergoing some sort of transition. The Indonesians (many of whom had been living in Malaysia) understood that they were going to Afghanistan mostly for training that they could take back to Indonesia to support the cause of Darul Islam. In fact, although some of the members of the first cohorts did fight against the Red Army (such as at the Battle of Jaji in 1987), they were explicitly told their primary mission was staying alive to take jihad back to Southeast Asia.[24] This nuance was initially lost on the Malaysians sent by Sungkar.

The first camp for the Southeast Asians was Camp Saddah, from 1985 to 1992. Sungkar was a good friend of Abdul Rasul Sayyaf (also known as Abu Sayyaf), the Afghan mujahidin commander most hospitable to non-Afghan fighters. Sayyaf provided land, weapons, and food within his Camp Saddah complex on the Afghanistan-Pakistan border. Camp Saddah was divided into three parts based on geographic origins, one of which was reserved for all Southeast Asians (Thais, Malaysians, Indonesians, and Filipinos), who were grouped together for the purposes of training in Malay and English. Until 1992, the Sungkar network sent recruits over in discrete classes for training in the regular programs, totaling at least seven classes (depending on how they are counted) by the time Camp Saddah was abandoned.[25] All told, the Indonesian government assesses that 360 Indonesian cadres were sent to Afghanistan and Pakistan.[26]

At the end of 1992, the instructors of the Afghanistan Military Academy packed up shop and moved to Afghanistan to take part in the new mujahidin government, and Camp Saddah closed. Abdullah Sungkar's network continued to benefit from Abu Sayyaf's munificence, and he allowed them to build a new camp in Torkham, in Afghanistan, which was isolated enough to "blow up a mountain" without anyone noticing.[27] This camp, which opened at the beginning of 1993, was open only to recruits of what was by now Jemaah Islamiyah. All of the instructors were Southeast Asian alumni from classes at Camp Saddah, including Nasir Abas, and taught much the same curriculum, although they seemed to have emphasized short courses over the three-year marathons offered at the previous camp. The newly arisen Taliban subsequently ordered Camp Torkham closed in 1995—it could not operate without some sort of support from the relevant state authority.[28] Because JI could not run large-scale training without government acquiescence, it did not use illicit routes in Afghanistan and Pakistan, and never built the structures usually set up to support those routes. Chapter 8 discusses the consequences this would have for JI as it set its sights beyond Indonesia in the late 1980s.

The Creation of Jemaah Islamiyah, 1993–1999

Command and Control: Formal Beginnings

From the time Jemaah Islamiyah was formally created in 1993 until 1999, when it moved back into Indonesia, the organization faced a political environment that, outside of Indonesia, was largely indifferent to its existence. In the late 1980s and early 1990s, the group's territorial ambitions had expanded from Indonesia to most of Southeast Asia. It spread across a vast geographic area, from Malaysia and Singapore in the west to Australia in the east, and was held together by a command and control network that relied on telecommunications and extensive travel along legitimate routes for face-to-face meetings. At least on paper, JI was a centralized, bureaucratic organization with regular promotions and the ability to transfer people between offices in different countries. When the group went operational in mid-1990s and began preparing to carry out attacks, the operational members were drawn from the hierarchy on an ad hoc basis, but they still remained subject to territorial and political considerations as they communicated and moved around Southeast Asia.

By 1992, the relationship between Abdullah Sungkar and DI Imam Ajengan Masduki was breaking down (and would remain as such until shortly before Sungkar's death). Other DI leaders charged that Sungkar was shaping the Afghanistan recruits to create his own faction, in part by having them swear *bayat* to him rather than to NII, while Sungkar charged Masduki with heresy.[29] The charges against Sungkar were not without foundation; Nasir's prior ignorance of NII is evidence of that.[30] By 1992, Sungkar and Ba'asyir's concept of the pan-Southeast Asian caliphate was fully realized, although Indonesia remained central to their focus. In Pakistan, other NII members explained to Nasir that Islam was without borders. Although Singapore and Malaysia would fall eventually, Indonesia was the priority, and non-Indonesians should help the Indonesian members of NII accomplish that goal. Sungkar himself came to Camp Torkham in 1992 and explained that Indonesia must be the first country taken over, and the rest would follow.[31] Such goals were laudable in the abstract to DI leaders, but strayed from the Indonesia-only concept of Darul Islam. With his grand plans and growing non-Indonesian base, it was only a matter of time before Sungkar became too big for Darul Islam.

In 1992 or early 1993, the NII recruits in Afghanistan were given a choice. They could choose Abdullah Sungkar and Abu Bakar Ba'asyir as their leaders, become part of a new organization called Jemaah Islamiyah, and stay in Afghanistan, or they could choose Ajengan Masduki and Darul Islam, and immediately go back to Indonesia or Malaysia. Given those two options by the military commander of JI Zulkarnaen, Nasir Abas chose to remain in Afghanistan, while, except for Imam Samudra, all the Indonesians chose Sungkar.[32]

So it was that Jemaah Islamiyah officially came into existence on 1 January 1993, according to Ahmad Sajuli, a witness in a Malaysian terrorism trial, in Serting, Negeri Sembilan, Malaysia. Ahmad Sajuli himself had first met Ba'asyir in 1989, and had been a member of JI since soon after the organization broke away from DI.[33] Either concurrently, or soon afterward, the formal structure of JI was set in place. In form, it was the result of lessons learned from the (dis)organization of the original NII structure, as well as aspects of military and Islamic hierarchies the Indonesians encountered in Afghanistan.[34] Only one of the four top councils was devoted to operations, the Majelis Qiyadah Markaziyah, the others were for other functions considered necessary for an Islamic government.[35] The *markaziyah* was a committee made up of the usual administrative officers plus the officers in charge of JI's *dakwah* unit, the education unit (which ran the JI-connected schools), the military academy in Afghanistan, and the units tasked with communications, political activities, and sending recruits off to conflicts.[36] To these were added the heads of the *mantiqi* (equivalent to military divisions), of which there were only two at JI's inception. Jemaah Islamiyah was never an organization entirely devoted to terrorist operations, but viewed the struggle for an Islamic state as multifaceted. The structure of the *markaziyah* reflected its simultaneous, interconnected campaigns of proselytization, education, military training, and later, blowing things up. Except for the JI-connected schools, such as Pondok Ngruki's Pesantren al-Mukmin, which were recruiting grounds for future members, all of JI's activities took advantage of the *mantiqi* structure in some way.

The *mantiqi* were structured like military organizations, although before about 1995 they did not engage in paramilitary operations per se. Each *mantiqi* had its own committee, the *majelis qiyadah markaziyah mantiqi,* with the usual administrative officers, *dakwah* units, education units, and in the case of Mantiqi I (which covered Singapore and Malaysia) and Mantiqi II (which covered Indonesia), officers in charge of fundraising. Below the *markaziyah mantiqi* were progressively smaller units, of which the most notable were *wakalah,* roughly equivalent to military brigades. Like the *mantiqi,* the *wakalah* were geographically based, but unlike *mantiqi* covered only specific provinces or cities in Indonesia or Malaysia (Singapore's JI cell was a *wakalah* within Mantiqi I).[37] *Fiah* were the actual terrorist cells that are commonly seen in popular media. They were generally fluid in membership, and consisted of six to ten people, who could be transferred between or work across different *fiah* when their skills were needed.[38] There were intermediate-level units, although it is unclear how rigidly the structure was followed between *fiah* and *wakalah.*[39] For example, seven operational *fiah* existed within the Singapore *wakalah,* leading to the conclusion that either Singapore's structure was still incomplete, or the structure envisioned by JI's leadership was an ideal type rather than reality.[40]

Such a system was optimized for the relatively open political environment that JI faced outside of Indonesia at its creation. The organization was comfortable moving across great distances and crossing many international borders along legitimate routes. Its hierarchical structure in theory allowed close control by Sungkar, but also required a great deal of communication between nodes within the group's network. Numerous face-to-face meetings, for example, helped build trust within the organization, but required extensive international travel. In essence, JI's strength in the 1990s, its ability to operate across Southeast Asia, was possible due to the technologies of globalization, but it was also only able to take full advantage of some of those tools in a politically open environment.

Suharto's Indonesia was still a no-go zone for Sungkar, Ba'asyir and the rest of the exiles, and any violent actions would have been met with the same force as they had been in the 1970s and early 1980s. Singapore and Malaysia certainly would not have countenanced violent attacks on their own soil, but as long as Jemaah Islamiyah appeared to be nothing but a non-violent *dakwah* network, they did little to stop it. Thailand and the Philippines, the "tail ends" of JI's supply chain, also had no specific policy against Sungkar and his network. Under Suharto, Indonesia had a strong anti-subversion law that allowed preventative detention, and used it liberally. The Indonesian government repeatedly asked for the extradition of Sungkar and Ba'asyir, but Malaysia refused. It also refused to use the Internal Security Act, Malaysia's equivalent of Suharto's anti-subversion law, to detain the clerics. The Malaysian government monitored both Sungkar and Ba'asyir, as well as returnees from Pakistan and Afghanistan, but did not suspect them of being part of a larger network.[41]

Abdullah Sungkar took the *usroh*-like *dakwah* structure he had spent ten years perfecting and expanding, first in Indonesia, then transplanted to Malaysia and by 1993 to Singapore, and subsumed it within a fairly rigid, military-like, hierarchical structure with some degree of centralization. Creation of new *wakalah* had to be proposed by the relevant *mantiqi* and approved by the *markaziyah,* as did appointment of *mantiqi* leaders and the creation of new operations. When Nasir Abas was made head of Mantiqi III (which was partially carved out of Mantiqi II, and covered eastern Indonesia and the Philippines), for example, he went to Solo and talked to Abu Bakar Ba'asyir personally.[42] Sungkar and other leaders' charisma brought cohesion to what would otherwise have been a scattered and incoherent network, while the structure was sufficiently bureaucratic for everyone from the amir on down to *wakalah* leaders to be replaced on a regular basis after short terms in office. In 1997, for example, Nasir Abas was assigned to the Johor *wakalah* (part of Mantiqi I) to teach Arabic language at Luqmanul Hakiem *Pesantren* (one of JI's religious schools, now closed by the Malaysian government). Then, on 30 August 1997, Nasir was transferred; he took his wife and moved to Sandakan, Sabah, Malaysia to head the *wakalah* there.[43] In many ways, JI acted like a multinational company that had decided not to register with the relevant authorities.

But Jemaah Islamiyah was destined for "greater" things than simply being able to hold itself together across an entire region. Abdullah Sungkar visited Afghanistan and Pakistan in 1993 or 1994, meeting many of al-Qaeda's leaders, including Osama bin Laden. Apparently it was a turning point for him, leading him to the conclusion that it was time for JI to start planning attacks. Sungkar pledged *bayat* to bin Laden, and following this visit, the JI leaders told Hambali (who would become the operations leader of JI) and Abu Jibril (who would become the head of Mantiqi I) to start cells throughout the region.[44]

The effect on the formal structure of JI was minimal. This is because specific attacks were apparently planned by people sent directly from the *markaziyah* and overseen by Hambali, who worked with members of relevant *fiah* without the knowledge of other *fiah* or *wakalah* members, or even the leaders of the *mantiqi* from which they were drawn. In this sense, specific attacks still used parts of the formal structure of JI, but were more ad hoc and flexible than the usual hierarchy. In Afghanistan, recruits were classified by Zulkarnaen according to how they would be most useful to JI, and it was the ones chosen for operations who became involved in the actual bombings.[45] Although all JI members continued in *dakwah* and religious training, the operational members began engaging in other activities in preparation for attacks.[46]

For example, operational members and their families took field trips and held family camps in Singapore and Malaysia. While the women and children were engaged in their own programs, the men would go off into the jungle and do physical and paramilitary training (with knives—they knew not to test the limits of either the Malaysian or Singaporean governments at this time).[47] They also began to think of certain targets around Singapore to attack, and started basic reconnaissance.

At least by the time JI went operational, and possibly before, the *dakwah* cells also began spreading back into Indonesia, using the Afghanistan veterans as the basis for the cells throughout western and central Indonesia. Very little is known about the pre-1998 Indonesian operations of JI, probably because it was secretive enough to confound even Suharto's security forces. Interestingly, unlike Mantiqi I, Mantiqi II does not seem to have gone operational in terms of training and attack planning until after Suharto fell. Jemaah Islamiyah recruited new members, especially from Pesantren al-Mukmin and its associated schools, and until just before Suharto fell, it seems to have been composed solely of *dakwah* cells, and recruiters. It was not impossible for them to get weapons, but the structure of JI in Indonesia was congruent with the political pressures of the time. The cells were located without regard to Darul Islam bases, though they covered many of the same areas: Sumatra (northern Sumatra, Lampung, and Pekanbaru), Java (with separate *wakalah* for West, Central, and East Java, Surakarta, and the Jakarta metropolitan area), and Nusa Tenggara.[48] This flexibility and non-territorial expandability aided JI as it spread outside of traditional DI strongholds into unknown territory such as Nusa Tenggara (the region east of Bali).

As events warranted, JI continued to expand. As with the 1985 escape to Malaysia, JI's choice of countries and cities where it would set up new cells seems to have been determined at least partly by the territorial needs of JI's transnational activities. In this vein, the *markaziyah* set up Mantiqi III, led by Mustapha, in 1997 to facilitate travel to the newly JI-only Camp Hudaibiyah, with *wakalah* in Sabah, Malaysia (including Labuan and Tarakan), at Nunukan in East Kalimantan, in North Sulawesi and Palu, Indonesia, and at Camp Hudaibiyah, in Mindanao.[49] In addition to their *dakwah* roles, the first two *wakalah* were essentially stops for JI members on the way from Sumatra, Java, Malaysia, and Singapore to Camp Hudaibiyah, and also were promising as way stations for smuggling weapons from the Philippines into Malaysia and Indonesia along illicit routes that ran through the many small islands of the Sangihe-Talaud Islands. The ways in which JI moved people to and from the Philippines for training, and how it moved weapons into Indonesia indicate how territory and political conditions affect various transnational activities.

Training in Mindanao

Jemaah Islamiyah's camps in the southern Philippines were significant not only for the training recruits received, but also for the connections that recruits formed there, connections that would later help them wage jihad in Ambon, Poso, and in the main JI attacks in Indonesia. This is certainly true, but more interesting is how the recruits got to and from the Philippines for training. In an open political environment such as the one JI experienced in the 1990s, combined with the fact that moving people is generally less suspicious than moving materials for attacks, JI still had incentives to create illicit routes and to make illicit use of legitimate routes. The networks that they used to transport people into the Philippines could also be used to bring weapons back across the border. But JI's experience also illustrates how sensitive a clandestine transnational organization is to political conditions: JI's operatives were not willingly illicit. Even in weak states, given the option, CTOs might choose to use legitimate routes and deal with the state. Even states with low state capacity cannot be entirely ignored when CTOs are crossing borders.

Camp Hudaibiyah in the southern Philippines island of Mindanao was not started by JI as a direct response to the loss of training areas in Afghanistan. Rather, it was a logical extension of the relationship between members of Jemaah Islamiyah and members of the Moro Islamic Liberation Front (MILF). Abdullah Sungkar and his recruits met MILF leader Hasyim Selamat and his followers when Hasyim lived in Lahore, Pakistan in the mid-1980s.[50] At some point, the MILF allowed Sungkar's NII recruits to claim they were Filipinos from the MILF in order to escape any notice by potential Suharto agents.[51] By 1991, Hambali and four other future JI members were living for periods of time in Mindanao on orientation trips with the MILF, where they learned fragments of some of the local (non-Tagalog) languages used by the Muslims of the southern Philippines.[52]

In September or October 1994, Nasir Abas and a number of other JI members, including Mustapha, were sent by the *markaziyah* to train the MILF fighters, not to establish a JI camp. Their journey illustrates the relationship between dependence on geography and varying political pressure. In JI-friendly Malaysia, Nasir, who was living in Johor Bahru at the time, took a flight from there to Kota Kinabalu, Sabah, and then an express bus to Sandakan in southeastern Sabah, where he met the other four people, including Mustapha. From Sandakan, they initially planned on taking an illegal route to Mindanao. A traditional boat owner from the Tawi-Tawi Islands between Sabah and Mindanao who ordinarily used the boat to ferry goods from Sandakan to the islands would take them to Bongao in Tawi-Tawi (The boatman was known to Nasrullah, one of the JI members who had lived among the MILF, from his previous trips to the Philippines.) After tarrying there for a night, they would then hop a domestic Filipino ferry to Zamboanga, and another one from there to Cotabato on the main part of Mindanao.[53]

Was the plan to pursue this complex and illegal way into the Philippines because they were afraid of being caught by the Malaysian or Philippine police?

Clearly not; they were not doing anything illegal in Malaysia, as evidenced by the first part of Nasir's journey. Perhaps they took the illegal route because of the laughable capacity of the Philippines' law enforcement, customs, and immigration agencies lowered the costs of the illicit route? As it turned out, not everything went according to plan. In Sandakan, Nasrullah and Mustapha decided to fly to the Philippines instead of hopping in the boat with everyone else, who were forced to travel without Nasrullah as a guide, much to their annoyance. Nasrullah and Mustapha flew from Kota Kinabalu to Manila, entered the country *legally* by getting visas on arrival (which were valid for twenty-one days), and caught a connecting flight to Cotabato, where they were waiting when the rest of the group arrived. Clearly the illegal, sea-based entry was not due to concern about being caught and identified as JI members. And if Philippine state capacity was so easily ignored, why bother to get a visa-on-arrival in the first place? Nasrullah and Mustapha explained that they flew into the Philippines legally because they were only planning on being in the country for a short time. In case they (high-level JI members) were called back for important business in Indonesia, they could fly back right away. Arranging illegal transport does after all take more time and care than using legal means. If they had to stay in the Philippines longer than twenty-one days, they explained they would have the MILF procure extensions of their visas.[54] Even in the Philippines, inarguably a weak state, JI behavior was determined more by the attitude of the government toward its activities than by state capacity. With no specific hostile policy against Jemaah Islamiyah in the Philippines, there was no reason that JI had to move about illegally if they could do so legally. Even the illegal entry of Nasir and friends is a testament to their responsiveness to specific pressure over state capacity. Because Nasir, Qotadah, Ukasyah, and Husain were planning to be in Mindanao for a long time to train the MILF fighters, they were not eligible for visas-on-arrival. They entered the Philippines illegally because they could not get visas for the length of time they needed in the country.[55] Jemaah Islamiyah was not illicit when it did not need to be; illicit routes not only robbed it of the use of air travel, and thus the ability to move quickly over large distances, but also had costs associated with setting up and using alternatives to legitimate transport. The illicit routes JI chose used the topography of the Philippines-Malaysia border to their advantage, but also meant they needed local contacts to support their travels, and could not travel as fast or as easily.

Once the two groups were reunited, they took a series of jeepneys to MILF territory, and walked several hours to get to the MILF village where they were supposed to train the fighters, only to find out, due to what was later termed a miscommunication, that the MILF leadership had not yet picked out the fighters to be trained. Miffed at this waste of their time, Nasrullah and Mustapha did in fact leave after several days, as did two other JI trainers, leaving only Nasir and Qotadah behind. On their own initiative, after the MILF did send some recruits for training, Nasir and Qotadah began a training camp. At first, they trained near the MILF village, but were constantly disturbed by villagers who came by and watched the fighters train; the exercises were apparently their only entertainment.[56] Perturbed, the JI trainers took advantage of an MILF rule that allowed whoever cleared land in MILF territory to use it as their own, whether for farming, or for training. They had the MILF fighters clear a plot of land, then build the beginnings of the newly christened Camp Hudaibiyah within the larger Camp Abu Bakar complex (a series of villages spread out over a large segment of MILF territory). Using a curriculum almost identical to that of the camps in Afghanistan, Nasir and Qotadah trained MILF fighters until Nasir was recalled at the end of 1996.[57]

At the beginning of 1997, in conjunction with the founding of Mantiqi III, the *markaziyah* made Camp Hudaibiyah the official JI training camp, which meant that only JI recruits actually trained there, while MILF fighters trained in another camp nearby, as did non-JI recruits from Banten (Darul Islam) and Sulawesi (Wahdah Islamiyah).[58] Abdullah Sungkar requested that Mantiqi I supply the funds to expand Camp Hudaibiyah within the larger Camp Abu Bakar, and by and large JI funded the operations through transfers from a Malaysian bank account.[59] The camp and its training were also highly organized and institutionalized. Jemaah Islamiyah landscaped the grounds, and added facilities (powered by a generator) where recruits could watch television and training videos, use computers, and communicate with the outside world (Nasir purposefully built the camp within walkie-talkie range of the MILF village). The twenty-four-hour per day curriculum was almost identical to that of the Afghanistan Military Academy, and offered three semester courses, plus short courses lasting anywhere from two weeks to six months. Recruits wore matching surplus Indonesian military uniforms bought in Indonesia or General Santos City in the Philippines.[60] An Indonesian JI member in Selangor, Malaysia sent recruits and scheduled classes. The JI instructors were mostly the same ones as during the later years in Afghanistan, and in some cases were transferred directly to the Philippines from their previous positions in Afghanistan. When JI leader Sardjiyo traveled from Afghanistan to the Philippines to help with Camp Hudaibiyah, for example, he apparently flew straight from Pakistan to Kuala Lumpur, then to Manila, and finally to Mindanao. He does not seem to have gone out of his way to conceal his movements.[61]

Before Camp Jabal Quba (the successor to Camp Hudaibiyah) was overrun, JI pushed through at least three eighteen-month classes (Kuliah Harbiyah Daurah) starting in 1998. Mantiqi II sent four classes for four-month sessions from March

1999 (Daurah Asasiyah Askariyah Yarmuk), while Mantiqi I sent six classes for sessions ranging from two weeks to two months from February 1999 (DAA Hithin). There was also a six-week session for five recruits from Ambon (DAA Uhud), plus a two-month session for at least one person from Mantiqi IV (which covered Papua and Australia), among others.[62] Again, the route by which the recruits entered the Philippines, and the legality of that route, were determined not by the need for secrecy so much as convenience. The Singaporean and Malaysian recruits (those from Mantiqi I who enrolled in the DAA Hithin courses) generally entered the Philippines using legal entry visas. Because they had full-time jobs in Malaysia and Singapore, they had to take vacation time to get jihad training, and could only make it for short periods of time.[63] They did not have the time to make the illegal trip, which could take up to four days each way. This is the manner in which Faiz bin Abu Bakar Bafana trained—he took a month off, in June 1998, and went to Camp Hudaibiyah to refresh his weapons skills, then returned to Malaysia.[64] The implication is that, had there been crackdowns in place that limited quick movement into Mindanao, the number of Singaporeans and Malaysians who trained would have decreased.

JI's training and logistics functions dovetailed in Mantiqi III. The same boat bought by JI operative Mubarok and a fisherman named Sardjono in the Sangihe-Talaud Islands in 1997 for weapons smuggling was also used to ferry recruits from Indonesia to the Philippines. Generally, one of the two routes for the recruits for Camp Hudaibiyah was to travel from Java to Manado, and from Manado through the Sangihe-Talaud Islands to Mindanao, using Sardjono's boat.[65] In the middle of 1998 (that is, soon after the fall of Suharto), Mustapha ordered Nasir Abas, who was in Sandakan at the time, to begin transporting JI recruits to and from the southern Philippines, by both legal and illegal means. This practice continued until the end of 2002, although it is not clear if Nasir Abbas was engaged in helping moving recruits to and from Mindanao the entire time.[66]

By February 2000, at least some non-JI recruits from Java took a different route. From Java, according to the International Crisis Group, they "went to Nunukan, East Kalimantan, crossed by boat to Tawao in Sabah, Malaysia, then on to Sandakan, Malaysia where they got a ferry to Zamboanga [in the Philippines]. From there they went to Cotabato and on to Camp Hudaibiyah [they probably went to the Darul Islam training camp]."[67] This is almost exactly the same route that the original JI instructors took in 1994, and probably one of the routes Nasir Abas used to ferry recruits, indicating JI's dependence on set routes and chokepoints. One of the recruits, Yusuf, had a passport, and it seems as if the major limiting factor at this time was the recruits' unfamiliarity with areas outside of Java—a series of guides accompanied them from Java to Camp Hudaibiyah—rather than worries about being apprehended (indeed, they had done nothing illegal in Indonesia).[68] Likewise, Nasir indicated that the primary factor in JI deciding whether to send its own recruits from Malaysia to the Philippines via legal or illegal means was the length of their stay, just as it had been in 1994 when Camp Hudaibiyah was first set up for the MILF.[69] The Philippines government, as weak as it was, was still enough of a presence to factor into JI's calculations, and for JI's part, it tried to follow the law unless there were extenuating circumstances. Illicit routes into the Philippines were possible, but, from JI's perspective, were sometimes too much work given other alternatives.

Weapons Smuggling

Until the mid-1990s, Jemaah Islamiyah was still in the training and *dakwah* phase, and its logistical network for ferrying weapons and explosives to its targets was essentially non-existent. About the same time that JI-only recruits began training at Camp Hudaibiyah in Mindanao, the group moved to take advantage of the agreeable topography of the islands between Mindanao and eastern Indonesia. Although JI had big future plans for blowing things up, they needed firearms and explosives to do that, and even in a place like Southeast Asia, this was easier said than done. It was not impossible to get weapons in Suharto's Indonesia (GAM was somewhat successful at it for decades before Suharto fell), but it was difficult enough that JI seems to have decided not to depend solely on stock that was procured domestically.

Despite the difficulties associated with operating in Suharto's Indonesia, Mantiqi III apparently was also tasked with bringing back weapons. For this they used Sardjono's boat. Moving from the hostile country of Indonesia to the JI-friendly southern Philippines for training purposes was not a problem for JI, except when the recruits did not have proper travel documents. Getting the weapons bought in Mindanao back to Indonesia was a bit trickier. The heavy breath of the Indonesian authorities on their necks may have slowed JI down, but it did not stop it from setting its operational plans into motion before Suharto fell.

Corruption played a role before May 1998 as well. Much of the Sulawesi network was not part of Jemaah Islamiyah, but performed certain tasks for members of JI, and provides an interesting illustration. A certain Suryadi, who was connected to JI through the organization Wahdah Islamiyah, also bought weapons in Mindanao between 1997 and 2001. In December 1997, Suryadi traveled in a "traditional boat" from General Santos City in the Philippines with three other men (two from Solo) and sixty-six bomb detonators to Nanusa in the Sangihe-Talaud Islands on the Indonesian side. After a brief incident in which the Nanusa authorities searched and found the bomb detonators, only to be paid off by Suryadi, the operatives proceeded on to Peta, Sangihe Island to make contact with

Sardjono. Sardjono sent them on their way to Tahuna, the capital of the Sangihe-Talaud Islands, and on to Manado. From Manado, Suryadi ended up in Makassar.[70] It was an arduous journey along the contours of the physical landscape; friendly factions of the state, in the form of corruption, nevertheless helped them navigate what otherwise would have been a precarious route. The technologies of globalization were of little help to Suryadi, and the experience was a sign of the difficulty JI would have of moving back weapons back into Indonesia, even in more favorable conditions.

Although JI had ambitions to move back operationally into Indonesia before Suharto fell, and was clearly trying to lay the groundwork for its eventual return, it did not move back in force until after May 1998.[71] Before Suharto fell, it was clearly possible to smuggle weapons into Indonesia, but smuggling a few weapons or a few people is quite different from establishing a far-flung network under the glare of a hostile government. Jemaah Islamiyah and its affiliates did smuggle some weapons into Indonesia, but it was dependent on illicit routes that closely followed the physical topography of the landscape: many small islands that made it easier to elude the power of the state. The networks needed to support these activities were not easy to set up, and JI's dependence on set routes also made it vulnerable to being interdicted. Although bribing corruption officials could resolve this problem to a certain extent, it was not enough to reestablish a major presence in Indonesia before 1998.

With the political openness that JI encountered in 1985 everywhere but Indonesia, it was free to expand over a number of different countries. There were no failures in JI's activities as such during this time, but even in its successes it proved susceptible to territorial and political constraints. Where it enjoyed complete openness, it was able to range far along legitimate routes—all the way to Pakistan and Afghanistan. Where it was operating under less friendly conditions, it was forced to find countries adjacent to Indonesia and use illicit, sea- or land-based routes through difficult terrain; it was unable to use air travel and open communications to get people, goods, and information and out of Indonesia. Even in the same journeys or the same areas, differing political conditions led to changes in how the group moved. Creating the structure to support illicit movement across borders was difficult and costly for JI, as when it smuggled weapons into Indonesia from the Philippines, and when it had the option of using legitimate routes, it often used those routes instead. Difficult terrain is less than optimal for weak states that want to maintain control of their borders, but it is also not the first choice for CTOs themselves. Even when they are successful, they are constrained. Witness, for example, how JI was dependent on airports in Malaysia and Pakistan during its training program in the 1980s. In short, even as the technologies of globalization helped it in certain activities, they were less useful when JI had a need to maintain certain levels of secrecy.

Jemaah Islamiyah's transnational command and control structure from 1993 to 1999 was impressive, but this was largely because it had an astonishingly open political environment outside of Indonesia. What it did with its newly expanded transnational support structure once Suharto fell from power in 1998 is the subject of the next chapter. Already we see the weaknesses in JI's network, weaknesses that resulted from its transnational links. These weaknesses would become more apparent as JI spread back into Indonesia, and later when its violent attacks led to successive crackdowns throughout Southeast Asia.

THE DECLINE OF JEMAAH ISLAMIYAH, 1999–2009

With the fall of Suharto in 1998 came the end of the subversion charges faced by Abdullah Sungkar and Abu Bakar Ba'asyir, and a chance to return to Indonesia. From May 1998, when Suharto resigned in the face of widespread protests and riots, and the loss of support from the military, until November 2001, when Singapore and Malaysia began arresting their respective *wakalah* members, Jemaah Islamiyah spread and operated with as little hindrance as could be expected for any secret group with violent intentions. Jemaah Islamiyah's scope and activities during this period show what a clandestine organization is capable of when it operates in a region where none of the governments are particularly hostile, and has highly motivated and competent members who know how to take advantage of the technologies of globalization. The leaders who returned from Afghanistan were trained well; they formed the backbone of an organization that was capable of replicating itself and carrying out terrorist attacks in what seemed like almost anywhere in Southeast Asia. Thanks to the political climate it faced, it did.

This chapter traces Jemaah Islamiyah's activities from 1999 until 2009, from the height of its power through the crackdowns that began in Singapore and Malaysia, and spread to Thailand, Indonesia, and the Philippines. Jemaah Islamiyah's territorial spread was not to be maintained for a prolonged period of time, or even for more than a couple of years. Political pressure after September 2001 meant that JI was robbed almost immediately of fast and convenient cross-border movement, and in order to maintain its transnational routes it resorted more frequently to subterfuge along legitimate routes, and illicit routes that hugged the contours of the landscape. The support structures for these routes often needed more political leeway than existed, and the routes were limited and subject to interdiction by even weak states. Jemaah Islamiyah discovered, for example, the difficulty of maintaining a permanent training program in the face of hostility from the local state in the Philippines. As state after state cracked down, JI became increasingly hemmed in by territorial constraints, and had difficulty maintaining the links across international boundaries that allowed it to be a transnational organization. As a result, the group was forced to contract, and arguably has ceased to exist as a coherent transnational organization.

Running Rampant, 1999–2001

Command and Control

In the post-Suharto political environment, Jemaah Islamiyah's replicable cells spread back into Indonesia, and the organization as a whole behaved somewhat like a (secret) multinational corporation. For a time, JI maintained what were effectively two headquarters with different functions. Abdullah Sungkar and Abu Bakar Ba'asyir did not actually return to Indonesia until 1999, a number of months after the end of Suharto's rule, and in any case, Abdullah Sungkar died within months of coming back. Abu Bakar Ba'asyir settled back in at Pondok Ngruki, with at least some of his network still intact. Although the group's top leaders moved back to central Java, the operational command under Hambali remained based in Malaysia until the Malaysian and Singaporean crackdowns. The headquarters were tied together by telecommunications and extensive legitimate travel, complete with business meetings. The technologies of globalization combined with political openness to allow a transnational bureaucracy to form, but Jemaah Islamiyah's reach was not unlimited, even then.

This was the period when Jemaah Islamiyah's structure attained full maturity, after years in exile. The *mantiqi* system was in full force, and Jemaah Islamiyah was so bureaucratic that it took months for the *markaziyah* to make decisions. At the end of January 2001, for example, Hambali's close friend Iqbal was arrested by the Indonesian police. Following Iqbal's arrest Hambali fled to Pakistan in order to avoid being captured, if indeed the police decided to look for him. He handed over leadership duties of Mantiqi I to Mukhlas. It was only in April 2001 that Ba'asyir officially appointed Mukhlas as head of Mantiqi I at a meeting in Pondok Ngruki.[1]

Because of the red tape, operations that demanded quick action were often started by JI members by themselves with the blessing (or lack of interference) of the *markaziyah*, and then, once they were mature, integrated into the command and control structure. This was how Nasir Abas started Camp Hudaibiyah, and it was also how some JI members became involved in the Ambon and then the Poso conflicts. Mustapha, for example, began Project Uhud to send fighters to Poso in October 2000, and ran it for several years before it was merged into Mantiqi III.[2]

Sungkar and Ba'asyir's move back to Indonesia meant that the highest-ranking leaders of JI were now in Java. But the wide-open political environment in Southeast Asia meant that the actual planning for JI operations remained centered in Malaysia, while JI operations members traveled and met throughout the region. Hambali and Imam Samudra in particular traveled especially frequently along legitimate routes without active support. The leaders would often meet in cities that were international transportation hubs, meaning that they could travel long distances, but were dependent on these same globalized chokepoints. The operations meeting in January 2002, for example, which was attended by Hambali, Abu Jibril, and Imam Samudra, among others, and would have been attended by Fathur Rahman al-Ghozi, JI's main contact in the Philippines, if he had not been arrested, was in Bangkok, a city without a functioning JI cell capable of supporting an actual clandestine meeting or illicit travel. Every participant had to travel internationally to get to Bangkok. It was, in short, the perfect example of a globalized terrorist organization, but more specifically it was the perfect example of a terrorist organization without strong concerns about being discovered. As amir, Ba'asyir traveled a fair amount himself, including trips to Camp Hudaibiyah in 2000 for the graduation ceremony of one of the classes, and to Kuala Lumpur for the Rabitatul Mujahidin meetings (described below) in 1999 and 2000.[3] Although it is not clear how he got to the meetings, he was the highly visible head of the school in Pondok Ngruki, and later the head of Majelis Mujahidin Indonesia. He was not one to slink around undetected, and that he attended meetings outside of Indonesia that were directly connected to Jemaah Islamiyah is a sign of how light the pressure was.

Jemaah Islamiyah's leadership was essentially part-time, with the exception of certain leaders like Hambali (with all the travel he did, it is difficult to conceive of him having a day job, aside from working as an itinerant preacher) and the instructors at Camp Hudaibiyah. The relative stability of the locations of many of JI's leaders would not have been possible in a situation where they had to go on the run, especially if their flight involved illicit routes. Nasir Abas's jobs as *wakalah* chief of staff, and later as head of Mantiqi III, occupied only part of his time. His day jobs were not covers so much as his primary means of supporting himself and his family. When he first returned to Malaysia from Afghanistan in 1994, he found employment as a construction worker, then as a carpenter making wardrobes and cabinets. After coming back from Mindanao to Johor (his native Malaysian state), he worked as a taxi driver in Johor Bahru until August 1997, when he moved to Sandakan by Mustapha's order. Until late 1998, Nasir sold vegetables at his mother-in-law's stand in the market in Sandakan. He then started his own small business, making homemade soya bean drinks and jelly, and doing quite well, even to the extent of employing other people. He continued his job until 2002, when he had to go on the run after the Bali bombing.[4] The jobs held by JI members were not covers for their activities so much as indications of how little the governments of the countries in which they operated knew about their other activities. Once they began to feel pressure and had to go on the run, steady jobs were the first to go.

Although Jemaah Islamiyah faced an open environment, it was not without territorial limitations, even in command and control. It found setting up cells outside of the central Malay-speaking areas to be somewhat more difficult than within Malaysia, Singapore, and Indonesia, as well as a waste of precious resources, given the presence of other Islamist groups in other countries. Without cells in those areas, JI would not have been able to support extensive illicit operations in those countries, other than hiding fugitives (in Thailand) and relying on local groups for training opportunities (in the Philippines). As a result, the JI leadership brought together Rabitatul Mujahidin, a group that met three times in 1999 and 2000, and achieved middling success.

Rabitatul Mujahidin was not an attempt to set up a new organization, but a recognition by JI that its ability to build its organization in every country in Southeast Asia was limited, even with the relatively lax political atmosphere that it encountered. Jemaah Islamiyah primarily wanted to avoid overlap with other jihadist groups, which is why it did not recruit Filipinos as official members, although it did have a *wakalah* centered around Camp Hudaibiyah, and a cell in the Philippines that bought weapons. There was also an informal network in Thailand sufficient to buy weapons and harbor suspects (one of the two Singaporean JI members who escaped in December 2001 went to Thailand).[5] But the *markaziyah* did not exercise command and control over any formal cells in Thailand or Myanmar, where the Rohinga Solidarity Organization was allied with JI, and its connection to Cambodia seems to have been solely for fundraising.[6] Abu Bakar Ba'asyir invited representatives from radical Islamist groups from the Philippines, southern Thailand, Myanmar, and Bangladesh as well as JI's core areas of Singapore, Malaysia, and Indonesia to attend the meetings in Malaysia in order to coordinate attacks, fundraising, and weapons procurement in Southeast Asia. The gathering decided to support the MILF's cause by attacking the Philippine ambassador's home in Jakarta in August 2000, and approved the Christmas Eve church bombings in December 2000. After this gathering the Rabitatul Mujahidin never met again.[7]

In a politically open environment, JI generally could communicate and move people around in legitimate ways, enabling it to spread over great distances, but its abilities were not unlimited. In areas where it encountered hostility, even at minimal levels, it needed cells to support its illicit activities. Setting up these cells was not without cost, and in many cases JI was content to cooperate with other groups rather than build its own infrastructure. For activities more threatening to states than simple meetings, JI had to create and staff its own illicit routes.

Weapons Smuggling

Contrast JI's command and control structure with its weapons smuggling efforts, even after Suharto fell. States are inherently hostile to violent groups smuggling guns into their territory, and we would expect JI to become dependent on illicit use of legitimate routes, or on illicit routes that traverse geographically advantageous features such as small islands and jungle. To move along these routes, JI needed to set up its own cells at strategic locations. These chokepoints persisted if successful, but they were susceptible to interdiction.

Given the difficulty of crossing international boundaries illicitly, JI had the option of not crossing them at all. Like Darul Islam and GAM, JI had a network that obtained weapons from Bandung's PT Pindad, Indonesia's official arms manufacturer. But the company did not seem to provide a steady supply of weapons or explosives.[8] Transnational activities are not necessarily preferred by clandestine organizations if they have domestic options, but domestic options are often unreliable.

Jemaah Islamiyah could also rely on factions within the government to increase its chances of success. This was particularly true when JI was involved in the Ambon and Poso. The conflicts were not entirely clandestine in that they were to a certain extent supported by elements of the Indonesian military looking to foment ethnic conflict for their own ends. According to one informant, soldiers would rent out their M-16s for 100,000 Rupiah (approximately US$10) per hour to (Muslim) fighters, and brokers obtained weapons through high-level military officials.[9] The problem was that this method of weapons procurement was not open to JI when it sought to stage other attacks in Indonesia (or elsewhere). Jemaah Islamiyah had to find ways to smuggle weapons transnationally.

In the face of hostility to smuggling, JI had to move weapons from countries either in its target area, or adjacent to the target area. For staging attacks in Indonesia, Singapore, and Malaysia, this effectively meant that it needed to get weapons from Thailand and the Philippines.

Jemaah Islamiyah may have smuggled weapons from Thailand to Malaysia, although in much smaller quantities. When Imam Samudra was in Batam in the run-up to the Christmas Eve 2000 bombings, he requested and received through the JI supply chain two pistols (with accompanying ammunition) from

Malaysia.[10] But these were not enough to do more than commit the occasional petty crime, and certainly not enough to start a small war. Although the border between Thailand and Malaysia sees a high volume of traffic, even in the wake of Malaysia's fight against the Communist Party of Malaysia and Thailand's fight against Muslim Malay separatists along their common border the area has not emerged as a major source of arms smuggling into Malaysia (as opposed to arms destined for other locales). Although JI built a major presence in the southern Philippines, it did not succeed in developing a network in Thailand that could do more than protect its fugitives and support planning meetings. This left JI to find other sources of weapons and explosives.

From 1999, Jemaah Islamiyah further developed the routes it had begun to set up before Suharto's fall. After Suharto resigned, the quantity of weapons JI smuggled in increased. The weapons brought in without a specific operation in mind seemed to have come via the original routes: from Mindanao in the southern Philippines, through the Sangihe-Talaud Islands into eastern Indonesia, from which they would be moved by courier service to Java or wherever else they were needed. The main challenge was getting them into Indonesia: compared to training in Mindanao, JI's dependence on advantageous geography was higher when smuggling weapons, and because the state was always at least somewhat hostile to smuggling, smuggling routes and methods varied less than those that supported training activities. Although JI recruits traveled to and from Mindanao by air or boat, depending on the length of their stay, it seems that pretty much all the weapons and explosives JI smuggled from the Philippines to Indonesia came by boat through the Sangihe-Talaud Islands to Sulawesi, and that re-entering Indonesia with explosives required more care than entering the Philippines with recruits.

The Sangihe-Talaud Islands, according to one source, were and are a major transit route for terrorists and smuggled goods. The islands have three major advantages for clandestine organizations. The geography of the islands, namely many small islands on the border between Indonesia and the Philippines, makes it easy to find places that are not patrolled. Standard border crossing is relatively simple, and corruption is such that border guards can be bribed if necessary. It is also possible to hire local fishermen to transport people and/or goods through the islands. Many mixed marriages also complicate enforcement. Although the Sangihe-Talaud Islands are in Indonesia, the population is Filipino.[11]

Jemaah Islamiyah had its own operatives smuggle when possible. Fathur Rahman al-Ghozi, for instance, purchased and shipped small arms, especially M-16s (probably locally made) from Zamboanga City to Ambon for use by the militant groups Laskar Jundullah and Laskar Mujahidin from 1999 on, although according to Philippine intelligence, he was able to get less than twenty weapons through to Indonesia successfully.[12] In mid-2001, according to Zachary Abuza, a shipment of M-16s was caught passing through Malaysian waters going from Zamboanga City to Ambon. In addition, at the time of his arrest seventeen M-16s were found in al-Ghozi's backyard in General Santos City.[13]

Jemaah Islamiyah did not rely solely on its people for weapons, but also depended on allied organizations, which would become important in later bombings. These organizations relied on the same transnational routes and methods as JI. Suryadi, the operative who was connected to JI through the organization Wahdah Islamiyah, continued buying weapons in Mindanao until 2001. As a cover for escorting recruits and/or weapons between the Philippines and Indonesia, Suryadi had started a cosmetics importation business, presumably to piggyback illicit smuggling onto legitimate activities.[14] Suryadi claimed under interrogation that upon meeting Imam Samudra in Pandeglang in Java in 2001 he was told to look into buying weapons from Libya.[15] No evidence exists that this potential arms deal ever came about, or that Suryadi had any idea how to get weapons from anywhere else but the Philippines. It is the only known instance where JI was even considering getting weapons from somewhere besides Southeast Asia.

By March 2000, according to the International Crisis Group, the Philippine military's assault on Camp Abu Bakar had made it difficult for recruits to get in or out. Two recruits were trapped there, and Suryadi was sent to bring them back. He was unsuccessful, but while waiting in Cotabato, he and someone from KOMPAK-Solo (one of the jihadist groups fighting in Ambon) managed to buy fourteen M-16s and AK-47s with the help of "Mustopa," most likely Mustapha, then head of Mantiqi III, in General Santos City. The two recruits were able to leave Camp Abu Bakar in August 2000, so they, Suryadi, and several others took a ship from General Santos City to Bitung in Indonesia. Rather than trying to bypass the checkpoints set up by both Indonesia and the Philippines, Suryadi preferred to take the risk of making illicit use of legitimate routes. They managed to smuggle the weapons into Indonesia by bribing Philippine customs officials and labeling the crate containing the weapons as "tuna fish." From Bitung, Suryadi then took the weapons to Makassar.[16]

It is dangerous for a CTO to depend solely on one source for weapons, and JI relied on several sources and methods through a variety of political conditions in the Philippines. Suryadi's ordeal with the recruits shows how tenuous a CTO's links between countries can be when one of the countries becomes a difficult place in which to operate. Although it is possible that some weapons were flown out of the Philippines, all the incidents I could find depended on them being shipped by boat from Mindanao to Sabah, Malaysia, or through the Sangihe-Talaud Islands to the rest of Indonesia. Success thus depended on the geographic advantages of the border. These topographic features were certainly there, but they channeled the flow of JI personnel and weapons along routes that that made the organization vulnerable to interdiction.

Jemaah Islamiyah no doubt moved many weapons into Indonesia by using open water and small islands to great effect. The cases discussed in this chapter show that JI weapons smugglers had to contend with the power of the Philippine and Indonesian states. In some cases they surmounted this power by bribing government officials, which raises the question of what might have been if the local authorities had applied themselves less corruptly to their jobs, even with their decrepit equipment and minimal manpower? One Indonesian police official claimed that JI avoided customs officials whenever possible, and to his knowledge, none of the explosives or weapons coming into Indonesia from the Philippines involved bribed officials.[17] This is almost certainly not true, but as with the training routes into Mindanao, JI did not take lightly crossing the border and dealing with officials in weak states.

Training in Mindanao

The sensitivity of clandestine organizations' transnational activities to political conditions in certain countries can be seen in the decline of JI's fortunes in Mindanao after 2000. Although it is easy to argue that weapons smuggling, inasmuch as it is always illegal, is constrained by territorial considerations, training, particularly moving recruits back and forth, is more problematic.

The fall of the Suharto regime seems to have had no effect on JI's Mindanao training activities. This applied to both the training itself and to the efforts to channel recruits from Indonesia, Malaysia, and Singapore to the Philippines. When the Philippine army overran Camp Abu Bakar in 2000, JI continued limited training. The numbers processed by JI, reportedly five to six at a time in each cohort rather than the hundreds that JI had trained from 1997 to 2000, meant that JI would have to look elsewhere for large training camps.[18] JI fugitives on the run, such as Umar Patek, found shelter in Mindanao, first with poorly controlled factions of the MILF, and then with the Abu Sayyaf Group (ASG). The role that the Philippines played in JI operations also shifted. From being the main location for large-scale JI training, the southern Philippines became a place where JI operatives could hide out from government authorities and perhaps continue to play some role in JI activities. It eventually became a place where they were hunted down and constantly on the move, no longer of much use to the larger JI network or, increasingly, to the MILF.

Large-scale training cannot exist in a vacuum; it requires at least the nonintervention of the relevant local government, which is not necessarily the internationally recognized government. This is a point that is missed by many discussions on state weakness. The question is not whether the government sitting in the capital city of a country is ready, willing, and able to suppress certain activities, but whether whoever controls a given territory is. Somalia, for instance, has governance without government. While there was no central government at all in the early 1990s, and the central government controls (and tenuously at that) a small portion of the country, more informal arrangements, often based on clans or local warlords, have sprung up. Just because there is not an international recognized state in a territory does not mean there is no one controlling it.[19]

An insurgency's control of a chunk of a nation's territory can be perceived as a sign of central state weakness, but illicit activities going on in the insurgency's territory without the insurgency's acquiescence should be taken as a sign of the weakness of the local state: the insurgency. In Southeast Asia, in particular, the more successful insurgencies, such as the MILF and GAM, have gone to great lengths to establish routine governance and state structures. Although the territory under their control is not lawful in the sense of being controlled by the central state, it is not necessarily any less lawless than central state-controlled territory, particularly given the corruption and capacity problems of the Philippines and Indonesian governments.

This can be seen in JI's training experiences in Mindanao. The southern Philippines is often characterized as one of those regions of anarchy that global jihad movements seize upon to further their goals with minimal outside interference. Yet Jemaah Islamiyah needed the approval of the MILF, the de facto local state, for large-scale JI training inside MILF territory, both before Camp Abu Bakar was partially overrun in 2000, and when JI established a second base along similar lines as Camp Hudaibiyah, known as Camp Jabal Quba, which was operating from 2000 until at least 2002. Two new trends began in 2001 and 2002.

First, the MILF had since 1997 been in peace negotiations with the Government of the Republic of the Philippines (GRP). Throughout the negotiations, the MILF denied offering sanctuary to Jemaah Islamiyah or any related terrorist groups, a claim that obviously did not stand up to scrutiny, given that Camp Hudaibiyah was initially set up by JI as a means of training MILF fighters. Gradually, however, from 2001 to 2005 the presence of JI members and radical Islamic recruits in the areas of Mindanao that it controlled shifted from being sanctioned by the top MILF leadership, to being ignored by the MILF leadership and allowed by local commanders, to irritating the MILF as it undercut MILF's claims to legitimacy as a non-terrorist negotiating partner. Thus, even though it had never publicly supported JI, the MILF began to distance itself from the terrorists in its midst. In 2004, the MILF leadership made a strategic decision to oppose JI. After being pushed by government negotiators, at May 2005 peace process consultative

gatherings with MILF supporters, MILF leader Al-Haj Murad made public statements condemning cooperation with JI and other Islamic extremist groups.[20]
The MILF also seemed to evolve away from an alignment with JI's stated goals.
When the MILF originally began cooperating with JI, the MILF's leader Hasyim
Selamat and eleven other top leaders were graduates of Islamic schools, and had
goals aligned with that of JI, although they remained concentrated on Mindanao. By 2005, only two of those Islamist leaders, Mimbantas and Umar Pasigan,
were left in the MILF structure.[21] Furthermore, the MILF's actual goals appear to
have shifted away from sympathy with JI. One Philippine government negotiator
noted that at no time during negotiations with the MILF were the words "Islamic
state" ever uttered.[22]

There were complications, to be sure. MILF state capacity was not zero, but
neither was it ironclad. Its leadership admitted to the Philippine government that
its control was limited whenever JI entered MILF territory.[23] Some Philippine
government analysts also commented that the MILF's factionalism was an im-
pediment in implementing any policy (such as the anti-JI policy) that might be
unpopular with stubborn and relatively autonomous local commanders.[24] Some
within the Philippine government also believed that the MILF was merely using
its more public attacks on JI and ASG for public relations purposes. They argued that the MILF had not been sincere in its comments on JI or ASG. Some
JI-affiliated operatives were reportedly still training MILF groups as of late 2005,
and the MILF had been considerably less cooperative in the operations and logistics of attacking JI. In addition, the Abu Sayyaf Group also harbored some JI fugitives, and would apparently do their bidding with the right monetary incentive.[25]
On the contrary, the MILF's factionalism was not such that local commanders
would actually consider breaking away from its leadership (and thus shelter JI
and ASG members with impunity) unless they were convinced that the leadership
was unable to get autonomy and other concessions for Moro civilians through a
strategy of negotiating with the Philippine government and turning against JI. As
of late 2005, no groups had formally broken away from the MILF.[26]

Still, the MILF's strategic decision, imperfect as it was, seemed to yield
changes in JI's overall training profile in Mindanao. In the process of negotiating
a peace agreement, the MILF and the Philippine government established a joint
coordinating committee, with seven members from each side—they monitored
the ceasefire, engaged in fact-finding, and most importantly, worked to isolate
JI and other criminals in the southern Philippines. Local monitoring teams in
thirteen conflict-afflicted provinces fanned out to monitor the process on the
ground, and in October 2004, an international monitoring team, composed of
Malaysians, and representatives from Brunei and Libya, arrived. The two sides
also formed an ad hoc joint action group, which shared intelligence on accused

criminals. Government negotiators hoped that the MILF would show increasing sincerity after its public anti-JI proclamation, and indeed, from the formation of the ad hoc joint committee until December 2005, the government and the MILF engaged in nine successful operations against criminals wanted by the government. In August and September 2005, the Armed Forces of the Philippines (AFP) informed the MILF leadership that a gang of ASG and JI members were hiding out in a marsh in Maguindanao. Complicating matters was the fact the marsh was located in difficult terrain, and housed three MILF groups with numerous civilians. Nevertheless, the MILF made way, and allowed the AFP to conduct operation for six weeks in the marsh. The three satellite camps vacated the area, and had to spoil their harvest as a result. Eight hundred MILF fighters moved to shelters, where their movement to and from their farms every day was monitored and regulated. During the operation, the AFP established a tactical coordination outpost where it laid out its plans to the MILF. The operation resulted in eight ASG members killed, and increased mutual trust between the central government and the MILF.[27]

This was not good news for JI's organized training activities. At some point Camp Jabal Quba became untenable for permanent training purposes, and it dropped off the Southeast Asian terrorist training map. The effect of the increasing MILF and AFP hostility was evident on JI's activities. Its members and other Southeast Asian militants continued to train in the southern Philippines, but they became more mobile, and moved around in small, semi-nomadic groups. The recruits trained in semi-permanent facilities in forested, mountainous territory, possibly in MILF territory, and used tents and other equipment that could be packed up and moved if necessary.[28] Some Singaporeans and Malaysians may have trained in the Philippines during this period, but in general it was Indonesia that was the primary supplier of trainees. Once the top MILF leadership began shifting away as the Islamist leaders disappeared, JI trainees were forced to embed themselves with local-level individual units of the MILF and ASG. After 2004, the Abu Sayyaf Group, and some MILF factions, replaced the mainstream MILF as the main benefactors of Jemaah Islamiyah. This allowed JI to continue operating, but robbed them of the valuable logistical support provided through general MILF cooperation. Maintaining a solid base camp became very difficult.

The Abu Sayyaf Group provided shelter and willing bombers in return for JI's training skills and collaboration on bombings. JI members who had contacts with the MILF and ASG found it easier to import ideology and military tactics than large numbers of trainees. In fact, it was ideology and tactics that worried the Philippine government more than whether Indonesians were getting terrorist training in Mindanao—the Abu Sayyaf Group's effectiveness and commitment to Islamist ideology tended to wax and wane with changes in leaders and interaction with JI ideologues.[29] By the end of 2005, the Philippine military assessed that twenty-nine JI operatives were active in central Mindanao, around the Mt. Cararao complex, training Rabitatul Sulaiman Mujahideen (RSM), MILF special forces, and Abu Sayyaf Group fighters.[30] It is unlikely that such a small number of JI operatives, cut off from the outside, constantly on the run, were all that useful to JI's operations in Indonesia. But they were quite useful to Abu Sayyaf and the MILF factions that continued to carry out attacks. After 2004, Philippine police described a number of bombings in the southern Philippines as joint Abu Sayyaf-JI operations.[31] Philippine police also arrested several JI members inside the country.[32] What is unclear is whether these JI collaborators were operating as part of some remnant of the Mantiqi III structure, were re-cruiting and training new JI members, either local Filipinos or Indonesians and Malaysians who made their way to Mindanao, or whether they were fugitives who were earning their keep by helping Abu Sayyaf's campaign.[33] They did earn their keep with a number of bombings from 2004 on, notably the SuperFerry bombing in February 2004, which killed 116 people, and the Valentine's Day bus bombing in Manila in February 2005, which exhibited a complementary use of the talents of different terrorist groups. In both cases, the Abu Sayyaf Group leadership apparently ordered and coordinated the attacks, while JI operatives trained members of RSM, a group made up of converts to Islam, to build and place the bombs.[34]

Despite the local success of JI's collaboration with ASG, RSM, and parts of the MILF, profound state hostility made transnational movement much more dif-ficult, not only when JI sought to move people, but also when it tried to move in-formation. The technologies of globalization were not useful to it under these conditions, and JI's structures in the Philippines and Indonesia lost touch with each other. Nasir Abas, as leader of Mantiqi III, had been the main JI contact for sending recruits to Mindanao, both legally and illegally, but he went into hiding after the Indonesian government's crackdown following the first Bali bombings in October 2002. By March 2003, Mantiqi III's function as the conveyor belt for JI trainees appears to have broken down. According to Singaporean intelligence sources, the movement of people between Indonesia and the Philippines contin-ued, and JI members and other Indonesian Muslim extremists looking for train-ing went to Mindanao, although the numbers were much smaller. The sources speculated that the movement persisted despite important arrests, indicating that either the numbers arrested were too small to provide a disincentive for JI and others to go to the Philippines, or that the Philippines was so important to Muslim extremists for training and weapons supplies that they were willing to risk the consequences to continue. The recruits did not go by themselves. There continued to be a coordinating mechanism that facilitated their journey to and from Mindanao.[35] As late as 2004, JI leaders were ordering operatives to go to the Philippines to help train Abu Sayyaf members, and to liaise with them for attacks.[36] But the mechanism seemed to be decentralized, and based more on personal contacts and informal alliances, such as with KOMPAK, than the formal, conveyor belt-like mechanism that JI had before.[37]

Greater pressure does not necessarily spell the end of all illicit cross-border movement and illicit activities, but state hostility tends to hamper transnational movement and communication, and forces people and information into precarious, interdictable illicit routes. Islamist militants' decentralizing response to crackdowns, the factionalism of the MILF, and the cooperation of the Abu Sayyaf Group allowed JI to continue some semblance of training, but drastically decreased their effectiveness and the numbers trained. The Philippine government did not (and does not) control large swathes of territory in the southern Philippines, in theory allowing militant training to continue to survive. But for large, organized, permanent bases, JI and other groups were dependent on the largesse of the relevant state authority in the region, the MILF. When the MILF as a whole turned ambivalent, and then hostile at approximately the same time as the crackdowns in Indonesia hampered the recruit sending mechanisms, JI adapted, but found it difficult to operate at the level to which it had previously been accustomed. The border itself was not necessarily any more hostile than before, but the structures on both ends that supported the illicit routes were destroyed or damaged, endangering the whole effort.

Retreat to Indonesia

Jemaah Islamiyah's overall decline outside of Indonesia and the Philippines began shortly after 11 September 2001, when the Australian, Singaporean, and Malaysian governments began rounding up JI members. The immediate effect of the crackdowns was to cut off the group from its funding sources in the three countries, and deprive it of the ability to plan and control operations in Singapore and peninsular Malaysia.[38]

The crackdowns also made JI change its bomb plans to the fallback countries of Indonesia and the Philippines, and move its planning activities to Thailand and Indonesia. The transnational routes used by JI were also more limited. They followed the contours of the landscape (either by land or sea), and involved using illicit means to pass through legal border checkpoints, or avoiding legitimate routes entirely, and moving through a series of adjacent countries.

When Faiz bin Abu Bakar Bafana was arrested in December 2001 in the wake of JI's Singapore bombing plots (see chapter 5), Hambali told Mohammed

Mansour Jabarah, an al-Qaeda and JI-affiliated operative, to go back to the original plan of attacking the U.S. and Israeli embassies in Manila. Luckily for JI, the original plan would not require the shipment of explosives across international boundaries. Jabarah was also to get out of Malaysia and go to Thailand, where the JI operational leadership planned to meet to evaluate the situation.[39] Mukhlas, then the leader of Mantiqi I, fled from Malaysia in January 2002 to escape the Malaysian police, who were looking for him as part of their general crackdown on Jemaah Islamiyah. He entered Thailand across the land border between Malaysia and Thailand, and was met by Zulkifli bin Marzuki, who was already living there, and who was JI's contact person in Thailand. Shortly thereafter, they were joined by Wan Min Wan Mat (who "had the same problem" of being on the run, according to Mukhlas), Dr. Azhari bin Husin, and Noordin Top.[40] Fathur Rahman al-Ghozi was supposed to join the group, but was arrested on his way out of Manila. Thailand was thus a place of refuge for JI, but did not have the support network necessary to support more than planning meetings. Inasmuch as Thailand was not adjacent to Indonesia, it was even less useful as a logistics node.

In February 2002, Wan Min Wan Mat, Hambali, Zulkifli bin Marzuki, Dr. Azhari, Noordin Top, and Mukhlas (and possibly Mohammed Mansour Jabarah) met in a rented house in Bangkok to plan strategies for jihad in Indonesia. They chose Mukhlas to be the leader of the *muhajirun* (a term loosely meaning "righteous fugitives"), because Hambali was wanted by the Indonesian police and had to stay in Thailand. Jemaah Islamiyah still felt confident enough in the political environment in Thailand not only to use it as a relative long-term safe haven for fugitives, but also to use it to bring together most of the top-level operational leaders for general planning sessions. By the end of March, Mukhlas decided it was time for the fugitives to relocate to Indonesia, where they would be under the command of Zulkarnaen.[41] Mukhlas would relocate to Tenggulun village in Lamongan, Java, Indonesia both so he could be with his family, and could better carry out jihad. Just before he left Thailand, Mukhlas met with Wan Min Wan Mat in the long-distance bus terminal in Yala, in southern Thailand. Wan Min Wan Mat, as Hambali's intermediary, gave him US$15,500 in cash for the purposes of carrying out jihad, with more money to come if needed. After taking the money, Mukhlas boarded a bus to Kuala Lumpur (how he got past Malaysian immigration at the border is unclear), then took another bus to Johor Bahru. In Johor Bahru, he took a taxi to a nearby beach whose name and location he claimed to have forgotten, and booked passage on a speedboat carrying fourteen illegal Indonesian workers back to Tanjung Pinang, Bintan, in Riau Islands province, arriving in the middle of the night. Presumably he then took another ferry ride to Tanjung Balai, Karimun, a major port between Batam and Sumatra, because it was there that Mukhlas tarried for several days in a cheap hotel (*losmen*) waiting for his wife and children to come from Johor. Together they took a ship to Jakarta, and from there a night bus to Surabaya, where they chartered a car that took them to Tenggulun village.[42]

What is interesting about Mukhlas's route is that, after he had escaped from a country that was pursuing him (that is, Malaysia), he actually re-entered the country and used it as a transit point. Although clandestine organizations do not completely avoid hostile territory, Mukhlas's behavior at first glance seems to be somewhat unusual. But it makes sense when we consider that Mukhlas was faced with state hostility in Malaysia and Singapore—and, if JI's activities became too obvious, Thailand—and needed to get back to Indonesia. Even in Thailand, there was some anti-JI state hostility, and flying out from Bangkok would have left Mukhlas too exposed. Jemaah Islamiyah members taking planes was not un-heard of during the "glory days" of 1999 to 2001, but it was rare after the first crackdowns began. The technologies of globalization were rapidly abandoning Jemaah Islamiyah; members had to stick close to the landscape, moving surrepti-tiously across land and sea borders. Thus, unless he wanted to charter his own boat, Mukhlas had no way of getting from Thailand to Indonesia without going through Malaysia. Because Mukhlas received money from Wan Min Wan Mat in the bus terminal in Yala in southern Thailand, then took a bus to Kuala Lumpur, he crossed into Malaysia by land, but it is unclear how he got past the immigration checkpoints. To get from Malaysia to Indonesia, he did not even risk the chance of being caught by Malaysian immigration, and chose a completely illicit route.

For some time after the Singaporean and Malaysian crackdowns, Mantiqi II members devoted their energies to aiding in hiding Mantiqi I fugitives who had fled to Thailand and Indonesia.[43] A number of the JI Singapore members escaped because the Singaporean government initially underestimated the size of the JI cell in the country. The escape routes of the Singaporeans suggest how dependent on topography and infrastructure (namely, land routes) the refugees became once the crackdowns began. Singaporean operative Mas Selamat bin Kastari escaped by land to Malaysia, then took a boat to Indonesia, presumably to Sumatra; he was ultimately captured in Pekanbaru. After he escaped from Sin-gapore, Mas Selamat, hiding in Indonesia under the name Edi Hariyanto, made plans to hijack a plane from Bangkok and crash it into Changi Airport. Before he was captured in February 2003, he was considered to be the JI member most dangerous to Singapore. After he escaped from a detention center in Singapore in February 2008, the designation presumably returned. Arifin bin Ali, a member of Fiah Tajnid, likewise escaped from Singapore through Malaysia. In January 2002 he hid in Thailand, where he was involved with some Thai Muslims he had met along the way in a plot to bomb embassies in Bangkok. He was arrested in May 2003.[44]

The Mantiqi I fugitives aside, the JI command and control structure continued to function normally up until the Indonesian crackdowns began in November 2002. Part of JI's target area was cut off, but given JI's extensive transnational structure, it was able to fail in one part, and reconstitute itself as an organization focused on Indonesia and the Philippines. The loss of Singapore and Malaysia were regrettable, but not critical to the survival of the organization.

Interestingly, the *wakalah* in Sabah, Malaysia, which was part of Mantiqi III, seemed to be unaffected by the Malaysian government arrests, a sign, perhaps, of how separate Mantiqi I and Mantiqi III were from each other. The transnational routes that connected Mantiqi I and Mantiqi III were not direct, but seem to have gone through Mantiqi II in Indonesia, providing some measure of insulation from the Mantiqi I fallout. One source claims that Nasir Abas, the head of Mantiqi III from April 2001, did not know about specific operations that Mantiqi I and II were planning, up until the Bali bombing.[45] After the Singaporean and Malaysian crackdowns, Nasir continued to do his job as before: transporting recruits, legally and illegally, to and from the Philippines for training, by this time to Camp Jabal Quba. Mustapha, having handed leadership of Mantiqi III to Nasir, ran Project Uhud, which continued to send JI fighters to Poso to take part in jihad. Mukhlas remained the head of Mantiqi I, even though he had few subordinates in Malaysia and Singapore who were not in jail.

The *markaziyah* meeting on 17 October 2002 in Tawangmangu, Solo, five days after the first Bali attack, was notable for its routine nature. The heads of the *mantiqi* gave reports on the status of their *mantiqi,* down to the *wakalah* level: how many people had been arrested where, which *wakalah* were still active, which ones had been destroyed, and what the active *wakalah* were doing at the time. Especially interesting was how JI handled the fallout of the collapse of Mantiqi I. Mukhlas reported that approximately seventy JI members had been arrested. He said that the remaining Mantiqi I fugitives were divided into three groups: those who remained entirely under the command of Mantiqi I, those who had transferred to Mantiqi II's structure, and those who were now subordinate to both Mantiqi I and II. Jemaah Islamiyah's leaders also discussed how to support Mantiqi I members and their families. While the Singaporean government was providing for the families of the Singaporean detainees, the wives of the Malaysian detainees needed money, so the *markaziyah* resolved to support the detainees' families financially. Nasir Abas, as head of Mantiqi III, was ordered to collect money from his *mantiqi.* Mantiqi I was in serious trouble, but JI appeared to be handling the situation according to the group's standard rules and regulations. Mantiqi II and III had barely been touched, and it was understood that JI members had standing orders to give sanctuary to any JI fugitives who came into their area, to the point of providing them with shelter, money, and a job.[46] Even if the overall structure was not involved in any given bombing, all of JI effectively became accomplices because they were under an obligation to help the bomb plotters in the messy aftermath.

Given that JI continued its formal operations even after the Bali bombing, it is possible, even likely, that the central command was not expecting such a strong reaction from the Indonesian police, and were counting on Indonesia as the long-term safe haven from which to relaunch its operations in Singapore and Malaysia. Jemaah Islamiyah did not fragment and drop the paramilitary structure until it was forced to by political pressure. Even though it had been forced out of Singapore and Malaysia, as long as it had a safe haven country, it would continue to operate. However, its transnational routes were under pressure. JI was now vulnerable to crackdowns in Indonesia and the Philippines.

Under Attack

The 2002 Bali bombing was too big for the Indonesian government to ignore, and it began an investigation immediately. The crackdown took a month in coming, in part due to delays in the police investigation, but after getting a break in the case, the government began arresting the bombing conspirators, and detained Abu Bakar Ba'asyir as an accessory to the plot. It should be noted that membership in Jemaah Islamiyah is not illegal in Indonesia. By April 2003, Indonesian police had captured eighteen major JI suspects, including Abu Rusdan, Abu Bakar Ba'asyir's successor as amir of JI, who was captured in Kudus in Central Java. On these suspects they found over seven thousand bullets of various calibers, a pistol, twenty-five kilograms of sulfur, fifteen kilograms of "potassium" (probably potassium chlorate), and detonators for making bombs.[47] With accompanying weapons, the cache would have been enough to start a very small war. The last two countries in Southeast Asia where Jemaah Islamiyah had a haven—Indonesia and the Philippines—had finally started to crackdown on JI presence in their territory. The means by which Jemaah Islamiyah adapted to the new security situation allowed some parts of it to survive intact, but also called into question whether JI was a transnational organization after 2005.

The crackdowns worked. Jemaah Islamiyah had nowhere to go. Its time as a coherent transnational organization with the ability to stage large-scale coordinated bombing operations was up. The central operational leadership of JI continued to meet and control ground-level operatives after the first Bali bombing, before and after the Indonesian crackdown, as the *markaziyah* meeting in Tawangmangu in October 2002 shows.[48] But here JI's behavior in part sowed the seeds of its own demise. At the Tawangmangu meeting, Nasir Abas asked

Mukhlas whether he was behind the Bali bombing. Mukhlas at first denied it, but later admitted that in fact he was. Others present at the meeting claimed this was the first time they had heard about JI's responsibility for Bali. This was the beginning of Nasir's dissatisfaction with JI, and one of the reasons he became "inactive," though he continued his duties as head of *Mantiqi III*. Other JI members also went "inactive" due to their revulsion at Bali.[49]

After Abu Bakar Ba'asyir's arrest, the *markaziyah* functioned well enough with Abu Rusdan at the helm, but the crackdown continued and began to take its toll. In January 2003, Malaysian police arrested two JI operatives in Sandakan, Sabah. The operatives had been involved in transporting personnel to and from Mindanao for training, but apparently had not done so for several months previously.[50] That same month, Nasir Abas and Abu Dujana (the secretary of JI) visited Abu Rusdan and Zulkarnaen (the military commander of JI) at Abu Rusdan's home in Java to update them on the progress made by Mantiqi III in incorporating JI's central Sulawesi cell (originally Project Uhud) into the *wakalah* structure.[51] Nasir and Abu Rusdan also discussed hiding Saad, also known as Abdul Roichman, in Palu, as Mantiqi III had remained relatively untouched by the crackdowns up to that point.[52]

In March 2003, Zulkarnaen, Dr. Azhari, and Dulmatin allegedly met on Sebatik Island near Borneo to assess JI's efforts and plan for the future. Forty-eight people were selected to carry out attacks between December 2003 and April 2004, including at tourist hotels in Jakarta, Surabaya, and Medan in December and January, and at a U.S. bank in February or March 2004. JI also launched its third recruiting drive since 1998.[53] The same month, Dulmatin, one of the principal Bali plotters, made his way to Poso with the help of KOMPAK. Nasir Abas met him on 23 March 2003 in Poso, and arranged to hide him for a period of time. Dulmatin asked Nasir not to tell anyone where he (Dulmatin) was, but Nasir felt that he had to tell Abu Rusdan, who was his commanding officer. Even under stress, JI's leadership tried to maintain a semblance of hierarchy, and went to great lengths to preserve the structures that supported illicit routes through the region.[54]

The *markaziyah* was still coherent enough to have another regular meeting on 7 April 2003, similar to the October 2002 convocation. At the meeting, in Puncak, a mountainous vacation area near Jakarta, the leadership pledged that JI would financially support the families of the Bali fugitives, and gave the usual update on *wakalah* activities.[55] But it would be the last such meeting; Nasir Abas was captured soon after, and Abu Rusdan was arrested in June. For his part, Hambali fled to Thailand. He was still in southern Thailand in March 2003, using the network he had developed there, but he largely shunned Muslim communities, and was arrested in August 2003 in a Buddhist area north of Bangkok.[56]

The crackdown led to disarray, but this is not to say that JI fell apart completely. It did not, and demonstrated an ability to replenish itself after Indonesia became inhospitable. In July 2003, Mantiqi II, serving western Indonesia, underwent a reorganization along functional lines, rather than geographic areas, and divided itself into education, *dakwah,* and military affairs branches, an indication, perhaps, that it did not have the manpower necessary anymore to staff the geography-based *wakalahs.* Because Mantiqi III was not involved in any bombing in Indonesia, it was less affected by the crackdown. When Mantiqi III members were arrested, it was generally on smuggling charges, hiding the Bali fugitives, or immigration violations. Nasir Abas, for example, was detained on immigration charges.[57] Mantiqi III *wakalah* teetered along until at least mid-2004, when they began to break down. They then may have been brought back into Mantiqi II.[58]

Outside of Indonesia and the Philippines, JI seems to have had an "insurance policy," but it too had territorial limitations. The detention of seventeen Malaysians and Indonesians, including Hambali's brother, in Pakistan in September 2003 suggests that Jemaah Islamiyah had at least an informal presence in South Asia after it shifted its training camps to the Philippines in the 1990s. Hambali's brother apparently arranged travel for Hambali to and from Pakistan and Afghanistan (presumably before he went on the lam in Thailand), but the operational activities of the group seem to have been minimal.[59] The group could bide their time and receive ideological and religious training in Pakistan, but unless they returned to Southeast Asia, there was little they could do to engage in violent attacks within JI's target area.

As of late 2005, JI's central leadership was focusing on reconsolidating the organization by laying low and training new recruits for the future. Jemaah Islamiyah as an organization had never concentrated solely on blowing things up. While the goal of all branches of JI was the eventual establishment of the pan-Southeast Asia Islamic caliphate, starting with Indonesia, the top leadership always saw the struggle in multifaceted terms. To that end, there were always equally important proselytizing, recruiting, and fundraising functions. The central leadership continued through all the crackdowns to direct the non-violent branches of the organization, but JI found itself to be overly weakened from the crackdowns in part because the *dakwah* and operational cells that carried out bombings were too closely intertwined. When so many top leaders were arrested, both the *dakwah* and operational branches suffered, and following the first Bali bombing crackdown, the leadership began concentrating on separating the operational cells from the *dakwah* cells, in order to rebuild the non-bombing parts of JI under a new centralized leadership.[60] Some of the members who wanted to continue to carry out Bali-style bombings began collaborating with Noordin Top and Dr. Azhari bin Husin, who went on to stage attacks in Jakarta in 2003 and 2004 (see chapter 5), in Bali again in 2005, and then finally in Jakarta in 2009.

The elements of JI apparently unaffiliated with Noordin Top after the Bali bombings faced their own set of problems in crossing borders, even though they were not planning attacks or trying to transport weapons or explosives. As of 2007, some kind of network ferrying Indonesians back and forth to Mindanao for training did exist, but it was unclear whether this was more than a remnant, or even part of JI at all, because Darul Islam has its own training connections with the Philippines.[61] Under such heavy political pressure, JI was forced to rely on illicit routes that depended on topographical advantages between adjacent countries. These routes in turn required structures at either end to support movement. The Philippines-Indonesia border, with the existence of some friendly factions of the MILF and Abu Sayyaf, provided the prerequisites, but the situation was precarious. It is unclear whether there was enough of a connection between the JI members in the Philippines and those in Indonesia to call JI a coherent transnational organization by 2007.

The next year, in February 2008, Mas Selamat, the detained head of JI's Singapore *wakalah,* escaped from the Whitley Road detention center in Singapore by climbing out of an open bathroom window. Helped, perhaps, by the Singaporean government's inept (but darkly humorous) handling of the situation, he was somehow able to get to Woodlands and the northern Singapore water boundary with Malaysia. After four days of hiding in Singapore, he swam across the Strait of Johor in the middle of the night (apparently by following the navigational buoys between Singaporean patrol boats stationed in the strait) to Johor Bahru. There he took refuge with two of his Malaysian friends in the town of Skudai, north of Johor Bahru, until he was captured in April 2009. Mas Selamat had indeed been thinking of going to the southern Philippines or Indonesia, but obviously had failed to carry out his plans.[62] Pursued by the police, apparently without a support structure in Singapore (or much of one in Malaysia), Mas Selamat had little recourse but to rely on the terrain between Singapore and Malaysia to escape. That he did successfully escape Singapore seems to have been a combination of luck and the Singaporean government's continuing incompetence, and every step of his short journey appears to have taken effort. Re-establishing a support structure in Malaysia does not seem to have progressed very far, and Mas Selamat did not take advantage of any of the technologies of globalization to leave Malaysia. His predicament became a reflection, in miniature, of that faced by JI as a whole as its transnational links fell away, one by one, after 2001.

At the apex of Jemaah Islamiyah's territorial expansion, the group's members were able to coordinate their activities across a number of different countries through extensive travel and communications. Getting weapons where they needed to go proved somewhat more difficult, and foreshadowed the problems JI would have in the event of a crackdown. Jemaah Islamiyah used the technologies of globalization to its advantage in the years following Suharto's fall, but it was an advantage contingent on an open political environment and depended on moving through legitimate chokepoints that became less useful when even weak states cracked down. Once the political window began closing, JI became more vulnerable to interdiction as it struggled to cross international boundaries using illicit routes that hugged the landscape. Repeated reorganizations in the face of crackdowns did little to halt the group's decline. Jemaah Islamiyah's travails suggest that operating covertly, or even without the support of at least some factions of the dominant authority in an area hampered its activities more than one would think given the mobility theoretically emanating from the use of modern technology.

To be sure, the Bali bombing played a significant role in JI's demise as a coherent transnational organization from 2002 on. Before the bombing, the Indonesian government could not have cracked down with impunity—it had cast doubts on the very existence of JI as a coherent organization, and was sensitive to being perceived as a Western stooge attacking Islamic groups at the behest of outsiders. After the Bali bombing, the Indonesian government had more political room to crack down and was able to receive counterterrorism aid from Western countries.[63]

The conflicts in Maluku and central Sulawesi from 1998 until 2002 had both created and sustained violent Islamist groups. The Bali bombing discredited such groups, even those that claimed to be defending Muslims. Flare-ups of violence in both Maluku and notably Poso continued for several years, but the signing of the Malino II Accords in February 2002 marked the end of the majority of the fighting in Ambon by the time of the Bali bombing. After the bombing, popular support for the continued existence of the jihadist groups evaporated; Laskar Jihad, the best-known Islamist militia fighting in Ambon and Poso, publicly announced its disbanding almost immediately after the bombing, although it was reportedly still training in other areas of Indonesia several years later.[64] Because there were now few places that could provide the video footage of Christians attacking Muslims that Hambali had used to rally the Christmas Eve bombing plotters (see chapter 5), an ideal aid for radical Islamist recruiting also disappeared.

For its part, the Indonesian government built public support for its anti-JI campaign through the transparent and relatively professional trial of the Bali bombing suspects. Even its missteps, such as when Abu Bakar Ba'asyir's conviction for being involved in the Bali bombing was overturned on appeal by the Indonesian supreme court, spoke to its attentiveness to the law, a change from the Suharto years.[65] In addition, repentant members of Jemaah Islamiyah have decried the group, encouraged current members to leave, and declared that what JI was doing was counter to Islamic teachings.[66]

The unpopularity of JI should not be overstated—according to one survey in 2006, 9 percent of those Indonesians surveyed considered the Bali bombing an act of jihad, while nearly 20 percent supported JI's general aim of establishing an Islamic state.[67] The group was thus opposed by the vast majority of Indonesians, but a significant minority supported the group and its aims; the Indonesian government had to tread somewhat carefully.

Jemaah Islamiyah as an organization was not dependent on, nor did it seek, mass support. Unlike some other terrorist organizations (notably the Palestinian Liberation Organization), JI kept its existence secret, did not as a rule publicly claim responsibility for its attacks, and did not attempt to provide social services as a means of building public support (unlike Hezbollah's extensive social welfare network in southern Lebanon).[68] Jemaah Islamiyah's logistical operations in particular relied on a relatively small number of members and allies manning support structures throughout Southeast Asia. The most direct effect of the unpopularity of the Bali bombing was that the Indonesian government had a freer hand in dealing with the group than it had before. It arrested members, broke up plots, and even engaged in deadly shootouts with fugitives, as happened to Dr. Azhari in November 2005 and Noordin Top in September 2009. Thus the government's rhetoric was turned into reality, creating a hostile environment for JI's transnational activities. External social and political factors help to explain why the Indonesian government was so successful against JI, and why recruiting may have become more difficult for JI. But we need to consider the role of territory to explain why JI's decline took the form that it did. Its transnational links were severed relatively quickly, and the rump groups in Indonesia and the Philippines had difficulty moving people and illicit goods around and between their countries even after they had recruited new members, leading to the drastic contraction of the territory where JI could feasibly operate.

But what about JI's actual bombing operations? In the abstract, we are interested in how political conditions and territory shaped JI's structures, but some analysts are more concerned with how the political geography of a region might lead to success or failure of specific attacks. Many of the training and planning meetings for which JI went to great lengths to organize were centered on building an ability to kill people. Transnational terrorist groups' use of violence, and their ability to project that violence over vast distances are, in the end, why we care about them at all. The next chapter analyzes four JI attacks between 2000 and 2003, and discusses the role that political conditions and geography played in their success or failure.

THE PLOTS OF JEMAAH ISLAMIYAH

Jemaah Islamiyah did not develop its command and control network, establish training camps, and smuggle weapons without purpose. Once the group went operational in the mid-1990s, it set about the task of staging violent attacks. But Jemaah Islamiyah was not only, or even primarily, an organization that bombed things. For the vast majority of the members of JI, studying the Qur'an, spreading radical Islamic fundamentalism, paramilitary training, and fighting to protect Muslims under siege across Southeast Asia were the reasons they joined the organization. Nevertheless, bomb plots are ideal detailed case studies of the state of a terrorist group's transnational activities, because they require bringing together people and materials in a specific place at a specific time, a task more complex than any single activity. Jemaah Islamiyah has been blamed for dozens of attacks since 1999, when it spread its operations back into Indonesia. Four plots are particularly illustrative of the challenges and opportunities JI faced at different points in time, how it adapted, and how it brought together the different components of the organization to wreak havoc.

The Christmas Eve 2000 bombings across Indonesia, and the failed Singapore plots in 2001 came after the fall of Suharto in May 1998, but before JI's existence became conclusively known to regional governments, giving the group relatively free reign of Southeast Asia. Portions of JI pulled off the first Bali attack in October 2002, after JI had been crushed in Singapore and Malaysia, but while the Indonesian government still claimed that JI did not exist in the country. Finally, the Marriott bombing in August 2003 came at a time when all the governments of Southeast Asia were on full alert, and JI was beginning to collapse as a trans-national organization.

Over time, JI was repeatedly forced to reconfigure its network, giving us a window into the changing effect that geography—both physical infrastructure and natural terrain—had on its operations as the regional political noose tightened. Before 2001, Singapore was not actively hostile to Jemaah Islamiyah's (secret) command and control activities, but the government was less friendly to the logistical activities that would be needed to smuggle explosives into the country. As a result, though the planners of the Singapore plots traveled frequently and openly throughout Southeast Asia, the logistics were considerably more difficult. Jemaah Islamiyah had plans to smuggle explosives from the Philippines across the politically open and geographically advantageous border with Indonesia, and then to get them into Singapore from Batam or Malaysia. Here their plans went awry due to the topography of the borders: there were no geographically advantageous illegitimate routes into Singapore, and the few legitimate routes were not amenable to large-scale smuggling. The plans failed.

By contrast, the Christmas Eve 2000 bombings solely in Indonesia succeeded from an organizational standpoint. Again, the planners traveled extensively throughout Southeast Asia, often by legitimate means, in the politically open climate. Moving the explosives from the Philippines throughout Indonesia was accomplished by limited use of illegitimate routes and the illicit use of legitimate routes, all of which stuck closely to the physical landscape. The plan worked, but it revealed weaknesses in JI's transnational structure. The 2002 Bali bombings, occurring at a time of openness in Indonesia, but of hostility in Singapore and Malaysia, were territorially constrained. Conversely, the 2003 Marriott bombing, coming after Indonesia's crackdown, was more precarious and territorially limited. It was becoming difficult for the violent factions of JI to move around, and the logistical routes in Sumatra and Java were highly susceptible to crackdowns, had the Indonesian government thought to look there.

Successful Integration: Christmas Eve Bombings

Although Jemaah Islamiyah had gone operational around 1995, and had begun trying to smuggle weapons into Indonesia in 1997, it did not engage in any bombings until 1999. But when it did, it began with a vengeance, hitting the Manila Metro, the Philippine ambassador's house in Jakarta, and in its most spectacular attack up to that point, thirty-eight different churches and Christian facilities in eleven different cities across Indonesia on Christmas Eve 2000.

Jemaah Islamiyah delivered bombs throughout central and western Indonesia, namely in Batam, Lombok, West Java (Ciamis, Jakarta, Bandung, Bekasi, Mojokerto, and Sukabumi), and northern Sumatra (Medan, Pekanbaru, and Pematang Siantar). The bombings were not successful in terms of mass casualties, competent bomb making, or delivery: the bombs killed "only" 19 people and wounded 120. Many of the bombs failed to go off, and some of the bombers died through careless accidents, including Abu Jabir, the leader of the Bandung plot. Jabir died when someone called his cell phone, which was wired to one of the bombs he was carrying.[1] The bombings were an astonishing success in terms of coordination: they all went off within ninety minutes of each other, and in fact an operation of that scope was something that JI would not pull off again. The operation's territorial spread was vast. Although all of the bombs were in Indonesia, much of the planning was done in Kuala Lumpur, and the explosives came from the Philippines. The governments of Southeast Asia had no idea that JI existed, and the fall of Suharto had opened up the way for JI to spread unimpeded back into Indonesia. As a result, the operation was JI at its freest; the plotters were surprisingly brazen in much of the planning and execution. This section concentrates on the planning that went into the attack on one location, Batam, the island in Indonesia immediately across from Singapore.

Preparation began with frugal investigative trips taken along legitimate routes several months before the attacks. In August 2000, JI members Imam Samudra and Syahid Jabir took a ferry from Jakarta to Batam, landing at Sekupang. The entire trip was done cheaply and quickly. They stayed in Batam for only two days, and used the time to develop a familiarity with the island, as well as get a passport for 700,000 Rupiah (about US$70).[2]

Jemaah Islamiyah at this period in its history was a bureaucratic organization that cherished planning meetings, and it held them whenever and wherever it could. This required extensive travel. At the beginning of September 2000, JI members Hambali, Mukhlas, and Zulkifli bin Marzuki met in Kuala Lumpur, where it was decided to put into action the earlier resolution of the Rabitatul Mujahidin. They pledged to support MILF's activities against the Philippine government by attacking its embassy in Jakarta, with explosives provided by Fathur Rahman al-Ghozi from the Philippines.[3] The next month, Hambali, Mukhlas, Dr. Azhari, and others met in Kuala Lumpur, and in addition to the embassy attack, made plans to attack churches in Indonesia, as well as U.S. military interests in Singapore. Hambali ordered his associate Faiz bin Abu Bakar Bafana to go to Solo to ask JI Amir Abu Bakar Ba'asyir for permission to carry out the attacks.[4] At the end of October 2000, Imam Samudra traveled from Jakarta to Batam, then took another ferry to Malaysia from Batu Ampar, Batam, using a passport under the name Abdul Azis, which was apparently his real name.[5] He was not worried about being caught.

The final meeting of the Rabitatul Mujahidin took place at the beginning of November 2000 at a resort in the Malaysian state of Perak, according to Faiz bin Abu Bakar Bafana. The plans drawn up earlier by the group in Kuala Lumpur were approved. Later that month, Faiz, Hambali, Abu Bakar Ba'asyir, and Zulkifli bin Marzuki met at a hotel in Solo, where they planned more details of the Christmas Eve church bombings, and attacks on U.S. military interests in Singapore, especially at Sembawang (that is, the Yishun Mass Rapid Transit [MRT] station). After the meeting, Faiz returned to Kuala Lumpur, and Hambali went to Jakarta.[6] The routes JI used during the planning certainly took advantage of the technologies of globalization as members held meetings all over the region. If JI's main purpose had been simply to run a command and control network across an entire region, it would have been a prime example of how modern transport and telecommunications have empowered non-state actors. But JI also wanted to blow things up.

Getting the bomb materials required a great deal of planning. At the November Rabitatul Mujahidin meeting, the JI leadership decided to get the necessary explosives for the bombings from Mindanao, and to transport them by boat, for which they allocated 15,000 Malaysian ringgit (about US$4,000) in addition to the money for the explosives themselves. Later in November, Faiz bin Abu Bakar Bafana, Hambali, Imam Samudra, Zulkifli bin Marzuki, and Abu Bakar Ba'asyir met in Solo for another planning meeting, not only for the Christmas Eve bombings but also for the Singapore operations.[7] If they could get away with it, JI was clearly intent on remaining active in Indonesia, the Philippines, Malaysia, and Singapore. It is unclear whether this was the same meeting where *Suara Pembaruan* claims that Faiz, Hambali, Imam Samudra, and Dr. Azhari met to discuss the bombings,[8] but after this meeting Hambali and others were dispatched to procure the explosives. Hambali and Faiz bought the explosives in Manila from unknown suppliers for some significant portion of 180,000 Malaysian ringgit (about US$47,000).[9] This was probably quite a significant amount of money for JI, but for almost forty bombs in eleven cities spread over a number of provinces in Indonesia, it cost little. By this time, JI had Sardjono's boat for moving weapons and recruits back and forth between Indonesia and the Philippines through the Sangihe-Talaud Islands, so it is possible, even probable, that this boat brought the explosives into Indonesia.[10] For an illegitimate route, JI had to provide its own infrastructure in order to evade state authority. A generally positive political environment did not necessarily significantly ease JI's logistics worries.

The lack of official scrutiny in any country meant that the planners and bombers (if not the bombs themselves) could move around Southeast Asia at little cost, with minimal concealment, and maintain personal control over each bombing. The leader of the cell in each city seems to have planned everything down to the bombs and personnel, leaving only the specific locations up to the foot soldiers. JI was certainly capable of using electronic communications (Hambali and Imam Samudra in particular talked many times on their cell phones before the bombings). However, they preferred to meet in safe locations with a JI presence (such as in Solo, Jakarta, and Kuala Lumpur), and this required a great deal of travel. If Imam Samudra's presence at all these meetings is correct, then in the space of three months he traveled to Jakarta, Solo, Kuala Lumpur several times, and finally to Batam, where he was in charge of the Batam bombs. Likewise Hambali was in Kuala Lumpur, Solo, Jakarta, Manila and/or Mindanao, Kuala Lumpur, and eventually went back to Jakarta, where he was in charge of the West Java bombs. Figure 5.1 shows the travel chokepoints and locations of planning meetings, and how the planners moved from place to place. The only locations that are geographically adjacent to each other are Singapore, Batam, and Johor. Without any outside pressure, Jemaah Islamiyah was comfortable using nearly its full territorial extent at the time to plan operations. Furthermore, the routes are similar to what one might imagine a small company with a limited budget using: direct plane trips to important meetings for the longer, non-adjacent routes, with a combination of much cheaper busses and ferries for the lower-level people (such as Imam Samudra) with more time on their hands, or for traveling shorter routes between close-by locations. In an open political environment, the technologies of globalization are quite helpful to terrorists: they can literally fly over international boundaries while making their plans.

While the high-level planners were calling meeting after meeting, the Batam plot began coming together. In the middle of November 2000, Imam Samudra returned to Batu Ampar, Batam from Johor, Malaysia, and then boarded a ship for Pekanbaru. After a night in Pekanbaru, he took a bus to Jakarta.[11] A few weeks later, Imam Samudra took the same route from Jakarta to Batam yet again, this time to settle in for the major part of the operation. He soon met with a JI member Iqbal, who was living in Batam. Also known as Basuki or, at times, Mahmud, Iqbal was one of the few JI associates in Batam. He provided temporary places to stay in the months before the bombing, and served as the fifth member of the Batam plot.[12]

Jemaah Islamiyah seconded low-level members from nearby cells to help with each bombing. In the case of Batam, Ja'afar bin Mistooki (alias Furqoon) traveled from Singapore to Batam with two other members of the regional command covering Singapore and Malaysia, Mantiqi I: Hashim bin Abas (alias Syamsudin), and Abdul Rahim (also alias Syamsudin).[13] They came on the orders of Hambali to help Imam Samudra with the church bombings at the end of November 2000,

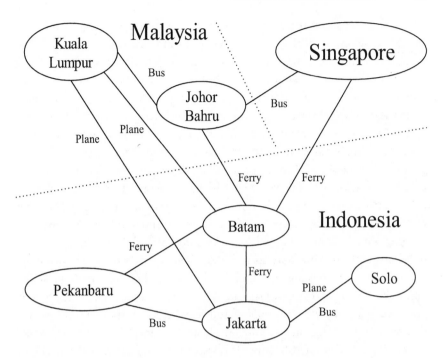

FIGURE 5.1   Batam bombings command and control locations and links, 2000

and returned on 25 December 2000.[14] Before going to Batam, the three Mantiqi I members took a side trip to Kuala Lumpur, where Hambali encouraged them by showing them a video of attacks on Muslims in Ambon.[15]

After the Singaporeans arrived in Batam, Hambali called them via mobile phone, and told them to find a house to rent. They rented out a room using local JI connections, in Happy Garden Block H, No. 3A, Kodya, after two days of looking. The Singaporeans were assigned the task of leaving the house in the morning, and returning in the evening, as if they were going to work, so that they would not arouse the suspicions of the neighbors. While at their "jobs," their assignment was to watch the movements of the police, survey the targeted churches, buy some components, such as suitcases and blenders, that would be needed to make the bombs, and help mix the bomb ingredients in the blenders. Imam Samudra gave the Singaporeans money for the components, and took the receipts to keep an accurate accounting of the money spent, an example of JI's scrupulous bureaucracy.[16]

The plotters received many visitors. In the middle of December, Mukhlas, who was a high-level Mantiqi I official at the time, flew into Batam, was picked up from the airport by Hashim, and gave a blessing to the plotters at the request of Imam Samudra, before leaving after a day for Johor via ferry.[17] After the plotters had been in Batam for three weeks, Hambali came to confer about the now imminent attacks on local churches. He also made an inspection of the safe house where the bombs were constructed.[18] Hambali's trip to Batam was not to bring money for the operation but to motivate the troops, as he had done in Kuala Lumpur. Dr. Azhari bin Husin also came to Happy Garden in the weeks leading up to the bombings armed with computerized pictures and charts showing how to build a bomb, and taught Imam Samudra much of what he needed to know, although Imam Samudra had had previous training in Afghanistan.[19]

Abu Jabir, the JI member in charge of supplies for the overall operation, sent an associate known as Tarmizi from Jakarta to Batam with a certain amount of TNT, two boxes of magnesium nitrate, detonators, and batteries. The other ingredients—potassium chlorate, sulfur, bolts, wires, and the other components—were bought in Batam.[20] Mahmud and Ja'afar then picked up Abu Jabir's package in Sekupang.[21] The Singaporeans mixed the ingredients, while Imam Samudra actually put the bombs together. It took Imam Samudra three days to make five bombs in the house at Happy Garden.[22] They then wrapped the bombs to look like Christmas gifts, and put them into suitcases.[23] All of the plotters dropped the bombs off at their designated churches and set the timers such that they would go off before 9:00 pm on Christmas Eve, which they did, and returned to Happy Garden by 11:00 pm.[24]

The day after the bombing, the Singaporeans returned to Singapore directly, and later met in Penang, Malaysia, with Imam Samudra. Ja'afar bin Mistooki went from Singapore to the house of Faiz bin Abu Bakar Bafana in Malaysia after the bombing for a wrap-up evaluation session attended by Mukhlas, Hambali, Imam Samudra, and several Malaysians.[25] The other bombing operations went off in virtually identical ways: Hambali and other high-level JI officials would stop by to oversee preparations personally, give instructions, and provide motivation, while local or nearby JI operatives would carry out the bombings in each city.

The Christmas Eve 2000 bombings are a classic case of a sophisticated, coordinated operation over large distances. But JI's moment of triumph also displayed the weakness of its operational model: it was only capable of working if no one was paying attention. The planning process for the bombings was characterized by numerous meetings in cities throughout Malaysia and Indonesia, with a TNT logistics network that extended from the Philippines through eastern Indonesia to Java, and back north to Medan and Batam. The primary planners, particularly Dr. Azhari, Hambali, and Imam Samudra, traveled constantly, using a number of different types of transport. Every time they crossed a border, and held a meeting, they would have put themselves in increased danger of being detected, if the relevant governments had been looking for them. In an indication of the easy political climate (or his lax operational security), Imam Samudra took the same boat to and from Batam at least three times. By comparison, in later bombings, such as the attack on the Marriott in 2003, the plotters were constantly traveling, but they moved across much smaller swatches of territory, and were more cautious, which limited their options in terms of the routes used.[26]

The bombings also illustrate that making a competent timed bomb is not as easy as it might appear in a country that has even minimal control over its territory. Many of the components of the bombs, particularly the TNT, could not be found in Batam, and had to be brought from Jakarta, or from the Philippines, via a circuitous route that took advantage of the geographical features of the Philippines-Indonesia border (or more specifically, the traditional trading routes that use the same features). In addition, the Batam operation was dependent on one bomb maker, Imam Samudra. Although Ja'afar bin Mistooki had also had a fair amount of training, it is unclear if he was capable of making sophisticated bombs, and even Imam Samudra needed the personal help of Dr. Azhari, JI's master bomb maker. If the plotters had not been able to travel extensively, if there had been a more restricted supply of bomb makers, and if the suppliers had not felt it politically feasible to transport illicit materials halfway across Southeast Asia, the Batam bombing operation would have been significantly impaired. Jemaah Islamiyah took advantage of the tools of globalization in the Christmas Eve 2000 bombings. The ease of travel and communications across Southeast Asia worked to their advantage, but the continuing importance of face-to-face contact, the low-level means of travel (by bus and ferry), and the lengths to which JI went to get supplies suggests a vulnerability that globalizing technologies were not able to remedy, and an opportunity for states to crack down.

Failed Integration: Singapore Plots

By comparison, the failed Singapore bombing plots of 2001, involving a number of the same people as the Batam plot, illustrate the infuriating difficulty (to terrorists) of operating across international boundaries in a geographically disadvantageous, politically hostile environment. JI's plans for attacking the Singaporean targets were among the first specific bombings conceived by members of the organization, in the mid-1990s. For several years, it seems that they were the centerpiece of JI's plans for terror. Khalim Jaffar, a Singapore *wakalah* member, first thought about attacking the Yishun MRT station (specifically the shuttle bus that took U.S. service members to Sembawang Naval Base from Yishun) in 1997, when JI Singapore went operational and was deemed ready to take part in terrorist attacks. In 1999, he and accomplices took video of the station from a public housing complex across the street under the guise of filming one of the accomplice's daughters. They were going to put the bomb in the baskets of bicycles that were parked near the station.[27] Faiz bin Abu Bakar Bafana took the tape to Afghanistan in 1999, and JI Singapore briefed al-Qaeda leaders in Afghanistan (which is why the Yishun MRT station video was discovered in the ruins of Mohammed Atef's house). Al-Qaeda was interested. The attack plans were approved by Jemaah Islamiyah's military council and supervised by Hambali.[28] Yet even though they were the longest-running plans JI had, they were not carried out. One could argue that their failure was due to the breakup of the cell by the Singaporean and Malaysian police, but the plans had already been in gestation for approximately four years before that. Why had they not moved on them? The answer is that the major limiting factor on the attacks was the logistical problem of actually getting the bombers and bomb materials into place.

The political environment in Indonesia, Malaysia, and Singapore in 2000 and early 2001, one of ignorance or benign neglect, was not going to get any better, and we would expect JI's command and control structure to move across large areas with little dependence on topographical features, or even topographical infrastructure such as roads and seaports. In concrete terms, this is what happened in both the Singapore and the Christmas Eve plots. As for logistics, the more limited routes provided by geography meant that JI had to find a chain of adjacent countries through which to smuggle its explosives along illicit routes (or by making illicit use of legitimate routes). The Batam bombings required smuggling the explosives only from the Philippines to Indonesia, and then through Indonesia. This was done without too much trouble, although it was not trivial. But when trying to get explosives into Singapore, Jemaah Islamiyah encountered a government that was virulently hostile to explosives smuggling in any form, even if it did not know that a terrorist group was behind the smuggling. This increased JI's dependence on topographical features when crossing Singapore's borders. But the tiny island city-state provided none that JI could easily use, rendering it logistically impotent for the amount of explosives it wanted to move.

The Singapore *wakalah,* equivalent to a brigade in JI's hierarchy, was either in existence at the formal creation of Jemaah Islamiyah on 1 January 1993, or it was set up soon afterward by Ibrahim Maidin, its first leader, known for his discipline and secrecy (and apparently magnetic effect over his subordinates).[29] From the early 1990s, the Singaporean government knew of some of JI's members, but did not necessarily know they were involved in the organization, a situation similar to that in Malaysia.[30] Jemaah Islamiyah was not a registered society—neither the operations nor the *dakwah* groups could legally exist in Singapore—which meant JI also faced a low hum of hostility, and took moderate security measures when within the country as a result. Aside from the Yishun MRT station, JI conducted several casings of U.S. houses, and on the family camping trips, they would charter buses to drive the entire group around. One member would have a camera, and would pretend to tape a friend or a child along on the trip in order to get video of the intended target. Jemaah Islamiyah also maintained electronic operational security, which would be akin to making illicit use of legitimate virtual routes. During their planning, JI members would use a single anonymous e-mail account, and save e-mails to be read by everyone in the draft box. No messages were sent, so none could be intercepted (so the theory went). They also put their shoes inside during meetings so as not to arouse the suspicion of the neighbors, and held the special operational classes only after regular Qur'an study groups had adjourned for the night.[31]

After the Singapore cell went operational, two plans reached the stage where cell members started worrying about procuring bombers and explosives: a series of simultaneous truck bombs against foreign interests, especially the Israeli, U.S., Australian, and British embassies; and the attack on the Yishun MRT station. JI's operational leadership first planned to attack the U.S. and Israeli embassies in a meeting in September 2001, after al-Qaeda's 9/11 terrorist attacks. They set a target date of either December 2001 or April or May 2002, and calculated that they would need twenty-one tons of ammonium nitrate. Information on the planned truck bomb attacks was initially confined to four members of Fiah Musa,[32] directed by Hambali and "Sammy," apparently an alias for Mohammed Mansour Jabarah, the Canadian-Arab JI and al-Qaeda operative.[33] The leadership had Sammy travel from Kuala Lumpur to Singapore in October to inform the Singapore cell of their plans against the U.S. embassy, the Israeli embassy, and U.S. naval forces in Singapore. The Singapore cell members added the British embassy and the Australian embassy, and conducted video reconnaissance, both together with Sammy and on their own.[34]

The actual suicide bombers for the attacks were to be supplied by al-Qaeda, presumably from outside of Southeast Asia, because at the time JI had no suicide bombers of its own,[35] but it was JI's role to handle the planning and other logistics. The Singaporean members of JI were deemed not ready for suicide bombing, although some of the Singaporean members did later express a willingness to be suicide bombers upon interrogation.[36] Actually bringing in the bombers would have involved simply flying them in.

This is when the logistics of staging violent attacks in a tightly controlled state like Singapore became an issue. According to the investigations of the Internal Security Department, the plotters did not manage to get explosives into Singapore.[37] There are three ways into Singapore: by air through Changi Airport (which was off-limits to JI); by sea from Johor, Malaysia or Batam, Indonesia; and by land across the Causeway (or, since 1998, the Second Link at Tuas). The two different sea borders encourage different kinds of smuggling methods. The narrow strait between Johor and Singapore can be crossed within sixty seconds by a speedboat, but such a small, swift boat can only handle a small load on each trip, rendering it unsuitable for safe passage of tons of anything. The more expansive waters between Batam and Singapore are more suitable for larger, slower, and stealthier boats that try to slip between Singaporean patrols, and this seems to be the option JI considered most seriously.[38] Because they already had plans to stage attacks in Singapore, at the same time as they were planning the Christmas Eve bombings in the latter half of 2000, the JI leadership (specifically Imam Samudra and/or Mukhlas) asked Hashim Abbas to observe the immigration post in Batam, with the goal of smuggling explosives into Singapore. Hashim Abbas duly took a ferry from Tanjung Putri in Johor, Malaysia to Batu Ampar in Batam, in order to see if it was possible to smuggle up to ten tons of TNT or C4 into Malaysia or Singapore from Batam, although he was at a loss as to where all these explosives would come from.[39] Nothing came of it, and facing a dead end by sea, JI turned to land.

The general bombing plans involved explosives from two sources: conventional TNT and ammonium nitrate, which presented acquisition challenges. Jemaah Islamiyah does not seem to have ever had any hope of buying TNT in Singapore, and it tried mightily to get foreign-bought ammonium nitrate into Singapore before resorting to a domestic supplier, which aroused the suspicion of Singaporean officials.

Others in JI got closer to working out plans for smuggling the Singapore explosives. At the beginning of July 2001, Faiz bin Abu Bakar Bafana and another JI operative by the name of Arkam, based in Kuala Lumpur, took a plane to Solo through Batam and Jakarta, to scout the route by which they would move the explosives intended for the Singapore attacks. The TNT would apparently be bought in General Santos City in the Philippines, then transported by ship to Manado in eastern Indonesia, on to Surabaya in Java, and finally Batam, where they would find some way to get it into Singapore. In Solo, another round of meetings took place at JI headquarters, after which Faiz flew back to Kuala Lumpur from Surabaya, and briefed Mukhlas (now head of Mantiqi I) on the plots.[40]

In the fall of 2001, in his role as the plot's non-Singaporean logistician, Faiz met with Fathur Rahman al-Ghozi in Kota Kinabalu, Sabah, Malaysia, and told him to buy explosives in the Philippines for use in Singapore, five to seven tons. Al-Ghozi subsequently ordered six tons of TNT from his supplier Hussein Ramos in Cebu starting in November 2001.[41] This is not unthinkable. Workers can easily pilfer detonators, a few kilograms of TNT, a length of detonating cords, and other materials for bombs from a mine over time by purposefully over-reporting how much they have used, and taking the difference for themselves, although

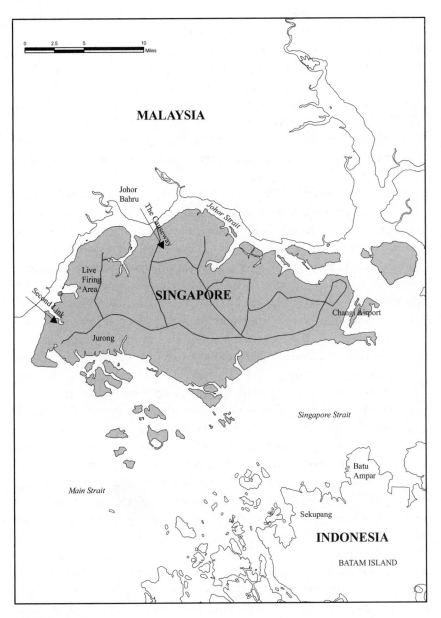

Map 5.1 Singapore

Credit: Ramachandra Sivakumar, Center for Geographic Information Systems, Georgia Institute of Technology

the large amount of TNT suggests a sophisticated operation.[42] After the wave of JI arrests in Singapore, with the plan still in operation in late December 2001, al-Ghozi apparently took possession of only 1,100 kilograms because he did not have enough money for the rest. His trip to Bangkok, for which he was about to leave when he was arrested, was not only for the JI meeting scheduled there in January 2002, but also to get the rest of the money for the TNT from the JI leadership.[43] The new plan was for al-Ghozi to move the explosives into Singapore by shipping it from the Philippines to Manado, Indonesia, thence to Malaysia, and finally over the Causeway between Johor Bahru, Malaysia and Singapore.[44] This differed from the original plan in that the explosives would go through Malaysia, but was no more successful than the plan to bring the explosives through Batam.

Figure 5.2 shows both of the planned smuggling routes that JI had mapped out for getting explosives into Singapore. The first plan was very similar to the route that had been used in the Christmas Eve 2000 bombings, and probably would have worked to get the explosives to Batam, at the very least. It is unclear from the second plan how JI was going to get the explosives from Manado to Johor Bahru. A ship is the most likely possibility, one that would not necessarily take a direct path between the two cities, but probably stop somewhere in Sabah, Malaysia. Manado is the key chokepoint in both plans, and for good reason. Terrorist groups' logistics are almost always more difficult than command and control—governments that do not care about seemingly harmless meetings care more about weapons smuggling, so it would be fair to say that weapons smuggling almost never encounters a truly non-hostile environment. As a result, a city with advantageous geography and an established network is especially valuable. Latent hostility encouraged JI's smugglers to be cautious, and they almost exclusively used the two waterways between the Philippines and Indonesia (the Sangihe-Talaud Islands) and between the Philippines and Malaysia (the area around Palawan), both of which are laced with tiny islands ideal for hiding boats and illicit goods. Chokepoints, even for illicit networks, are sticky. Manado is the first major city in Indonesia for boats illegally plying the waters between the Philippines and Indonesia, and is convenient for getting to the rest of the country. Although the province is mostly Christian, it contained a Jemaah Islamiyah safe house, and was one of JI's transit points for recruits going to the Philippines for training, and coming from the Philippines with weapons. None of region's governments knew it at the time, but cracking down on smuggling through Manado in 2000–2001 might have stymied Jemaah Islamiyah's plots before they ever got to Singapore or western Indonesia.[45]

Ammonium nitrate was easier for the plotters to get, but presented its own problems. The embassy bombing plan was to acquire six trucks, build giant

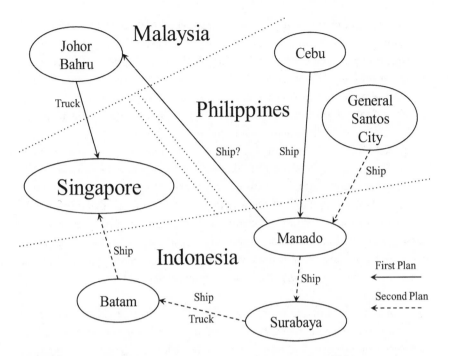

FIGURE 5.2 Planned TNT smuggling routes in the Singapore plots, 2001

ammonium nitrate (more than three tons each) bombs in them, and leave each for the suicide bomber to pick up at a location near the target. JI had already acquired four tons of ammonium nitrate locally in Malaysia, and a man known only as "Sabah" was holding it there.[46]

Jemaah Islamiyah planned to smuggle both the TNT and the ammonium nitrate across the Causeway into Singapore, making illicit use of a legitimate route. The plotters considered putting the ammonium nitrate in large barrels, possibly camouflaged among cosmetics boxes. When the Singaporean government cracked down, they had not yet gotten the trucks, the necessary chemicals, or the detonating cords.[47] But bringing almost twenty tons of ammonium nitrate into Singapore over the Causeway was no simple matter. Conventional explosives (TNT) remain stable for years, and can be stored for a long time. On the contrary, ammonium nitrate degrades to the point where it is unusable relatively quickly. If the Singaporean bombers wanted to use ammonium nitrate in their truck bombs, they would have had to bring in large amounts each time. Bringing in small amounts in multiple shipments would have been more secure, but would have taken more time, and the first shipments would have degraded by the time the last shipments arrived.[48] Aside from the degradation, each trip across the Causeway increased the chance that the plotters would be caught.

Stymied by the problem of getting Malaysian (or Filipino) explosives into Singapore, Sammy ordered one of the Singaporean cell members, Ellias, to find warehouse space in Singapore for building the bombs, and to acquire seventeen tons of ammonium nitrate in Singapore. Both projects were unsuccessful. They were in the process of finding someone to receive the explosives and store them, and were looking for a warehouse to store the explosives and trucks when the crackdown came.[49] Ellias talked to a friend of his who knew of a company that would sell him ammonium nitrate. The company manager told Ellias to come in person to arrange the order, but Ellias was arrested before he could do so.[50] A Singaporean source notes that there are only three or four sources of ammonium nitrate in Singapore, thus limiting the terrorists' procurement options.[51] With the wave of arrests, the four tons of ammonium nitrate that JI had obtained were missing, causing Malaysian and Singaporean officials headaches looking for it. It turned up in early 2003 buried at a rubber plantation in Malaysia, but had degraded to the point where it was not very usable as explosives, just as JI had presumably feared.[52]

In an indication of the open political environment that existed outside of Singapore, the planning aspects of the Singapore plots were in some sense even more geographically widespread than the Batam plots. Al-Qaeda in Afghanistan was briefed on some of the Singapore plans, which included operatives coming down from Kuala Lumpur, operatives going up to Johor Bahru, explosives buying in the Philippines, and a planned meeting in Bangkok. The Arab suicide bombers to be provided by al-Qaeda would fly in the day before the embassy bombings and proceed to their destinations.[53] But geography and politics got in the way of JI's machinations. Although JI had plans to attack targets in Singapore from at least 1997 on and had conducted reconnaissance on all the targets, it was consistently presented with the problem of how to transport explosives from a country with a lax environment to a more weapons-hostile environment and finally to a supremely weapons-hostile environment, a problem it never overcame. Singapore, being a small island city-state with a high level of state capacity, might be significantly more difficult for a terrorist group to penetrate than a larger, weak country such as Indonesia. This is true, and to a certain extent I chose the Singapore plots as a comparative case because the island's geography provides clear smuggling routes that can be analyzed easily.

Yet dependence on geography for less than legitimate routes still holds for other parts of JI's activities. Although JI found it easier to move explosives and people from the Philippines to Indonesia, it had to take the time and bear the costs of setting up its own smuggling cell, using its own boat, and depending on the many small islands separating the two countries to evade authorities. The operation was by no means trivial. Moreover, many of its safe houses and support cells were based in cities, such as Manado, that were also legitimate transportation hubs. This use of a combination of semi-legitimate and illicit routes had the effect of lowering JI's chances of being caught. It also meant that even if JI avoided the security apparatus of the state at the border by depending on topographical advantages, it still often ended up in a city from which it pursued more legitimate options, providing more constraints on the routes it could realistically take. After October 2002, as the political environment worsened, these problems were to become even more acute.

Retrenchment and Integration: The First Bali Bombings

The first Bali bombing in October 2002, which killed 202 people, was Jemaah Islamiyah's most infamous attack, and the catalyst for the Indonesian government to crack down. Ironically, the plot was planned and executed in a relatively open environment *inside Indonesia*. Following the crackdowns in Malaysia, Singapore, and the Philippines (or rather, the areas of the Philippines controlled by the Manila government), Jemaah Islamiyah was reduced to Thailand, western and central Indonesia, Mindanao, and Mantiqi III, which continued to transport trainees through East Malaysia to Mindanao for training at Camp Jabal Quba. The drastic uptick in hostility from Malaysia, Singapore, and much of the Philippines had thrown a wrench into JI's operations, such that *no* transnational command and control or logistical activity was particularly easy.

The operation itself is less interesting than the planning that went on before the bombing. Mukhlas, still technically head of Mantiqi I, apparently felt free to work and travel openly in Indonesia for most of 2002, after he moved to the Javanese village of Tenggulun. He even used part of the money that Wan Min Wan Mat had given him in Thailand to go to Ambon for about a week in July 2002 to check on the jihad situation there.[54] Wan Min Wan Mat sent two more batches of money, via courier, to Mukhlas. One, totaling $10,000, arrived in June or July 2002 at Mukhlas' house, carried by Tamin, an Indonesian worker who had been living in Malaysia. The final batch was carried by Noordin Top, and arrived at Tenggulun at the end of September 2002.[55]

Nothing much seemed to happen until August, when Amrozi mentioned to his brother Mukhlas that Imam Samudra had a plan to conduct a bombing operation in Bali.[56] The brothers Ali Imron, Mukhlas, and Amrozi then took a car down to the house of one Hernianto, in a village in Sukaharjo, where they held the first planning meeting for the Bali bombing. According to Mukhlas, Imam Samudra, Dulmatin, Idris, and Umar (also known as Abdul Ghoni) were also in attendance (according to Amrozi, Zulkarnaen and Utomo Pamungkas were also there).[57] It was there that Mukhlas doled out tasks, each to his own expertise, and promised enough money to fund the operation. In the year or so after the Bali bombing, the Indonesian government arrested more than eighty people in connection with the attacks, but for our purposes we are primarily interested in the main actors who were involved in planning and carrying out the bombings. In early September, Amrozi, Idris, Dulmatin, and Imam Samudra were among those who attended a more limited motivational and logistical meeting inside the An Nahel mosque near *Pesantren* al-Mukmin in Pondok Ngruki, near Solo in central Java. Several days later, Amrozi, Idris, and Ali Imron bought the white Mitsubishi L-300 that would serve as the car bomb.

Getting most of the components for the bombs was not a problem. Amrozi purchased the chemicals that would be used for the bomb at a chemical store known as Tidar Kimia in Surabaya. All told, he bought one ton of potassium chlorate, 40 kilograms of aluminum powder, and 100 kilograms of sulfur between 18 and 23 September. Amrozi then used the Mitsubishi, and the other car the plotters had at their disposal, a green Suzuki Vitara, to transport the chemicals, divided into a number of cartons, to long-distance busses traveling from Surabaya to Denpasar, where he paid to have them sent as unaccompanied baggage in five separate batches. Interestingly, Amrozi paid only 235,000 Rupiah (about US$20) for all the baggage costs.[58] Although Mukhlas had a total of US$30,500 for the operation at his disposal, the actual transportation of the main bomb components seems to have been a small part of the total cost. There were no international borders across which it needed to be smuggled, and the low level of political hostility the plotters were facing in Indonesia allowed them to use regular courier services along legitimate routes (notice that they moved along roads, not through airports, even inside Indonesia) rather than more expensive illicit carriers.

Within Central and East Java, and Bali, the plotters moved around quite frequently, following a pattern set in the Christmas Eve bombings. Amrozi went to Bali twice, first at the beginning of September with Imam Samudra, Dulmatin, Ali Imron, Idris, and Utomo Pamungkas to scout for targets, safe houses, and other local logistical needs. The second time, nearly all the main plotters were concentrated in one place in Denpasar. Amrozi, Utomo Pamungkas, Idris, Ali Imron, and Dulmatin drove the Mitsubishi L-300 and the Suzuki Vitara together to Denpasar from Surabaya on 5 October, arriving in Denpasar the next day. On the way, they stopped to buy filing cabinets in which to place the explosives. In Denpasar, they loaded the Mitsubishi with the explosive materials. Dr. Azhari, Little Umar, Big Umar (Abdul Ghoni), and Imam Samudra arrived in Denpasar separately. The entire team came together in a garage—Dr. Azhari had apparently designed the bombs, Dulmatin put together the electronics for the bombs, and the Umars loaded the explosives into the filing cabinets.[59]

According to Ali Imron, Dulmatin and Abdul Ghoni provided the TNT, which was used as a booster for the homemade explosive mixture. The TNT came from Dulmatin and Abdul Ghoni's time waging jihad in Ambon. Given Dulmatin's ties to the southern Philippines (which is where, if still alive, he was hiding as of 2008), it is possible the TNT had been smuggled in from the Philippines earlier, or that it had originated with someone else in Ambon.[60] In any case, Dulmatin was able to get the TNT from Ambon to Bali without too much trouble.[61] Amrozi, Dr. Azhari, and Dulmatin left Bali on 10 October, leaving only Ali Imron, Idris, and Imam Samudra, plus the two suicide bombers.[62] Mukhlas took the bus to Denpasar on 9 October, and stayed for three days to oversee preparations, tour the target sites, and bless the operation. He was homeward bound on 11 October.[63] On 12 October, Idris remotely detonated the non-suicide bombs (including the one outside the U.S. consulate), and Ali Imron drove the suicide bombers Iqbal and Jimmy most of the way to the targeted nightclubs, before getting out. Jimmy went into the nightclub, and Iqbal drove the rest of the way, where he detonated the car bomb. Imam Samudra, Ali Imron, and Idris left Bali by long-distance bus on 13 October.[64] The actual preparations, consisting of buying chemicals from a regular store, buying or renting vehicles, and sitting on long-distance busses, were quite pedestrian.

The plot to bomb Bali took place almost entirely in Java and Bali itself (where the plotters did not spend more than about a week and a half), even though the plotters were drawn from both Mantiqi I and Mantiqi II. There does not seem to have been major JI activity in Thailand (excepting Hambali's escape there), for example, after Mukhlas and the others left in March 2002. Thailand was still useful for refuge and general planning meetings, but its distance from the center of JI in Indonesia made it less useful for anything else. Thus, Dulmatin's provision of TNT may well have come from his personal contacts that extended outside of JI, but if in fact the TNT did come from the southern Philippines, the Bali plot used the one remaining transnational illicit logistical route available to the extended JI network.

The Bali bombing also betrayed a marked stress on Jemaah Islamiyah. Although it killed far more people than the Christmas Eve 2000 bombings, and the bombs were considerably more sophisticated than the Christmas Eve 2000 bombs, as a plan, Bali was relatively simple compared to what JI had pulled off earlier. In part this was due to the small number of primary plotters—without the cooperation of a non-trivial portion of Mantiqi II's operational apparatus, the plotters could not pull off more than one city at a time. Hambali, who had coordinated the Christmas Eve 2000 bombings across different cities through extensive travel, was in no position to do more than provide money, given that he was still on the run in Thailand. Indonesia's open political environment allowed the Bali plotters relative freedom of movement in Java and Bali, and they *did* move around, but the Malaysian and Singaporean crackdowns had the (at the time unanticipated) effect of hindering much of the rest of JI's transnational network. Thus, changing political conditions, combined with the geographical constraints that JI had already run up against in its previous attacks, shaped the operation behind the first Bali attack, and thus shaped the Bali bombing itself. Far from being JI's high point, Bali was a sign of its accelerating decline.

Increasingly Constrained Integration: The First Marriott Bombing

As JI came under increasing strain in the Philippines and in Indonesia, and became constrained as a coherent operational clandestine transnational organization, the bombings attributed to it from 2003 on followed a similar pattern. The non-territorial aspirations of JI's violent breakaway faction should have made Noordin Top and Dr. Azhari's operations more flexible and rendered them ready and willing to move out of Indonesia to stage violent attacks in a more hospitable locale. And in fact, because both Dr. Azhari and Noordin Top were Malaysian, they had even less reason to remain in Indonesia. But extreme political pressure constricted the territory in which the terrorists could feasibly stage bombings, an activity requiring the physical movement of people and materials. As a result, their situation was precarious.

Jemaah Islamiyah may have been involved in a bombing of the Davao airport in the Philippines on 4 March 2003, due to the similarities between that bombing and the one in Manila in 2000.[65] It is unclear, though, if later JI bombings in the Philippines were actually on the orders of anyone in Indonesia. The Marriott, the Australian embassy, and the second Bali bombings, perpetrated by a faction of JI with tenuous connections to the JI central command, were essentially Indonesia-only operations, and are of interest mainly as a control group of bombings. They show what happens to a group's operational capabilities as it comes under increasing political pressure. The logistics networks for major bombings since the first Bali bombing are interesting for where they are not—namely outside of Sulawesi, Sumatra, Java, or Bali. To maintain his operations, Noordin Top—the leader of the violent faction—had to reach out to outside organizations, who did not necessarily have the same territorial aspirations or goals as he did. When the outsiders did not come through, he was limited to Java, resulting in strains to his faction in its ability to be an operational transnational network.

The 5 August 2003 bombing against the JW Marriott hotel in south Jakarta was apparently the last JI attack for which planning was known beforehand by members of the JI central command (*markaziyah*). Noordin Top, the perpetrator, began taking classes at Luqmanul Hakiem, the Jemaah Islamiyah *pesantren* in Johor, Malaysia in 1995, joined the organization in 1998, and, for legal reasons, later became the putative director of Luqmanul Hakiem. The Malaysian government forced the closure of Luqmanul Hakiem as part of its ongoing crackdown on JI in early 2002, and Noordin Top moved first to Riau, Indonesia, then to Bukittinggi, West Sumatra. After the Indonesian crackdown in November 2002, Dr. Azhari, then JI's top bomb maker, moved to Bukittinggi to join Noordin Top. In December 2002, after the Indonesian crackdown began, the JI cells on Sumatra began feeling pressure as well. A JI member known as Toni Togar was still holding onto explosives from the Medan portion of the Christmas Eve 2000 bombings. Toni wanted to get rid of the explosives, and told Noordin Top of his plan, but Noordin Top instead decided to use the explosives to stage another bomb attack.[66]

For the attack, Noordin Top used JI members from Bengkulu, Lampung, and Riau, all locations in or near Sumatra, to carry out a bombing in Jakarta, on Java. What is interesting is that under conditions of a high degree of state hostility, the planning and logistics for attacks (this would also be the case for the next two bombings) all took place in one general location, in this case, Sumatra, and the actual attack took place in an adjacent location in the same country. The plotters and the explosives could be moved to near the target only a short time before the attack, without crossing any international boundaries, although they did take a trip to Jakarta in the month before the bombing to scope out targets and rent safe houses before returning to Lampung.[67] Although command and control is the activity least attached to the physical landscape, given the political situation and the need to maintain operational security, the planning for the attack began to follow the same pattern of constricted territory and geographical dependence that logistics activities more commonly follow.

In February 2003, Noordin Top's team arranged for the explosive ingredients (aside from the TNT and detonators) to be sent as "unaccompanied baggage on an ordinary intercity bus" from Dumai to Pekanbaru to Bengkulu, essentially down the length of Sumatra, ever closer to Jakarta.[68] Separately, Mohammad Rais, one of the plotters, and Dr. Azhari picked up the TNT and detonators in Padang; they were apparently put together with the chemicals and other ingredients, and sent to Bengkulu. In June, Asmar Latin Sani, the future suicide bomber, and another plotter accompanied the bomb ingredients (hidden in bulk cigarette boxes) on a long-distance bus from Bengkulu to Lampung, just across from Java.[69] It was Lampung that served as the center of the bombing, and where all the bomb ingredients eventually came before being sent to the Jakarta safe houses, along with almost all the plotters, to prepare for the attack. In the months leading up to attack, more and more members of the attack team were arrested—the Indonesian government was actually cracking down—but Noordin Top did not abandon his plans.[70] The arrested plotters were peripheral, and here I would argue that the lack of any need or ability to coordinate across great distances actually helped Noordin Top's plot. Because he and the explosives were already in Indonesia, no international chokepoints and only one domestic chokepoint—the ferry from Lampung to Java—had to be crossed.

In an indication that the secret, structurally flatter side of Jemaah Islamiyah was still operational, Hambali sent money by courier to Dumai, where a Noordin Top associate picked it up and brought it to Lampung, where the attack team met on 4 June 2003. The team did not decide on a target until they had gotten to Jakarta and had surveyed a number of potential locations. Azhari and Noordin Top informed members of the JI top leadership, notably the secretary of the central committee, Abu Dujanah, and Qotadah (possibly the same person who had helped to set up Camp Hudaibiyah in 1994), on 7 June 2003 about the plot in a hotel in Lampung. After the attack, the four met again in Bandung for an evaluation. Abu Dujanah apparently "tried to mobilize the JI network to protect the perpetrators" after the attacks, but the JI hierarchy dropped out of the operational narratives of Noordin Top's plots.[71] Jemaah Islamiyah as a whole was under too much stress, and Noordin's group, the faction of JI that wanted to return to its quiet proselytizing roots wanted no part in the bombings.

Inasmuch as the Indonesian police were actively seeking to arrest or kill them, Noordin Top and his followers were under great pressure as they planned the Jakarta attack. As a result, they stayed close to the landscape when they moved about, and pursued a systematic means of getting people and explosives to Jakarta through the most logical chokepoints as they progressed down the length of Sumatra. Noordin Top's faction was resourceful enough to put together the attack, but the way in which the planners went about the plot suggests that they were logistically vulnerable in the face of state hostility: the technologies of globalization were almost entirely absent from the course of the plot. As almost no non-hostile countries were left adjacent to Indonesia (with the exception of parts of the southern Philippines), the group had little ability to maintain a substantial transnational network anymore.

Pulling off one clandestine transnational activity is not trivial for a terrorist group, even in the best of circumstances. Simultaneously holding and planning meetings in more than one country, buying and shipping bomb ingredients, and moving people and goods to the right locations, all while one or more governments are trying to stop you, are all difficult activities. Thus, it is little wonder that JI's violent faction operated on a once-a-year bombing schedule within Indonesia from 2002 to 2005, and then waited four years before successfully carrying out its next plot in 2009. In the case of the four plots outlined in this chapter, JI faced varying political and geographic conditions as it tried to stage violent attacks, first across Indonesia, then in Singapore, in Bali, and finally in Jakarta, and the structure of each plot shifted as a result, not always successfully. Although Jemaah Islamiyah did not proclaim its existence and was uninterested in publicity, when it came to operations, it did not seek any more secrecy than was required. Secrecy has a high cost when one is seeking to integrate command and control, logistics, and to a lesser extent training, into an explosive whole. Whenever it had the political openness to do so, JI behaved much like a small multinational corporation, and benefited from the technologies and processes often associated with globalization: cheap plane trips, cell phone calls, e-mail, and generally lenient border controls. When growing hostility forced it to act more like the clandestine group that it was, those technologies and processes proved less helpful, and JI had to fall back on any geographic advantages, the presence or lack of which determined the success or failure of its attacks. Sometimes moving along illicit routes helped JI operate, sometimes it was able to use legitimate routes within countries even under pressure, but in all cases, JI's dependence on topographical features and infrastructure rendered its logistics vulnerable to interdiction. The next section of the book shows that this is true even for groups that do control some territory, as in the case of GAM, and even for groups that have no obvious attachment to territory, as in the case of transnational organized criminals.

Part III

EXTENSIONS: SOUTHEAST ASIA AND BEYOND

GERAKAN ACEH MERDEKA

Jemaah Islamiyah was the most territorially expansive terrorist group ever based in Southeast Asia, which makes the problems it had with crossing international boundaries surprising. One might be tempted to attribute JI's woes to its status as a terrorist organization—it had no territory to call its own (as most insurgent groups do), and its explicitly political and religious goals may have led it to exclude methods and routes that more open-minded groups, such as criminal syndicates, are willing to exploit. In chapter 1, I compared the different ideas of a terrorist organization Jemaah Islamiyah, a separatist insurgency GAM, and transnational criminal organizations, in the form of maritime pirates and smugglers. I now expand my analysis of territorial constraints to include the two comparative cases. Although GAM and organized criminals have ideas about why they exist, and what they want to accomplish, that are both radically different from each other and from Jemaah Islamiyah, the logic by which political conditions and territory constrain their behavior remains similar throughout.

Over its thirty-year history, GAM rose up three times, in 1976, 1989, and 1998, twice after almost being pummeled into oblivion by the Indonesian army. The organization arose indirectly from the remnants of the Acehnese branch of Darul Islam in the mid-1970s, and declared independence from Indonesia on 4 December 1976. After the first insurgency, GAM was able to retreat outside of Indonesia (and indeed, outside of Southeast Asia) to rebuild its organization. It took advantage of training in Libya in the late 1980s, and returned to Aceh to start the second insurgency in 1989. This time it was better organized and better armed, and had operations outside of Aceh in other parts of Indonesia, as well as Singapore and Malaysia, mostly commanded from its base in Sweden. Nevertheless, the Indonesian government declared martial law, and by 1996 was able to put down the second rebellion. In 1998, after Suharto's precipitous fall, GAM rebelled again, and spread throughout Aceh. This insurgency was by far the best armed and most organized of its attempts, and, despite a failed peace process, GAM and the Indonesian military were still fighting in December 2004 when the Boxing Day Tsunami hit Aceh, and the two sides finally made peace.

Not all CTOs are willingly clandestine, or willingly transnational. GAM was a classic separatist organization. If it had had its druthers, it would not have left Indonesia, and it would have acted as much as possible like the legitimate guerrilla organization it claimed to be. But it did not have its druthers. It is likely that many CTOs are not willingly transnational—leaving their country of origin is a means of survival rather than a preference. GAM differs from the other cases in this book in two important aspects: throughout its entire life, GAM never changed its target area, and it was a mostly legitimate organization outside of Southeast Asia.

Air travel and modern telecommunications allowed GAM to recover from setbacks outside of Indonesia, and made it easier to run a large part of its command and control structure on a global scale in politically friendly countries. It was wholly illegitimate inside Indonesia, but had neutral (if not positive) relationships with Southeast Asian countries, and positive relationships with other governments. But this was only moderately helpful when it came to getting back into Aceh, for people and especially for weapons. No matter how globalized the command and control structure was, the much less territorially expansive logistics network that followed illicit sea routes from Malaysia and Thailand, and roads from Indonesia proper, was also instrumental in determining GAM's ability to fight. In the north and west, Aceh is bounded by open ocean, on the east by the Malacca Strait (and further afield, Thailand and Malaysia), and on the south by the rest of Sumatra, and hence Indonesia. Aceh's isolated position meant that GAM's options for moving people and goods into Aceh by making illicit use of legitimate routes and creating illicit routes were limited and prone to being cut off. In part GAM tried to right this situation by avoiding transnational routes when possible, something it was occasionally able to do because it enjoyed the help of friendly forces within Aceh and Indonesia as a whole. Even with this assistance, GAM was ultimately unable to overcome the political and geographic vulnerabilities it faced. Although it quite willingly accepted provincial autonomy in 2005, it failed to achieve its goal of independence for Aceh.

It is easier to study GAM than JI. Unlike JI, GAM's leaders always tried to paint their organization as legitimate, and were willing to talk to outsiders even during the war. After the definitive end of the conflict in 2005, they became relatively transparent about their prior activities, and because it had no connection to external terrorist groups, research on GAM has largely remained the province of area studies specialists rather than security generalists. As a result, the literature on GAM is less focused on figuring out what the group was doing than on the roots of the Acehnese rebellion. In general, authors emphasize how Aceh historically has been different from the rest of Indonesia—it was connected to trade routes outside of the Indonesian archipelago, the Acehnese fought the Dutch more tenaciously than many of the other ethnic groups of the East Indies, and the sultanate of Aceh promulgated its own independent treaties.[1] Analysts usually consider the rebellion to be a response either to economic exploitation and the centralization of political power that occurred during Suharto's rule,[2] or to long-standing identity issues rooted in nationalist and religious grievances.[3] More recent research, however, has centered on the cyclical pattern by which Indonesian government crackdowns played a role in constructing Acehnese culture and identity as fundamentally different from Indonesian culture and identity.[4] Proponents of the political-economic exploitation thesis often draw a line between Darul Islam in the 1950s and GAM in the late 1980s and early 1990s, while supporters of the Acehnese identity argument usually find historical continuity in GAM's grievances, an idea lent credence by GAM leader Hasan Di Tiro's obsession with history. The two perspectives are not mutually exclusive. Economic exploitation, especially in the form of natural resource extraction, and political marginalization could certainly have played a role in crystallizing pre-existing Acehnese nationalist identity based on a shared religious and ethnic history, and could have convinced the rebels that independence was the only option, in part because government exploitation made its concessions on autonomy non-credible.[5] For the most part, all authors agree on what GAM wanted by the time the rebellion was in full swing—total independence from Indonesia.

The second body of literature on GAM deals with the course of the insurgency, Indonesia's response, and the structure of GAM. The conduct of the Indonesian military in its crackdown on GAM in the second insurgency created grievances among the Acehnese population that exacerbated the third rebellion and led to more widespread support in the early 2000s than GAM had ever had before.[6] For its part, GAM's tactics included a number of human rights violations, even as it was able to build a support base within the province.[7] Rather than focus on GAM's activities inside Aceh, as the other authors do, I concentrate almost entirely on what was happening with GAM outside of Aceh, both its activities in other countries, and its attempts to cross borders into the province itself.

The Indonesian government and GAM twice attempted to make peace, from 2000 to 2003, and in 2005. They succeeded the second time. A third group of literature argues that the peace process failed in 2003 in part because neither side was willing to compromise enough to satisfy the other, and because the level of trust was quite low.[8] The 2004 Boxing Day Tsunami is generally taken to be the catalyst for the beginning of the second round of peace talks,[9] although GAM's military position was deteriorating even before the tsunami.[10] I take no specific position on why the 2005 peace talks succeeded, although this chapter does give some insight into the political geographic factors that led to the logistical situation in which GAM found itself immediately before the tsunami.

In this chapter, I look at GAM's transnational activities during five periods in its history: its first insurgency, from its preparation in the early 1970s to its demise in 1979, its time in the wilderness until 1989, through its second insurgency starting in 1989, and finally, through its third rebellion until 2005, when it made peace with the Indonesian government. In each period, I generally detail GAM's transnational command and control structures, training programs (where applicable), and logistical networks, how GAM was forced to adapt its routes and methods, how it was dependent (or not) on geography and infrastructure, and the effect of varying political conditions in the states from which it operated.

Building GAM and the First Rebellion, 1971–1979

Command and Control

After he had received Daud Beureueh's blessing, Hasan Di Tiro returned to Aceh via Medan three times between 1971 and 1976.[11] The Acehnese community in Medan accorded him respect as "a local boy made good" and a number of people were receptive to his ideas. In Banda Aceh he had an audience with the governor over a business deal for his company. But his trip was mostly to build support for his independence movement and make contact with what would become the leaders of GAM, such as Malik Mahmud, the long-time GAM representative in Singapore.[12] Di Tiro publicly and formally left Indonesia via Medan at the end of September 1976, but apparently slipped back into Aceh illegally by boat, landing at a village in Pidie, on Aceh's northeast coast (the district from which Di Tiro originated).[13] That Di Tiro would choose to enter Aceh illegally when he was not technically yet an outlaw in Indonesia is interesting; clearly, for what he knew would be a treasonous activity, he wanted to operate as secretly as possible, and used an illicit route. The contrast between Di Tiro's two routes is telling: the public business trips followed no limits, while the final trip to start the insurgency used a route that would become common for GAM in the years to come.

In its first rebellion, GAM was not a fully realized transnational organization, nor was it even a full-scale armed rebellion. Di Tiro was focused completely on Aceh, although even before events drove him overseas, he had the structure in place necessary to support a transnational insurgency. His business in the United States allowed him to support the movement financially from overseas, and his pre-GAM meetings in Singapore and Medan built the first traces of a logistics network outside of Aceh. As was the case with the groundwork laid by Abdullah Sungkar in Malaysia to support his Darul Islam efforts in Indonesia, the network built up by Hasan Di Tiro outside of Aceh to support GAM's impending fight in Aceh allowed GAM to become a transnational network very quickly. Just as with Jemaah Islamiyah, the support structure made a transnational GAM thinkable. GAM's external network did not lead to an expansion of its target area, but the locations of its external support structure did point to where it could have gone upon fleeing.

Much like Jemaah Islamiyah, GAM's structure was one that functioned well either in close proximity, or in hospitable political environments, although initially GAM had problems operating under pressure. Although the independence proclamation was issued on 4 December 1976, the full cabinet (minus the members in Singapore) did not meet until 15 August 1977 because they had trouble getting together.[14] This is not to say GAM was inactive in the first year. GAM leaders moved from place to place propagandizing and organizing members down to the village level.[15] But it was slow going. GAM had problems communicating and moving across large distances under pressure. In the 1970s, the technologies of globalization, such as satellite phones, that would have enabled it to do so were not yet available.

Operations and Logistics

GAM's activities through 1979 were almost exclusively limited to propaganda and intimidation—the organization's structure was largely oriented toward command and control. GAM had few weapons when it began, enough to demand protection money from foreign companies operating in Aceh (which it did), but insufficient to do anything more than annoy the Indonesian security apparatus. After seeing the beach where Di Tiro intended to land with the weapons, Daud Beureueh had given timid Tiro money for the purpose of buying a boat to haul the weapons. On one of his trips to Aceh before the 4 December 1976 proclamation, Hasan Di Tiro had promised the people who would make up

AGAM—the military wing of GAM—including Fauzi Hasbi Geudong, that he would use his resources to bring back weapons for the fight. Two months later, he took them to look at a building owned by company PT Arun, and promised them that, a year from then, they would own the facility. For those looking to engage in violence, this was good news. Unfortunately for them, it turned out when he returned he had only brought back two pistols and two rifles, causing consternation and disappointment.[16] In addition to the foreign weapons, Edward Aspinall's source estimates that GAM in its first rebellion had about twenty domestically procured weapons left over from Darul Islam.[17] Many judged GAM as an organization built on propaganda; it needed a workable logistics network to be taken seriously. This was especially disappointing (apparently) to Teungku Fauzi Hasbi Geudong, who was an admirer of Daud Beureueh, and he exclaimed to his followers that Di Tiro's war was a "pure lie."[18] By staying out of logistics, GAM could avoid physically moving along transnational routes, but it was also prone to losing people like Fauzi Hasbi Geudong. Di Tiro explained that GAM's fight would not be like a regular war, but would be holistic, embodying political, diplomatic, and especially economic struggles, in addition to the guns and grenades. But, explained Di Tiro, they had to work on propaganda and organization first, so they had no need of guns for now.[19]

Di Tiro's strategy was not unreasonable: simply running in and starting to shoot things would have been useless in liberating a people who did not yet know they were supposed to be liberated (under GAM direction, of course), which was the point of the propaganda campaigns. Later GAM did succeed in killing some people, and forming ad hoc armed guerrilla groups somewhat later in the first rebellion, but its initial strategy was designed by intellectuals with no military background.[20] Indeed, Di Tiro's first training program, for fifty cadres, was a three-week class in ideology, and economic and political development held in September 1977.[21] Most of GAM's initial supporters were also intellectuals, and in the first rebellion, GAM received little support from the Acehnese mainstream.[22] Estimates differ, but in the initial phase, GAM's strength apparently averaged about 100 active members.[23] The Indonesian military's crackdown came hard for such a small and ill-trained group, and it quickly blockaded GAM's supply routes. Although GAM was already more transnational than most fledgling insurgencies, this is one of the problems such organizations face. Given their small target areas and the cost in money, time, and effort of crossing international boundaries, they have often not built up robust supply routes. Against an Indonesian military willing and able to do almost anything to accomplish its objectives, propaganda was not nearly as powerful as it must have seemed while Hasan Di Tiro had been proselytizing in Medan or Lhokseumawe.

Fleeing into Exile

In dire straits, in August 1978 GAM sent an operative to Medan to raise money and build a logistical network to acquire weapons. The operative was captured by Indonesian security forces, and GAM's situation deteriorated.[24] The next month, Di Tiro sent Husaini Hasan and Zaini Abdullah on a mission out of the country to rally diplomatic support, but after two weeks the envoys had failed to find a way past the Indonesian security forces, and they returned to GAM's stronghold in Pidie.[25] By December 1978, GAM's stronghold was under attack by the Indonesian military, and Di Tiro instructed his subordinates to begin preparations for him to leave Aceh for three months in order to pursue diplomatic options and find sources for weapons. On 15 March 1979, Di Tiro met with his cabinet, and vested power in several subordinates while he was out of the country. Less than two weeks later, on 28 March, Di Tiro set off from Jeunib beach in eastern Aceh across the Strait of Malacca in the motor boat *Teruna,* accompanied by several other boats, with GAM members serving as guards.[26] Di Tiro's destination was Singapore, but the accompanying boats returned to Aceh through a port in neighboring North Sumatra. Thereafter, most of the other senior GAM leaders either escaped, as in the case of Husaini Hasan, who fled by boat from the same beach to Penang, Malaysia in 1980, or were captured or shot, as in the case of Muchtar Hasbi. By the middle of 1982, no senior GAM leaders were at large in Aceh.[27] Under hostile conditions, GAM leaders fled using illicit routes that followed the physical contours of the landscape to adjacent countries. It is clear that setting up such routes is difficult, and once in place, the organizations tend to keep using them until they can no longer do so. Di Tiro and Husaini's use of the same beach is a case in point. If GAM wanted to survive in Aceh, it would have to do better.

GAM's first insurgency is notable for the progressive deterioration in its position, and the changes in its routes and methods as it moved closer to clandestine action, and incurred ever greater state hostility. Whereas Di Tiro first flew into Medan as a returning hero, he crossed illegally by boat from Malaysia in order to establish GAM's illicit base, and escaped illicitly by boat to Singapore at the end. GAM viewed Medan as a crucial chokepoint for transport into and out of Aceh and Indonesia, for both people and weapons, but their access to it, via illicit use of the Aceh-Medan highway, was shaky at best. Although many of the nodes, Singapore, Medan, and Penang, and the routes, by boat from eastern Aceh to Malaysia or Singapore, were evident in GAM's early years, GAM clearly did not have well-developed networks outside of Aceh, and was not yet skilled in the use of all the means at its disposal. If they were under illusions about the difficulty of the task they were facing before, GAM leaders were under no such illusions when they regrouped in exile.

Years of Exile, 1979–1989

Command and Control

Thanks to the diplomatic prowess of Hasan Di Tiro, and GAM's relatively innocuous message, its leaders were able to flee to a number of different countries. Di Tiro left Southeast Asia for Mozambique, then returned to his home in the United States before moving to Sweden. Husaini Hasan escaped Aceh virtually penniless, and settled in Sweden because that was the first country that would accept his application for refugee status. Others remained in Singapore and Malaysia. Not all leaders were happy with GAM's expatriation, but there was little they could do.[28] Essentially, GAM had become little more than an Acehnese advocacy organization with offices outside of Indonesia. Perhaps ten to twenty guerrillas remained in the Acehnese jungle, moving among remote villages and spreading GAM's message via low-level propaganda.[29] How much the leadership outside of Aceh knew about the remnants in the province is unclear, but the ability of the leadership to direct operations in the province does not seem to have been particularly strong. In 1985, for example, Di Tiro sent a letter to a colleague by the name of A. Razak in Perak, Malaysia asking how many GAM members were left in Aceh, and what they were doing.[30] The high levels of state hostility in Indonesia made it nearly impossible to maintain an ongoing command and control structure in Aceh over long distances. GAM as of yet had little communications technology, so the only ways into Aceh were by boat or on land. This stood in contrast to GAM's later command and control achievements using modern technology.

However, GAM was essentially a legitimate transnational organization outside of Indonesia during this period, with the exception of some of its activities in Malaysia, and to a certain extent analysis of its organizational structure passes out of the bounds of clandestine transnational networks and into the realms of legitimate transnational NGOs. The benefit for GAM was that it got much better at controlling its members across great expanses, as the primary nodes in the network in the 1980s were only Sweden, Libya, and Malaysia, and GAM leaders traveled among them with impunity. In an open environment, GAM could use legitimate physical and virtual routes for communication around the world. Other countries with Acehnese immigrants or refugees were the locations of GAM advocacy organizations, either explicitly as branches of GAM, or behind thinly veiled, but plausibly deniable, front groups. In some cases, GAM's leaders located themselves strategically around the world. Malik Mahmud was already a Singaporean citizen when GAM began its war, and Husaini Hasan (and many others) were Malaysian citizens, leading to natural bases in both countries. In others, the connection was almost due to happenstance. One GAM informant claimed that the organization had based itself in Sweden because it was the first country that took GAM in.[31] Otherwise Sweden is indeed an odd place from which to run a Southeast Asian insurgency. But GAM had no choice.

Aside from reconsolidating its structure, GAM was involved in traditional, and legitimate, advocacy activities. GAM supporters held demonstrations outside the Indonesian embassy in Stockholm, and the leaders, especially Hasan Di Tiro, wrote tens of pamphlets and articles for a variety of publications. GAM also made contact with other Indonesian separatist organizations, including the Republik Maluku Selatan (RMS) and Fretilin, the East Timorese insurgency, both of which were at the time based in the Netherlands.[32] But GAM still did not know how to fight a war, and for this it needed training.

Training in Libya

In the 1980s, Muammar Gaddafi, the eccentric dictator of Libya, was using his country's intelligence services to engage in acts of terrorism, culminating in the bombing of the nightclub in Berlin that killed two U.S. servicemen and led to the U.S. bombing of Tripoli. Among Gaddafi's other extracurricular activities was his support of liberation movements. If all the liberation movements the world over were successful, using their Libyan training and support, they could then set about demolishing the U.S. empire. That was the idea, at least. In reality, many of the liberation movements Libya trained had nothing to do with the United States, as friend or foe. GAM never had an anti-U.S. agenda. Indeed, it was actually counting on the support of the international community in its fight against the Indonesian government. Even its supposedly Islamic foundations were mostly an instrument to gain the support of Acehnese who cared for such things; the 4 December 1976 declaration does not mention Islam or God, and some GAM members abandoned Di Tiro precisely because they thought him too secular. During the 1980s, a number of Muslim national liberation movements trained in Libya at Gaddafi's behest, including the Moro Islamic Liberation Front. It is possibly that it is here that GAM's connection with the MILF first began.[33]

Nonetheless, when Libya offered to train GAM, apparently with no strings attached, Di Tiro accepted. By 1985, GAM was essentially finished as a fighting force in Aceh. Because of its weakness in the 1980s, and the relative lack of rage-producing Indonesian military operations, GAM initially recruited trainees by going from village to village, and asking the heads of families for volunteers. The recruits were drawn from the young (male) population and had to satisfy certain requirements. They had to be sufficiently healthy, and had to demonstrate an understanding of what GAM was fighting for.[34] In 1987, the organization recruited around fifty young men for a year's training in Libya.[35] Recruits also came from Acehnese living and working (sometimes illegally) in Malaysia.

GAM's international network made it easy for it move people from Malaysia to Libya, and the numbers trained expanded rapidly.[36] In 1988, according to a recruit named Darwis, approximately 700 GAM recruits were training in Libya. After a year in Libya, Darwis returned to Aceh via Singapore and Malaysia in order to help with GAM's operations at the beginning of the Indonesian military's new campaign. He had to flee Aceh for Malaysia at the end of 1990 and ask for political asylum. According to GAM spokesman Sofyan Daud, about one thousand GAM members trained at Tajura, about fifteen kilometers southeast of Tripoli.[37]

Although there is some disagreement among sources, GAM seems to have received both small arms training, and ideological, tactical, and strategic warfare education.[38] Exiled GAM leaders such as Daud Paneuek, who excelled at recruiting and mentoring, inspired and guided the recruits in Libya.[39] Hasan Di Tiro also went down to Libya to encourage the recruits, and train them in the ways of GAM. For nearly all the recruits, it was the first time they had ever met the president of the organization for which they were fighting.

GAM stopped sending recruits to Libya for training by 1991. The immediate effect of the training was to produce skilled fighters well suited for high positions. The first recruits came back to Aceh in 1988 and started a new round of violence, in part by leading others in attacks, and in part by training the GAM recruits who were not able to go to Libya.[40] They were also tasked to carry out specialized missions. Ligadinsyah Ibrahim, for example, graduated from school as an electrical engineer in 1986, joined GAM the same year, and went to Libya for four months of training in 1988. According to the prosecutor at his trial, he was trained to be a "commando," and upon his return to Aceh was assigned to obtain explosives with which to bomb government buildings.[41] Not all GAM leaders went to Libya for training, nor was it necessary to be a Libya alumnus for advancement within the organization. Teungku Abdullah Syafie, the military commander of GAM until he was killed in 2002, did not go to Libya, nor— according to his spokesman—ever left Aceh. With that said, many of the Libyan alumni did become mid-level leaders of GAM, and their presence was felt in the increased effectiveness of the organization's operations in the late 1970s.[42] Muzakkir Manaf, GAM's military commander from the death of Abdullah Syafie until the signing of the Memorandum of Understanding, is a Libya alumnus.[43]

From a logistical viewpoint, GAM's Libyan training experience was similar to JI's experience in Afghanistan and Pakistan. Different levels of state hostility and dependence on topography dictated different types of routes, even within the same trip. For both organizations, once they were outside the grasp of the

Indonesian government, the exact location of their training was not so material, a testament to the glories of globalization and modern aviation, and the flexibility in training routes relative to logistics. As legitimate organizations outside of Southeast Asia, they were also globalized organizations. Jemaah Islamiyah was increasingly lax about its movements and security the farther it was from Indonesia, and, as time went by, recruited from young men in Malaysia to avoid dealing with the Indonesian government. GAM tried to avoid dealing with the Indonesian government by recruiting in Malaysia, thereby minimizing the need to cross the Strait of Malacca. Acehnese who ended up in Kuala Lumpur generally flew in from Aceh through Medan, in order to avoid Indonesian government suspicion, while Acehnese in Penang (genuine political asylum-seekers) usually came by boat from Aceh.[44] Upon arrival in Malaysia, recruits were taken in by the extensive Acehnese community, and then sent on their way to Libya, all expenses paid. In fact, upon graduation, the Libyan alumni were given several hundred dollars as a stipend, and then returned to Aceh.[45]

Like JI, GAM may have used its training experiences to build informal networks with other like-minded insurgent groups. Unlike JI's training experiences, however, GAM's time in Libya did not contribute to widening of its territorial or ideological aspirations. In fact, given the split within GAM several years later over its abandonment of its Islamic roots several years later, if anything, the training might have solidified GAM's nationalist ideology. GAM's time in exile was almost wholly legitimate. Malaysia continued to be key to smuggling recruits into or out Aceh by boat, and Medan was a useful transit point when GAM felt comfortable sending people by plane, but once GAM members left Malaysia, they faced no hostility at all, and often received help from the state (as in the case of Libya). As a result, even while they remained focused on Aceh, the actual GAM network spread out farther around the globe than any other organization discussed in this book. GAM was in good standing to stage a return to Aceh.

Daerah Operasi Militer, 1989–1998

GAM's second insurgency began in 1989, and was largely crushed by the Indonesian military by 1992—after it declared Aceh to be a military operations zone (*daerah operasi militer*). However, sporadic fighting went on until the beginning of the third insurgency in 1998. This time, the insurgents were better armed and better organized than they had been in 1976. Although the military took about the same amount of time to finish them off, it had to invest more energy in the enterprise, and encountered (and created) problems that would come back to haunt it in 1998.

Command and Control

As soon as the first GAM recruits graduated from Camp Tajura in Libya, they began infiltrating back into Aceh, and eventually became active in four districts, again primarily in northeastern Aceh. Whereas the first generation of GAM members had been intellectuals, the second generation of GAM recruits was made up of fighters who established a paramilitary presence on the ground in a way that the original insurgents had not been able to do. The first insurgents went from place to place giving out pamphlets, while the second generation was able to put GAM's elaborate plans for governance structures into practice in accordance with its territorial intentions, such that GAM acquired two formal structures: the civilian structure in Sweden, and the parallel military and civilian administrations in Aceh.[46] In 1988 and 1989, Yusuf Ali and Yusuf AB, the two main leaders on the ground for the second insurgency, returned to Aceh, and secured control of an isolated village in Idi Rayeuk. From there they became the points of contact for GAM members coming across the Strait of Malacca into Aceh, both to fight and to smuggle weapons.[47] Even unarmed, GAM was able to infiltrate a large portion of the countryside in the four northeastern districts, and give the impression that it was everywhere.[48] By the time the government began its crackdown in 1990 within the four districts where GAM was active, only the urban areas were under direct Indonesian government control.[49]

GAM was heavily dependent on Malaysia as its main sanctuary, and the GAM leaders who were directly supervising AGAM's efforts moved back and forth (presumably by boat) across the Strait of Malacca at the height of the fighting.[50] Di Tiro stayed in Sweden but nearly all of GAM's senior leaders, whether they were based in Sweden or not, visited Malaysia on a regular basis. For getting into Aceh, physical, illicit routes that emanated from the relative freedom of an adjacent country were necessary, even if the GAM members had flown from Sweden, the classic deterritorialized command and control center. The movements also went the other way. Malik Mahmud, who was based in Singapore, in turn traveled frequently to Sweden.[51] GAM used its relative freedom in Malaysia to recruit fighters from the sizable Acehnese laborer population, raise money—both from the Acehnese residents and from businesses run by its members, and spread propaganda.[52] Although GAM seems to have had cells in Medan and Jakarta, these do not seem to have been decisive in 1989. Instead, GAM operated openly outside of Indonesia, and resorted to illicit boat trips to get into and out of Aceh. As a result, it was especially dependent on Malaysia for its command and control. Because it does not appear to have used telecommunications such as satellite phones or e-mail during the second insurgency, all communication had to come through land telephones or in person across the Strait. GAM's cross-Strait command and control structure worked, but it was precarious.

For a while, GAM's fight was made slightly less precarious thanks to the existence of factionalism within the state, friendly forces within the Indonesian government and military, an advantage it had not had during the first insurgency. Some village administrations actually aided GAM operatives in their quest to infiltrate isolated areas. According to Indonesian commanders, Acehnese soldiers who had family members in GAM would make half-hearted patrols through the jungle, and sometimes actively assist GAM in its efforts.[53] These friends within the Indonesian government could weaken the military's hold on Aceh itself, but they could not control transnational routes. Thus, they could do nothing to help GAM as it moved between Malaysia and Indonesia, nor could they sabotage Indonesia's efforts to pressure Malaysia about GAM.

Operations and Logistics

Libya's aid to GAM did not include actual weapons. In any case, Di Tiro rejected outside states' help with weapons because Aceh was a naturally "rich" country. Unsurprisingly, then, GAM was chronically short of weapons, especially whenever it was launching a new insurgency.[54] GAM's main source of weapons during the second insurgency seems to have been the Indonesian military itself, although the initial contributions were involuntary. In May 1989, GAM felt confident enough about its return to Aceh that a small unit attacked several Indonesian soldiers and took their guns. Over the next year, it followed up with a number of other similar attacks, and must have built a small weaponry stash.[55] If possible, GAM preferred to avoid going transnational entirely, and here the friendly elements of the Indonesian military and government were instrumental. Not only did some military and police deserters join GAM, but as the second insurgency petered out, a number of soldiers and policemen were convicted of providing GAM with guns, ammunition, and, in one case, more than ten kilograms of TNT.[56] But even covert supporters within Aceh were not enough to overcome GAM's weaknesses.

Stealing or buying weapons from the military was insufficient to satiate GAM's hunger for weapons. This is why some organizations go transnational in their logistics supply routes—domestic sources are inadequate. As a result, GAM began building the network necessary to smuggle guns in from across the Strait of Malacca. The village controlled by Yusuf Ali (and presumably others once GAM expanded its control) certainly played a role on the Acehnese end, but on the other end, GAM built up a network where the operative Teungku Usman coordinated buying weapons from Kuala Lumpur.[57] In addition, GAM members raised money in Malaysia from 1991 on to organize weapons procurement networks that managed to buy seventy-six AK-47s and M-16s in Thailand, then ship them directly to Aceh (a route that prefigured the route that GAM was to use a decade later).[58] From at least 1993 until 1996, Malik Mahmud apparently organized part of the operations from Singapore.[59] The origin of the weapons is unclear, although some of them may have been traded for ganja.[60] What is interesting here is that GAM coordinated weapons buying from a number of locations in countries adjacent to Indonesia, but it was still limited to one route for actually getting the weapons into Aceh, across the Malacca Strait. This made it vulnerable to interdiction.

Denouement

Within two years after Indonesia declared a military operations zone in Aceh, it had succeeded in isolating GAM's units inside the province. By late 1991, several hundred fighters were fleeing to Malaysia and requesting asylum.[61] The flow of refugees from the crackdown, combined with the Libya veterans who did not return to Aceh, meant that the number of Acehnese in Malaysia sympathetic to nationalist messages increased rapidly.[62] By the end of 1991, 200 people had asked for permission to stay in Malaysia, and by the end of 1993, 684 people had applied for refugee status.[63] In response, Indonesia stepped up operations on the northern and eastern coasts of Aceh to cut off refugees, and was still blockading the coast in April 1992.[64] Unlike at its debut, GAM was not completely destroyed after the second insurgency, but in the mid-1990s, the situation was dire, and by mid-1994, fighting was only sporadic.[65] By some reports, the GAM members left in Aceh numbered in the tens, and they had to fend for themselves, either by growing ganja, or by robbing banks.[66]

Times were difficult in Malaysia as well. In July 1994, younger GAM members held a meeting in Malaysia, and wondered openly where the guns and money promised by Hasan Di Tiro were.[67] Furthermore, Husaini Hasan felt that GAM had abandoned its commitment to Islam, and split from Hasan Di Tiro over that and succession issues to form Majelis Pemerintahan-Gerakan Aceh Merdeka (MP-GAM).[68] The split did not extinguish GAM, but it was clear that remaining an advocacy organization for another ten years was not an option for Di Tiro's organization. Worse, in December 1996, Indonesia finally persuaded Malaysia to get serious about the Acehnese illegally working in the country, which led many GAM leaders to ask for asylum in other countries, especially Europe, the United States, and Singapore, and to set up branches of GAM outside of Sweden and Malaysia, notably in the United States and Denmark.[69] Malaysia never completely cracked down on GAM because it was too useful as a bargaining chip with

Indonesia. However, the mid-1990s showed that GAM had to do several things to survive and return to Aceh as a fighting force without angering the Malaysian government. It had to find a better way to run operations in Aceh without physically going through Malaysia, and it had to find sources of weapons that did not leave such a huge footprint in the same country. Relying on a single illicit water route between Malaysia and Aceh worked for a while for GAM, but it was a precarious situation, one easily cut off by the Indonesian military and withdrawal of neutrality by Malaysia, and was not enough to sustain a full-fledged insurgency. GAM would have to become even more transnational. Evolving technology and the changing political situation in the rest of Southeast Asia allowed this to happen.

War and Peace, 1998–2005

By 1998, the crackdown, however bloody, seemed to be working. GAM had disappeared as a fighting force, and martial law was ended. At the end of that year, however, GAM began its third insurgency.

From its second crisis period in the mid-1990s, GAM revived itself and overcame the MP-GAM split to become, by the early 2000s, larger and more effective than ever before, with control of the lion's share of Acehnese territory, and operations spread throughout the world. After several years of fighting in the third insurgency, the Indonesian government and GAM agreed to a humanitarian pause so that they could negotiate an end to the war, but a series of missteps indicated that the trust and the structural conditions for peace were still not there, and fighting re-erupted in 2003. After the 2004 Boxing Day Tsunami, however, GAM and the government began negotiations in earnest once again, and the two sides finally signed a Memorandum of Understanding (MoU) that ended the war. The peace process is not the concern of this section. Rather, I look at how GAM operated across many different countries, and the advantages and challenges that it faced as it fought against the Indonesian government in a globalizing world. It is also during this time that we can see most clearly the role, whether through corruption or genuine conviction, that friendly actors within the Indonesian (and to a certain extent Malaysian) governments played in GAM's struggle. At no time were the friendly factions strong enough to change the configuration of GAM's transnational structures, but in providing weapons and ammunition in Aceh, they lessened GAM's dependence on sources for weapons outside this territory. GAM's experiences with countries outside of Indonesia during this period also illustrate the extent to which, even as a semi-illegitimate organization, it was sensitive to political conditions and certain chokepoints.

GAM's political environment changed a number of times from the mid-1990s until the end of the war in 2005. The Swedish government throughout this period allowed GAM to operate, and no Western countries, where a number of GAM advocacy cells were active, ever took action against the organization. In Southeast Asia, however, Indonesia was unremittingly hostile to any GAM activities, although a small number of openings remained. The 1997 Asian Financial Crisis knocked the Indonesian government on its heels, and the turmoil surrounding the fall of Suharto in May 1998 meant that the government in Jakarta had more important things to worry about than guerrillas in the jungles of Aceh. The mid-1990s were not kind to GAM, and the Indonesian military had been confident that GAM had retreated into obscurity and ineffectiveness. Its re-emergence in 1998 came as such a surprise to a distracted government caught in the instability of the post-Suharto period that at first the military was not entirely sure what to do, leaving political space for GAM's activities. Later, during the failed peace negotiations, the relative lack of fighting gave GAM (and the Indonesian military) breathing room, but GAM's negotiators still met with Indonesian representatives in neutral countries to avoid repercussions.

During this time, GAM maintained a delicate relationship with the Malaysian government. Although Malaysia found GAM useful as a bargaining chip with Indonesia, it wanted nothing to do with Acehnese refugees, and did not legalize GAM as a registered organization. GAM was able to move around Malaysia, and used it as a base for many activities, but it was leery of doing anything that would seriously annoy the Malaysian government. Although GAM did in fact irritate the Malaysian government on a number of occasions, its tenuous position in the country affected its activities in interesting ways.

Thailand, as the base of GAM operative Zakaria Zaman, had a somewhat different trajectory in its relations with GAM. Under the leadership of Prime Minister Chuan Leekpai, the Thai government was neutral toward GAM, and GAM got away with a fair amount of illicit activity. When Thaksin Shinawatra became prime minister in 2001, the Thai government grew considerably more hostile, until Thaksin forced Zakaria out of Thailand in 2003. Thereafter, Thailand largely fell off GAM's radar.

GAM was finally able to use telecommunications to transmit information into and out of Aceh, but we can still see the limits of the tools of globalization. As GAM's network became more globalized, it became more dependent on Malaysia as a hub. It had to take flights in and out of Malaysia, and make illicit trips from Malaysia into Aceh. The command and control network can tell us a little about the logistics network—Malaysia was a hub for both—but the need to move weapons along routes that followed the contours of the topographical infrastructure and natural terrain of the region through adjacent countries of varying friendliness limited the spread of the logistics network, and hence GAM's ability to fight.

Command and Control

GAM's command and control structure in the third insurgency was something of an achievement, spread as it was over dozens of countries around the globe, often embedded in local expatriate Acehnese communities. GAM was never able to establish the international advocacy network that East Timor's Fretilin had (even though, in sheer organizational and warfighting abilities, GAM was much stronger than Fretilin), but its global activities were still impressive.[70] Its advocacy network was mostly legitimate and rather far-flung.

GAM had a presence in many of the countries where Acehnese refugees settled. The organization did not exist between countries, but rather within different countries, and its nodes were embedded in ways that accorded with the political environment. The Acehnese community in Sweden, where the GAM leadership was based, was not that large, but was very powerful, partly because Scandinavian countries were among the few countries willing to take in the GAM leadership when they fled from Aceh. Denmark also had a large Acehnese presence. Stavenger, Norway had a strong Acehnese community thanks to money provided for refugees. In Norway, GAM was camouflaged as a refugee organization, and in a number of countries, its advocates were not formal members of the organization. One member of GAM's negotiating team in Helsinki, for example, was not one of "the three-thousand," the registered members in GAM's database.[71]

GAM's footprint was smaller in other countries. In New Zealand, there were only three Acehnese, but they were vocal enough to be granted audiences with high-ranking members of the New Zealand government. For its part, Australia had a vocal Acehnese community before 11 September 2001, but afterward the Australian government became less tolerant of supporters of any insurgency, regardless of whether it was related to al-Qaeda. In North America, GAM's activities were mostly limited to lobbying, although Canada at one point took Acehnese refugees.[72] In the United States, a GAM supporter operated an information center out of Harrisburg, Pennsylvania, but in general, North America did not play a huge part in GAM's struggle.

Some of the technologies that accompanied the rise of globalization in the public consciousness in the 1990s also allowed GAM, an early technology adopter, to build new lines of communication into and within Aceh, such that it became possible to run day-to-day operations there from Sweden. GAM members began to use satellite phones and laptops before the Indonesian military did, and made extensive use of cell phones in the third insurgency. This obviated the need for much, but not all, of GAM's illicit travel that was solely for command and control purposes. It did not obviate the need for guns or bombs.

With the new equipment, most of which came from Singapore,[73] the GAM leadership in Sweden maintained a coherent command and control structure halfway across the world that combined top-down control with local autonomy. The GAM government was divided into seventeen territories, and the GAM leadership formally had direct contact with the top leader in every province.[74] In practice, GAM Sweden was in contact with the TNA's (Tentara Nasional Aceh [the Acehnese National Army], the new name adopted for AGAM during the third insurgency) commander-in-chief every day by phone, providing a framework and rules of engagement for the local commanders and civilian leaders to follow. Yet even at the height of martial law, TNA commanders were given enough autonomy to take the initiative.[75] In 2002, a reorganization of TNA formalized this structure; TNA was divided and sub-divided on a territorial basis in a hierarchical military structure.[76]

Within Aceh, GAM reached its greatest territorial extent. At its height in the early 2000s, GAM physically controlled more than 80 percent of Aceh's villages although it remained semi-mobile.[77] There was no stationary headquarters for Aceh's military operations. Instead, the commander-in-chief of TNA would move around near whatever area of Aceh he happened to be from.[78] As GAM spread throughout Aceh, the organization chart of the formal positions in the parallel military and civilian structures was finally filled out for most of Aceh's provinces, even if in some cases only several dozen GAM members were in a province.[79]

In concert with the formal, territorial structure, GAM maintained an informal network that was less tied to specific territory. The network operated within Aceh, and connected Aceh to the outside for most activities besides formal command and control, and military operations within the province. Over time, for example, GAM claimed that it built an intelligence network on the village level throughout Aceh, and could easily detect the arrival of Indonesian intelligence operatives.[80]

There were also GAM leaders in Aceh who monitored the loyalty of GAM members on the ground, and acted as an informal intermediary between frontline military commanders and GAM Sweden if the formal chain-of-command was being intransigent. In fact, the military leadership depended on the informal intermediaries to get logistical support, supplies, money, and staff. Toward the end of the conflict, intelligence chief Irwandi Yusuf and Zakaria Zaman served as the backdoor liaisons. This is a tribute to the miracle of modern telecommunications, because Zakaria was in Thailand until 2003, and Irwandi was in Jakarta (or in jail) for much of the time. GAM Sweden also used this informal network to sound out ground-level commanders and members about their thoughts on signing the Memorandum of Understanding (and officially giving up the goal of absolute independence), and then to enforce discipline and prevent schisms after the decision was made.[81]

The presence of two parallel structures for GAM Sweden to control and supply its forces in Aceh illustrates the organization's geographic problem. The formal structure was mostly territorial, inasmuch as each of the units was expressly designed to operate in Aceh, with the exception of the cabinet-level civilian leaders, who were all outside of the province. By contrast, the informal structure, which covered intelligence, fundraising, training, and logistics, was not intentionally territorial. GAM was indifferent as to the locations of the nodes and connectors for its informal structure, except that whatever was being moved ultimately had to begin or finish in Aceh, which limited the flexibility of the informal structure. With the fall of the Suharto dictatorship, GAM operatives were able to move more easily around Indonesia and Southeast Asia more generally, but this increased their dependence on predictable chokepoints. As ease of travel increased and GAM was able to run more of its organization further from Aceh, the networks in Medan, Jakarta, Kuala Lumpur, and Penang seem to have taken on greater importance. The new communications technologies allowed GAM to establish new, more direct lines of communications, but it did not rely totally on telecommunications to run the network. Given the fragile political conditions in Malaysia and Indonesia, it would have been foolish to do so.

Instead, GAM continued to move people by illicit means, and increasingly through the use of legitimate routes. Acehnese going between Aceh and Malaysia would usually take the ferry from Medan, or would fly.[82] GAM members also traveled through Batam or Jakarta using local fake ID cards. Relatively easy flights around Southeast Asia allowed GAM to establish more solid presences in cities far away from Aceh, but it also meant that the cells were concentrated in larger cities with easy access to air travel, and more important, that there was a limited number of routes from those cities into Aceh. In effect, the further that GAM's network got away from Aceh, the more its movements were funneled into routes between a few chokepoints when it wanted to move progressively closer to Aceh. The major chokepoint (if an entire country can be considered a choke point) continued to be Malaysia, and its importance to GAM only grew as the group expanded its activities outside of Indonesia and Southeast Asia, as it became GAM's hub not only for illicit travel, but also for movement along legitimate routes.

The Importance of Malaysia

As the country immediately across the Strait of Malacca from Aceh, Malaysia was the logical place for GAM to flee, but its importance even after GAM had begun using new communication technologies is an indication of GAM's continued dependence on geography, physical movement, and the limited options it faced when trying to enter or leave Aceh. GAM received most of its financial support from Malaysia, used it as a way station for refugees (and occasionally weapons), and ran an intelligence network from the country.[83] There has long been an Acehnese presence in the Malaysian state of Kedah, but the largest community was in Penang. During the conflict, GAM's presence was a sensitive issue in Malaysia, so much so that the Malaysian government turned over the problem of Acehnese refugees to the United Nations High Commissioner for Refugees (UNHCR), and washed its hands of the matter.[84] At one point in 1997, hostility from the Malaysian government grew to the point where Malik Mahmud told hundreds of Acehnese to return to Aceh to fight rather than be caught in Malaysia.[85] Due to political sensitivities, GAM was not a formal organization in Malaysia, and when it held meetings, it did so quietly; whether the meeting was broken up was up to the discretion of individual policemen.[86] As a result, GAM did not have a specific headquarters in Malaysia, but moved around as its operations warranted.[87]

The Acehnese community in Malaysia was large enough to provide some measure of support to GAM. Before the Memorandum of Understanding, an estimated 40,000 Acehnese were living illegally in Malaysia, plus perhaps another 20,000 legal Acehnese.[88] According to UNHCR, in 2004 approximately 8,000 Acehnese had a refugee protection card, and 11,000 were waiting for the card. As long as Acehnese could find a boat to take them across to Malaysia, they could get into the country. An Acehnese refugee organization would then aid new arrivals, and teach them how to hide from the Malaysian police.[89] The Acehnese refugees were insular, and created their own community rather than living with other Indonesians.[90] They were also supportive of GAM. One senior member of GAM's negotiating team estimated that perhaps 80 percent of the Acehnese refugees in Malaysia sympathized with GAM's cause, and provided some financial support. In fact, it was rich Acehnese in Malaysia and elsewhere who provided the financial backbone of GAM's struggle.[91] One expert estimates that approximately 5,000 Acehnese, concentrated in Kuala Lumpur and Penang, sent money to GAM.[92] This base of support, even if slightly illicit, along with Malaysia's geographic centrality to GAM's transnational network, encouraged the concentration of GAM's activities in Malaysia. Although GAM was a globalized network, the very act of globalizing encouraged the organization to centralize its activities for both legitimate and illicit activities. When tracking clandestine transnational organizations, it would behoove us to look at countries that are at the nexus of legitimate and illicit routes. These countries are where high-flying groups must go to ground to get back into their target area.

The Intelligence Network

This was also true of GAM's non-territorial intelligence network, which existed wherever GAM had interests and could get away with violent activities. One of the functions of GAM's intelligence network was to find and take out (that is, assassinate) GAM's enemies, a task that required operations in Aceh, Malaysia, and occasionally Indonesia proper. Within Aceh, the intelligence network was tied to GAM's quasi-governmental formal, territorial structure, and detecting GAM enemies and Indonesian agents was straightforward (or rather, it was easy for GAM to kill those it suspected).[93] According to a GAM leader, whenever a newcomer entered a village with no visible business, and remained for more than a couple of hours, the local GAM operatives would enquire as to the visitor's business and origin. Even if the newcomer spoke Acehnese well and without a visible accent, GAM could detect Indonesian intelligence agents through asking them about various archaic Acehnese words that no one who had learned Acehnese through school lessons would know. Once found out, GAM would interrogate the prisoner, and generally he would lead them to several more operating within GAM's territory before he was "taken out of operation." By this means, GAM was able to weaken the Indonesian government's intelligence network in Aceh.[94]

Singapore was also an important part of GAM's command and control and intelligence structures given that it was the base for GAM's Prime Minister Malik Mahmud, who was the only Singaporean citizen in the GAM leadership.[95] GAM did not dare to conduct assassinations or any major subterfuge in the island city-state, but Singapore was a long-time safe haven for GAM, and thanks to Malik, was also important as a node in its command and control network.[96] As for Malaysia, before martial law, GAM had a number of agents who were mostly engaged in counterintelligence work against Indonesian intelligence operatives in Malaysia (who were themselves presumably engaged in espionage activities against GAM leaders and sympathizers in Malaysia). The GAM operatives had a fair amount of success detecting the Indonesian agents and taking them out of operation. It should be noted, however, that what GAM considered Indonesian agents also included supporters of splinter factions such as MP-GAM, and Acehnese who had engaged in deals gone bad with GAM. Teungku Usman Ibrahim (possibly the same Teungku Usman who had previously been a weapons buyer for GAM), for example, donated money to GAM's cause for the purchase of guns through Malik's associate Ismail Syah Putra, such that the money made its way to Malik Mahmud in Singapore. Years elapsed, but none of the promised guns were forthcoming. Usman went to Malaysia, and talked to a GAM operative there, who told him that Malik Mahmud had the money. Usman then unsuccessfully tried to find Malik, but Malik refused to meet with him unless he had more money to offer. Usman then asked for his money back, which was refused. In April 2000, he was killed by GAM in his house in Gombak, Malaysia.[97]

GAM was also capable of more public action when it felt particularly threatened, even in Malaysia, but it took action sparingly. Teuku Don Zulfahri is probably the best known GAM defector assassinated by the organization, because of the spectacular nature of his death. On 1 June 2000, while he was dining in a public restaurant in Kuala Lumpur, two men walked in, shot him twice, and escaped through the back door. Don Zulfahri was a cosmopolitan who had graduated from high school in Medan, and lived in the United States before settling in Malaysia and going into business for himself, eventually becoming quite wealthy and taking three wives, including a Chinese woman. In 1996, he returned to Aceh to look for business opportunities, and was warmly received by the local government, but he remained supportive of Acehnese independence. At some point he became involved in MP-GAM, and advocated returning GAM to the idea of an Islamic state in Aceh, taking responsibility for the damage the organization had done, and lobbying for independence in a less oppositional way.[98] This apparently angered GAM, which ordered his assassination. Two of the GAM members who were part of the conspiracy had entered Malaysia illegally, and did not have work permits. Seven others were held by Malaysian police in connection with the case.[99] Although Don Zulfahri's high-profile assassination showed the strength of the organization's intelligence network outside of Aceh, GAM was careful not to carry out too many killings on Malaysian soil.

The Story of Irwandi Yusuf

The geographic spread of GAM's intelligence network, the opportunities provided by the technologies associated with globalization, and the political and geographic challenges faced by GAM as it moved across international boundaries are well illustrated by the story of Irwandi Yusuf. As intelligence chief and an important strategist, immediately before the reignition of hostilities in 2003, Irwandi was ordered to move the intelligence headquarters to Jakarta. Even as GAM fought in Aceh, it felt confident enough to operate one of the main logistical and intelligence connections between Aceh and the outside world from the capital of the country they were fighting, hundreds of miles away from the front.

On the fifth day of hostilities in 2003, Irwandi was arrested. At the time, he was the only contact between the field commanders in Aceh and the media, relaying news from the commanders, and arranging access for journalists when possible. Juggling so many responsibilities, he forgot to change the SIM card in his mobile phone, and Indonesian intelligence tracked down his phone number without knowing his identity or his activities. On the day he was arrested, the police came three times, and checked his ID, but were not sure if they had the right person. Much to his regret, Irwandi confirmed that the phone number was his, and the police went to get an arrest warrant. At the police office, Irwandi made sure to be very cooperative with the investigators—he freely admitted to things they obviously already knew, and sowed disinformation among what they did not. At one point, for example, his interrogators showed him a GAM video, and asked him to identify the people in the video, including Sofyan Daud, one of the TNA's top commanders. The leaders of GAM were well known in Aceh, but astonishingly, Indonesian intelligence apparently had little idea of what the leaders or field commanders even looked like, let alone how each person fit into the overall GAM structure. Irwandi willingly "helped" by misidentifying all the leaders, and told his interlocutors that he was just an innocent Acehnese who had met GAM leaders when he was hired to be the interpreter for a U.S. freelance journalist. Grateful for such valuable information, the police allowed him to stay in the relative luxury of the office of one of the commanders. The next day, news of Irwandi's arrest appeared on television, and his sister, who was living in Jakarta at the time, came to visit him. On her next visit the following day, she passed him a new mobile phone, which he used to communicate with Sweden and Malaysia. He would talk in the office's bathroom, and store the charger behind the sofa—the police did not check his person or anywhere else in the office.[100] Human error, rather than the inexorable march of technology, prevented the Indonesian government from stopping Irwandi's activities. At the same time, modern technology allowed GAM to coordinate across vast distances and maintain the network, even under hostile circumstances. In fact, Irwandi continued to coordinate the intelligence network from his prison cell nearly as easily as if he had been free. As a result, when he finally escaped from prison, the network was intact.[101]

Irwandi was in prison in Banda Aceh when the 2004 Boxing Day Tsunami came, and was one of the few people to survive as the wave tore apart the prison. In the ensuing confusion, he escaped. His brother came from Bireuen to pick him up. Irwandi then took a public bus to Medan, which had to pass through three checkpoints on the way (this was down from the usual ten checkpoints, but the tsunami had caused a general breakdown in order). Luckily for Irwandi, it was nighttime, and the soldiers were primarily looking for young men of fighting age, so he was able to flash a pack of Marlboro cigarettes as his Indonesian national ID card at all the checkpoints. From Medan, he caught a flight to Jakarta.[102] GAM's presence in Jakarta, and the difficulty that it had in getting across the boundary between Aceh and Medan suggests that the power of a hostile state is often most pervasive at the border. It would have been nearly impossible for Irwandi to fly out of Aceh given political conditions there, even if the tsunami

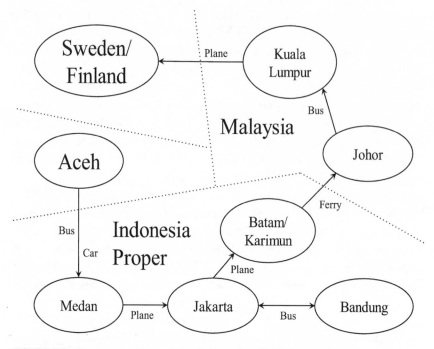

FIGURE 6.1   The travels of Irwandi Yusuf, December 2004–January 2005

had not destroyed much of western and northern Aceh's infrastructure. Forced to make use of a legitimate land route, Irwandi had only one choice, and only luck saved him from being detected. Once inside Indonesia proper it was a simpler matter to fly to Jakarta, as no border had to be crossed. Borders limit the options of transnational organizations and force them to confront or slip past state authority, and the Indonesian government (unwittingly) missed its greatest opportunity to catch Irwandi when he slipped out of Aceh.

In prison, Irwandi had befriended a female journalist. Over time, she had become sympathetic to the Acehnese cause, thinking he was a TNA field commander who was actually free and roaming the jungles of Aceh. Irwandi told her many moving but utterly false stories of his combat exploits sitting in his prison cell, and the journalist, who was married to a Kopassus (Indonesian special forces) officer, passed along useful information on the movements and disposition of Indonesian government forces in Aceh. She invited Irwandi to come and visit if ever he was in Jakarta; he told her in October 2004 that he would be vacationing in Jakarta in either December or January. Upon his arrival in Jakarta in January 2005, Irwandi sent her a text message. She put him up in hotel room, and took him around to the *AcehKita* magazine offices several times.[103] The presence of friendly factions within Indonesia certainly did aid Irwandi in his travels, but only in specific ways. They did not get him out of prison, nor were they that helpful in helping Irwandi evade conviction once he was captured. However, in prison, Irwandi was able to run the intelligence network thanks to sympathetic guards, and his connections with the journalist not only helped GAM's position in Aceh itself, but also aided him when he escaped to Jakarta. In short, friendly factions within the state were useful for the internal movement of people, and for pure communications, both of which held the network together in Aceh and Indonesia, but factions were less instrumental in GAM's efforts to hold the network together on a transnational basis.

In Jakarta, Irwandi moved around from place to place, staying with friends and people in his network, and even visited a friend in prison in Bandung, using a fake ID he had had made in Jakarta.[104] But big things were afoot, and soon GAM Sweden ordered Irwandi to come to Sweden to help with the Helsinki negotiations. Thereupon he took a flight to Batam, and tried to use a fake passport, but was rebuffed.[105] Irwandi then mobilized GAM's intelligence network in Malaysia to get him out of Indonesia. The GAM intelligence operatives came down to Batam and Karimun, and arranged his passage through the Indonesian checkpoints (probably by paying off officials, or finding sympathizers) at Batam, and then Karimun, from whence he took a ferry to Johor Bahru and freedom. The rest of the trip was simple: Irwandi flew directly from Kuala Lumpur to Sweden.[106]

Here again, the greatest friction encountered by Irwandi was not inside of Indonesia itself, but in his efforts to cross Indonesia's borders. It is unclear what Irwandi's operatives did to get him to Malaysia, so I will draw no conclusions about the existence of friendly factions, but what is more interesting is Irwandi's relationship with territory. The topography of the terrain covered by Irwandi in his travels became important mostly when he was crossing hostile boundaries—between Aceh and North Sumatra, and between Indonesia and Malaysia. Although Irwandi was clearly clever enough to fly around Indonesia, even as a fugitive, the boundaries in some sense brought GAM's network "back to earth" and limited its territorial extent. Under hostile conditions, the topography of the terrain between nodes on different sides of borders also channeled Irwandi's movements: the ferry route from Karimun to Malaysia is short, and Karimun itself is a haven for smugglers. In addition, the highway from Aceh to Medan is the only way to leave Aceh quickly, if one is trying to get to Jakarta, where much of GAM's intelligence network was located. But, as Irwandi's experience showed, moving along the route through hostile areas is quite precarious, and Irwandi got through due to the confusion of the tsunami, and the obliviousness of the soldiers. This precariousness of movement in hostile conditions can be seen even more clearly as we look at the challenges GAM struggled to overcome to get the weapons it needed during the third insurgency.

Weapons Smuggling

Although GAM was an ideological organization, it was indifferent about where its weapons came from, as long as it could get them cheaply. Thus, over the course of its thirty-year struggle it dealt with a number of organized crime organizations, and developed the most sophisticated and organized arms smuggling network in Southeast Asia. Although the explosive devices Jemaah Islamiyah built were more sophisticated than any of GAM's bombs, Jemaah Islamiyah was not able to match GAM's resourcefulness in weapons procurement.[107] With that said, the organization's creativity was severely tested by Aceh's physical position within Indonesia and Southeast Asia, as well as the limitations imposed by the need to stage violent attacks. Figure 6.2 shows the two major smuggling routes GAM operated from 1998 to 2005, one from Cambodia through Thailand to Aceh, and another that ran to the province through Java and Sumatra. Both reveal GAM's dependence on chokepoints, land- and sea-based infrastructure, and natural terrain for its nodes and flows within the network as it moved from its limited realistic weapons sources into Aceh. Despite some overlap with GAM's command and control structure in Southeast Asia, the group's experience demonstrates that success in one does not mean success in the other.

INDONESIA AS ITS OWN WORST ENEMY

As much as possible, when buying guns, bombs, and bullets, GAM tried not to leave Indonesia at all, or even Aceh, which is how it ended up buying perhaps 20 percent of its weaponry from within Indonesia.[108] Every time GAM crossed an international border (which included, from its point of view, the border between the areas of Aceh that it controlled, and North Sumatra), it risked discovery, and for an organization that did not have more than 3,000 weapons even at its height, even the loss of one shipment was painful.[109] GAM bought most of its ammunition from sources in Java, not necessarily solely in Jakarta or Bandung, but the largest single source of GAM's weapons and ammunition was PT Pindad, the notoriously leaky company in Bandung that is the official supplier of small arms and ammunition to the Indonesian military.[110] GAM had its brokers in residence in Bandung who would arrange to buy "excess" weapons from PT Pindad.[111] In August 2001, for instance, Bandung police captured four GAM weapons brokers, who had already smuggled several shipments to Aceh.[112] The next month, acting on intelligence, police captured one GAM broker during an attempted weapons buy in Bandung. Two others escaped, but the police found a house containing

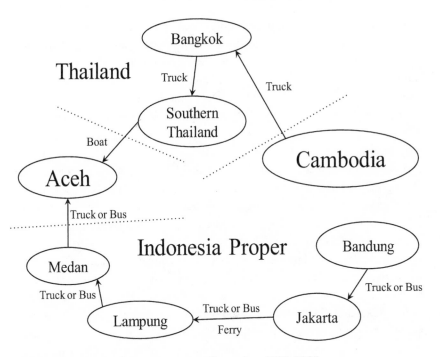

FIGURE 6.2   GAM's major weapons smuggling routes, 1998–2005

all sorts of gun-related apparatuses.[113] Guns in Bandung are a cottage industry that extends beyond PT Pindad. In Cipacing, a village near Bandung, suppliers also sell homemade air guns, which could be converted (often in GAM's own workshops) into guns that fire bullets.[114]

How GAM got the weapons from Bandung to Aceh is another exercise in ingenuity, but also shows how dependent GAM was on the infrastructure built (and often controlled) by the Indonesian government. The captured conspirators in the 2000 Jakarta Stock Exchange bombing case described how they had transported weapons they had bought inside the gas tanks of a succession of trucks and cars between Bandung and Aceh. At least one of the transfers occurred in a building owned by a GAM conspirator.[115] In another incident in December 1999, GAM had infiltrated a long-distance bus company. Unbeknownst to the passengers, the driver, conductor, and a passenger on a bus between Jakarta and Medan were found to have loaded pistols, ammunition, walkie-talkies, and chargers destined for Aceh. Police grew suspicious when the bus came right off the ferry in Lampung (the city that is the terminus in Sumatra for the Java-Sumatra ferry) and tried to go ahead through the police checkpoint (the police were specifically on the lookout for GAM smugglers). When asked for papers, the driver apparently made an attempt to bribe the police.[116] Thus, GAM's smuggling activities, which made illicit use of legitimate routes from Bandung to Aceh, often worked, but GAM was in a precarious position. Given the geography of the land route from Bandung to Aceh, there was one primary highway GAM could use, and a number of chokepoints, such as Medan and Lampung, where it was at risk of interdiction by even a minimally competent Indonesian government.

Indeed, Medan was one of GAM's principal chokepoints in Indonesia. GAM had a number of hangouts in Medan where its members and sympathizers were known to meet, but Medan has a well-deserved reputation for smuggling and corruption that exists irrespective of GAM. The expectation might be that chokepoints become less important along an illicit route as a CTO tries to evade the government by moving through terrain that is difficult for the government to police. In fact the experiences of GAM and JI show that chokepoints, either those created by the CTO, or regular transit hubs, continue to be important to illicit operations. Because a knowledge of the culture and language, and a network of local contacts are needed, it is difficult to create illicit chokepoints, and CTOs tend to depend on them as long as they can. Chokepoints that are at the nexus of legitimate and illicit routes are even better than normal ones. It appears that GAM's smuggling activities were dependent on Medan as a chokepoint because it was the transportation hub that linked the land routes that GAM was forced to take from Bandung to Aceh due to state hostility. Weapons coming from Java were transported by truck through Medan.[117] GAM then made extensive use of the road from Aceh to Medan, approximately a twelve-hour drive, using local IDs they had bought on the black market to pass through checkpoints.[118] In April 2003, for example—as a result of an investigation in the Medan-Banda Aceh bus terminal—police discovered a red suitcase destined for Aceh, and containing nearly 500 rounds of ammunition, two hand grenades, and half a kilogram of ganja in a hotel room.[119]

Smuggling between Thailand and Malaysia, and Medan is a popular activity, given the existence of Tanjung Balai Asahan (relatively near to Medan) as the crown jewel of smuggling ports in the area of Sumatra, and this probably influenced GAM's choice of routes. The smuggling boats are owned by "businessmen" in Medan and Pekanbaru. They legally travel to Thailand on business, and when they come back, they bring guns and, often, motorcycles (which are much cheaper in Thailand, given the taxes in Indonesia).[120] The exact price of the guns was subject to supply and demand. In 1998–1999, as GAM was emerging from hibernation at the end of Daerah Operasi Militer, it had to replenish its weapons supply, but had only one channel, which offered AK-47s at 4,000,000 Rupiah per piece (about US$400). As they developed more channels, the price came down to a more manageable US$100 for each AK-47. GAM did buy some M-16s in Java, but those had come from outside of the island (and presumably from outside of Indonesia).[121] These numbers varied widely. Other sources put the price of M-16s and AK-47s purchased between Aceh and Thailand and in Indonesia at between 19,000,000 and 27,000,000 Rupiah.[122] Likewise, a gun brought over to Medan in 2005 in smuggling boats from Thailand could be bought for 500,000 Rupiah. Previously the going rate had been 5,000,000 Rupiah.[123] These figures were confirmed by GAM leaders, although it is unclear how many guns they were actually able to get from Medan, at this price or any other, once the Indonesian military started closing in, and Thailand was cut off to GAM as an organization.[124]

Friendly forces within Indonesia were of use to GAM in lessening its dependence on the dangerous transnational routes. GAM bought guns from elements of the Indonesian military (Tentara Nasional Indonesia, or TNI, in Indonesian), referred to as "our Acehnese friends in TNI," who were generally in the "organic" components of TNI's Acehnese forces. It also supplied ganja to TNI in exchange for guns. Sometimes, however, it was able to buy directly from TNI combat troops, using money.[125] Elements within TNI, and not just individual soldiers in Aceh, sold weapons and ammunition to GAM. During the third insurgency, for example, a huge batch of weapons and ammunition went missing on the way from Bandung to Surabaya, and ended up in Aceh.[126] Indonesian military personnel were also caught red-handed trying to ship guns to Aceh from Bandung, including the airmen who made repeated deliveries of weapons made in the Air Force's factory in Bandung in December 2001.[127] In Aceh, Indonesian soldiers would go off on a mission (or not), fire some bullets into the air, then claim they had used a great deal more, whereupon they would sell the excess bullets to GAM.[128]

GAM also made its own weapons in dire circumstances, but this does not seem to have been its preferred method, if only because of the crude nature of the weapons, and the fact that this did not solve its ammunition problem. Aceh has home workshops that use traditional workers to produce crude guns. In one incident, a member of TNI-AU (the Indonesian air force) from Aceh gave such a worker a sample of a pistol and asked him to make tens of copies.[129] In July 2001, in another incident, TNI found a GAM gun-making factory in Pidie district with electric generators, grenade launching machines and guns, and ammunition, and proclaimed the guns to be operational, but far worse quality than what TNI used.[130] Although GAM often publicly played up the connections it had within Indonesia as a way to embarrass the government, it could not rely solely on sources within the country, and had to fall back on transnational routes.

TRANSNATIONAL ROUTES: MALAYSIA AND THAILAND

One of GAM's main source of weapons was always Indonesia: either from rogue elements of the Indonesian military, or from sources in Java and Medan. But given that the Indonesian government at least had nominal control of these sources, and could strangle them with effort, GAM was forced to diversify. GAM's sources of weapons and ammunition in its third uprising from 1998 to 2005 were not substantially different from those in the early 1990s, but it clearly had to rebuild its networks every time it made a comeback, as evidenced by the fact that it had only one supplier when it began to rebuild in 1998.[131] With every new insurgency, its networks were more sophisticated and allowed the group access to more sources of weapons, but the routes remained the same, and were subject to political geographic considerations. In both Malaysia and Thailand, GAM was sensitive to political conditions, given the centrality of Malaysia in the organization's Southeast Asia command and control structure, and of Thailand as a source for weapons. Smuggling from Thailand involved crossing a border and traversing the country by land, while smuggling from both Malaysia and Thailand required finding sea-based routes across the Strait of Malacca to Aceh. Because of the difficulty of these smuggling routes, GAM tried to minimize the actual territory traversed and the borders crossed when possible, in order not to anger the Thai or Malaysian governments. When it actually did end up angering the Thai government, it was forced to shift its tactics considerably.

Under the Chuan Leekpai government (1997–2001), Thailand was a hospitable place for peaceful GAM activities, even though the Thai government was not ecstatic about weapons intended for Aceh crossing Thai territory, or being stolen from Thai military arsenals. Zakaria Zaman for years was GAM's official representative in Thailand, and lived quite openly in a house in Bangkok.[132] GAM did some smuggling in this period, but Zakaria did not procure most of its weapons. With that said, he was certainly capable of getting weapons, and did so on occasion, although he did not move the weapons himself.[133] Zakaria obtained weapons via routes heavily tied to the landscape and transportation infrastructure: he had weapons moved from the Cambodia and Vietnam borders, trucked them across Thailand, and sent them via GAM's small "navy" of fishing boats from beaches in northern Malaysia and southern Thailand to beaches such as Percut in Aceh Timur.[134]

Even given the favorable political conditions, GAM tried to avoid shipping weapons across Thailand, or being directly implicated in weapons smuggling. In effect, even the fear of a crackdown constrained GAM's illicit routes and methods. Thus it was that on a number of occasions, GAM avoided crossing borders, and bought weapons from the Thai mafia. The gangsters would send GAM GPS coordinates, and two ships would meet in the middle of the Malacca Strait to exchange guns and money. The weapons GAM brought directly from Cambodia were cheaper than weapons obtained from the Thai mafia, but the mafia's weapons supplies were safer, more reliable, and less politically risky.[135]

The organization also had professional smugglers and members of the Thai military smuggle the weapons for them, who were also tied to the same routes and favorable terrain. Two low-ranking Thai soldiers were caught smuggling weapons in May 2001, for example, when they were found to be driving two trucks stuffed with ammunition, thousands of guns, TNT, and forty-six land-mines in Songkhla province in southern Thailand. They were about to offload the loot onto a fishing trawler waiting for them in Songkhla harbor, although conflicting reports indicated that they were headed for an island in Sathun prov-ince.[136] They had successfully run the smuggling route a number of times before, in connection with an Acehnese broker who had gone to Yala (the southern-most Thai province, bordering on Malaysia) to buy firearms stolen from a Thai military depot.[137]

When Thaksin Shinawatra became prime minister in 2001, Thailand-GAM relations nosedived. Zakaria was forced to flee in 2003, and the Thai authori-ties ransacked his house in Bangkok soon after.[138] Although GAM continued to smuggle weapons from Thailand, it seemed content to use intermediaries who were directly in contact with the group's brokers in Aceh. A huge stash of weapons destined for Aceh was found in July 2002 in Sathun province, located directly west of Songkhla in the Isthmus of Kra, facing Aceh across the Strait of Malacca.[139] This was not an isolated instance—Sathun seems to have been the preferred transaction and jumping-off point for GAM's weapons purchases. Probably in late 2003 or early 2004, someone in Thailand sold caches of weapons to the Daud Rampok Group, a small Acehnese gang, for 7,000,000 Rupiah per gun (US$500–700). An associated gang, the Daud Puteh Group, then sold the guns to GAM. By the time the two gangs were rounded up at the end of January 2004, they had already concluded five separate transactions with GAM, totaling ninety-nine guns. The gangs transported the weapons (presumably by fishing boat) from Sathun province's Adang Island, one of the Thai islands closest to Aceh and Langkawi (and, incidentally, within a national park).[140] The gangs had apparently supplied GAM with AK-47s, M-16s, and pistols on four previous oc-casions since 2001, each time having sailed from Thailand to Aceh's Idi Rayeuk region. The fifth and final time, for reasons that remain unclear, the gang decided to move the weapons through Medan's Tanjung Balai Asahan port, where some of them were caught. Several other members of the gang were caught in Java, in-dicating the group's geographical spread.[141] Thus, when the Daud gangs chose an illicit route that took advantage of the difficult physical landscape and avoided legitimate routes or chokepoints, they were successful. But when the Daud gangs went through a legitimate chokepoint in a hostile country, they failed.

Fishermen also worked for GAM. In December 2004, fisherman Pawang Rahman jocularly described how he had gone to and from Malaysia and Thailand several times to buy weapons for GAM. In Thailand, he bought guns from a po-liceman known only as Silat. GAM's trade in weapons through these areas had started in 2004, and continued through at least November 2004. The money for buying the weapons was acquired once a month from a boat owner near Belawan port in Medan.[142]

Pawang Rahman also mentioned Malaysia. According to him, in Malaysia, one could buy guns on Pulau Batu Putih in Perlis state (near Langkawi).[143] GAM claimed it was wary enough of arousing the Malaysian government's ire that its operatives tried not to route any weapons through Malaysia, preferring the high seas method, even though it was more expensive.[144] Although GAM got away with using Malaysia as a base for much of its command and control, finance, and some counterintelligence operations, arms smuggling was something that the Malay-sian government strongly disliked. Rumors circulated about Malaysian weapons being smuggled from the Langkawi and Penang areas, and Jemaah Islamiyah managed to obtain ammonium nitrate in Malaysia. But aside from Pawang Rah-man's assertions, I can find no public records of specific GAM smuggling in-cidents from Malaysia other than pistols brought back by expatriate Acehnese returning from Malaysia.[145] This is not to say that the smuggling did not happen. According to another source, GAM received many weapons from Penang with the connivance of Malaysians.[146] But it lends credence to GAM's claim that it minimized the presence of weapons in Malaysia so as not to encourage the Ma-laysian government to stage a real crackdown on GAM. GAM had to keep quiet and move from place to place in its operations in Malaysia, but no major GAM leader was ever arrested in Malaysia and shipped back to Indonesia, even though every GAM fugitive went through Penang or Kuala Lumpur at some point. GAM informants generally said that the major obstacle for them was getting into or out of Indonesia, not anything to do with entering or leaving Malaysia.

GAM was sensitive to the politics of both Thailand and Malaysia. In both countries it tried to minimize the need to transit weapons through their terri-tory, both by minimizing them as sources, preferring to allow Indonesia to sup-ply them, or by minimizing the territory crossed and the official GAM role in weapons trafficking in Thailand and Malaysia, such as by meeting the Thai mafia halfway across the Strait of Malacca. When Thailand turned hostile after 2001, nothing GAM could do would mollify the government, so GAM continued to smuggle weapons from Thailand. But it clearly had a more difficult go of it—Thai police began catching more brokers inside of Thailand, and Zakaria was not physically present in the country to arrange for transport, having returned to Aceh after escaping from Bangkok.[147] It was not an optimal situation for a nominally globalized insurgency, which had limited options if it wanted to fight a war, given the geographic position of Aceh. GAM had many different weapons sources—the military, smugglers, the mafia, and fishermen—but it still had to funnel weapons through essentially just two routes due to its reliance on infrastructure and natural terrain.

THE LIMITS OF RESOURCEFULNESS

The crackdown in Thailand put GAM in a precarious position. Previously almost all of GAM's non-Indonesian weapons had gone through Thailand, coming from either Thailand or Cambodia (or according to some reports, Vietnam). Flying the weapons was not an option, and the farthest it seems that GAM could hope to transport the weapons by sea was across the Strait of Malacca (none of the ships owned by GAM or smugglers associated with GAM were long-distance ocean-going cargo ships). Malaysia was not a viable option both because of political sensitivities, and the lack of enough weapons to start a war (even the armed groups that have operated within Malaysia recently have not gotten their weapons domestically). Indonesia's status as a supplier was also precarious, inasmuch as an uptick in Indonesian military effectiveness in curbing TNI corruption in Aceh, stopping leakage from Bandung, breaking GAM's network in Jakarta and/or Medan, or blocking GAM smuggling boats from getting across the Strait of Malacca, could deprive GAM of any reliable source of weapons and ammunitions. There are many indications that, despite the best efforts of many incompetents in the Indonesian government, this is in fact what happened.

The Indonesian navy's radar was bad, but not completely ineffective. By staying close to shore on the east coast of Aceh, they made it difficult for GAM boats to run the blockade, and though they occasionally made it through, GAM members were also sometimes killed.[148] Publicly, GAM leaders denied that any of their boats were getting through because the Indonesian navy's blockade was so successful. (In fact they did not acknowledge that their weapons came from anywhere but Indonesia until the war was officially over.) This made smuggling directly from Thailand more difficult, even as Thailand grew more hostile. Even if GAM successfully got guns to Medan, it still had to find a way to get them overland through a series of checkpoints on the Medan-Banda Aceh highway. From GAM's point of view, the border between North Sumatra and Aceh may as well have been another heavily guarded international boundary.

GAM found creative ways to get around its weapons limitations. Guerrillas would work in shifts; one group would blend into society and build the local logistical support network, while the other would fight. GAM had only to show that it still existed and could kill its enemies when it wanted to. This strategy, combined with the shift-oriented means of fighting, led to waves of violence in approximately three-month intervals, which decreased the necessity of loads of guns and ammunition for everyone, all the time.[149]

Such tactics apparently confused the Indonesian military greatly, and at times it vastly over-reported GAM's material strength. In early 2000, the Indonesian military estimated that GAM had about 3,000 weapons, including shoulder-launched missiles and Stingers. In fact, according to GAM sources, the number was then close to about 300, and GAM certainly did not have any Stingers. Many GAM members would even put hammers in holsters to give the impression that they were armed with pistols. Fighters would also ambush Indonesian army units using only two or three weapons, get on a motorbike, go down half a kilometer, and fire again in order to perpetuate the illusion of great numbers.[150]

Still, TNI's aggressive efforts to find and destroy weapons had an effect. GAM admits to having had 3,000 weapons destroyed or captured by TNI. At its high point, GAM had about 15,000 fighters with 3,000–4,000 weapons, according to one GAM source, which differs somewhat from other estimates.[151] The general conclusion, however, is that GAM fighters greatly outnumbered weapons. By the end of the fighting, the Indonesian military was capturing GAM weapons that were clearly handmade. GAM was hurting for weapons and particularly ammunition.[152] In the Memorandum of Understanding, GAM committed itself to handing over for destruction 840 arms, the number that the Indonesian government claimed that GAM had. In fact, it had difficulty reaching even this number. In total, GAM had an estimated 1,000 weapons at the beginning of 2005, but many of these had been buried by people who had later been killed, and not even local commanders knew where the weapons were buried. Before coming up with 840 weapons, GAM spent a lot of time digging fruitlessly in various locations around Aceh looking for guns.[153]

By the end of the fighting, even given GAM's gun shortage, its most concerning material shortfall was the lack of ammunition: many of the people in their Jakarta network had been arrested before the 2004 tsunami.[154] This was evident during the weapons handovers during the peace process, when the 840 weapons were accompanied by only 7,000 rounds of ammunition, less than nine bullets per gun.[155] GAM was able to manufacture guns, but ammunition is much harder to make without precision machinery and had to be imported from Thailand or Java, which is why GAM informants stressed that the lack of ammunition, more than lack of guns, impeded their ability to fight. They could have gone yet another round of disappearing into the jungle for five years, only to re-emerge yet again, ready for another uprising, but this time the leaders judged this not to be the most prudent course of action.

GAM's situation is a testament to the importance of seemingly peripheral logistical issues. GAM's strength—its transnational network—in time became its weakness, for it depended on supplies from these same international sources (including other parts of Indonesia) that were susceptible to being cut off.

Outside of Indonesia, GAM was either an ambiguously illegal organization (in Singapore, Thailand, and Malaysia), or a legitimate entity (in the rest of the world). This reality, combined with its avowed pragmatism about the specific countries it used for its activities meant that its activities were more geographically widespread than either JI's or the organized crime syndicates discussed in the next chapter. At the same time, the configurations of GAM's command and control, training, and logistical structures reflected GAM's attempts to move people, information, and weapons into Aceh. The closer GAM got to Aceh, the more political conditions and the geographic landscape limited the routes and methods it could viably choose. Even as GAM became a globalized organization that took advantage of innovations in transportation and communications, and that was able to survive repeated failures in Aceh itself, it became dependent on certain countries and cities, especially Medan and parts of Malaysia, as chokepoints, for both legitimate and illicit activities. GAM's pragmatism about support and supplies in theory made it willing to get what it needed from anywhere, but its logistical needs locked it into somewhat predictable sea- and land-based routes between contiguous countries, with methods that were either illicit or made illicit use of legitimate infrastructure. GAM was sensitive to changes in the political climate in large part because of the geographic vulnerability of this supply chain, and tried to avoid being transnational whenever possible.

It is evident from GAM's experience that the ability to go transnational is a mixed blessing for a clandestine network. Although a more globalized structure allows clandestine organizations to escape crackdowns in a given country, if their target remains in that country and they need to move people and illicit materials to the target, they face a logistical problem. Every hostile border they must cross has the potential to scuttle the operation. If they are crossing great distances, they generally need to move through legitimate chokepoints that are controlled by potentially hostile states. If they are closer to the target, they can try illicit means, but they then become vulnerable to interdiction as their routes become dependent on geographic features and built infrastructure for success and failure, and hence more predictable.

TRANSNATIONAL CRIMINAL ORGANIZATIONS IN SOUTHEAST ASIA

Whereas JI and GAM are (fairly coherent) single organizations whose evolution can be tracked across time, countries, and varying political conditions, individual criminal organizations are ephemeral and often ad hoc, coming together as a coherent entity for one or two operations and then dispersing. The names of criminal syndicates and the roster of personnel are constantly changing or non-existent, making them different beasts than many terrorist and insurgent organizations. R. T. Naylor goes so far as to argue that even the well-known hierarchical, permanent organizations such as the Chinese triads, the Colombian drug cartels, and the Italian mafia are in fact better described as "parallel governments" that provide some measure of internal governance for their members, but do not control them in any systematic, top-down manner. As "associations of criminals," rather than "criminal associations," it would be difficult to track their development over time and changing political conditions in the same manner as JI and GAM, to say nothing of more diffuse organized crime.[1] Indeed, books that treat both terrorism and crime as manifestations of non-traditional security threats often lapse into aggregate statistics and descriptions of general trends when they turn to crime after focusing on individual terrorist groups.[2]

As a result, this chapter is necessarily less ambitious than the chapter on GAM, to say nothing of those on Jemaah Islamiyah. Nonetheless, once a given set of criminals has come together for an operation—once they want to move across borders—the challenges they encounter are the same as for JI and GAM. They must establish support structures in multiple countries, and figure out how to move surreptitiously between those countries using the transportation and

communications infrastructure provided. Where possible, I use focused miniature case studies of small areas or individual groups to illustrate these constraints.
I compare smuggling routes into Singapore with those into Batam, and examine
the command and control and logistical networks of two specific hijacking incidents in Southeast Asia. Strictly speaking, these specific pirate and smuggling
syndicates cannot substitute for other criminal groups, but they provide evidence
that the logic of the argument does actually play out successfully in real life.

The choice of small-time smugglers and big-time pirates as exemplars of
criminal organizations is deliberate. Both small-time smugglers and big-time
pirates deal with local political authorities, particularly when corrupting officials through bribes, but they are more economic than political actors. Clearly
criminal syndicates that are embedded in the legitimate political landscape and
as such have legitimate political activities exist—for example, the drug traffickers
of northeastern Myanmar, who are well integrated into autonomous local ethnic power structures, particularly in the Wa state.[3] Such organizations, however,
cease to be non-state actors, and as such no longer have a fundamentally adver-
sarial relationship with the state. By contrast, though the smugglers and pirates
of this book interact with various factions of the state, in no case are they able to
operate as blatantly as the drug traffickers of the Wa state. This denies them the
full and open use of the state's legitimate infrastructure, and allows them to be
ushered in as cases to compare with Jemaah Islamiyah and GAM.

Naylor distinguishes organized criminals from regular criminals by the relationship that they have to markets: namely, organized criminals need one to
make their money, either because they are sapping money from legitimate businesses, or because they are distributing illicit goods. To support their market-
based activities, like legitimate companies, organized criminals often create their
own distribution networks.[4] In more extreme cases where the state is essentially
absent, organized criminals may even play a role in building market institutions,
as happened in Russia in the 1990s.[5] This book is about transnational organizations, and the pirates and smugglers in this and in the next chapter make their
money by moving goods across international boundaries. Just as with Jemaah
Islamiyah and GAM, this leads to the need for transnational support structures
with roots in more than one country.

Both smugglers and pirates face the same dilemma once they have acquired
their illicit goods, be they cigarettes or hijacked ships, namely how to sell them
profitably. Unlike drugs, the goods in which pirates and small-time smugglers
traffic are not illegal, or at least not initially so. Although pirates and smugglers
need markets just as much as drug traffickers do, unlike drug traffickers, they
can afford to make use of legitimate markets to ply their wares. If, as analysts
argue, organized criminals are parasitic on the state—they corrupt officials, raise

the level of ambient violence in a country, and hinder economic development—organized criminals that depend on the existence of a functioning state for transportation, communications, and markets are especially interesting.[6]

The choice of small-time smugglers and big-time pirates also parallels the scope of the territorial ambitions of the first two cases in this book. Whereas GAM remained focused on a small portion of Indonesia for its entire history, the smugglers discussed here have small-time ambitions. They want to get everyday items—oil, rice, pirated video compact discs (VCDs)—from one place to another to sell at a profit. Usually this involves crossing just one border, in contrast to cocaine trafficking networks, which, in substantially more ambitious operations, move cocaine from Colombia through Central America to the United States, or to Africa, and thence to Europe.[7] Like Jemaah Islamiyah in the 1990s, the maritime piracy hijacking syndicates have support structures in a number of different countries as they struggle to hijack, disguise, and sell off cargo and ships.

Like Jemaah Islamiyah, maritime pirates in particular have attracted many journalistic accounts, but theoretically oriented analysts of smugglers and pirates generally take one of two contextualizing approaches: an organizational approach or a financial approach. Both approaches allow us to compare criminals to terrorists and insurgents. First, in the past several decades, thanks to their increasingly adept use of technology, transnational criminal syndicates might best be understood as often loosely coupled, structurally flat, ad hoc networks that can come together for a specific venture before dispersing.[8] The implication is that organizational structure determines adaptability, and that networks are inherently more adaptable. As the next chapter shows, the territorial spread of the organization is also relevant for adaptability, at least in terms of how a syndicate is arrayed over the physical landscape. Just as in the cases of JI and GAM, here I am more concerned with how criminal syndicates move people, goods, and information from country to country than with how members of those syndicates are related to each other.

This is not to say that organizational approaches do not have something to say about how we situate criminal syndicates in space. Although his book is focused on the social networks within drug trafficking syndicates (and terrorist groups), Michael Kenney goes into great detail about all the nodes in Colombian drug traffickers' supply chains, from farmers to transporters to street distributors. From Kenney's description, it is clear that one of the enduring problems traffickers face is how to get their processed drugs across borders to their destinations. For this task they have both "transportation distributors" and "aviation/maritime transportation rings" that vary their routes and methods to avoid state scrutiny.[9] The technologies of globalization are often assumed to have empowered transnational criminals who, even more than terrorists, can piggyback on legitimate communications and transportation infrastructure to move around the world.[10] Phil Williams argues that one of the properties of networks (versus hierarchical organizations) is their ability to transcend boundaries, including physical boundaries.[11] This ability to leap across jurisdictions makes it difficult for states, which are often jealous of their sovereignty, to cooperate and compromise in order to fight them, as Mak Joon Num shows in his research on anti-piracy cooperation in the Strait of Malacca.[12]

The ease with which criminal networks cross international borders is emphasized even more when analysts take a financial approach to transnational crime. Brian Fort acknowledges that both criminals and terrorists have some vulnerabilities, such as money transfer reporting requirements. At the same time Fort is worried about the transnational nature of maritime piracy, and crime in general. Transnational financial flows are an area where both criminals and terrorists overlap, thus presenting powerful security threats, even as states still consider criminals to be a matter solely for the police, and particularly virulent terrorists to be a matter of national security.[13] Large amounts of money generated by criminal activities can be used to corrupt local officials, buy legal protection, and take advantage of weak banking systems, thus guaranteeing criminals a friendly reception in some weak states.[14]

Perhaps neither approach provides an accurate view of the nature of organized crime because they are focused on the wrong things. Far from proclaiming criminal networks as the dark vanguard of a newly globalized world, Naylor instead portrays organized criminals as arms-length, opportunistic networks of somewhat resourceful losers. They are indeed adaptable, but rarely are able to do so on the scale and with the speed attributed to them by analysts. The absolute volume of criminal money is not enough to corrupt the global financial system, and the manner in which criminals behave nowadays is not qualitatively different from decades past.[15]

These studies have turned an eye toward the transnational nature of many criminal enterprises, and the threat this development poses. I continue the process by situating pirates and smugglers' activities in space, and seeing where the technologies of globalization have helped them. Crossing borders does provide criminals with some opportunities, but it also presents them with problems grounded in territory and political conditions. Because the criminals are ultimately moving physical goods, having a good grasp of global financial flows is of limited use when analyzing some of their activities. Moreover, because the constraints exist on the activities (rather than on the organizations per se), the story of success or failure in criminal organizations can be told without regard to how horizontal or vertical their structures are. Just like JI and GAM, neither pirates nor smugglers are as freewheeling as they appear at first glance.

In this chapter, I first tackle smugglers: their structure, and the routes and methods they use to operate. To illustrate the constraints smugglers face conditional on political and territorial considerations, I look at the outcomes in smuggling into Singapore and Batam, and explain what this means for the smugglers' dependence on geography. In the second section, I look at pirates, and explain what goes into hijacking a ship and disposing of its cargo. Large-scale operations seem to require territorially widespread operational areas, but though pirates have shown an ability to use the tools of globalization to their advantage, they remain subject to territorial restrictions for a number of reasons, mostly related to the pirates' continuing need for sophisticated legitimate market infrastructure.

Mundane Smugglers

Structure

The structure of mundane smuggling syndicates is simpler than that of any of the other organizations examined in this book. The terrorist and separatist groups' command and control, training, and logistics structures are often clearly delineated; maritime piracy gangs' command and control networks are often sharply different from the people who actually hijack the ships; and smuggling syndicates' command and control and logistics networks are often unified. The entire operation has no other purpose other than moving material goods from one country to another. For small-time smugglers, these goods are often those that would not otherwise be illegal, or at least do not appear illegal. In 2003 and 2004, for example, joint Malaysian-Indonesian maritime patrols apprehended smugglers who were moving timber, cars, used clothes, and *sembako* (that is, *sembilan bahan pokok,* or the nine daily necessities) between Malaysia and Indonesia (generally the cars were sent to Malaysia, and everything else was sent to Indonesia).[16] Around the same time, Indonesian police caught smugglers who were attempting to bring buffalo meat from India through Malaysia into Kalimantan Barat by truck.[17] Likewise, in March 2004, Indonesian border police intercepted a truck containing hundreds of chickens when it attempted to enter Kalimantan Barat from Sarawak, Malaysia through a border checkpoint. The truck first aroused suspicion because the chickens looked different from those usually found in Kalimantan Barat, as well as being too old to lay eggs, which was their declared purpose. The driver presented a letter from a local official that purported to give permission for the chickens to be imported, but this was problematic: parts of the letter were handwritten, the official in question had already retired, and in any case, permission for such a transaction had to come from Jakarta.[18]

The mundane nature of the goods has two effects. First, it seems the network does not need to be very large, as disposing of the goods in the destination country is often as simple as selling them in a regular market. It would appear that syndicates are not any larger than they need to be. Second, smugglers encounter highly variable levels of state hostility. All states in Southeast Asia are nominally against drug trafficking, but some might not devote the same level of resources to fighting illegal rice or chicken imports. As a result, the smugglers make use of a wide variety of routes and methods to move their goods, depending on how the states in which they operate view what they are smuggling.

Operations

The routes and methods used by small-time smugglers are in many ways similar to what we already seen in the logistics activities of JI and GAM. JI and GAM often moved along illicit routes when transporting explosives and guns across international boundaries, while smugglers of mundane items seem more comfortable trying to get through customs with some level of subterfuge. As would be expected, open use of legitimate routes is uncommon among smuggling syndicates (which decreases the use of air routes), thus limiting the overall transnational territorial spread of the networks. But illicit use of legitimate routes is quite widespread, and the smuggling of mundane goods involves more shades of gray than is evident in the other logistical activities seen in this book.

One retired Indonesian customs official explained that three types of smuggling exist in Indonesia: so-called administrative smuggling, physical smuggling, and a combination of the two. Administrative smuggling essentially consists of making illicit use of legitimate routes for moving goods into the country. Importers lie on the customs manifestos that must accompany shipments about what the containers are holding, change the document to claim a lesser value, or fail to declare some of the goods. If discovered, they claim to have made a mistake. Physical smugglers, on the other hand, bypass the state entirely, and use completely illicit routes.[19]

Administrative smugglers in Indonesia have been known to use some creative tactics. They can use false documentation, and change the value of their goods from U.S. dollars to Singaporean dollars, or delete a zero or two on the manifest. They can also underestimate the horsepower of imported automobiles or motorcycles. The cost of adjudicating the dispute plus the penalty they have to pay if caught is still less than the regular duty.[20] One foreign executive estimated that perhaps 30 percent of the consumer electronics in Indonesia were smuggled, primarily through under-declaring the value of the contents of imported containers, while possibly 90 percent of high-technology products overall were smuggled.[21] Of course, although under-declaring a shipment is certainly smuggling, it would be difficult to describe those who engage in it as smuggling syndicates per se. Legitimate companies have perverse incentives to smuggle. According to the foreign executive whose company makes cell phones, the small shops that actually sell cell phones do not report their sales to the central government, so the distributor receives a value-added tax bill from the government, and tries and fails to collect money from the retailers, which leads to a government audit. In response, the distributor must close down and change its name as often as every six months. Importers are thus placed into situations where they are almost required to break the law, and it would be easier to avoid government regulations if possible.[22]

Aside from false declarations, smugglers can also bring shipments into port, and forward the documents to the customs station, but immediately send the goods to smuggling clearing houses or local markets. As a rule, at least one customs official is in on the scam—the advantage is that the importers have legitimate documentation, but have no inspections that could disprove their declarations. Finally, smugglers can send both documentation and the goods through customs, and declare them to be destined for free-trade zones or duty-free stores, then arrange to have them diverted to local markets for sale.[23] For legitimate importers, none of these methods require a logistical network over and above what they would otherwise have in place to import and distribute their goods. Only the second method requires the complicity of anyone outside of the company. In addition, these methods of smuggling do not depend on geographical advantages as the smugglers are using legitimate ports and even interacting with the state on what would from a distance appear to be a legal basis. This lack of a network plays a key role in how smugglers respond to changes in state policies. The strength of semi-legitimate smuggling is that there is essentially no network to compromise. This is also a weakness. The necessity of allies within the state and a legitimate transportation node limits the route to the location of that agent, making it simple to crack down (assuming the state has the capacity to fight such corruption).

Other smugglers try to avoid dealing with the state at all by creating their own illicit routes across international boundaries, and here physical topography becomes important. Although they are freed from the limitations of a political ideology, mundane smugglers still generally use the same smuggling routes to and from Indonesia that Jemaah Islamiyah and GAM used in their operations. First, they sail between Singapore and Indonesia via the many islands of the Riau Islands province. Many of the consumer electronics smuggled into Indonesia come from Singapore due to the short distance.[24] Smugglers also move between Indonesia and Malaysia via the Malacca Strait (if by sea), and from Sarawak and Sabah (if by land). There are "rat ports" (*pelabuhan tikus*) in Malaysia, for example, from which speedboats can move from Dumai to Medan in about an hour and fifteen minutes.[25] Smuggling also occurs via the Sangihe-Talaud Islands between the Philippines and Indonesia. In fact, the Sabah-Mindanao-Manado triangle contains many smuggling networks that operate along traditional maritime routes that have been used for hundreds of years. Sulu, Bugis, and Bajau traders do not recognize borders, and move back and forth with ease.[26] Both JI and GAM had to construct complex smuggling routes for their weapons and explosives that crossed, at times, thousands of miles and a number of international borders, but mundane smugglers minimize the distance they travel and the number of borders they cross. If a profit can be made by bringing goods from one country to a market in an adjacent country, little need exists to set up a bigger network. This is true even for large, expensive goods. In February 2004, for instance, Indonesian navy ships intercepted a wooden ship, manned by seven crewmen, that was smuggling eleven used cars from Singapore to an illegal port in southern Batam Island, a distance of perhaps twenty miles.[27] Given these small networks, their non-territorial ambitions and limited geographical scope, and the wide variety of routes and methods adopted by mundane smugglers, it is useful to see the constraints smugglers face. A look at the political geography of smugglers' routes into Singapore and Batam, paralleling JI's plots examined in chapter 5, provides a useful case study.

The Political Geography of Smuggling

The actual geography of Singapore and Batam's borders is the same as for JI's plots when we consider mundane smuggling, but the nature of the goods is quite different, and that means that smuggling syndicates move in somewhat different ways from Jemaah Islamiyah. Jemaah Islamiyah had to figure out ways to get highly illegal explosives into Singapore and Batam (ultimately, the explosives smuggled into Batam entered Indonesia via illicit routes from the Philippines). Conversely, the otherwise legal nature of mundane smuggled goods tends to give regular smugglers more options when it comes to taking advantage of geography. Singapore and Batam are particularly good comparison cases for mundane smuggling because both areas are both origins and destinations for illicit goods. Singapore has high levels of state hostility to smuggling, while Batam is somewhat less hostile. Consequently, the routes used by smugglers into Singapore are highly dependent on topographical features of the physical landscape, but those used by Batam smugglers somewhat less so. Instead, Batam smugglers are more comfortable using the transportation and market infrastructure provided by the state to move and peddle their goods.

SINGAPORE: HIGH HOSTILITY, HIGH DEPENDENCE ON TOPOGRAPHIC ADVANTAGES

Singapore clamps down on smugglers by making it not lucrative. Because Singapore is a largely tariff-free country, smuggling non-luxury goods hardly makes sense. According to police sources, cigarettes and alcohol are the two primary smuggled goods, as they are among the few goods that actually have duties placed on them.[28] The non-declaration of imported items so common in Indonesia is not a problem in Singapore, because there is no point in hiding the value of imported goods.

As a rich country that has a labor shortage and is surrounded by poorer countries, Singapore *does* have a people-smuggling problem. In the south, illegal immigrants come up from Indonesia, and in the north, they come down from Malaysia. From a police perspective, the geographies of the northern coast and southern coast of Singapore present different law enforcement challenges (and hence different incentives for certain methods of smuggling). In the north, the Strait of Johor between Malaysia and Singapore is shallow enough and the strait narrow enough (at one point constricting to 600 meters) that it requires special fast patrol boats and surveillance systems. The Singaporean government has also set up barriers in the strait itself, at Lim Chu Kang, and just north of Pulau Ubin, among other places.[29] The problem in the north, then, is that potential smugglers can race from the Malaysian side. In a fast boat, the run could conceivably be made in less than a minute, and it then becomes a cat and mouse game. Because the Singaporean government has a strong policy against smuggling of people, weapons, and drugs, it has cracked down on them in draconian ways since at least 1993. As a result, the people smugglers have become more creative, and have become even more dependent on the geographic and infrastructural characteristics of the north coast, namely the existence of the causeway and pipeline linkages between Singapore and Malaysia, and the narrowness of the strait. Thus, illegal migrants have come in by hiding in vehicles crossing the causeway, and until police took steps to close down that route, walked along the pipes that carry water from Malaysia to Singapore.[30] A number of migrants have also landed in the unpopulated northwestern side of Singapore, in the Live Firing Area—a military training region full of jungle and Singaporean soldiers—where they have been rounded up rather quickly. Finally, some people try to swim to the Singaporean side from the Malaysian side in the middle of the strait. As of 2005, for 400 Singaporean dollars (about US$250), smugglers would take illegal migrants to the middle of the strait, give them two inflated trash bags for flotation, and tell them to swim to the other side.[31] Thus, smugglers have solved the problem of high state hostility (and capacity) by effectively not dealing with it all. These illicit routes do use geographical advantages along Singapore's coast, but the route that smugglers can then take are limited and known to the police.

The southern coast of Singapore presents its own problems. The gap between Batam's outer islands and Singapore is wider than the gap on the north coast, but it is still narrow. Moreover, unlike the north coast, the Singapore Strait on the south coast is one of the world's major shipping passages, and smugglers (or pirates) can slip out of the stream of legitimate traffic passing through Singapore's waters and make a break for it, often for Pasir Panjang on the southern coast. In the past, smugglers have attempted to outrun the Police Coast Guard (PCG) in fast but expensive boats capable of carrying twenty people at a time. In a number of instances the PCG, cooperating with the Navy and the port authorities, captured and confiscated the boats, causing major financial losses for the smugglers.[32] Some smugglers have responded by changing the type of goods they move (if we consider people to be a type of good). According to sources who have been involved in smuggling to and from Batam in the past, if there are apparently only otherwise legitimate goods on a boat (excepting a reasonable-size crew) moving around Singapore waters, they are less likely to be stopped by the Singaporean authorities than a boat that obviously contains more people than is sufficient to crew it.[33] To cut off illegal migrants, the government has also cracked down hard on the land-based recruiters in Singapore who find jobs for the illegal migrants, and allowed migrants to come to Singapore more easily through legal channels. As a result, the smuggling syndicates have largely disappeared in the south due to lack of profit. What smuggling takes place now is carried out in wooden rowboats costing only sixty to seventy Singaporean dollars (about $US40 to US$45). Because the southern smugglers have to rely on stealth rather than speed, and Singapore has a good surveillance system, the chances of being caught are high, but the potential financial losses in any given failed operation are low.[34]

Smugglers into Singapore, then, do adapt their tactics to Singaporean state hostility and the topography of its borders. As with Jemaah Islamiyah, mundane smugglers into Singapore face the final mile problem: however much they are able to use the technologies of globalization to their advantage before the final leg, when confronted with political hostility, modern technology abandons them. Greater hostility generates greater dependence on routes that take advantage of geography, notably Singapore's extensive coastline relative to its total land area, and proximity to Malaysia and Indonesia. Unlike Jemaah Islamiyah, mundane smugglers can indeed get their goods into Singapore in small quantities and with acceptable penalties if they are caught, but the routes they can realistically take are still somewhat limited and predictable.

BATAM: LOW HOSTILITY, LOW DEPENDENCE
ON TOPOGRAPHIC ADVANTAGES

Even more than Singapore, the geography of Riau Islands province, of which Batam is a part, would seem to be ideal for piracy and smuggling. Hundreds of small islands, many uninhabited, flank shallow straits through which the majority of the world's shipping must pass, and Batam is so close to Singapore that the Singapore skyline is actually visible from northern Batam. Riau Islands province is infamous in Indonesia for smuggling and pirate attacks. Smugglers in Batam, for example, often cater in cigarettes, electronics, white rice, cars, and sugar from Singapore and Malaysia.[35] One would expect, at first glance, that smugglers use these small, isolated islands to move their goods, and some of them do. But what is remarkable is how many of them do not—the relative lack of state hostility means that smugglers often do not take advantage of geographical features that would otherwise help them elude the authorities.

A visit to Batam in August 2005 revealed the extent to which smugglers were relying on covert routes that sometimes bypassed state power but did not rely on Batam's geography (notably its small islets nearby and its stretches of isolated coastline). At night in Batam, smugglers can load and unload illicit goods at many *pelabuhan tikus*, as long as the relevant authorities receive kickbacks. There are sixty-four *pelabuhan tikus* on the island, with locations well known to the relevant authorities.[36] For example, there was a large *pelabuhan tikus* a five-minute drive from a naval base through a *kampung* (village) near Batu Ampar, one of the major legal ports in Batam. Another *pelabuhan tikus* lay next to an industrial area, including a major pipe-making factory. In other words, it was in an ordinary location. At Batu Ampar itself, legal goods from Singapore are brought in during the day, and illegal goods are brought in at night by the same docks. If the situation permits, they are brought in simultaneously.[37] At the time of my visit, the port police station was situated approximately fifty yards in front of the part-time *pelabuhan tikus,* with a police patrol vessel in port. Some attempt at secrecy is made when smuggling illegal goods into the legal ports of entry in Batam. Some smugglers, for example, put crates of vegetables from the outer islands on top of the illegal goods, so that when the police come to inspect, they look only at the top layer of crates, and ignore the rest. One source recounted how he was once on a boat carrying white onions between Singapore and Batam. In the middle of the night, men came to offload the illegal goods, which were hidden under the legitimate items, and shortly thereafter, the police arrived and took a bribe.[38] According to other sources, the major disadvantage of using the legal ports as entry points for smuggling is that it is difficult to bring in more than a couple of crates at a time.[39]

Even if the police have been paid off, discretion is still necessary. There is little resistance, for instance, to bringing cars from outside of Indonesia to Batam, for Batam is a low-tariff zone. If goods stay in Batam, they are mostly duty-free. If they leave Batam for the rest of Indonesia, the importers must pay the relevant duties and taxes.[40] As a result, moving goods between Batam and Indonesia can be treated analytically as a transnational activity. Some smugglers who do move "used" luxury cars from Batam to Jakarta disguise the cars by giving them military-issue license plates, and completely covering them in decals the color of Indonesian military vehicles (generally dark blue or green) to avoid being questioned by authorities, then shipping them to Jakarta, where relevant officials are paid off. Once safely off the ship, the smugglers peel off the decals and sell the cars, which due to tariffs can be as little as half the cost of a luxury car legally sold in Jakarta.[41] Barring such masterful displays of subterfuge, less organized smugglers turn to completely illegitimate *pelabuhan tikus,* where they can bring in entire boatloads of goods at a time. Yet the relative lack of enforcement only shows that the authorities are doing little to stop the pirates and smugglers. Are they also incapable of doing so?

In Batam, the local police can only be effective with backup support from the Riau Islands provincial police, but they are not necessarily unable to enforce the law.[42] When queried about smuggling non-dangerous contraband (i.e., not guns or drugs), both Singapore and Batam sources said that as long as the smuggled goods were not otherwise dangerous, they had bigger things to worry about, although Singapore in particular obviously puts a fair amount of resources into stopping the smugglers. One police source, for instance, said that he knew who the main VCD smugglers in Batam were, and knew that the VCDs were produced in Batam and Jakarta, but acknowledged that if the police were to crack down too hard, the masses, who cannot afford to buy legal DVDs, would complain.[43] But hostility is not necessarily constant over time. The authorities can and do crack down. The results of those crackdowns will be discussed in the next chapter.

The smugglers in Singapore and Batam try to cross only one border. In this they stand in contrast to both JI, with its large target area, and even GAM, which, though it had a small target area, had very specific items it needed to smuggle, and thus at times had to bring them from sources far afield. But the small-time smugglers nonetheless exhibit a similar relationship with territory and political conditions as JI and GAM: where they can use legitimate infrastructure in service to their activities, either openly or by finding allies within local governments, they do. Smugglers are in a double bind. Where they seek to avoid dealing with the state (or its infrastructure) entirely due to state hostility, they become dependent on geographical features that increase the time and effort needed to smuggle goods, features that may or may not be there, and that are known to the authorities. When, in places like Batam, the political environment is favorable enough to allow some use of legitimate infrastructure, smugglers must still use some sort of subterfuge to move their goods. This increases their operating costs, and inasmuch as their smuggling routes pass through a few legitimate choke-points, makes them vulnerable to crackdowns.

Because the target areas of mundane smugglers are so small, the constraining effect of territory is not necessarily all that noticeable. But what about piratical hijacking syndicates—organizations with larger target areas, with greater ambitions that stretch across a number of countries, but still no desire to control or govern territory? How do they organize their networks in response to territorial and political considerations?

Piratical Hijacking Syndicates
Command and Control

Large-scale transnational piratical hijacking syndicates are a recent phenomenon. Pirates who seize ships are nearly as old as shipping itself, the second oldest profession of the shipping world. Traditional Malay pirates have roamed certain parts of the Southeast Asian seas for centuries, preying on unsuspecting trading ships to make a living from loot. But organized syndicates that plan an attack from one country, carry it out in another, and sell the cargo in a third (or fourth) have really only come to the fore since the 1980s, with the rise of globalization and the decrease in cost and time of international transport. The command and control structures of these groups likewise stretch over multiple countries, and are held together by the movement of information and people through virtual and physical space, along, for the most part, legitimate routes. In some sense, they should be the poster children for the expansion of opportunity that the technologies of globalization have allowed criminal organizations. When observed closely, however, their behavior does not bear this out.

In a given operation in Southeast Asia, a few financiers from within or near the region will pitch in funding of perhaps around US$500,000 (which makes some transnational hijackings more expensive than almost all terrorist attacks).[44] The investment is highly leveraged, and failure could result in bankruptcy for the financiers.[45] The top people seem to come from a few places around Asia: mainland China, Hong Kong, Jakarta, East Malaysia, and the Philippines, although at least some financing has apparently originated with individuals associated with the insurance industry in Bangkok. Hong Kong used to be a center for piracy financing, but has declined in recent years.[46] Indonesian officials also whisper darkly that some pirate gangs are actually international syndicates from the insurance business, which stage attacks in Indonesian waters to make it unsafe for ships, and thus drive up the premiums they charge.[47] One source also claimed with some frustration that a few Singaporean financiers are involved in the schemes, the identity of at least one of whom is known by the Singaporean government, which does nothing because he has not broken any Singaporean laws.[48]

The general geographical pattern of financing reinforces the notion that command and control are not as nearly as tied down by territorial concerns as the actual operations and logistics of the attacks, but are not untethered from territory either. Operations within Southeast Asia can be financed from almost any business center within the region. Other pirate syndicates exist in the world, notably in West Africa, where the hijacking of phantom ships is financed by Lebanese businessmen, and in the Gulf of Aden, where goods stolen off the coast of Somalia are sold in Dubai. These syndicates do not appear to be as sophisticated as the Southeast Asian networks, and they largely keep to themselves.[49]

Like GAM, pirate syndicates have made good use of the technologies of globalization to keep their networks together. Pirates have been known to use GPS and radio transmitters to coordinate with each other, and avoid naval forces. One syndicate actually rented a hotel room and filled it with communications equipment for this purpose.[50] Although the shipping industry is globalized, the maritime piracy industry is not. In all likelihood, this is probably because, like Jemaah Islamiyah, piracy syndicates' command and control functions are intimately tied with their operations and logistics networks. Modern technology in theory allows pirates to be globalized, but the illicit logistics of their operations limit their reach. The networks are only as big as they need to be in order to dispose of the cargo and ships—disposal usually requires a transnational network, but not a global one. The financiers use contacts from their own legitimate shipping networks to sell their goods, always taking care to dissociate themselves from the operations, and they rarely have such contacts outside their home region.[51] The hijacked ships also usually operate within a single region given the prevalence of transshipment hubs, especially within Southeast Asia (Singapore and Hong Kong in particular).[52]

Once the financing for the operation has been secured, the financiers (or their middlemen) sometimes contact a pirate broker, who is usually located closer to the planned attack. In some cases, the pirate brokers actually double as pirates themselves. Once formed, the pirate syndicates identify the ship to be hijacked by its value and the ease with which the cargo can be sold covertly. The pirates generally attack ships with cargo that is relatively easy to transfer, and/or ships that are easy to hide.[53] The targeting of ships is similar to how the nature of smuggled goods affects routes and methods used. Smaller general cargo ships, which are often twenty-five to thirty years old, are off the radar of the international ship-ping community, and are generally restricted to sketchier, but legitimate ports, where officials might be more compliant.[54] Fishing boats do not usually have embossed numbers, so it is easy to change their names quickly. Tugs and barges are also popular targets, as they are useful both for the cargo they may contain (which can be just as profitable as larger cargo ships), and for their carrying capacity if empty.[55]

On occasion, pirates have been known to take orders for specific ships and cargo.[56] Competent pirates, like ship owners, wait for contracts before they move their ships. Like airlines, they only make money when their ships are on the move and carrying cargo. Different ship owners tend to specialize in certain cargos—such as grain, dry goods, oil, gas, iron ore, containers—making them more or less attractive to certain pirates.[57] The pirates may also target certain ships, or their owners, for other reasons, such as extortion rackets. In the late 1990s, a small tanker disappeared from the waters around Kalimantan. At about the same time, a sister ship owned by the same company approached a pilot station in the area of Sabah and East Kalimantan (probably in the Tawau/Sandakan area), and asked for help. The ship had been attacked, and everything had been taken, including the carpeting, the crewmembers' clothing, and the curtains from the rooms.[58]

Having found a target, the financiers (or their middlemen) create false docu-ments, appoint forwarders, and find buyers, who are often legitimate but incuri-ous businessmen. Such people do exist. One informant associated with the Hong Kong shipping industry notes that he sometimes receives suspicious e-mails of-fering for sale certain amounts of crude oil with no clue as to their origin.[59] When the one ship was finally recovered off the coast of Malaysia in August 2005, for example, having been hijacked two years earlier, the current Hong Kong owner said he had bought the ship from the previous "owner" for US$10,000. He appar-ently had not bothered to inquire further about such a great clearance item, and was so uninterested in the outcome of the piracy investigation that he refused go to Malaysia to meet with the authorities. In another incident, stolen cargo was traced to a buyer in Singapore, who had known something was wrong, but had bought the cargo anyway at 30 to 40 percent below market value.[60]

The actual task of hijacking and disposing of the ship is arranged by middle-men. Middlemen can come from any number of countries in the region, includ-ing Indonesia and South Korea, while foot soldiers can come from Myanmar, Indonesia, and the Philippines, but often seem to be recruited from the country nearest to the attack site.[61] Recruitment is a simple affair. In one incident, un-employed Indonesian seamen in Batam were simply asked by the recruiter if they were interested in taking part in a hijacking operation.[62] Having recruited pirates, syndicates next go about attacking ships and stealing their cargo.

Operations: Seizing the Ship

The two primary tools of pirates are boats and weapons. Pirates generally use boats that are ideal for stealth, or speed, or some combination of the two. For attacks that are close to shore, and less logistically complicated, pirates prefer to set out from a hidden location on shore with speedboats. Some pirates in the Philippines are highly organized and well equipped, and have handguns and automatic rifles. Their double-engine speedboats are capable of twenty-five to thirty-five knots, can easily outrun Philippines naval ships, and can slip into hidden coves for protection. They roam the seas in gangs of as many as three boats, looking for prey.[63]

If pirates are further from shore, or if the attack involves more than stealing money and other valuables from the ship's safe, the pirates might use a so-called mother ship—a fishing boat, or a larger ship disguised to look as if it could be one. The pirates use this ruse as a means to approach unsuspecting ships, then at the last minute release smaller, speedier boats from which they actually attack their prey. In June 2004, armed pirates in a fishing boat hijacked the *MT Pematang* in the waters of Berhala, in North Sumatra, while the ship was waiting for a dock in Belawan. The captive crewmembers managed to contact the Indonesian navy, who responded rapidly, and then attacked the ship when it did not respond to Morse Code hails.[64] The next month, the tug *Global Semesta I* and the barge *Global Semesta IV* were traveling from Palembang through the Bangka Strait when a nearby fishing boat suddenly turned and followed an intercept course. The gun-toting pirates launched a wooden boat toward the *Global Semesta*s, and quickly climbed aboard, where they surrounded the crew, then put them off the ship, and took the hijacked tug and barge toward the Malacca and Singapore Straits.[65] Other ruses have also worked. The leader of one pirate gang active in Jakarta harbor in 2004 described how the pirates attacked ships. With nine pirates on two ships, the gang would send one ship to a target ship to offer its services as a ferry from the anchored ship to the mainland. As the first ship ferried a portion of the crew to Jakarta, the other ship would approach, and armed pirates would board and rob the remaining crew of any possessions and spare parts that could be sold.[66]

If they maintain the element of surprise, the pirates might simply try to sneak aboard, or if the crew senses their presence, the pirate ship might fire warning shots to encourage the target ship to stop. This happened with the *Motor Cipta Karya* when it was waylaid in the Malacca Strait in November 2004 by pirates, who subsequently made off with money, cell phones, and three crewmembers, but not the ship.[67] Although some pirates might be armed only with machetes, and others with firearms, and in some cases, machine guns mounted

on the front of their speedboats, this does not indicate that better-armed and/
or more violent pirates are actually more competent, or part of more organized
syndicates. In 2005, in an infamous incident, a group of Somali pirates fired a
rocket-propelled grenade at a cruise ship in an attempt to get it to stop.[68] An informant affiliated with the Hong Kong shipping industry expressed incredulity at
their plan. Rocket-propelled grenades are poor weapons with which to threaten
individuals. Cruise ships also make poor targets. They have far too many people
to hold hostage conveniently, and the money and jewelry that is the usual loot of
non-hijacking pirates is spread out among hundreds of cabins rather than kept
in a central safe, as on most cargo ship and tug boats. Eventually, the cruise ship
used a directed sound weapon to repel the pirates. The informant noted that,
aside from actual warships, cruise ships are the most heavily protected ships in
the world—their freeboards are too far above the waterline for pirates to easily
clamber aboard, they often have electrified anti-pirate fencing along the deck of
the ship, and their owners have constant knowledge of their location and disposition.[69] Looking at the logistical sophistication of pirates' operations is a better
way to make conclusions about their organizational abilities than the weapons
they use, or the ships they target.

Just as terrorists and separatists might benefit from friendly forces within
governments, sometimes pirates have help from somewhere within the organization that owns the ship that they are targeting. This could allow them to have
specific information about a given ship, its cargo, and its location at any given
time. An International Maritime Bureau official recalls a case in which a syndicate attacked three tin-hauling cargo ships owned by the same company in the
Bangka Strait, leading to suspicion that the syndicate had a mole in the company.[70] A mole on the ship could also lower ropes so that the pirates can clamber
on board more easily, although an informant stressed that this was unnecessary;
pirates are quite capable of boarding a hostile ship themselves, and are often willing to attack a ship without any inside man.[71] Once on board, pirates have standard operating procedures: they hold the crew at gunpoint, and steal anything
of value off the ship. If they intend to hijack the ship, they put the crew either
in a lifeboat or on an island, kill them, or hold the crew hostage while they head
for a port to offload the cargo. If they intend to take hostages, in Southeast Asia
they generally seize the captain and engineer (as the most valuable crewmembers), and make off toward areas unknown.[72] The different types of pirate gangs
do not usually overlap—mere sea robbers are not the same people as hijacking
syndicates, but sudden changes of plan can occur. In February 2003, for instance,
pirates boarded the tugboat *TB Wisdom* in the waters around Pontianak, West
Kalimantan, and finding nothing of value, took the boat instead, putting off the
crew in the waters of Riau Islands province.[73]

Although the act of seizing the ship is less logistically complex than actually disposing of the ship and cargo, the attack is not without territorial considerations. The fuel capacity, size, and speed of the pirates' boats help to determine the proximity of their attacks to land. Speedboats might not have the range or strength necessary to operate on open water, while fishing boats do not have the speed to attack ships. Philippine pirates operating in the open waters of the Moro Gulf, for example, use sturdier boats than those in other parts of the country.[74] Areas with many small islands provide hideouts for pirates, and enable them to minimize the time they spend on the water, when it is difficult to mask their activities, especially after they have made away with the loot. In April 2004, Indonesian police captured a syndicate composed of seven people, including the leader. Their modus operandi included moving from island to island, and attacking ships carrying palm oil, and solar, as well as standard cargo ships.[75] Another captured pirate, whose gang had preyed on fishing boats in the waters between Sumatra and the Riau Islands, an area that is studded with hundreds of small islands, admitted that there were four coherent pirate gangs that originated from Tanjung Balai Asahan (one of the main ports in the area), each with their own designated territory for piracy. Due to the crowded conditions for passing ships, he boasted that his gang was able to attack at least twenty fishing boats in the course of five hours before being caught.[76] In addition, the many narrow straits of Southeast Asia mean that ships must slow down to pass through, making them easier targets for pirates. Many of these straits are shared by two countries— Singapore, Malaysia, and Indonesia in the west, and the Philippines, Indonesia, and Malaysia in the east. Most pirate attacks, from looking at the International Maritime Organization data, do not take place in international waters, but when pirates have borders nearby, they often take advantage of them.[77] These factors lead to piracy hot spots, although in general, the larger syndicates are able to attack ships in open water, at full speed. For the hijacking syndicates, disposal of a ship and its cargo is often a transnational operation, and once they seize the ship, they immediately set about crossing the border to another country.

Logistics: Disposing of the Ship and Cargo

What the pirates do with the ship and cargo after the deed is where pirate syndicates intersect with what we have already seen with large-scale terrorist organizations such as Jemaah Islamiyah. Solving the problem of moving people and material across international borders under state hostility requires friends within the relevant governments, or a support network and geographic advantages along the relevant borders. When it was moving explosives and recruits between the Philippines and various parts of Indonesia, Jemaah Islamiyah took great care to use legitimate routes when possible and to build illicit infrastructure when necessary. Where it could attack was largely a function of these support structures' continued existence.

The pirate syndicate structures for disposing of hijacked ships and cargo are as territorially widespread as they need to be to do the job. Certain kinds of cargo and ships require more complex networks, and thus more territorially expansive support structures. The causation is not entirely one way—syndicates with large networks would presumably be more likely to seize high-value ships. But the point stands: as with Jemaah Islamiyah, the pirate syndicates that wow the world and convince analysts of the triumph of the technologies of globalization find it necessary to build extensive networks to move along illicit routes or pass through legitimate state-controlled chokepoints. In the process they become vulnerable to interdiction and, under pressure, find it difficult to hold specific transnational links together when the crackdowns begin.

When hijacking a ship, and disposing of the cargo and the ship itself, the pirate syndicates operate on top of pre-existing merchant networks. Ship owners establish connections with brokers, ports, and ship repair firms around the world so that they can more efficiently move their cargo and repair their ships as they sail through the more commonly used shipping routes. This network is invaluable for legitimate ship owners in avoiding the choking formal bureaucracy that characterizes so many developing countries, especially in Southeast Asia. The dark side of red tape-cutting informal networks is the small cargo brokers and ship repair firms that deal with anyone who brings in a ship and cargo with no questions asked, even if it is obvious that something is not quite right about the ship.[78]

It is unusual for competent pirates to hijack a ship and its cargo without having a pre-arranged buyer (assuming it is not intended for their own use), or a quick and convenient way of selling off the loot. In this they mirror the legitimate shipping industry, where ship owners specialize in certain kinds of cargo, and do not move their ships without having cargo and a destination in hand.[79] Before they hijack a ship, syndicates often have buyers for the cargo and ship, agents for the new crew, and ports for alterations lined up. Any falsified documents needed for transactions are also prepared in advance so that the new "owners" can become overnight ship owners, using temporary registrations from Belize, Panama, or Honduras. Although some pirates have been incompetent enough to hijack a ship before finding a buyer, they do not waste any time shopping a phantom ship around after they have captured it.[80]

Some cargos are more difficult to dispose of than others, especially if the cargo is not a common commodity. Different kinds of cargo require larger or smaller operations to dispose of them. This can affect the size and spread of the network—with logistically more complex cargos, some pirates may choose to take a pass, especially when a crackdown is in progress. Others will try to pull it off. In June 2005, ten pirates boarded a diesel oil tanker—en route from Singapore to Myanmar—off the coast of Langkawi, Malaysia, having been alerted to the ship by two members of the crew. Police hypothesized that an international syndicate was responsible, because unloading the tanker's diesel would require a large buyer.[81] When the pirates make off with more moderate amounts of oil or gas, they can sell it in a nearby village, and in theory they can always divide the cargo and repackage it to avoid suspicion. But any kind of cargo in sufficient quantity could generate suspicion. When in 2005 660 tons of tin ingots worth US$4.5 million were hijacked by pirates, the International Maritime Bureau notified ports in the region to be on the lookout for that amount of tin.[82] In the case of oil or other chemicals, the pirates often have other ships on standby, ready to transfer the oil at sea.

One of the larger pirate gangs in Indonesia, for example, led by a certain Captain Buang, hailed from Palembang in southern Sumatra, and attacked ships in the Bangka Strait more than once. On the night of 23 April 2003, the twenty pirates of the gang lay in wait in the Bangka Strait after having left in two speedboats from their base near Sungai Musi. Upon arriving in Tanjung Buyut, they waited for two hours until the *MT Tirta Gama* happened by, with 2,000 tons of palm oil and nineteen crewmembers, bound for Cirebon from Palembang. Sixteen pirates from the two speedboats then climbed up and took the ship at gunpoint, eventually herding the crew into one room inside the ship. The hijacked ship headed for Malaysian waters, and after three days was met by the *MT Soraya*, onto which the pirates spent eight hours offloading the palm oil.[83] Every transnational link involves crossing a border, and means having to deal with or evade another state. At-sea transferring has the advantage of minimizing the number of different states (or local authorities) that the pirates have to deal with, because the transfer takes place in international waters, or at the least, out of the sight of naval warships, but increases the operation's logistical intricacy. This is the same situation faced by GAM once it ran into hostility in Thailand—it minimized any contact with Thai authorities as it smuggled weapons across the Strait of Malacca by meeting the suppliers halfway across the Strait. The disadvantage of this approach is plain for both pirates and GAM: the organizations had to provide their own logistical infrastructure, and their territorial scope was limited inasmuch they could not easily use legitimate infrastructure to move around.

Agents can arrange warehouses for temporary or more permanent storage of the pilfered cargo, find buyers if necessary, and handle distribution from the warehouses. Sometimes the syndicates also need people in a given port to hide the ship, although this is not always true. The intricacies of disposing of

cargo can be illustrated in the foibles of a 2005 tin ingot-stealing pirate syndicate. The Indonesian syndicate hijacked at least three ships carrying tin ingots,
and owned by the same owner, in the Bangka Strait area, which is probably an
indication that they had an insider within the organization, or were based locally in the Bangka Strait. In one incident, in April, they hijacked a ship going
toward Singapore, and sailed it to Pasir Gudang, in southern Johor, Malaysia.
Their pre-planning was typical of pirate syndicates: they had an agent or agents
who secured a warehouse in Pasir Gudang in which to store the ingots, and even
found a pilot to guide the ship into the port. Once docked, the pirates forced the
crew at gunpoint to stay silent and move the tons of tin to the warehouse over
of several days. Their mistake was to sail the ship into Indonesian waters, and let
the crew and ship go before they had split up the tin cargo and moved the ingots
away from Pasir Gudang. Police found the tin still in the warehouse, and caught
the pirates. It was unclear how the pirates managed to have their false documents
accepted by the Pasir Gudang port authorities.[84]

The Pasir Gudang incident illustrates how even large-scale pirates depend on
legitimate infrastructure unless it is necessary to use illicit routes. Assuming the
pirates are not prepared to offload the cargo at sea (which requires at least one
cargo ship of their own, plus additional equipment), they have to find a port. It
is extremely difficult to sell cargo straight off a hijacked ship, which is why pirates
so frequently look for ports to store the cargo before sending it to the buyer.[85]
In recent years, most transformations have been done in shipyards, where the
pirates grind the label off the ship.[86] Usually, but not always, the offloading and/
or repainting port is not in the same country as the attack or, if it is in the same
country as the attack, at least nowhere nearby. In years past, Malaysia, or at least
its border regions, seemed to be the country of choice for repainting and re-
naming ships hijacked around Indonesia. One analyst said that in Tawau, East
Malaysia, he asked officials about the ships that were repainted and renamed in
the area, and the Malaysian officials denied that they had anything to do with it.
Rather, they said, the transformation of the hijacked ships into phantom ships
took place just off Tawau, on the island in the river that separates Indonesia from
Malaysia, on the Indonesian side.[87] The Tawau area is poorly controlled by both
Malaysia and Indonesia.

To solve the problem of pirates repainting ships, in theory, all larger ships
should have embossed registration numbers that can be seen through binoculars, and are extremely difficult to remove. Smaller ports, however, often do not
enforce the law, as this requires crosschecking the registration and paperwork
they would rather avoid.[88] Thus, pirates who do not have the resources to offload
cargo and disguise the ships at sea must use legal ports. They are dependent on
the transportation infrastructure of the host nation, on the physical geography

of the region (border areas with confusing jurisdictions), and on the host nation's ports thinking little of the threat of piracy to ignore sketchy ships. The advantage for them is that they do not need to provide their own infrastructure. The disadvantage is that their options are limited—they can either bribe officials, or if that is impossible, hope to avoid the attentions of the state. Their situation is precarious.

The target areas of the pirate syndicates affect their choice of port for repainting and offloading. If the pirate syndicate is planning on selling the cargo or ship far away from the attack, its contacts have to spread out accordingly, and the intermediate port might be at a third point removed from either the attack or the destination port. The larger operations go quite far afield. The less sophisticated, and smaller-scale operations might not stray very far when disguising their stolen ships. One informant talked about how his boss's ship was once stolen in Batam, and his boss had had to hurry over to a certain *pelabuhan tikus,* also in Batam, where pirates were known to take their hijacked ships, in order to recover it before it was altered in such a way that even the owner could not identify it. Reportedly, the entire process would not have taken more than a couple of days.[89] In another case in June 2005, the tug and barge combination *Sumber Power VI* and *Limin XII* were hijacked from a port in Batam. Several days later, the Indonesian navy was successful in buying the ships through a sting operation. The syndicate, which included at least four people, and was led by one Dedy, had been planning the attack for a month. They had already changed the names of the ships, and created false documents.[90] Why do not all pirate gangs leave the country from which they hijack a ship? Pirates can evade the state by crossing borders and moving into a different port, but this increases the size of the target area, and the complexity of the operation.

Pirate syndicates do take advantage of the tools of globalization for communication and the movement of people. The logistics of disposing of ships and cargo present two countervailing territorial pressures. Depending on the pirates' ambitions and the type of cargo and ship to be sold, they may require a territorially expansive network. Conversely, when they actually hijack a ship or take its cargo, they must move across the ocean, and depend on geographical features that are difficult for states to police, or on legitimate ports that have high thresholds for illegal behavior, and this limits their overall movements. We will see how this plays out in two case studies.

Integration: *Bahar XI* and *Bahar XXVIII*

In March 2005, a Singaporean who referred to himself as Mr. Lee contacted a pirate broker in Batam, and met with him in Kedai Kopi Indah, behind Hotel

Harmoni, in Batam to negotiate for pirates to hijack a specific pair of ships.[91] On 23 April 2005, Mr. Lee took a ferry from Singapore to Batam, and met with the pirate broker, Doni, from 10 am to 11 am, first at the Fortuna Hotel, and later in a nearby café. Here Mr. Lee gave Doni the departure time, location, and route of the tug and barge combination to be taken, the *Bahar XI* and the *Bahar XXVIII*, as well as a down payment for his gang's piracy services. The remaining balance was due upon successful delivery of the targeted ships to an unspecified port in Thailand, where a foreign buyer had already agreed to take possession of the barge and its cargo.[92] After the meeting, Mr. Lee apparently returned to Singapore, and the pirate broker and his friends, all of whom were unemployed Indonesian sailors, gathered weapons and rented a small, fast boat.[93] That night, the *Bahar XI* and the *Bahar XXVIII* left Batu Ampar, carrying tin ingots bound for Kalimantan, and were followed by the pirates. Shortly after leaving Batu Ampar, the pirates set upon the ships in the waters around Karas Island, between Batam and Bintan.[94]

As it was the middle of the night, most of the crewmembers were sleeping, and they were taken by surprise. The pirates threatened the crew with homemade weapons, and at first asked only for the ships' official documents, but then demanded not only the documents, but also the ships themselves. The crewmembers surrendered, the pirates put them ashore on an empty island (*pulau kosong*) near Lindung Island off the coast of Bintan. Unfortunately for the pirates, the *pulau* was not *kosong* enough, and the crew went to get help. One of the crewmembers had a SIM card with him, and inserted it into the cell phone of the village headman, whereupon he called the ship owners, Habco Primatama, in Pekanbaru, who in turn called Batam's marine police. The marine police immediately set out and caught up with the hijacked tug and barge combination north of Bintan, as the pirates were trying to leave Indonesian waters, bound for Thailand. The pirates worked fast. In the eight hours that they had possession of the *Bahar* twins, they had already repainted the tug boat from black to white, and had renamed it *Ayu*.[95] Five of the pirates escaped in the rented boat, but seven were caught, including the pirate broker.[96] According to the police, the syndicate would have stood to make the equivalent of US$1,000,000 from the sale of the tin ingots if they had gotten away with it. The Batam police attempted to find Mr. Lee by combing the immigration records for that day, but too many Mr. Lees had entered on ferries from predominantly Chinese Singapore, even if that was his real name, and the trail went cold.[97]

The *Bahars* incident illustrates the complexity associated with transnational piracy syndicates. This particular operation was quite typical: the syndicate operated from a third country, and had taken an order before the hijacking took place. That the pirates also had excellent information about the movements and timing of the ships is especially interesting inasmuch as the ships were brand new—they had just been constructed in the PT Bandar Victory Shipyard in Sekupang, Batam.[98] Knowledge of the ships' movements could not have been derived from observing their past behavior. Such inside knowledge suggests a complex operation. The nerve center of the syndicate appears to have been in Singapore, and the financier (or one of his underlings) had arranged for a buyer to take possession of the barge and cargo in Thailand, a country different from the location of the financier, the pirates, and the *Bahars,* which were being employed solely within Indonesian waters. Note here, however, that the portion of the plot's command and control structure that required the greatest amount of secrecy—the negotiations about the exact details of the hijacking, and the down payment—took place via a face-to-face meeting after a ferry ride between Singapore and Batam. As with many of Jemaah Islamiyah's plots, although the tools of globalization allow the command and control structure of an organization to be anywhere in the world, in practice, command and control, and the actual logistics of the operation are territorially linked due to the plotters' desires for secrecy and face-to-face meetings. From the authorities' side, the tools of globalization, in the form of cell phone calls from a small, rural island in the middle of Indonesia to a company in yet another part of the country, allowed them to close in and capture the pirates before they were able to get to Thailand. Modern technology does not always make illicit transnational organizations stronger.

Integration: *Petro Ranger*

Even more territorially expansive operations are not unheard of. On 17 April 1998, the *Petro Ranger,* owned by a Singaporean company Petroships Ltd., was hijacked by a gang of pirates after it had left Singapore. It was to deliver 11,000 metric tons of kerosene to Vietnam.[99] Two southern mainland Chinese refined oil smugglers decided that "they wanted to smuggle someone else's oil," and organized a one-off syndicate to do just that.[100] They contacted Indonesian Chinese middlemen, who proceeded to hire ethnically Indonesian pirates, and equipped them with modern boats and communications gear. The pirates then hijacked the *Petro Ranger* in the South China Sea, and brought lighters—smaller cargo ships, which were Chinese-registered—in order to siphon off the kerosene.[101] It was here that they realized their logistical mistake when it turned out the *Petro Ranger*'s cargo was more than their own ships could handle. They were only able to offload 4,000 metric tons of kerosene at sea before they headed to their destination of Haikou, Hainan province, where the syndicate heads were planning on offloading and selling the rest of the kerosene. During the entire time the pirates controlled the ship, they held the original crew hostage. When the Chinese officials came aboard at anchor in Haikou, one of the hostages managed to convey the situation to the police, who then arrested the pirates. The original crew was eventually freed with the ship, but the Chinese government offloaded and impounded the remaining 7,000 metric tons of kerosene, supposedly as insurance to make sure the crew testified. The Vietnamese owner of the kerosene refused to deal with the Chinese government, leaving the insurers to take a big loss, while the Indonesians were released without charges several months later. The syndicate heads were charged with an unknown crime, but were soon released as well.[102] At this point, piracy was not a priority for the Chinese government.

Clearly the pirates had good information, excellent coordination skills and communication technology, and an expansive transnational network, with nodes in Indonesia, China, and either Singapore or Vietnam. Yet the *Petro Ranger* incident highlights the logistical complexity of a hijacking operation. The pirates themselves, even as professional smugglers, were overwhelmed by it, and incorrectly calculated their ability to absorb so much oil. Creating their support infrastructure, as they did when offloading the kerosene, was difficult enough that the pirates took the ship to a legitimate port to complete the deed, where they ran into trouble. Even in a politically friendly environment (as China during the incident was), large-scale transnational piracy is not as easy as it looks, although it is territorially spread out. This becomes especially important as we look at how pirate syndicates respond to crackdowns, and the political environment that pirate syndicates would encounter once the Chinese central government began to take a darker view of local government corruption and organized crime in mid-1998.

The effects of modern technology are not as evident for groups with as small an operational area as for mundane smugglers. However, they face the same tradeoffs between efficiency and stealth as groups with larger ambitions. For their part, large-scale pirate syndicates make use of modern transportation and communications, just as JI and GAM did, to establish networks in countries that are sometimes far apart, although a paucity of information limits our ability to draw strong conclusions about the nature of many parts of these syndicates. Yet when it comes to the logistics of hijacking and disposing of a ship, the pirates are just as dependent on geography and friendly political conditions as terrorists and separatists are, perhaps even more so.

When GAM smuggled weapons into Aceh, and when Jemaah Islamiyah set off bombs in Indonesia, the main problem they faced at the transnational level was crossing borders. Once they had actually crossed the final international border, their dependence on the state for modern transportation and communications infrastructure or, barring that, the costs associated with avoiding state power, both declined markedly.

Both pirates and smugglers, however, have an additional step after crossing their final border and reaching their destination: they must find a way to dispose of their ships or illicit goods profitably, and for this they must often depend on a legitimate, or at least semi-legitimate market infrastructure. Even if criminals have completely open access to telecommunications and air, land, and sea routes, if they have no one to buy their goods, their operation is a failure. This dependence has the effect of increasing the salience of legitimate chokepoints, as market infrastructure, for obvious reasons, is often co-located with communications and transportation infrastructure. Unlike JI and GAM's (costly and slow) illicit infrastructures, pirates in particular cannot set up markets on their own that can absorb entire ships or thousands of tons of purloined cargo. Terrorists, separatists, and criminals share many of the same routes and methods as they move around Southeast Asia, but it is pirates who would theoretically be the least tied to any given piece of territory. This is because they have large target areas, no desire to control or govern territory, and are both the most constrained by and dependent on the chokepoints created by the technologies of globalization. The stories of both the *Petro Ranger* and of the *Bahars* are of syndicates that moved from legitimate port to legitimate port in the planning and execution of the attack, and disposal of their loot, hoping that they could slip in under the radar. Where they actually did avoid state-controlled infrastructure, they were either overwhelmed or did a poor job of hiding their tracks. Despite their radically different motivations, the logic by which technology and territory affect the transnational activities of smugglers and pirates is the same as for terrorists and separatists.

FLUIDITY AND RIGIDITY
IN CLANDESTINE TRANSNATIONAL
ORGANIZATIONS

The political environments of clandestine transnational organizations change, if for no other reasons than because formerly friendly states crack down or because hostile states fall apart or turn their attention elsewhere. In large part because of crackdowns, the groups discussed in this book have a checkered record of success: Jemaah Islamiyah's leaders Abu Bakar Ba'asyir and Abdullah Sungkar fled into exile in Malaysia, GAM was kicked out of Aceh, pirate syndicates were rolled up, and smugglers faced increased and unwanted police attention. This chapter traces what happens to the groups next, and seeks to answer some vexing questions. How did Jemaah Islamiyah transform from an Indonesian-based branch of Darul Islam into a multinational organization fighting for a pan-Southeast Asian Islamic caliphate? Why did it contract so precipitously after 2001? Why did GAM not evolve in the same way? What happens to pirates and smugglers' transnational footprints when governments crack down on different parts of their support networks? Although the technologies of globalization do allow groups to move around the world, not all CTOs have global or even transnational ambitions. Furthermore, not all groups move out of the way (to other countries) when crackdowns come. Sometimes they successfully shift their tactics and locations; sometimes they simply disappear.[1]

Clandestine groups under pressure can adapt their tactics, targets, and organizational structures, all of which present both benefits and risks for illicit groups. Changing the organizational structure of a group makes sense, as certain kinds of organizational structures can make terrorist groups or criminal syndicates more adaptable. This is, in fact, the main point of much of the literature on clandestine organizations as networks, although not all networks are equally adaptable.[2] Wheel-based networks, with a leader at the center who coordinates most of a syndicate's activities, are more efficient at moving illicit goods, but are susceptible to takedown when the leader is removed from the network. Conversely, snake-like networks are more difficult to destroy, but are less efficient, and take longer to adapt, due to the absence of a central coordinating body.[3] Yet a structural approach does not explain all of a CTO's behavior. Both Jemaah Islamiyah and GAM could be loosely described as wheel-based networks, but only JI metastasized into a major transnational threat.

Counterterrorism analysts also examine changes in CTOs' tactics and targets.[4] Terrorist groups, for instance, appear to have shifted toward high-casualty attacks on softer targets over the past few decades.[5] They have also attempted to switch to forms of communication that are more difficult for state intelligence and police agencies to compromise, and have turned to suicide bombers in response to hardened targets.[6] Adaptation in tactics and targeting, like that in organizational structure, need not be of one type. Jemaah Islamiyah, for instance, incrementally improved its operational security from 2000 to 2004, and made its bombs both more reliable and higher in explosive power, although it did not adapt particularly well in its choice of targets given its incremental change in tactics, which explains the relative ineffectiveness of the 2004 attack on the well-fortified Australian embassy.[7] Seen another way, although its targeting effectiveness improved only marginally, JI's shift from supporting Muslims in religious conflicts (which led to its involvement in Poso and Ambon, and the Christmas Eve 2000 bombings) to putting together major bomb attacks, such as the Bali bombings, represented a major innovation in targeting as part of a larger strategy.[8] Examining targeting preferences and tactics is particularly useful for counterterrorism analysts who are trying to determine how terrorist groups might adapt their behavior in response to increased physical protection measures and law enforcement scrutiny. This approach is less useful when comparing how different kinds of groups adapt: smugglers as a rule do not blow things up, so an analysis of changes in the nature of bomb attacks would not be germane.

Conceiving of CTOs structurally as aggregations of transnational activities, and thinking of transnational activities as consisting of nodes connected by flows complement what we know about structural adaptation, at least in terms of how CTOs' structures, regardless of whether they are networks or hierarchies, are arrayed across different countries. Whether a given group is better described as a network or a more coherent organization, the cells that make up the group have to be located somewhere, and they have to find ways to move people, goods, and information between those cells. We can also build in the geographical dimension of shifts in tactics and targeting, if we consider tactics to be the methods that CTOs use as they move along legitimate or illicit transnational routes, and targeting to be the countries within CTOs' target areas. Understood in this way, we can thus conceptually subsume changes in the organizational structure, targeting, and tactics of a CTO within changes in its transnational territorial configuration and ambitions.

What actually causes illicit groups to adapt varies. Learning can, for instance, be precipitated by astute analysis of the successes and failures of previous operations. The improvement in the reliability of Jemaah Islamiyah's bombs from attack to attack is evidence of this.[9] Organizations can also learn from training programs or combat experience, both of which benefited JI and GAM over the years. External allied groups can also introduce operational and ideological innovation. Al-Qaeda's support for Jemaah Islamiyah is a case in point.[10] But not all groups have been driven to adapt their transnational footprints or their ideas about territory by training or experience with outsiders. This chapter suggests that groups' openness to changes in the location and scope of their territorial ambitions via these (and other) external factors is determined by the nature of their preexisting conceptual relationship with territory. If they are indeed to open to change, change can be catalyzed, or at least made possible, by the success or failure of their activities, and the process by which they attempted to carry out those activities. In essence, changes in CTOs' transnational territorial configurations can lead, indirectly, to them expanding, contracting, or shifting not only the locations, routes, and methods of their transnational activities, but also their ideas about where they should be.

Success, Failure, and Changes in Territorial Ambitions

State hostility and subsequent failure in the face of a lack of geographical advantages mean that there is often a difference in where a CTO wants to be, and where it actually is. This opens up the possibility of changes in the location and size of the CTO's target area. The CTO's territorial intentions and the initial size of its target area affect the susceptibility of that target area to change. The network's target area is rigid if it has smaller territorial ambitions and concrete plans to govern territory. However, the network's target area is flexible if it is focused on achieving its goals over larger areas, and has no concrete plans to govern (whether it eventually seeks control of territory or not).

For an organization that has small, localized ambitions, and is focused on only part of one country, no matter what the group's territorial intentions, it is unlikely to change its target area. It is often not transnational by choice, but has been driven to reach outside of its target area for political or economic expediency. It often has a support structure in neighboring countries (or even countries far away), but it never loses sight of its original mission. For groups that seek to control territory, this is often because the small size of their target area allows them to dare to dream of seizing and holding a non-trivial portion of the territory. The criminal gangs that have no desire to control territory often maintain just enough contact with people in other countries to get the job done and make money, but do not necessarily have an established network of their own outside of their preferred region. As previous chapters demonstrated, no matter what one's goal, it is difficult to set up transnational links without ample resources, and the links tend to break easily under pressure.

Conversely, a CTO with aspirations that span a number of different countries is likely to be flexible in its territorial ambitions. When a CTO has a large target area that ranges over several countries, if it encounters resistance in one part of that territory, it can move to another part, or even further afield, while still keeping hope alive that it will soon return to its former glory. Furthermore, if the CTO's support structure is extensive enough that only part of the network is taken down in any given crackdown, the CTO can use the rest of the network to revive itself. Effectively, the larger the target area, the greater leeway the CTO has to fail in any given smaller area, and still survive. As new countries are opened up to the CTO, it may choose to build on its already expansive transnational links, and expand outward.

But the scope of a group's ambitions is not the sole determinant of its territorial or ideational adaptability. Groups that have made plans or have set up governance structures are unlikely to move from their original target area. Even if governance is not feasible, the network has organized itself in such a way as to govern a specific piece of territory, and the structure is not amenable to being replicated. It has ambitions to be an alternate state to the one currently in power, and states, even imaginary ones, do not often transpose themselves well onto other countries. In a sufficiently large country, under significant state pressure, the organization might be unable to keep itself together even in one country, and might break up into a number of semi-autonomous regional groups with smaller target areas (as happened with Darul Islam).

A similar group that has no plans to govern, or a group that has no desire to control is much more likely to change its target area under pressure. In hostile situations, like its more territorially grounded cousin, it can be exiled from its target area to more favorable political climes. But unlike organizations that have plans to govern, this kind of group (notably terrorist organizations) has a structure that is designed to spread relatively easily. Although the group's goals are concentrated in one country, nothing in the structure of the network is tied to that particular territory, and the structure itself is replicable in different contexts. Once the group is exiled, the leaders either look for better places to operate, or they continue to spread the cells in the new country (often in order to move illicitly back into the original country), and eventually it becomes realistic to expand the target area into new countries. In short, for groups with flexible target areas, their territorial ambitions often follow their illicit support structures, rather than the other way around.

I argue that outcomes of transnational activities can initiate changes in the CTO's target area. This is how seemingly minuscule groups can become transnational behemoths, and how an organization can disappear, only to reappear in a different country. In essence, although a CTO's goals influence how and where it wants to carry out which kinds of activities, and state hostility and geography affect the outcome of those operations, the operations themselves create new facts on the ground that in turn shape the CTO's target area. The more an operation requires illicit methods, the more likely it is that a successful operation in a given country will entrench that country within the network's territorial ambitions. Successful activities that make legitimate use of legitimate routes will not entrench a country in the network's target area because there are virtually no costs to the CTO, while successful activities that make illicit use of legitimate routes or that use illicit routes will. Conversely, failed operations have the potential to remove a country from an organization's target area; failed activities keep the CTO from entrenching itself in a country at all. When a CTO does have a flexible target area, failure is likely to result in the target area shrinking or being reconfigured away from the country where the CTO failed. Not only are support structures destroyed, but as the CTO rebuilds, its remaining members may demand greater focus on their own areas, leading to a contraction of the group's ambitions. This is exactly what happened to Jemaah Islamiyah after 2001.

Throughout the book I argued that building up the structures necessary to support illicit activities is harder than it looks. Less legitimate routes usually require more time, money, resources, and crucially, a network in the countries through which the CTO is moving. Although state hostility might succeed in forcing out a CTO entirely, if the CTO is nonetheless successful in operating in hostile conditions, this paradoxically could entrench it in the hostile state even more. When the CTO makes illicit use of legitimate routes, and even more so when it creates its own illicit routes, the networks that it creates to sustain its operations require a deep understanding and connection with the geography, people, and culture of the area in which the CTO is moving. When it comes to creating illicit routes, rather than simply connecting with allies over whom it has no control, the CTO might have to plant its operatives on a permanent basis if it wants to have secure access to the route. It might have to buy its own transportation equipment, and establish relationships with corrupt or sympathetic government officials. It needs safe houses, vehicles, outside sympathizers, knowledge of idiosyncratic customs, and relationships with suppliers, brokers, and buyers. In short, when the CTO's target area is flexible, the act of successfully evading the government does much to entrench the CTO in a given country, and move that country into the CTO's sights.

Jemaah Islamiyah, GAM, pirates, and smugglers all reacted differently to success and failure, but the logic of adaptation was the same. Jemaah Islamiyah metastasized into a larger, more dangerous organization because it was not focused on governing specific pieces of territory, and its replicable cells made expansion a realistic option once it encountered pan-Islamist ideology in Afghanistan. The group then contracted once again when it began to lose its support structures in country after country. For its part, GAM did not metastasize because it wanted to govern Aceh, and had set up structures to that end. Similarly, the flexibility of maritime pirate syndicates shows how they can fail in one country and then reconfigure their support networks, while for many small-time smugglers, the effort to build a new network in a country that has cracked down may be too much to bear.

Jemaah Islamiyah

Becoming Jemaah Islamiyah

How did Jemaah Islamiyah become Jemaah Islamiyah? The shift from a branch of Darul Islam to the pan-Southeast Asian Jemaah Islamiyah was not immediate. Abdullah Sungkar began establishing his network in Malaysia in 1985 primarily to get back into Indonesia, and to support the cause of Darul Islam there. He arranged with sympathetic Malaysian businessmen for construction jobs for Indonesian members of the network, which necessitated expanding his own personal network in Malaysia. Muzahar Muhtar, for example, worked as a construction worker whenever he was in Malaysia,[11] and during his stays in Indonesia, one of his tasks was to bring *tenaga kerja*, or Indonesian guest workers, to Malaysia to work, where they could earn money for the *jemaah* (society), and by extension, the cause in Indonesia.[12]

Sungkar and Ba'asyir also began traveling around Malaysia and replicating the *usroh* network they had built in Indonesia. Nasir Abas describes how fifty Indonesians suddenly appeared at his *pesantren* in Johor Bahru in 1985. They apparently already knew his teacher (indicating that at least some connections existed between the exiles and Malaysian Islamist clerics), and proceeded to sell (or hand out) Islamist books from Indonesia, as well as invite students to discuss Islamist thought and jihad.[13] The *usroh* structure's portability and lack of geographical anchors were an asset as the Indonesians sought to build support. The structure also gave them a power base separate from their original base in Central and East Java (and Jakarta). In Sungkar and Ba'asyir's absence, Pesantren al-Mukmin was continuing to churn out students ready for jihad (although, it should be emphasized, most students had no such interest). The time it took to build the *dakwah* network can be seen in the delay in sending Malaysian recruits to Afghanistan. Nasir says that he and another Malaysian were the first non-Indonesians sent by Sungkar, and they were part of the third class.[14]

In November 1987, with the Darul Islam Imam Adah Djaelani in jail, a committee of DI leaders met in Bakaban Ciamis and made the decision to elect a new acting imam. Ajengan Masduki maneuvered his way into the top position. He appointed Ba'asyir as minister of justice, and set Sungkar in charge of bringing in foreign political and monetary support. It is not clear what Ba'asyir was supposed to do about administering justice in Indonesia from Malaysia, but Sungkar's location suited him for the job. Within the DI leadership, he had a position that virtually necessitated him building ties outside of Indonesia, which could only enhance the decreasingly Indonesian nature of his network. Another DI leader was appointed to run the program to send jihadis to Afghanistan. Due to the continuing harsh political conditions in Indonesia, Darul Islam saw in Afghanistan the opportunity for training.[15]

Sungkar and Ba'asyir's experience in Malaysia comports well with the argument up to this point. Having been forced out of Indonesia, the pair sought a country from which they could establish transnational links along both legitimate and illicit routes that avoided the power of the Indonesian state. As a geographically proximate country, Malaysia was ideal. To support these activities logistically and financially, they had to establish a new network in Malaysia, a network that would not have been necessary if they had been able to get back into Indonesia without any problems. They were able to build the network relatively quickly because the structure of their branch of DI was not concerned with governing territory, and so was replicable in new locations.

Whereas CTOs with local goals are unlikely to change either the location or scope of their ambitions, and CTOs with expansive goals are flexible in both their transnational footprints and their ideas about where they should be, groups that are focused on only one country occupy an uncomfortable middle position. Both Darul Islam and what would become Jemaah Islamiyah wanted to bring about an Islamic state in all of Indonesia. However, Darul Islam's desire to govern Indonesia and the structures it set up for that purpose contrasted with Sungkar and Ba'asyir willingness to set up cells not tied to specific pieces of territory. It was this difference that led to their divergent paths. Sungkar and Ba'asyir had a flexible target area, and an entrenched network in Malaysia. They were ripe for an expansion of their territorial ambitions into Malaysia, at the very least. What they needed was an immediate catalyst. This came in the form of the group's training in Afghanistan.

The Importance of Afghanistan

The story of JI's training experiences in Afghanistan, and the routes recruits took to get there, suggest why, when Jemaah Islamiyah later expanded its territorial ambitions, those ambitions included Malaysia but not Afghanistan or Pakistan. Moving between Indonesia and Malaysia, Sungkar's recruits and couriers encountered a great deal of state hostility, and had to build networks that would allow them to take illicit routes dependent on topographical features (such as the Strait of Malacca) and less policed routes (such as the ferries that operated in the same area).

There were no such concerns moving from Malaysia to Pakistan, as evidenced by Nasir's trip on Aeroflot. Abdullah Sungkar traveled a number of times to Pakistan and Afghanistan, and in fact he had the alumni from the first classes of Camp Saddah set up a DI reception center specifically for meeting, acclimatizing, and transporting recruits to the camps. Zulkarnaen was in charge of this aspect of the network's operations, and was so overt as to live in a house in Pabbi village near Peshawar, and bring his wife over after some time. What is interesting is the sensitivity of the training to the political environment. In 1989, after the death of mujahidin-friendly Pakistani leader Zia ul-Haq, the new Prime Minister Benazir Bhutto was considerably more hostile, and no new recruits arrived that year. They preferred to avoid Pakistan entirely rather than come covertly.[16] Members of the network were told to conceal their movements or identities in the initial stages of transiting Malaysia. When questioned by Arabs and Afghans in the camps in Afghanistan, the Indonesians were told to identify themselves as Malaysians, or as "Filipino mujahidin" for fear that Suharto's intelligence operatives might hear about them and come looking. Although Suharto's tentacles did not extend to South Asia, fear of him apparently did.[17] But except for these extreme security measures, because it was difficult to do large-scale training on the Pakistan-Afghanistan border without at least a neutral Pakistani government, the recruits took a legal route and did not build an illicit support network in Pakistan or Afghanistan. Consequently, Jemaah Islamiyah did not entrench itself in the country.

Yet Jemaah Islamiyah did expand its ambitions as a result of its time in Afghanistan. Sungkar's network went into Afghanistan in 1985 as a faction of Darul Islam, and came out as Jemaah Islamiyah, working toward a pan-Southeast Asian caliphate. Sungkar began sending recruits to Afghanistan almost as soon as he got to Malaysia. But according to Nasir Abas, when he arrived in Afghanistan in 1987, he and Mat Beduh were the first Malaysians sent by Sungkar. The previous two classes and the other students in Nasir's class were all Indonesians sent through Malaysia, suggesting that for at least two years after Sungkar and Ba'asyir escaped to Malaysia, they were still focused on Indonesia and NII rather than a wider Southeast Asian caliphate, or at least remained dependent on an Indonesian-dominated network to recruit fighters for training.[18] How did this change happen? One theory is that the shared experience of being in Afghanistan solidified a sense of Southeast Asian-ness among the recruits. Segregated as they were from the rest of the non-Afghan mujahidin, not usually speaking Arabic, Dari, or Pashto in a country with a plethora of strange new experiences, they built a solidarity that differentiated them from the Arabs and Afghans.[19] The only common language spoken among the Southeast Asians was English, and in some cases dialects of Malay. But as Nasir notes, at first he thought himself quite different from the Indonesians (and presumably the Thais and Filipinos). However, through time and shared experiences, he became used to their culture, mannerisms, and ways of speaking, and developed a loyalty to the others in the camp that transcended the more ethereal notions of jihad and caliphates.[20] Many of the transnational personal connections that were to show up later in Southeast Asia were forged in Afghanistan. It was here that Fathur Rahman al-Ghozi met two MILF mujahidin—a connection that International Crisis Group argues played a role in JI's decision to move its training base to Mindanao.[21] In addition, Hambali's first contacts with al-Qaeda occurred while he was serving in a liaison capacity in Pakistan, and he was a member of al-Qaeda's leadership committees by 1996.[22]

Socializing with Arabs, Afghans, and other Southeast Asian mujahidin in Afghanistan and Pakistan probably helped solidify a Southeast Asian identity and allowed for transnational personal relationships that would later prove instrumental in JI's spread. However, this cannot fully explain the transformation. Although all the recruits in Afghanistan would most likely be willing to work toward an Islamic state, not all were interested in fighting for it outside of their countries. Out of the Southeast Asians who trained in Afghanistan, only Sungkar's network actually made the leap to regional ambitions. The Filipinos, Thais, and other Indonesians were glad to accept help from outsiders to build their Islamic states in Mindanao, Pattani, and Indonesia as part of the global caliphate, but they did not have visions of being members of an actual transnational organization.

Although Sungkar's group had ambitions to control an entire country (Indonesia), it had no structures designed to govern specific pieces of territory. With such a non-territorial structure, the group was open to new target area-expanding ideologies, and it encountered that in al-Qaeda's pan-Islamic ideology in Afghanistan. Sungkar's network was the only group sending recruits to Afghanistan from Southeast Asia that was physically separated from its original target area. With an organizational structure that was capable of top-down command and control, but was also geographically portable and scalable, and the beginnings of a Malaysian network Sungkar and Abu Bakar Ba'asyir had built up to support the DI cause in Indonesia, the infrastructure for a transnational network was in place to make the shift from Indonesia to Southeast Asia realistic.

As Sungkar attracted more non-Indonesian recruits, his proclaimed goal expanded to all of Muslim Southeast Asia, with Indonesia as the initial base from which was to spring the forces that would conquer or convert the rest of the region. It is unclear whether the change was initially only instrumental. Nasir recounts how when he first went to Afghanistan, he was concerned that all the other recruits seemed to talk about was Negara Islam Indonesia. Nasir states that if Abdullah Sungkar had been solely focused on Indonesia, he would not have joined—an admission that NII was simply not enough to motivate non-Indonesians. Nasir was assured that true Islam did not have borders, and that Indonesia was merely the first country that had to be converted; the rest, including Malaysia, would follow.[23] If the original shift was instrumental, by the time Jemaah Islamiyah was founded as a separate organization, the transformation was complete, solidified by the personal ties built in Afghanistan: the network had not only Indonesian, but also Malaysian and Singaporean members, and Filipino affiliates.

Post-2001 Contraction

Jemaah Islamiyah actually has arguably changed its territorial ambitions twice, not only in exile in the 1980s, but also since 2001, when it has contracted to a shadow of its former self because it failed in too many places. The group's decline outside of Indonesia and the Philippines began shortly after 9/11, when the Australian, Singaporean, and Malaysian governments began rounding up JI members. The immediate effect of the crackdowns was to cut Jemaah Islamiyah off from its funding sources in the three countries, and deprive it of the ability to plan and control operations in Singapore and peninsular Malaysia.[24] Yet, over time, the crackdowns also removed those countries from JI's operational area, and began the organization's conceptual return to its Darul Islam roots. With such a widespread network, JI could afford to fail in one country, and still operate as a coherent organization in the remaining non-hostile areas, but its lack of successful illicit routes into those countries gradually made it less realistic for it to consider those countries part of its target area.

The most straightforward reason for JI's shift was a clearheaded assessment of its options. JI operatives conceded that for the present time Singapore, Malaysia, and Australia were out of their reach. It lost significant fundraising capabilities, but it did not collapse.[25] It remained unbowed, and it was still able to launch significant attacks in the countries remaining open to it, namely Indonesia and the Philippines. In early 2002, an alleged operative for JI claimed that JI's mistake had come in miscalculating the ability of the Malaysian and Singaporean governments to crack down on the organization's cells operating within their borders. He said that JI had also overestimated the degree to which Malaysia and Singapore's Muslim communities would be moved to support groups like JI after the United States began its operations in Afghanistan, an assessment confirmed by Malaysian officials.[26] Indonesia, he said, would be different, because even moderate clerics were strongly against U.S. operations. As a result, JI had shifted to an Indonesia-first strategy, and would let Singapore and Malaysia alone for the time being.[27]

Jemaah Islamiyah also had less strategic reasons for contracting. Largely cut off from other countries, except for the Philippines, where it had no formal Filipino members, JI was forced to replenish its top ranks from Mantiqi II members. The crackdowns in Malaysia and Singapore had robbed JI of most of its Singaporean and Malaysian members. Many of the Mantiqi I members who fled to Indonesia, such as Mukhlas, were actually Indonesian. Just as a growing non-Indonesian constituency in JI's formative years had helped along an expansion in the group's territorial ambitions to include all of the Muslim parts of Southeast Asia, so the crackdowns meant that the impetus for such an expansive target area no longer remained, and it contracted.

The non-bombing cells were still committed to violence, but they made a tactical decision to stop bombings and engage in jihad in Poso as they built the foundations of the Indonesian Islamic State.[28] The Indonesian wing of JI also planned to grow connections to other radical groups in Indonesia, which only served to re-emphasize its Darul Islam roots.[29] The violent parts of Jemaah Islamiyah increasingly relied on non-JI networks to operate, networks that were focused exclusively on one country as their target area, whether it was Indonesia or the Philippines. As JI's operational branch came to be personified by Noordin Top and Dr. Azhari in the popular media, the two reached out to Darul Islam members and other young men who could be radicalized in order to find willing participants for their bombings. Sympathetic preachers and others would bring young men to the attention of Noordin Top, who would whip them up into a suitably radical fervor, and prepare them for death, while Dr. Azhari would build the actual bombs.[30] Ring Banten, for example, one of the most militant Darul Islam factions, which had its own conduit to Mindanao for training and weapons, assisted in the Australian embassy bombing in Jakarta on 9 September 2004.[31] Jemaah Islamiyah's territorial aspirations thus shifted decisively to Indonesia.[32]

Jemaah Islamiyah had essentially ceased to exist as a CTO capable of blowing things up. It is perhaps better to think of it from this point on as three overlapping domestic networks: one concentrated in Indonesia and dedicated to ongoing bombings (its future uncertain after the death of Noordin Top in September 2009),[33] another covering the same area but more reticent about violent attacks (outside of waging jihad in Poso), and the third violent group operating in the Philippines, with limited movement into and out of Indonesia (Dulmatin was apparently able to return to Indonesia, only to be killed by police outside of Jakarta in March 2010).[34] Assuming that JI's central leadership was still operating, and engaging in education, *dakwah,* and recruitment activities, it had essentially reverted to something similar to what it was before Sungkar and Ba'asyir fled to Malaysia: a group loosely affiliated with Darul Islam, waiting for the day when its members, or their children, could rise again to continue the fight for Negara Islam Indonesia. Once a CTO has metastasized, it is not a given that it will forever remain a regional or global menace.

Gerakan Aceh Merdeka

Only so much can be said about GAM in this chapter as it managed to stay fixated on Aceh through a thirty-year insurgency. The most basic explanation for why GAM's target area never changed is that it was an ethno-nationalist organization that wanted independence for Aceh, and few separatist organizations move away from their original aspirations unless they criminalize or are swept up in larger ideological movements. This is especially true if, as some argue, GAM actually became less Islamic and more nationalistic over the course of the insurgency.[35] Extracting the territorial aspects from GAM's separatist ideology can help in making an explanation of GAM's lack of change more than a tautology, especially when compared with other groups discussed in this book. Why, after all, do separatist organizations seem so impervious to changes in their territorial ambitions?

Like Darul Islam, GAM from the beginning set up formal governance structures that were grounded in specific places in Aceh, with provincial governors, ministries, and parallel military command. Although it would be a stretch to say that GAM actually controlled any territory prior to the second rebellion, it certainly expected that, with the support of the people, it would be able to eventually. These formal structures, in effect a government-in-exile, were unique to

Aceh and could not be replicated. Like small-time smugglers, GAM was sufficiently small that it was possible for a government crackdown to push it out of its target area. In GAM's case, unlike with many smugglers, it initially lived on to fight another day. Like Jemaah Islamiyah, in its exile, GAM set about creating the structures and routes necessary to get back into its target area. But unlike Jemaah Islamiyah, the illicit smuggling, intelligence, and command and control structures it built from Thailand, Malaysia, and Indonesia proper into Aceh were different from those in Aceh itself. The GAM cells outside of Aceh were informal, often ad hoc, had more direct contact with the leadership in Sweden, and were not territorially grounded. Because GAM's reason for being was ultimately to govern territory, even if they had wanted to expand their target area to other countries or other parts of Indonesia, they would not have been able to do so on the same terms as within Aceh. The illicit structures outside of Aceh were not suitable for governing territory, and as such could not be more than peripheral to Aceh's main mission. By contrast, Jemaah Islamiyah's cells in Malaysia were similar to those in Indonesia. When Abdullah Sungkar began thinking in terms of a pan-Southeast Asian caliphate, he had the structures in place outside of Indonesia to make his campaign more than a mere fantasy.

What about external catalysts for change, such as contact with groups with different aspirations? GAM portrayed itself to the outside world as a secular nationalist organization, and although its image inside Aceh was somewhat more Islamic, mainstream GAM was sufficiently secular that the factions that broke off did so in part because they felt that Hasan Di Tiro and his allies had abandoned the idea of an Islamic state.[36] Given its secular orientation, GAM was poorly suited to ally with al-Qaeda or even tap into the idea of a larger Islamic caliphate.

But there is reason to believe that even if GAM had allied with al-Qaeda, it would not have changed the scope of its territorial ambitions. Consider the Moro Islamic Liberation Front, like GAM a separatist organization that sought to control and govern a small piece of territory. The MILF apparently sent fighters to train in Pakistan during the 1980s, just as GAM sent fighters to train in Libya. But unlike Jemaah Islamiyah, the MILF never metamorphosed into a transnational organization. Its formal governance structures could not be replicated outside of Mindanao, and it saw no benefit in recruiting non-Moros as integral members.

The desire to control and govern territory would seem to be important in how organizations adapt their transnational configurations to crackdowns and political openings. But criminal organizations typically have no desire to become anything like either GAM or JI. As we will see, the size of the networks that criminal syndicates build also matters in terms of how they adapt to state hostility.

Maritime Pirates and Smugglers

Pirates' Response to Crackdowns

With Jemaah Islamiyah and Gerakan Aceh Merdeka, it is a fairly simple matter to figure out how a given clandestine transnational organization responds to crackdowns, as both JI and GAM are fairly coherent, long-standing organizations. Primary source documentation and interviews with JI and GAM members allow us to draw solid conclusions about their thoughts at the time. With pirates, it is considerably more difficult to see how given groups adjust to changing political conditions, due to the transient nature of specific hijacking syndicates and the secrecy surrounding especially the higher echelons of the syndicates. To see how piracy syndicates fit into the argument, I look at general trends in how pirates have responded to crackdowns, and then focus on a series of three hijackings in 1998 and 2000 that suggest that large-scale syndicates do in fact adjust the configuration of their transnational support networks in response to changes in the political climate.

States and private companies can crack down in a number of ways on maritime piracy, particularly hijacking syndicates, although some of these methods are problematic. States can increase the chances of pirates being caught, and increase the penalties they receive if they are caught. They can also interfere with the usefulness of the nodes within the syndicates' logistical networks, in the form of lower police and coast guard corruption, and better enforcement at ports. For their part, ship owners can increase the difficulty in taking the ship, through anti-piracy technology, and decrease the (illicit) value of the ship and/or the cargo. In essence, they can make ships less attractive to pirates.

The immediate logical response by governments is to arrest pirates, and to increase patrolling, as Singapore, Malaysia, and Indonesia did in the Malacca Strait in 2005 and 2006 after Lloyd's of London declared the Strait a war zone, thus raising insurance premiums on all ships passing through the area.[37] But the patrols cannot go on forever, and crackdowns are rarely sustained. If no robust response comes from the authorities, pirates can entrench themselves in a region. But as with mundane smuggling, state capacity is not irrelevant, and weak countries can crack down in specific places at specific times to break groups' links, which can affect groups with small target areas disproportionately, because they have no room to fail. In East Malaysia, for example, in the early 2000s, police in Sabah arrested several local pirate gangs, and piracy declined markedly.[38]

Ship owners have been just as concerned about pirate attacks as governments, and have been somewhat more successful in making life more difficult for pirates worldwide. The International Maritime Bureau's (IMB) Piracy Reporting Centre in Kuala Lumpur, for example, is wholly funded by large shipping companies, and manned by Royal Malaysian Navy personnel twenty-four hours a day. The shipping industry has made a number of reforms, such as requiring internationally recognized ID numbers for larger ships, embossing the names of ships on their hulls, encouraging enforcement of the registration system, and installing GPS locators in their fleets. It is very difficult to change a ship's name and number when it is embossed on the stern of the ship, and can be seen through binoculars. The industry also encourages flagship states, many of which are weak, to crack down on rogue ships. In Hong Kong, in order for a ship to be added to the registry, it has to be inspected and evaluated according to risk analysis standards, and produce valid certificates, including the deletion certificate from the previous owner.[39] In addition, modern ships are often equipped with a GPS locator (ShipLoc) hidden somewhere on the ship, which can tell the owners exactly where the ship is at any given moment. Pirates can switch off the beacon if they find it, but this raises questions.[40] Inasmuch as they decrease the value of a stolen ship (and its cargo) and make it more difficult for pirates to hide once they have made off with their loot, it is possible that these measures have had more direct effect on hijacking syndicates' activities than naval or coast guard patrols. What kinds of responses should these crackdowns produce?

As with Jemaah Islamiyah and GAM, hijacking syndicates would be expected, under increasing state hostility, to move along illicit routes and to make illicit use of legitimate routes, and to depend on the physical terrain and the physical infrastructure for success. In practice, this should mean that command and control structures are less encumbered by territorial constraints than the logistics of seizing and disposing of ships and their cargo. Hijacking syndicates are limited in their command and control, because the logistical points they use are often part of their legitimate commercial networks, which are limited in scope. In theory, a banker in Rotterdam could order a ship to be hijacked in Indonesia. In practice, he probably does not have the contacts necessary to dispose of the ship in Southeast Asia.

Under pressure, Jemaah Islamiyah found its territorial ambitions shrink as its support structures were destroyed or crippled in successive countries, and its non-Indonesian members were replaced by those focused on Indonesia alone. The target areas of pirate syndicates are connected even more intimately to their actual support networks, because a region without a support network is by definition a region where no money is to be made for a syndicate; therefore such a region is outside of the syndicate's target area. In response to crackdowns both from ship owners and from states in the region, Southeast Asian hijacking syndicates appear to have adapted in two ways. First, they have moved toward operations that are less logistically complicated, and by extension require fewer transnational activities. Second, evidence indicates that they have moved into new, more politically lax geographic areas.

Many pirates have moved to less logistically complicated attacks. In practice, this means that the attacks also cross fewer international borders. They require fewer nodes spread out over fewer countries, and involve moving materials that are more difficult to detect—cargo and small boats, rather than large ships. Hijackings in Southeast Asia have declined overall, from twenty-three in 2004 to just five in 2007.[41] International Maritime Bureau officials also claim that hijackers have shifted from attacking larger ships to attacking smaller boats—tug-and-barge combinations and fishing boats—that fall below the threshold for international attention.[42] Thus, hijackings now differ in kind from those of the past. The IMB's Piracy Reporting Centre claims a success rate of 90 percent or higher in recovering hijacked cargo ships and tankers, but a very low recovery rate for smaller tugs and barges, which can be quickly disguised with the addition of a funnel or ventilator.[43] On December 31, 2004, International Maritime Organization regulations came into effect that required Automatic Identification System transponders "aboard all ships of 300 gross tonnage and upwards engaged on international voyages, cargo ships of 500 gross tonnage and upwards not engaged on international voyages and all passenger ships irrespective of size."[44] The upshot of these regulations is that the only ships not equipped with some sort of tracking device (and thus susceptible to hijacking) are fishing boats and smaller general cargo ships, which are often decades years old, are off the radar of the international shipping community, and are generally restricted to sketchier ports.[45] As a result, the IMB advises smaller boats to get ShipLoc, but the costs are too expensive for smaller operators.[46]

Ships are also hijacked solely for the cargo, which simplifies the logistics of the operation. With the new identification numbers and tracking devices, pirates are finding it more difficult to sell off hijacked ships. If there is no market for the ship, the value of the ship disappears. Thus, pirates are increasingly scrapping the ship, putting the cargo on another ship, and selling off the cargo. The pirates who unloaded the cargo in Pasir Gudang (see chapter 7), would fit this description. In 2005, just such a scuttled ship was found at the bottom of the Bangka Strait.[47] In the case of tugs, barges, and fishing boats pirates do not have to sell the ships—they can use them for smuggling operations and fishing, negating any decline in resale value. Although some groups with large target areas are capable of shifting their operational areas, the fact that they often adapt by simplifying logistics suggests that moving across the whole region under pressure is difficult. Just as JI lost close control of its network in the Philippines under pressure, anti-pirate crackdowns complicate transnational ties, either by making them precarious or cutting them off entirely. The technologies of globalization are of little help.

For instance, some pirates in Southeast Asia responded to crackdowns by moving into logistically simpler kidnapping. Kidnapping is popular in Somalia, as well as in areas of Southeast Asia with low state capacity.[48] Kidnapping requires only two nodes—the attack on the ship, and a hideout on land. Pirates can grab a captain's cell phone, and call his family demanding a ransom, thus decreasing any need for the pirates to use their own communications infrastructure. In the Malacca Strait, pirates have been known to meet people bringing the money halfway in the Strait after one week of negotiations.[49] The kidnapping pirates also run protection rackets, which are not so easily captured with incident-based data. One Malaysian researcher who did work with fishermen in the Strait of Malacca in the early 2000s found that 40 percent were paying protection money to pirates. In the event of non-payment, pirates can strip everything from the boat, and take it back to their village.[50] Merchant ships will not necessarily report a minor attack, especially in the case of quick kidnapping, or hostage taking, because they do not want to lose time. An increase in reports of attacks also increases their insurance premium.[51] In all these cases, the shift in tactics—hijacking smaller ships, kidnapping, and selling just the cargo—allows a decrease in the number of support cells, and thus in the number of transnational routes that must be used, even if the networks remain geographically spread out. But the pirates can also move to politically friendly areas. That is, they can change the location of the nodes, something the small-time smugglers do not do.

On 27 September 1998, the *Tenyu,* carrying fifteen Chinese and South Korean crewmembers, and US$15 million worth of aluminum ingots, left Kuala Tanjung in Sumatra bound for South Korea, and promptly disappeared. Three months later, Chinese police found a vessel called the *Sanei 1* moored in Zhangjiagang in China's Jiangsu province. *Sanei 1* aroused suspicion for several reasons. The crew was entirely Indonesian; the ship was largely rusty, with the exception of several freshly painted places; a *Sanei 1* did exist, but operated solely in Japan; and the *Tenyu*'s serial number was on the ship's engine.[52] The Indonesian crewmen claimed that they had come on board the ship in Myanmar on the orders of a Singaporean, and had no idea that the ship had been hijacked. Despite the fact that the real crew had disappeared, and was presumed murdered, the Chinese government released them without charges, and repatriated them to Indonesia in July 1999, to the outrage of the IMB and the shipping industry.[53]

Three months later, at least one of the Indonesian pirates in the *Tenyu* incident was found to be sailing another hijacked ship, the *Alondra Rainbow.*[54] This provides an opportunity to observe the transnational behavior of at least part of a hijacking syndicate over time (although there is no evidence either way that the same financier was behind both hijackings). The *Alondra Rainbow* incident is perhaps the best-known pirate hijacking in recent history, and an analysis of the incident should help illustrate the transnational structure of a well-developed hijacking syndicate. Like many other ship hijackings, the actual hijackers were not the instigators of the plot. On 4 October 1999, a chief engineer, Burham Nanda, and a master, Christinous Mintando, both presumably Indonesian, met with an "employment agent" at a café in Batam to plan the hijacking. Soon after, the pirates left from Jakarta for Batam on the *MV Sanho* with thirty-five people, of whom twelve had swords and/or guns. After getting supplies in Batam, on 22 October the *MV Sanho* arrived in Kuala Tanjung, still in Indonesia, the same port where the *Alondra Rainbow* was taking on 7,000 metric tons of aluminum ingots. That same day, the *Alondra Rainbow* left for Miike, Japan, taking with it a pirate who had slipped on board during the loading process. Once the *Alondra Rainbow* was out to sea, the armed pirates hopped into a speedboat that was attached to the *MV Sanho,* and crept up in back of the target. At that point, the stowaway pirate let down a rope, whereupon those in the speedboat clambered aboard, and tied up the very surprised seventeen members of the *Alondra Rainbow*'s crew. After the *Sanho* pulled up next to the *Alondra Rainbow,* the pirates moved the original crew to the *Sanho.*[55]

The *Alondra Rainbow,* now with an all-pirate crew, sailed to Miri, East Malaysia within three days. They had already renamed the ship *Global Venture,* and at Miri repainted the hull black from the original blue. The day after the *Global Venture* arrived in Miri, the pirates moved 3,000 of the 7,000 metric tons of aluminum ingots to the *Bonsoon II,* which then sailed to Subic Bay in the Philippines and unloaded the ingots for a buyer. Apparently the pirates were in at least intermittent contact with the syndicate liaison, because he ordered them to go to Karachi, Pakistan (although the captain of the ship, when captured, said they were heading for Fujairah in the United Arab Emirates). They got as far as the eastern Arabian Sea before they were spotted—despite the fact that they had changed the name to the *Mega Rama*—and captured by the Indian navy on 16 November.[56] Once again, the crewmembers claimed that they were legitimate sailors, and had no idea of the provenance of the ship.

The syndicate associated with both hijackings clearly had a large target area, with contacts in many countries. The *Tenyu* incident involved pirates from Indonesia hijacking a ship bound for South Korea, and taking it to China, possibly with a financier from Singapore. The *Alondra Rainbow* network was even more extensive, with the pirates hired by someone of unknown nationality,[57] traveling through Indonesia with several support ships, disguising the ship en route and in East Malaysia, then sending the cargo to the Philippines and Pakistan and/or the United Arab Emirates. Notably missing from the hijacked *Alondra Rainbow*'s itinerary was China, in the 1990s the destination of choice for hijacked ships. Clearly the syndicate had contacts in China; why did it not use them, instead of trying to reach South Asia?

The answer is arguably connected to events in China before and after the *Cheung Son* incident. The *Cheung Son* was a Hong Kong–owned ship hijacked south of Taiwan in the South China Sea in November 1998, on the way from Shanghai to Malaysia. This was after the *Tenyu* disappeared but before the *Sanei 1* was discovered. When the bodies of the original crewmembers began washing up on the Chinese coast, police tracked down a Chinese fisherman in Fujian who had rented out his boat to a gang of pirates who were at the time celebrating in Shenzhen (across the border from Hong Kong). Upon being apprehended in a karaoke bar, the leader of the gang, all of whom were Indonesian, admitted that "an Indonesian named Roger, who worked for a Singapore shipping company" had given the gang US$350,000 for the ship and cargo.[58] This time, however, rather than releasing the pirates back to Indonesia, the Chinese government sentenced twelve of them, plus the owner of the rented boat, to death in December 1999, with the sentences being carried out in January 2000.

The *Tenyu* pirates were released after *Cheung Son* was hijacked and the *Alondra Rainbow* was stolen before the *Cheung Son* pirates were sentenced, but China's political climate had begun to change for the worse for pirates before the *Alondra Rainbow* was taken. As China's economic reforms progressed in the 1990s, local government corruption approached dangerous levels. By July 1998, the then prime minister Zhu Rongji had had enough, proclaiming at a conference of the central leadership the beginning of a large-scale crackdown on corruption, particularly in southern China, where economic development had been focused, More important for the present discussion, that was the destination of most hijacked ships that ended up in China.[59] To drive the point home, in October 1998 Zhu ordered the firing of six hundred officials in Guangdong on corruption charges.[60] Suddenly corruption, and certainly collaboration with pirates, were officially frowned on, and a number of local officials were executed.

China had turned hostile to organized criminals and the officials on whom they depended for support. The relevance of this crackdown for piracy syndicates became clear when the Chinese delegate to the International Maritime Organization outlined the measures her government had taken against pirates, including the arrest on 15 August 1999 of the kingpin of the *Cheung Son* network. This occurred on 4 October 1999, coincidentally the same day that Burham Nanda and Christinous Mintando were meeting with the pirate broker in Batam to plan the *Alondra Rainbow* attack. The International Maritime Bureau pronounced itself unsatisfied with China's anti-piracy measures, especially because the government had released the *Tenyu* suspects.[61] Nonetheless, the anti-corruption campaign, and the Chinese government's public stance against piracy seems to have made an impression on pirate syndicates who had previously used southern China as either a market or a base.

By the time the *Tenyu* syndicate took *Alondra Rainbow,* it had modified its transnational support network to bypass China, although other nodes, such as Kuala Tanjung, seem to have remained intact. Unlike small-scale smuggling gangs, transnational hijacking syndicates do not disappear under pressure—they change their tactics to render their operations less logistically intensive, and/or they shift their transnational territorial footprints to more favorable areas. Similar to JI's 2001 loss of Singaporean and Malaysian members, pirate syndicates likely found that their friends within local governments and businesses in southern China were unwilling to help. The transnational ties seem to have been cut relatively quickly, given that China has essentially disappeared from the piracy world after 2000. Denied either a market for their goods, or the port infrastructure to support disguising and turning around hijacked ships, large-scale pirate syndicates reconfigured themselves based on the remaining support nodes, and began to build support nodes and market ties in other countries.

Smugglers' Response to Crackdowns

Smugglers have the same problems with crackdowns that JI, GAM, and pirates face: transnational links break easily, legitimate infrastructure becomes risky, even unusable, and the costs of avoiding crackdowns can drastically shrink where they operate. Because small-time smugglers are often crossing only one border, if one country becomes inaccessible to them, they run the risk of shutting down entirely.

Unlike Jemaah Islamiyah or even GAM, where the government is not realistically capable of giving the organizations what they really want, fighting mundane smuggling is more straightforward, but if anything is more difficult. If states want to stop smuggling, they can first and foremost remove the reasons smugglers have for existing. They can get rid of tariffs (or at least lower them) on imported goods, so as to decrease the difference in price between two adjacent countries. When the Indonesian government lowered tariffs on electronics imports, for example, it found that the quantity of electronics smuggled decreased.[62] However, because tariffs are such a major portion of many governments' revenues, it is unlikely tariffs will be eliminated entirely, to say nothing of the interest domestic producers may have in keeping tariffs high.

States can also increase the chance smugglers have of being caught, by cracking down on corruption, or by increasing their law enforcement capabilities. Increasing state hostility should also increase the dependence that smugglers have on geographic advantages along the borders, and thus limit their methods and routes. But increasing state capacity is a much bigger problem than smuggling, and is outside the scope of this book. The Indonesian government is certainly capable of doing this in targeted areas at a local level, but certain second-order consequences of cracking down could actually spur more smuggling. When the central government cracks down on corruption, according to one knowledgeable source, the local police agencies lose their illegal income. As a result, they must operate strictly on the formal budget, and have to reduce their effective policing area, as well as operating hours.[63] Several sources also noted the hesitancy of local police forces in both Riau and Kalimantan, two of the most active smuggling areas, to crack down on smugglers too harshly because of the large numbers of local people dependent on it for their livelihood.[64] A police source in Batam, for example, said he was reluctant to shut down smugglers completely because the poor people of the island have no other way to acquire affordable everyday goods.[65]

The question of how individual smuggling syndicates respond to crackdowns or changes in state hostility requires a somewhat different answer. Organizations with larger target areas can afford to fail in one area and reconfigure their networks around the hostile country or region because they have built a transnational network of personal ties and business contacts that can successfully support activities elsewhere. By contrast, the small smuggling syndicates we are studying have not developed such outside networks. Near Medan, for example, Tanjung Balai Asahan is the primary smuggling spot. According to a practitioner source, the routes used by smugglers change with every new Sumatra Utara police chief, who cracks down on smuggling initially, and is effective for approximately a year before the smugglers figure out ways to get past him.[66] In Indonesia, especially around Sumatra, the physical landscape, in the form of many small islands, provides advantages to smugglers. But these illicit routes still move into Medan, just in less convenient and presumably more covert ways. Oftentimes, a given smuggler might not have even developed any route besides the one he uses—the smugglers who move between Malaysia and Sumatra are not the same as those who shuttle from Mindanao to Sulawesi. As we have seen in all of the case studies in this book, building a new illicit route requires not just advantageous geography, but also a support network that may be beyond the abilities of clandestine actors of limited means.

Thus, political pressure gives small-time smugglers three options. First, they can shift into goods that face less hostility. If, say, the police are cracking down on pirated VCDs, the smugglers might start bringing in rice and cooking oil. Second, they can move along more covert routes, perhaps shifting entirely to illicit routes that depend on geographical advantages of the border. Finally, they can decrease the volume of their smuggling, or even shut down their operations entirely. If the state is sufficiently competent, of course, the smugglers could have their operations forcibly shut down for them. The first and third options imply a decrease in overall smuggling for a given good in a particular location. Smugglers with small target areas have less room for failure, and they might disappear in the face of a crackdown. For the second option, we would expect that successfully shifting to more covert routes and methods might actually entrench a group in its target area, further explaining why small-time smuggling syndicates are so much less flexible than large-scale piratical hijacking syndicates or transnational terrorist groups.

To see how this actually plays out in the real world, I return to Batam to see how small-time smugglers adapt to crackdowns. Evidence shows that even in Indonesia the police are capable of applying enough pressure to criminal activities to make it not worth the smugglers' while, at least during a highly publicized crackdown. The story of Edi perfectly illustrates this point.

Over root beer floats, Edi, one of the biggest pirated VCD smugglers in Batam, described how he went about his work.[67] He originally started out small, with just a camcorder in a movie theater, and a need to feed his wife and two small daughters. But over time his operation grew, and he set up a factory in Batam to produce pirated VCDs. The smuggler boasted that he could have a VCD for sale on the streets of Batam within a day or two of a movie's opening in the United States. Someone—not employed by the Batam smuggler—would record the movie via camcorder in a theater in the United States on opening day, and burn a master VCD. The VCD would then be flown over to Indonesia—probably by overnight airmail—where the smuggler's factory would churn out copies and the network would transfer the VCDs to stores all over Riau, including in Tanjung Pinang, Tanjung Balai, and Nagoya, for retail. Some time ago, a local police crackdown forced Edi to move the factory to Jakarta. This, however, added an extra link in his distribution chain, so at the time of the interview, Edi was flying the VCDs from Jakarta to Batam, probably via courier or unaccompanied freight on commercial flights.[68]

When Indonesian president Susilo Bambang Yudhoyono came into office, he and his head of police vowed to crack down on pirated CDs, DVDs, and VCDs, especially because, according to Edi, in August 2005, an agreement came into force requiring Indonesia to do so. Indeed, several weeks later, pictures began appearing of the millions of pirated VCDs, DVDs, and CDs that were confiscated.[69] According to Edi, times were hard due to the crackdown, and in fact, Edi had been forced to curtail his activities considerably. He said half-jokingly not to put his picture in any magazine, or else he would "hang." But he was not terribly worried. For one thing, he had alternative sources of income, namely running karaoke parlors and video gambling dens. For another, Edi was fairly confident that this latest crackdown, too, would pass. Before, Edi said, smugglers could just pay off the police during crackdowns with a little money; the police would then give a heads-up when the situation cooled down.[70] Higher-level corruption also helps the smugglers. Another source noted that if it became evident a given police officer was serious about enforcing the law, the more politically connected smugglers could call his superior and rectify the situation. The source boasted that he had once had an officer reassigned within twenty-four hours.[71] But, in the case of the 2005 pirated VCD crackdown the orders came the chief of police, making bribing more difficult. Edi would keep his head down, and wait for the political pressure to let up before ramping production back up. Nevertheless, Edi and the other major pirated VCD producers on Batam had banded together in order to better respond to the crackdown by using optical technology to mark the VCDs as products of their group. If VCDs began popping up in Batam that were not so marked, Edi intimated that action would be taken against the interlopers, although it was unclear what kind of action he meant.[72]

Edi was not always so focused on VCDs. Originally he also sold cars imported from Malaysia. A group unaffiliated with him would steal the cars in Malaysia and transport them into Singapore. The cars would then be shipped across to Batam, where Edi would receive them and sell them to buyers on Batam. Selling the cars in Jakarta was another thing altogether, said Edi, and he apparently never dealt in that aspect of the "secondhand" car market. Eventually, he said, the Malaysian supplier felt political pressure from his government, and could no longer guarantee his side of the bargain, so the relationship was severed.

Edi's actions make sense. His target area was quite small but he showed himself able to establish both transnational and long-distance domestic connections, with suppliers outside of Indonesia, and with his own factory in Jakarta. The factory shows that he was flexible and willing to move some activities out of his target area to stay afloat. This move did not translate into a larger target area, however; all outside links appear to have been merely to supply his Batam operation. Under greater pressure, this time on a national level, Edi chose to stop producing illegal VCDs and instead concentrate on other businesses rather than become more transnational. Likewise, Edi's car business, though transnational, was focused only on Batam. Once the Malaysian link was cut, Edi exited the business rather than try to establish a new link—the network to move around outside of Indonesia was simply not there, and his overall Batam operation was not threatened.

A desire to control and govern a small amount of territory often leads to territorially bound governance structures that bind a group to that area, rendering its target area inflexible. But small-time smugglers, who usually have no desire to control, let alone govern territory, also remain focused on one area, suggesting that there may be a common mechanism that leads such different groups to the same outcome: the nature of the transnational networks they build due to their humble territorial ambitions. When moving information, people, and goods into a very small area—a single province in the case of GAM, or a single city in the case of many smugglers—the support structure for such a network is often composed of essentially just people from that small area. GAM had a geographically extensive operational area, but all of its operations were oriented to moving back into Aceh, and every contact within its support structure, except for some of the initial weapons suppliers, was Acehnese. GAM existed in a number of different countries but because it made no effort to recruit non-Acehnese, it did not embed itself outside of Aceh. Likewise, small-time smugglers like Edi build networks that cross international boundaries but are not embedded in other countries. Edi opportunistically worked with a Malaysian supplier to deal in stolen cars, but his own network simply received the cars in Batam. Once the Malaysian supplier became unreliable, the flow of cars stopped, and Edi had no other contacts in Malaysia to continue.

By contrast, with a target area of an entire country, Jemaah Islamiyah before 1993 was perfectly content to use operatives from any part of Java, or any part of Indonesia as part of its network. Trying to build a network that could target different points throughout an entire country both required and encouraged constituencies who were not focused on a single point but rather had knowledge of and experience in Java, Sumatra, Sulawesi, and other places. The replicability of Abdullah Sungkar and Abu Bakar Ba'asyir's networks' *usroh* cells, and their lack of ties to specific territory, further encouraged flexibility in their target area.

Crossing borders illicitly is hard work. It is hard enough that when CTOs do it successfully, it is generally because they have built a support network from one country to another. This serves them in good stead should they have flexible territorial ambitions. Thus Sungkar's desire to keep commanding his organization in Indonesia from Malaysia led him to replicate the cell structure of his branch of Darul Islam. This made it realistic for him to expand JI's mission into most of Southeast Asia once he began recruiting non-Indonesians. By contrast, although it spread around the world, GAM did not have replicable structures that were central to its mission. The structures GAM set up in Aceh to govern the province remained its focus in no small part because they were not only tied to territory in general, they were tied to very specific pieces of territory.

If CTOs have large enough ambitions, they can afford to fail in one area, and still have residual structures with which they can operate somewhere else. Such is the case with some pirate syndicates, who are often compelled to establish support nodes in a number of different countries due to the complexity of making money off the sale of a hijacked ship. Without large-scale territorial ambitions, CTOs have little incentive to bear the costs in time, money, and effort in building widespread transnational connections. Thus, mundane smugglers go out of business or lay low when a crackdown comes, rather than try to expand into another country. Both types of criminal organizations, and at times both JI and GAM, have tended to react to crackdowns by adopting tactics and structures that reduce the need to cross borders illicitly. It seems that the technologies of globalization are a sufficiently ambiguous boon to illicit groups that there are times when they prefer not to use them at all.

CONCLUSION

Blowing things up matters. Categorical statements are dangerous, although less so than actual bombs. But violence or the threat of it, and state hostility to that violence as well as to activities (e.g., smuggling) that are both illicit and physical in nature, separate clandestine transnational organizations from legitimate transnational advocacy groups and multinational corporations. Whereas advocacy groups must move only information or people around the world, usually legally, and where corporations build and maintain efficient logistical networks that are facilitated by states, illicit transnational organizations by definition face hostile states. The infrastructure that makes possible the existence of far-reaching logistics networks, and hence forms the engine of globalization—telecommunications, airports, seaports, highways, railroads—has a dark side, inasmuch as it can also be used by illicit groups to move the explosives, weapons, people, and communications necessary to carry out violent attacks.

Yet many parts of this infrastructure are built and controlled by states. The farther and faster a group wants to move around the world, the more dependent it is on chokepoints, such as international airports, where they can be interdicted. Globalization means non-state actors can move quickly around the world, but it also means they cannot move randomly. In a situation where states are hostile, this places significant impositions on clandestine groups' operations, impositions that show no sign of being ameliorated by the technologies of globalization. Planning can certainly be done from across the world via e-mail, phones, and faxes, but all the e-mail access in the world will not get the guns, explosives, or drugs to the desired target. Under political pressure, CTOs can shift their activities to routes that cross international boundaries in ways that avoid state power, or that take advantage of specific aspects of state weakness. They then become dependent on features of the physical geography and infrastructure of the region that tie them to the landscape and otherwise constrain their activities. In essence, state hostility robs CTOs of the tools that they need to carry out the activities that are the most direct means of accomplishing their goals: concentrated acts of violence and crime.

This book has moved beyond assertions that territory matters to explanations of how and when both territory and ideas about territory matter. "What do CTOs want?" is certainly an important question, but just as crucial are questions "Where do they want it?" and "What do they want to do there?" Even in a globalizing world, if we understand how a given CTO thinks about territory, we can then think about the group's relevant area of operations, whether it might seek to take over territory, and what it might do if it actually does. Ideas about territory also give us a sense of how a group might respond to changes in the political environment, how it might move over physical territory, and how the scope of its territorial ambitions might change. Shorn of technology in hostile situations, CTOs must maneuver across the physical landscape. This can restrict their geographical spread, and their transnational movements. Even for the most globalized of organizations, the politics of individual countries continue to matter. Clandestine transnational organizations must "come down to earth" at some point—they exist in territory, not over it, and they operate from country to country, not between them.

Territory and Clandestine Organizations Outside of Southeast Asia

In this book I have focused on Jemaah Islamiyah and to a lesser extent other illicit groups in Southeast Asia. The weaknesses that were latent in al-Qaeda before 2001 were real in Jemaah Islamiyah, GAM, and Southeast Asian pirates and smugglers. Yet perhaps the region is unique in some way. The very characteristics that make Southeast Asia such a fertile area to study—its patchwork of strong and weak states, tens of thousands of islands, relatively robust communications and transport infrastructure, connections to the global economy, and history of illicit transnational movement—also mean that the illicit groups that roam its highways and byways, and the challenges those groups face, might be unusual. As a result, in three miniature case studies, I extend the argument by moving outside of Southeast Asia and relaxing some of my assumptions about the nature of clandestine transnational organizations.

First among these is al-Qaeda. It is a terrorist organization with even grander territorial ambitions than Jemaah Islamiyah which, post–9/11, was forced by attacks from the United States and its allies to become something akin to a social movement and a rallying cry for ideological sympathizers rather than remain a coherent transnational organization. Second are pirate hijacking syndicates in Somalia, who while being blissfully free of state hostility, operating as they are from the territory of a collapsed state, are also frustratingly free of the state-provided infrastructure that provides the foundation for the technologies of globalization that would allow them to engage in sophisticated hijackings. Finally, I look at the Liberation Tigers of Tamil Eelam, the separatist insurgency in Sri Lanka who fought a twenty-five-year war for independence. The struggle was ultimately unsuccessful, but because they controlled a substantial amount of territory and functioned as what was effectively a state, they were able to achieve logistical wonders never even dreamed of by most other insurgencies. In some cases, my argument travels outside Southeast Asia quite well. In others, more research, as ever, is needed.

Al-Qaeda

Up until 11 September 2001, al-Qaeda at least had pretensions of being a fairly centralized, bureaucratic organization that maintained at least periodic control over branches in a number of different countries, although on a much grander scale than JI: al-Qaeda's territorial ambitions ultimately included the entire globe.[1] First it would establish a safe haven where it could establish an Islamic state. From there, it would spread out to rebuild the Islamic caliphate across the Muslim world, and finally convert the rest of the world.[2] Because its target area overlapped with smaller groups with more localized ambitions, al-Qaeda was ready and willing to cooperate with other jihadist organizations, and in some sense functioned as a venture capital firm and force multiplier for local terrorist groups, giving them funds for particular bombing operations, and providing military training to their members. Its adventures in Somalia in the early 1990s, when al-Qaeda operatives infiltrated the Ogaden region straddling the border of Somalia and Ethiopia in order to train Ogaden separatists, stand as a case in point.[3]

Before the United States attacked Afghanistan, al-Qaeda felt little political pressure, and consequently its command and control structure was able to run some operations from its headquarters in Afghanistan, such as the U.S. embassy bombings in Nairobi and Dar es Salaam in 1998, the USS Cole attack in 2000, and ultimately the 9/11 attacks.[4] Documents captured in the ruins of al-Qaeda safe houses in Afghanistan show an organization with an executive committee, functional directorates, application forms for members, bylaws, and even pension and vacation plans.[5] Like Jemaah Islamiyah prior to 2001, al-Qaeda functioned much like an illicit multinational corporation. Inasmuch as it was dependent on the communications and transportation infrastructure controlled by states to move people, goods, and information among its cells in different countries, al-Qaeda had weaknesses that remained latent until 9/11.

After the United States began bombing Afghanistan in October 2001, many of these latent weaknesses came to the fore. The central leaders of al-Qaeda were either killed (e.g., Mohammed Atef), captured (e.g., Khalid Sheikh Mohammed), or forced into the territory on either side of the border between Afghanistan and Pakistan. Like central Mindanao, Pakistan's Northwest Frontier Province (NWFP), particularly the Federally Administered Tribal Areas (FATA), have long had areas where central state penetration is minimal at best. Unlike central Mindanao, the transportation routes within FATA NWFP are rather robust, and people within those regions have access to communications networks.[6] With that said, it is unclear to what extent al-Qaeda is able to take advantage of that infrastructure, as opposed to allied Taliban militias, and indigenous Pakistani militant groups, who have staged attacks from within FATA and NWFP against targets inside Pakistan.[7]

Two things have happened in the wake of the retreat of al-Qaeda's core into the Afghan-Pakistan border area. First, groups that are aligned with al-Qaeda's ideology and enamored with its fight against the United States, and the West more generally, have proclaimed themselves to be local franchises of the organization. Al-Qaeda in Iraq (AQI), which grew out of Abu Musab al-Zarqawi's group, and al-Qaeda Organization in the Land of the Islamic Maghreb, which emerged from the Salafist Group for Preaching and Combat, both rebranded themselves and launched attacks after 2004 in Iraq and North Africa, respectively.[8] Because the new al-Qaeda franchises did not start out as branches of a centralized al-Qaeda, one would not expect the leadership in Afghanistan to exercise close control over the groups, but even matters of strategy were difficult for headquarters to handle from such isolated territory, in such hostile political conditions, across such great distances. A letter purportedly from Ayman al-Zawahiri in 2005, for instance, to AQI complained about the latter's strategy of taking harsh measures with Iraqi Sunnis and attacking Shiite civilian targets as counterproductive.[9] Later in a video interview, al-Zawahiri referred to those who attacked civilian targets as traitors.[10] Al-Zawahiri appeared to be impotent to stop such behavior from Afghanistan, and while AQI was successful in stoking a Sunni-Shiite civil war in Iraq between 2005 and 2007, its behavior also drove away Sunnis in al-Anbar province, arguably leading to the Sunni Awakening and contributing to the success of the U.S. shift in counterinsurgency strategy from 2007 on.

Second, other groups have adopted al-Qaeda's tactics and ideology without franchising at all. Ian Lesser and his colleagues speak of an emerging "new terrorism," one that is characterized not only by increased body counts, but also a departure from the traditional hierarchical and largely self-contained terrorist groups. Increasingly, terrorists have fractured into structurally flat, decentralized cells that share a common ideology and stay connected across great distances by using information technology.[11] Attacks in Europe since 9/11—notably the Madrid train bombings in March 2004, and the London bombings in July 2005—seem to have been committed by cells made up of a mix of individuals who were in ideological sympathy with al-Qaeda's goals but had no apparent connection to al-Qaeda's command and control structure, and individuals who had actually participated in al-Qaeda in the past, but whose connections to al-Qaeda's central leadership during the bombing operations were questionable.[12]

The "new terrorism" may present terrorist groups with some previously unheard of ways to strike and evade government authorities, but it comes with a cost. After al-Qaeda began to devolve after 2001, despite attacks continued around the world, it sacrificed some degree of reliable command and control. Across borders and under pressure, the principal-agent problem reared its ugly head, even in a world with technologies of globalization.

Of course, groups may not need a coherent transnational command and control structure to accomplish their goals, but the experiences of clandestine organizations in Southeast Asia suggest that there is a limit to what the technologies of globalization can accomplish under hostile conditions. Some transnational groups, including al-Qaeda, may find that their transnational links begin to fray when they are under attack and that they are losing control of their far-flung branches and suppliers. As long as its enemies do not relent, al-Qaeda will likely find it difficult to rebuild itself as an illicit multinational corporation. It has been forced into a decentralized, structurally flat form of transnational terrorism, with all the strengths and weaknesses that entails, regardless of whether it prefers that or not.

In addition to the command and control issues, the European attacks raise the question of whether transnational conspiracies can make do with domestic logistical networks. For example, some Moroccans were in the group that carried out the Madrid train bombings (perhaps implying some sort of transnational command and control structure), but they bought the explosives for the bombs in Spain.[13] However, one-off events are different in their requirements than the ability to apply continuous pressure, either through bombs or the use of small arms. It is unlikely that a terrorist group would be able to carry out an extended insurgent campaign in Western Europe without at least some transnational movement of weapons or materiel. The Provisional IRA, for instance, had to import weapons into Ireland during the Troubles.[14] Even less developed parts of the world do not necessarily have sufficient supplies of locally produced weapons. If Southeast Asia were truly awash in guns and explosives, the southern Philippines would not be such an attractive place for so many terrorist groups, Islamist groups would not have rented rifles from the Indonesian military during the ethnic conflicts in Maluku, and GAM would not have built such an extensive and costly weapons supply network. If a transnational logistical network is in fact necessary for a group to accomplish its goals, it will encounter many of the same problems that GAM, criminals, and Jemaah Islamiyah encountered in Southeast Asia.

Maritime Piracy Hijacking Syndicates

Southeast Asia is not the only part of the world frequented by pirates. Today, outside of Southeast Asia, pirate attacks are largely concentrated in India and Bangladesh, in West Africa off the coast of Nigeria, and in East Africa off the coast of Somalia.[15] West Africa and East Africa are the only regions besides Southeast Asia that have significant numbers of hijackings, the most logistically intensive type of pirate attacks (see table 9.1). The preponderance of hijackings in East Africa is particularly interesting as an extension of the argument vis-à-vis maritime piracy.

Whereas Southeast Asia is populated by countries that have either relatively high levels of state capacity (Singapore and Malaysia), or at least are not the worst of the worst (Indonesia and the Philippines), Somalia is the most comprehensively failed state in the world.[16] It has not had an effectively functioning central government that exercised de facto control over anywhere but Mogadishu since the collapse of the Mohamed Siad Barre government in 1991, and the UN-sponsored Transitional Federal Government has often had to meet outside the country because it has no de facto control over any territory.[17] Some regions have declared independence from Somalia, and others serve as battlegrounds for nearly constant warfare among hostile factions. Governance does exist in some places at the regional level, but it is an open question whether the governments of Puntland or Galmudug, for instance, have any significant ability to control what happens on the ground within their territory. Whatever qualities of state failure central Mindanao or northwestern Pakistan might have are doubly true in the case of Somalia.

But this presents a potential problem for extending the lessons of maritime piracy hijacking syndicates in Southeast Asia to East Africa. The transnational support structures that maritime pirates use to dispose of their loot require a fair amount of time and effort to set up, and render the groups vulnerable to interdiction. But the syndicates' transnational links are only weaknesses inasmuch as the relevant states are capable of cracking down on their support structures and severing the links. If there is no functioning government, as in the case of Somalia, then perhaps transnational links are not a weakness after all. Perhaps hijacking syndicates can use the technologies of globalization without worrying about crackdowns in failed states, because such states are incapable of providing the hostile conditions necessary to force CTOs to sever their transnational links and make them stick close to the landscape. Indeed, there is widespread concern that failed states might serve as incubators of global dark actors like organized criminals and terrorists precisely because their governments are incapable of stopping organized criminals or terrorists from making their territory into safe havens.[18] Terrorists and criminals can spend less time and fewer resources evading the authorities in a failed state, but they must also spend more time and energy providing for their own security.[19] More important for criminals, a state that is unable to broadcast power over its territory (as determined by the borders recognized by the international community) is also a state incapable of providing the political and economic infrastructure, in the form of not only administrative offices to regulate markets but also the physical transportation infrastructure necessary to move people and goods around territory in a relatively efficient manner, and the commodities markets where sellers can hawk large quantities of non-subsistence commodities. While state hostility as a means of constraining criminals' movements may be lacking in failed states, so too is the transportation and market infrastructure that would otherwise make possible those same criminal syndicates' sophisticated operations.

This is seen in the variation in the sophistication of maritime pirate hijackings in East Africa and Southeast Asia. Two types of pirate attacks rise above mere muggings by sea in their logistical intricacy. First, hijackings where the pirates seize the ship and cargo and sell one or both of them predominate in Southeast Asia (see chapter 7). Second, hijackings where the pirates seize the ship and hold both the ship and crew for ransom predominate in East and West Africa. Table 9.1 tabulates hijackings by type in various regions of the world from 2000 through 2007.[20]

Kidnappings for ransom differ in two respects from ship and cargo seizures. First, they are less logistically complicated than ship and cargo seizures. Over and above the financiers, middlemen, and pirates, Southeast Asian hijacking syndicates need support personnel who can repaint and recertify hijacked ships, store cargo, and sell both the cargo and the ship, often in different countries, and safe locations in which to do all these things. Kidnappings for ransom, by contrast, require only the rather minimal assets needed to stage the attack, the communications equipment to contact the ship owners, and a safe haven to keep the ship and crew while negotiations are ongoing.

Second, kidnappings for ransom take more time than ship and cargo seizures. Whereas pirates in Southeast Asia attempt to dispose of the ship and cargo as

Table 9.1 Hijacking incidents by region, type, and year

REGION	TYPE	2000	2001	2002	2003	2004	2005	2006	2007	TOTAL
Strait of	S/CS	1	2	5	7	1	0	1	1	18
Malacca	KFR	0	3	2	3	13	5	3	1	30
South China	S/CS	0	3	3	7	6	6	3	3	31
Sea	KFR	1	4	1	0	3	1	2	0	12
East Africa	S/CS	0	0	0	0	0	0	0	2	2
	KFR	2	3	3	1	2	12	5	10	38
West Africa	S/CS	2	0	0	1	1	0	0	1	5
	KFR	0	0	0	6	3	0	6	7	22
Mediterranean	S/CS	0	1	1	0	0	0	0	0	2
Sea	KFR	0	0	0	0	0	0	0	0	0
South America	S/CS	1	0	0	1	0	0	0	1	3
	KFR	0	0	0	1	0	0	0	1	2
Indian Ocean	S/CS	0	1	0	3	2	0	1	0	7
	KFR	0	2	0	4	4	1	0	0	11
Total incidents		7	19	14	33	35	25	21	27	183

Notes: S/CS = ship/cargo seizure; KFR = kidnapping for ransom
Source: Justin V. Hastings, "Geographies of State Failure and Sophistication in Maritime Piracy Hijackings,"
Political Geography 28, no. 4 (2009), p. 219; published with the permission of Elsevier.

quickly as possible in order to evade law enforcement (even from weak states), pirates in Somalia have fewer concerns about enforcement actions, either because they are acting on behalf of local warlords, or because the probability of foreign state intervention is low. The result is that pirates often take months to negotiate ransoms once they have taken hostages.

Because Somali pirates have time and little fear of enforcement but also little economic or political infrastructure to support the networks that would be necessary to dispose of a hijacked ship and cargo, they choose instead to engage in kidnappings for ransom. This is generally true of pirates in failed states, who disproportionately engage in kidnappings for ransom instead of ship and cargo seizures.[21]

Evidence indicates that it is the infrastructure available that limits piracy hijacking sophistication, rather than the competence of the pirates themselves, as Somali pirates are quite sophisticated. They have demonstrated an ability to strike moving targets up to 450 kilometers from land using fishing boats and hijacked ships as mother ships that release speedboats close to the targets. They operate in paramilitary-style organizations, track passing targets with radios and GPS devices, provide full meals to their captives, and give interviews to major world media.[22] Even more crucially, some pirate organizations have the ransom money they raise deposited into bank accounts in Dubai, indicating the existence of transnational support networks that nonetheless are unable (or unwilling) to dispose of ships and cargo.[23]

The lack of interest in the ships and cargo is even more remarkable when we consider that at least some of the Somali pirate gangs are acting on behalf of local warlords and thus, with exception of infrequent foreign intervention, can act with the knowledge of the local government.[24] There have even been instances where pirates have set upon ships immediately after they have discharged their cargo, indicating a lack of interest in taking the cargo itself.[25] Although local warlords can provide security for the pirates, they cannot provide adequate transportation infrastructure or large-scale commodities markets. It is an open question whether ship and cargo seizures or kidnappings for ransom are more dangerous to sailors and world trade, but the experience of Somalia's pirates suggests that the logic of how the technologies of globalization constrain CTOs' activities carries over outside of Southeast Asia. In areas with even minimally functioning states, CTOs dealing with hostile governments have limited access to fast and cheap communications, and transportation and market infrastructure because of state control and regulation. In areas with failed states, CTOs have limited access to such technologies because they often do not exist. Either way, illicit organizations face constraints.

Liberation Tigers of Tamil Eelam

GAM was quite resourceful in its day, but the ingenious solutions it developed to solve the problem of moving people, goods, and information around the world through often hostile territory were arguably topped by at least one other insurgent movement: Liberation Tigers of Tamil Eelam (LTTE), more colloquially known as the Tamil Tigers. Over the course of the civil war with the Sri Lankan government that lasted from 1984 until 2009 and killed an estimated 70,000 people, the Tamil Tigers did not waver from their goal of controlling and governing an independent ethnic Tamil homeland carved out of the northern and eastern parts of the island.[26] This single-minded goal remained unchanged despite a demonstrated ability to strike far from Sri Lanka, notably when the Tigers used a suicide bomber to kill Indian politician Rajiv Gandhi in 1991, which implied at least a minimal support structure in India.[27]

Unlike GAM, most of the main LTTE leadership, notably Vellupillai Prabhakaran, the charismatic and enigmatic top leader, never left Sri Lanka, largely because they were able to seize and hold a significant chunk of territory early on in the civil war. As a result, the Tamil Tigers did not have the same transnational command and control problems—where the leadership was in exile—that GAM did. Like GAM, they built an extensive transnational network rooted in their ethnic diaspora and dedicated to fundraising.[28]

The Tigers' logistical challenges were somewhat different from and, in some respects, even more restrictive than the ones GAM faced. As with GAM, the Tamil Tigers operated on the periphery of an island, with the only land route out of their territory being the one that led into the territory of the state that they were fighting. As with GAM, the nearest neighboring country—in the Tigers' case India—had other members of the same ethnic group who could provide the basis for a transnational support structure. But Indian government was ambivalent at best about the Tamil Tigers, and after its failed peacekeeping intervention from 1987 to 1991, declared the LTTE to be a terrorist organization. The Tamil Tigers' nearby options for sources of weapons ended there, thanks to Sri Lanka's geographical isolation at the southern tip of the Indian subcontinent. Yet by 1987, the Tamil Tigers gained military parity with the Sri Lankan military, and neither side was able to defeat the other outright. This had several important implications for how the Tigers conducted the war, and how they went about setting up their transnational support structures.

First, the conventional nature of much of the war meant that there were pitched battles and relatively well-defined front lines. This is not to say that they did not resort to unconventional tactics—in certain areas the Tamil Tigers behaved more like guerrillas. The group is (in)famous for inventing suicide belts, and pioneering the widespread use of suicide bombers (including female bombers).[29] But away from the front lines, unlike traditional insurgent guerrillas, the Tamil Tigers were able to hold significant chunks of territory, including most of Sri Lanka's northern and eastern coasts, unmolested for long periods.

Second, given its long-term uncontested control of territory and its relatively strong financial position, the LTTE was able to administer its claimed territories in ways that GAM could only dream of, even so going so far as to establish a de facto capital in Killinochi. Although the LTTE did not start with governance structures in place, it developed them relatively quickly, and had well-defined functional and territorial divisions that administered different areas, meted out justice according to an explicit legal code, and collected taxes, including from passing ships.[30] Militarily, the Tamil Tigers were one of the few insurgent movements to establish sophisticated naval (the Sea Tigers) and air force (the Air Tigers) units. These units operated from relatively fixed (although camouflaged) bases and conducted sophisticated, coordinated operations.[31] The Sea Tigers were particularly effective, often engaging in head-to-head battles with the Sri Lankan naval vessels, and besting them. Over the course of the insurgency, the Sea Tigers reportedly destroyed as much as 50 percent of the Sri Lankan navy's ships and made the northern and eastern coasts largely off-limits to naval infiltration.[32]

Third, the LTTE did not achieve international recognition of their sovereignty (and so were denied external sovereignty), but because they were able to control territory (particularly territory with a lengthy coastline) unmolested, they successfully set up nearly all of the structures essential to effective governance. The Tamil Tigers also were one of the few separatist insurgencies that not only controlled the means to move people, goods, and information across international boundaries, but also the infrastructure and territory that were required to use those means in a relatively efficient way. In short, the Tamil Tigers crossed the threshold from non-state actor to state, and were not dependent on other actors to enter or leave their territory. Hezbollah, Hamas, the Moro Islamic Liberation Front, and militants in Pakistan's Northwest Frontier Province could also arguably fall into this category, although none of them are or were transnational to anywhere near the extent that the Tamil Tigers were.

Not only was Sri Lankan state hostility less relevant in how the Tigers crossed borders, but in fact it was the Sri Lankan navy, which for years struggled to resupply the army's garrison in Jaffna by ship due to an LTTE siege on land, and denial tactics at sea, that had trouble crossing borders. The LTTE used its own boats to move people and weapons from its bases in Tamil Nadu, a state in southern India immediately across from the Tigers' territory. The LTTE had a number of cargo ships registered under false names in Honduras, Panama, and Liberia. It used these phantom ships to move weapons from suppliers in Thailand, Myanmar (where they had a base for several years), and Cambodia across the Indian Ocean without passing through any areas that were not either international waters or controlled by the Tigers.[33] The organization did not have major port facilities along its coastline, but it was able to transfer weapons and supplies offshore from the cargo ships onto smaller boats.[34] So well-organized was the Tigers' transnational acquisition network that in 1997 they were able to divert a shipment of mortars destined for the Sri Lanka government by bidding on and winning the contract to transport the shipment from the manufacturer in Tanzania, then sailing instead for Tamil-held territory.[35] In May 2009, at the end of the war, Sri Lankan authorities announced that they had captured 100,000 LTTE small arms, 1,000,000 rounds of ammunition, and a tank, an astonishing cache for a fighting force that numbered around 10,000.[36] As far as moving people, rather than being reliant on using the roads, rails, and airports built and controlled by states to move its personnel, the LTTE used its own sea-based troop transports. These transports successfully battled Sri Lankan navy ships and landed fighters along the coast behind enemy lines during the Battle of the Elephant Pass in 2000, resulting in a strategic defeat for the Sri Lankan government.[37]

With the breakdown of the ceasefire in 2006, the Sri Lankan military gradually advanced against the Tigers, retaking the eastern part of the country and the entirety of the Jaffna Peninsula in the north. By January 2009, the Tigers lost Killinochi, their de facto capital, and retreated into small northern parts of the country. On 16 May, the Sri Lankan military overran the Tigers' last territorial stronghold, killing Prabhakaran and other leaders, and the Tigers conceded defeat. Most important from a logistical standpoint, the Sri Lankan army gradually choked off the Sea Tigers, and by February 2009, when the Sea Tigers lost their base at Chalai, they were down to a few miles of coastline, all of which was blockaded by the Sri Lankan navy.[38] By May 2009, the LTTE had lost access to the coastline entirely, cutting them off from outside reinforcements.

That the Tamil Tigers were able to amass such huge caches of weapons and air and sea equipment, and fight off the Sri Lankan military for nearly twenty-five years (unlike GAM, which was essentially crushed three times over approximately the same period) is a testament to what happens when we stretch the assumptions of the argument in this book.[39] Although the LTTE was arguably in at least as difficult a position geographically as GAM, its status as a state, with control over infrastructure and territory, spared it many of the limits that the technologies of globalization place on other illicit groups. The Tamil Tigers' astonishingly effective top leadership and their innovative tactics served in good stead, and arguably set them apart from less capable insurgent movements, but their experience serves as a cautionary lesson for the extent to which globalization does help violent groups once they have control of territory and infrastructure.

Note, however, the rapid collapse of the LTTE quasi-state once they lost access to strategic territory and the transport infrastructure contained therein, and were in essence forced to revert to non-state status. The Tigers lost much of their governance apparatus when Killinochi fell in January 2009, and they lost control of the terrain and transport infrastructure needed to bring in supplies from the outside world the next month. Within two months, the LTTE had lost the war. Clandestine transnational organizations can indeed take full advantage of the fruits of the technologies of globalization if they have crossed the threshold into state status, but those fruits can quickly be taken away if the groups fall below the threshold.

The Future

The importance of territory has implications for how we analyze clandestine transnational organizations. They are not merely disparate examples of non-traditional security threats that have arisen from the miasma of an increasingly chaotic and fast-paced globalizing world, but can in fact be compared systematically. Terrorists, criminals, and insurgents often want very different things—money, converts for their ideology, power for themselves, independence for their ethnic group—and these goals are often not directly comparable. But these groups all have ideas about territory, and all are limited by physical territory and political conditions in systematic ways. Our expectation is that in moving similar things between countries with similar policies against them, different CTOs—no matter how diverse in their goals—will take similar routes and use similar methods. If Jemaah Islamiyah had wanted to smuggle weapons in Medan (where it had a cell) from Thailand and Malaysia (where it had few weapons sources) once the Indonesian and Malaysian governments had turned against it, in all likelihood, it would have had to use the same routes and methods as GAM did. Moreover, as we have seen, groups with similar goals, such as Darul Islam and pre-1993 Jemaah Islamiyah, can have very different territorial trajectories, while those with different goals, such as post-1993 Jemaah Islamiyah and large-scale pirate syndicates, can respond to political conditions in similar ways.

We can also think about how CTO might react to changes in their political fortunes, either in the form of crackdowns or more political openness. Some structural conditions (such as geography) are largely beyond the control of any practitioner reading this book, and some factors are determined by the CTOs. CTOs can decide a great many things, but they are significantly constrained by factors that states can control, notably states' hostility toward the CTOs and the factions within states that might help the CTOs. Indirectly, through manipulation of the political environment, states can also determine CTOs' dependence on topography and infrastructure, and ultimately encourage failure in certain aspects of their operations.

With knowledge of a CTO's goals and ideas about territory, we can assess whether the CTO is likely to be open to changes in its territorial aspirations. We can also identify countries that might be at risk for infiltration and entrenchment. Where can the CTO fail and still recover? How far afield is the CTO willing to try to go for certain activities? If a neighboring country is friendly, would the CTO be likely to move in? Would cracking down in one country result in the CTO dropping it from its target list, or would it fixate on returning from exile? Would the CTO building a support structure in a country make that country a target? Crackdowns could ultimately provide the opportunity for some types of CTOs to metastasize outside of their home territory, much as Jemaah Islamiyah did after being evicted from Indonesia in 1985. One lesson we can take away is that if a state decides to crack down on a CTO with flexible territorial ambitions, it should make sure that it gets everyone in the group and prohibits their return. Half-hearted crackdowns have the potential to be even more harmful to state security than no crackdown at all. If the CTO triumphs in adversity, and succeeds in building illicit routes, it can entrench in a new country. Barring that, the hostile state should have sufficiently cooperative relationships with neighboring countries to make sure that the CTO cannot use their territory for operations. If Malaysia had been more hostile to Abu Bakar Ba'asyir and Abdullah Sungkar's activities in the 1980s and 1990s, perhaps Jemaah Islamiyah would not have become a regional threat.

The good news is that in the future, even as the world becomes more globalized, and international communications and transportation become ever faster and cheaper, not much will change. Weak states are not completely powerless in the face of the increased movements of people, information, and goods across their borders, especially if they make good strategic decisions in their choice of allies in the fight against terrorism, insurgency, and crime. It is not easy to hold together a violent clandestine organization together in the face of state hostility, even with the help of modern technology. With continued vigilance, such groups will hopefully become the exception rather than the rule.

Notes

PREFACE AND ACKNOWLEDGMENTS

1. See Duncan McCargo, *Tearing Apart the Land: Islam and Legitimacy in Southern Thailand* (Ithaca: Cornell University Press, 2008), xvi.

2. Graham Brown is particularly concerned about the official anonymous sources, government documents, and regular news reports that serve as the basis for most recent research on Jemaah Islamiyah. See Graham Brown, "The Perils of Terrorism: Chinese Whispers, Kevin Bacon and Al Qaeda in Southeast Asia—A Review Essay," *Intelligence and National Security* 21, no. 1 (2006): 150–82.

INTRODUCTION

1. The translation used in the epigraph at the beginning of the text can be found in Osama bin Laden, "Declaration of War against the Americans Occupying the Land of the Two Holy Places," *Al Quds Al Arabiy,* August 1996, www.pbs.org/newshour/terrorism/international/fatwa_1996.html.

2. Kurt M. Campbell, "Globalization's First War?" *Washington Quarterly* 25, no. 1 (2002): 7–14.

3. Kenichi Ohmae, *The Invisible Continent* (New York: HarperBusiness, 2000); Thomas Friedman, *The World Is Flat* (New York: Farrar, Straus and Giroux, 2006).

4. Susan Strange, *The Retreat of the State: The Diffusion of Power in the World Economy* (New York: Cambridge University Press, 1996).

5. Benjamin Barber, "Plenary Roundtable: The Clash of Cultures and American Hegemony," paper presented at the American Political Science Association Annual Meeting (Philadelphia, 1 September 2006).

6. Janice E. Thomson, *Mercenaries, Pirates, and Sovereigns: State-Building and Extraterritorial Violence in Early Modern Europe* (Princeton: Princeton University Press, 1994).

7. See, for example, Stephen D. Krasner, *Sovereignty: Organized Hypocrisy* (Princeton: Princeton University Press, 1999), 3–42, who discusses different understandings of sovereignty, not all of which include perfect control of cross-border movement.

8. Peter Andreas, "Redrawing the Line: Borders and Security in the 21st Century," *International Security* 28, no. 2 (2003): 78–112.

9. Robert Gilpin, *Global Political Economy: Understanding the International Economic Order* (Princeton: Princeton University Press, 2001), 362–76.

10. Stephen D. Krasner, "Power Politics, Institutions, and Transnational Relations," in *Bringing Transnational Relations Back In: Non-State Actors, Domestic Structures, and International Institutions,* ed. Thomas Risse-Kappen (Cambridge: Cambridge University Press, 1995), 268; Samuel P. Huntington, "Transnational Organizations in World Politics," *World Politics* 25, no. 3 (1973): 333–68.

11. Audrey Kurth Cronin, "Behind the Curve: Globalization and International Terrorism," *International Security* 27, no. 3 (2002–2003): 30–58.

12. Nasir Abas, *Membongkar Jamaah Islamiyah: Pengakuan Mantan Anggota JI* (Jakarta: Grafindo, 2005), 38.

13. Author Interview, GAM Negotiator, Banda Aceh, January 2006.

14. "Edi" is a pseudonym, and will be used without quotation marks in all future references to the individual.

15. Author Interview, Chinese-Indonesian Smuggler, Batam, Indonesia, August 2005.

16. Peter Andreas, for example, contrasts the near invisibility of border checks for high-flying executives with the obstacles they pose for poor would-be illegal immigrants. See Andreas, "Redrawing the Line," 110.

17. Friedman, *The World Is Flat*. See also Waleed Hazbun, "Globalisation, Reterritorialisation, and the Political Economy of Tourism Development in the Middle East," *Geopolitics* 9, no. 2 (2004): 310–44.

18. Alexander Murphy, "The Space of Terror," in *The Geographical Dimensions of Terrorism*, ed. Susan L. Cutter, Douglas B. Richardson, and Thomas J. Wilbanks (New York: Routledge, 2003), 49.

19. Andreas, "Redrawing the Line," 78.

20. Jeffrey H. Norwitz apparently does not include mundane smugglers in his definition of armed groups for this reason. See Jeffrey H. Norwitz, ed., *Armed Groups: Studies in National Security, Counterterrorism, and Counterinsurgency* (Newport, RI: U.S. Naval War College, 2008).

21. John Arquilla and David Ronfeldt, eds., *Networks and Netwars: The Future of Terror, Crime, and Militancy* (Santa Monica, CA: RAND, 2001).

22. Work on transnational social movements might be more useful here. See Donatella Della Porta, ed., *Social Movements and Violence: Participation in Underground Organizations*, vol. 4: *International Social Movement Research* (Greenwich, CT: JAI Press, 1992); Donatella Della Porta and Sidney G. Tarrow, eds., *Transnational Protest and Global Activism* (Lanham, MD: Rowman & Littlefield, 2005).

23. For information on pirate warlords, see Xan Rice, "Focus: Ocean Terror: How Savage Pirates Reign on the World's High Seas," *Observer* (UK), 27 April 2008.

24. Combating Terrorism Center, *Al-Qaida's (Mis)Adventures in the Horn of Africa* (West Point, NY: Combating Terrorism Center, U.S. Military Academy, 2007), 19, 23.

25. Dian H. Murray, *Pirates of the South China Coast, 1790–1810* (Stanford: Stanford University Press, 1987).

26. Paul J. Smith, ed. *Terrorism and Violence in Southeast Asia* (Armonk, NY: M.E. Sharpe, 2005), 5. This tendency to categorize groups by their objectives is common. See, for example, T.X. Hammes, "Armed Groups: Changing the Rules," in Norwitz, *Armed Groups*, 447–56.

27. For recent sources on al-Qaeda, see Rohan Gunaratna, *Inside Al Qaeda: Global Network of Terror* (New York: Columbia University Press, 2002); Peter L. Bergen, *The Osama Bin Laden I Know: An Oral History of Al-Qaeda's Leader* (New York: Free Press, 2006); Peter L. Bergen, *Holy War, Inc.: Inside the Secret World of Osama Bin Laden* (New York: Simon and Schuster, 2002); Daniel Byman, "Al-Qa'ida as an Adversary: Do We Understand the Enemy?" *World Politics*, no. 56 (2003): 139–63; Bruce Hoffman, "The Changing Face of Al Qaeda and the Global War on Terrorism," *Studies in Conflict and Terrorism* 27, no. 6 (2004): 549–60; and Brad McAllister, "Al Qaeda and the Innovative Firm: Demythologizing the Network," *Studies in Conflict and Terrorism* 27, no. 4 (2004): 297–319. For books and articles on pirates, see Charles N. Dragonette, "Lost at Sea," *Foreign Affairs* 84, no. 2 (2005), 174–75; Carolin Liss, "Maritime Piracy in Southeast Asia," in *Southeast Asian Affairs 2003*, ed. Daljit Singh and Chin Kin Wah (Singapore: Institute of Southeast Asian Studies, 2003), 52–70; William Langewiesche, *The Outlaw Sea* (New York: North Point Press, 2004); Gal Luft and Anne Korin, "Terrorism Goes to Sea," *Foreign Affairs* 83, no. 6 (2004); Graham Gerard Ong, "'Ships Can Be Dangerous Too': Coupling Piracy and Maritime Terrorism in Southeast Asia's Maritime Security Framework," Institute of Southeast Asian Studies Working Paper, Singapore, 2004; Corey Pein, "Hijacking the Pirate Menace,"

Slate, 12 September 2006; and Peter Chalk, "Low Intensity Conflict in Southeast Asia: Piracy, Drug Trafficking, and Political Terrorism," *Conflict Issues* 305/306 (1998).

28. Much of the literature on Jemaah Islamiyah has this trait. See Zachary Abuza, *Militant Islam in Southeast Asia: Crucible of Terror* (Boulder, CO: Lynne Rienner, 2003); Zachary Abuza, *Political Islam and Violence in Indonesia* (New York: Routledge, 2007); Greg Barton, *Jemaah Islamiyah: Radical Islamism in Indonesia* (Singapore: Singapore University Press, 2005); Kenneth Conboy, *The Second Front: Inside Asia's Most Dangerous Terrorist Network* (Jakarta: Equinox Pub., 2006); Maria A. Ressa, *Seeds of Terror* (New York: Free Press, 2003); Smith, *Terrorism and Violence in Southeast Asia;* and S. Yunanto et al., *Militant Islamic Movements in Indonesia and South-East Asia* (Jakarta: Friedrich-Ebert-Stiftung, 2003).

29. Jason Seawright and John Gerring, "Case-Selection Techniques in Case Study Research: A Menu of Qualitative and Quantitative Options," *Political Research Quarterly* 61, no. 2 (2008), 297.

CHAPTER 1

1. See, for example, Domenico Tosini, "Sociology of Terrorism and Counterterrorism: A Social Science Understanding of Terrorist Threat," *Sociology Compass* 1, no. 2 (2007): 664–81. See also Ariel Merari, "A Classification of Terrorist Groups," *Studies in Conflict and Terrorism* 1, no. 3 (1978): 331–46.

2. Barbara Walter and Andew Kydd, "Strategies of Terrorism," *International Security* 31, no. 1 (2006): 49–80.

3. For information on the Abu Sayyaf Group, see "Terrorist Organizations," in Office of the Coordinator for Counterterrorism, *Country Reports on Terrorism* (Washington, DC: U.S. Department of State, 30 April 2008).

4. David Rohde, "2nd Record Level for Afghan Opium Crop," *New York Times,* 28 August 2007. See also "Jemaah Islamiyah in Southeast Asia: Damaged but Still Dangerous" (Jakarta: International Crisis Group, 26 August 2003), 24–25.

5. Tamara Makarenko, *The Terror-Crime Nexus* (London: C. Hurst, 2007).

6. Timothy Hoyt, "Adapting to a Changed Environment—The Irish Republican Army as an *Armed Group,"* in *Armed Groups: Studies in National Security, Counterterrorism, and Counterinsurgency,* ed. Jeffrey H. Norwitz (Newport, RI: U.S. Naval War College, 2008), 47–59.

7. See Peter A Fleming, Michael Stohl, and Alex P. Schmid, "The Theoretical Utility of Typologies in Terrorism: Lessons and Opportunities," in *The Politics of Terrorism,* ed. Michael Stohl (New York: CRC Press, 1988), 153–96. The chapter classifies typologies of terrorism and takes them to task for their lack of analytical and functional utility.

8. For an account of how terrorists can use non-violent means, see James A. Lewis, "The Internet and Terrorism," Proceedings of the 99th Annual Meeting of the American Society for International Law (2005).

9. Brian Jackson, "Groups, Networks, or Movements: A Command-and-Control-Driven Approach to Classifying Terrorist Organizations and Its Application to Al Qaeda," *Studies in Conflict and Terrorism* 29, no. 3 (2006): 241–62; Shaul Mishal and Maoz Rosenthal, "Al Qaeda as a Dune Organization: Toward a Typology of Islamic Terrorist Organizations," *Studies in Conflict and Terrorism* 28, no. 4 (2005): 275–93. Both studies classify terrorist organizations by organizational structure.

10. Martha Crenshaw, "Theories of Terrorism: Instrumental and Organizational Approaches," in *Inside Terrorist Organizations,* ed. David C. Rapoport (New York: Columbia University Press, 1988), 19–26.

11. Boaz Ganor, "Terrorist Organization Typologies and the Probability of a Boomerang Effect," *Studies in Conflict & Terrorism* 31, no. 4 (2008): 269–81.

12. Hoyt, "Adapting to a Changed Environment," 47–59.

13. Joseph Camilleri and Jim Falk, *The End of Sovereignty? The Politics of a Shrinking and Fragmenting World* (Brookfield, VT: Edward Elgar, 1992).

14. Christopher Brown, *Sovereignty, Rights and Justice: International Political Theory Today* (Cambridge, UK: Polity Press, 2002).

15. Donald Black, "The Geometry of Terrorism," *Sociological Theory* 22, no. 1 (2004): 14–25.

16. Ravinatha Aryasinha, "Terrorism, the LTTE and the Conflict in Sri Lanka," *Conflict, Security & Development* 1, no. 2 (2001): 25–50.

17. If there are no hostile states within a CTO's target area, the organization is not a CTO.

18. International Crisis Group, "Al Qaeda in Southeast Asia: The Case of The 'Ngruki Network' in Indonesia" (Jakarta: International Crisis Group, 8 August 2002), 3–4; International Crisis Group, "Recycling Militants in Indonesia: Darul Islam and the Australian Embassy Bombing" (Jakarta: International Crisis Group, 22 February 2005), 2–3.

19. See International Crisis Group, "Al Qaeda in Southeast Asia," pp. 3–4, for a short discussion of the South Sulawesi component.

20. International Crisis Group, "Recycling Militants in Indonesia," 5.

21. Ibid.

22. International Crisis Group, "Al Qaeda in Southeast Asia," 5; International Crisis Group, "Recycling Militants in Indonesia," 6–7.

23. Ibid., 7.

24. International Crisis Group, "Al Qaeda in Southeast Asia," 6–7, 9.

25. International Crisis Group, "Recycling Militants in Indonesia," 12.

26. International Crisis Group, "Al Qaeda in Southeast Asia," 9–10; International Crisis Group, "Recycling Militants in Indonesia," 12–14. Sungkar and Ba'asyir were not the first or only ones to use *usroh,* but they seem to have been the best at using them.

27. Edward Aspinall, *Islam and Nation: Separatist Rebellion in Aceh, Indonesia* (Stanford: Stanford University Press, 2009), 32–33.

28. M. Isa Sulaiman, *Aceh Merdeka: Ideologi, Kepemimpinan Dan Gerakan* (Jakarta: Pustaka al-Kautsar, 2000), 12–13. See also Aspinall, *Islam and Nation,* 41–42.

29. Sulaiman, *Aceh Merdeka,* 15.

30. Tim Kell, *The Roots of Acehnese Rebellion, 1989–1992* (Ithaca: Southeast Asian Program, Cornell University, 1995), 61–63.

31. Al Chaidar, *Gerakan Aceh Merdeka: Jihad Rakyat Aceh Mewujudkan Negara Islam* (Jakarta: Madani Press, 2000), 148.

32. See GAM and the Government of Indonesia, "Memorandum of Understanding between the Government of the Republic of Indonesia and the Free Aceh Movement" (Helsinki: GAM/Government of Indonesia, 15 August 2005).

33. Sulaiman, *Aceh Merdeka,* 18, 20.

34. Moch. Nurhasim et al., *Konflik Aceh: Analisis Atas Sebab-Sebab Konflik, Aktor Konflik, Kepentingan Dan Upaya Penyelesaian* (Jakarta: Lembaga Ilmu Pengetahuan Indonesia, 2003), 40–41.

35. See Al Chaidar, *Gerakan Aceh Merdeka,* 150–52; Sulaiman, *Aceh Merdeka,* 29; Aspinall, *Islam and Nation,* 64–65.

36. See Alan Dupont, "Transnational Crime, Drugs, and Security in East Asia," *Asian Survey* 39, no. 3 (1999): 433–55 for a discussion of drug markets and routes.

37. Richard N. Cooper, *Tariffs and Smuggling in Indonesia* (New Haven: Economic Growth Center, Yale University, 1974).

38. Author Interview, Buddhist Pandita and Chinese-Indonesian Businessmen, Cipayung, Bogor, Indonesia, July 2005.

39. Author Interview, Government-Linked Economist, Jakarta, July 2005.

40. Author Interview, Buddhist Pandita and Chinese-Indonesian Businessmen, Cipayung, Bogor, Indonesia, July 2005.

41. Author Interview, Riau Islands Provincial Police Official, Batam, Indonesia, November 2005.

42. Author Interview, Capt. Noel Choong, Head, International Maritime Bureau-Kuala Lumpur, Kuala Lumpur, July 2005.

43. Eduardo Ma R. Santos, "Piracy and Armed Robbery against Ships: Philippines Perspective" (Quezon City: Philippines Center for Transnational Crime, n.d.).

44. Author Interview, Think Tank Researcher on Piracy and Smuggling, Kuala Lumpur, July 2005.

45. Author Interview, Official, International Maritime Bureau, Kuala Lumpur, May 2005.

CHAPTER 2

1. Brynjar Lia, *Globalisation and the Future of Terrorism: Patterns and Predictions* (London: Routledge, 2005).

2. Neil Brenner, "Beyond State-Centrism? Space, Territoriality, and Geographical Scale in Globalization Studies," *Theory and Society* 29, no. 1 (1999): 39–78.

3. Stephen Paul Haigh, "Globalization and the Sovereign State: Authority and Territoriality Reconsidered" (paper presented at First Oceanic International Studies Conference, Australian National University, Canberra, Australia, 14–16 July 2004), 8.

4. Colin Flint, "Terrorism and Counterterrorism: Geographic Research Questions and Agendas," *Professional Geographer* 55, no. 2 (2003), 164.

5. Nurit Kliot and David Newman, eds., *Geopolitics at the End of the Twentieth Century: The Changing World Political Map* (London: Frank Cass, 2000), 151.

6. Flint, "Terrorism and Counterterrorism," 164.

7. Paul Ganster and David E. Lorey, eds., *Borders and Border Politics in a Globalizing World,* xi.

8. See Anthony Reid, *Southeast in the Age of Commerce, 1450–1680.* Vol. 2: *Expansion and Crisis* (New Haven: Yale University Press, 1993), 202–66. In terms of the relative unimportance of land per se, I visited the Banda Islands in the summer of 2008, and was amazed at how small they are. Even the largest, Banda Besar, can be traversed on foot in a few hours. The local inhabitants continue to harvest and process nutmeg for export.

9. Reid, *Southeast Asia in the Age of Commerce,* 202–66.

10. Eric Tagliocozzo, *Secret Trades, Porous Borders* (New Haven: Yale University Press, 2005), 1–19.

11. James Warren, *Pirates, Prostitutes and Pullers: Explorations in the Ethno- and Social History of Southeast Asia* (Crawley, Western Australia: University of Western Australia Press, 2008), 309–15.

12. James F. Warren, *Iranun and Balangingi* (Singapore: Singapore University Press, 2002), especially 1–85.

13. Janice E. Thomson, *Mercenaries, Pirates, and Sovereigns: State-Building and Extraterritorial Violence in Early Modern Europe* (Princeton: Princeton University Press, 1994), 21–42; Warren, *Iranun and Balangingi,* 58–64.

14. Tagliocozzo, *Secret Trades,* 365–66.

15. Author Interview, Singaporean Internal Security Officials, Singapore, November 2005.

16. If the state is actually aiding and abetting the CTO's activities, the organization has many more tools at its disposal, but my argument is only concerned with groups that have been denied the resources of a state.

17. The top ten global ports by tonnage in 2004, for example, were located in Hong Kong, Singapore, China, South Korea, Taiwan, the Netherlands, the United States, Germany, the United Arab Emirates, and Belgium. The governments of some of those countries certainly suffer from corruption problems, but none of them would be considered failing states in any sense of the word. See Deutsche Bank Research, "Container Shipping: Overcapacity Inevitable Despite Increasing Demand," (Frankfurt: Deutsche Bank, 25 April 2006).

18. For the general literature on weak and failed states, see Daniel C. Esty et al., "The State Failure Project: Early Warning Research for US Foreign Policy Planning," in *Preventive Measures: Building Risk Assessment and Crisis Early Warning Systems,* ed. John L. Davies and Ted Robert Gurr (Boulder, CO and Totowa, NJ: Rowman and Littlefield, 1998), 27–38; Gary King and Langche Zang, "Improving Forecasts of State Failure," *World Politics* 53, no. 4 (2001): 623–58; Robert Rotberg, "The New Nature of Nation-State Failure," *Washington Quarterly* 25, no. 3 (2002): 85–96; Robert I. Rotberg, ed., *State Failure and State Weakness in a Time of Terror* (Cambridge, MA: World Peace Foundation, 2003); Tatah Mentan, *Dilemmas of Weak States: Africa and Transnational Terrorism in the Twenty-First Century* (Aldershot, UK: Ashgate, 2004). For a list of failed and weak states, see Fund for Peace, "Failed State Index" (Washington, DC: Fund for Peace/Foreign Policy, 2008), which considers Indonesia to be a weak state, and Somalia to be a collapsed state.

19. Jeffrey Herbst, *States and Power in Africa: Comparative Lessons in Authority and Control* (Princeton: Princeton University Press, 2000), 254.

20. Rotberg, "The New Nature of Nation-State Failure," 85–96.

21. Flint, "Terrorism and Counterterrorism," 165.

22. James A. Piazza, "Incubators of Terror: Do Failed and Failing States Promote Transnational Terrorism?" *International Studies Quarterly* 52, no. 3 (2008): 469–88; Ray Takeyh and Nikolas Gvosdev, "Do Terrorist Networks Need a Home?" *Washington Quarterly* 25, no. 3 (2002): 97–108.

23. Combating Terrorism Center, *Al-Qa'ida's (Mis)Adventures in the Horn of Africa* (West Point, NY: Combating Terrorism Center, U.S. Military Academy, 2007), 14–15; See also Kenneth Menkhaus, "Somalia and Somaliland: Terrorism, Political Islam, and State Collapse," in *Battling Terrorism in the Horn of Africa,* ed. Robert I. Rotberg (Washington, DC: Brookings Institution Press,2005), p. 39 and Ken Menkhaus, *Somalia: State Collapse and the Threat of Terrorism* (Oxford, UK: Oxford University Press, 2004).

24. Herbst, *States and Power in Africa,* 161–72.

25. Angel Rabasa, et al., *Ungoverned Territories: Understanding and Reducing Terrorism Risks* (Santa Monica, CA: RAND, 2007), 134–36.

26. Combating Terrorism Center, *Harmony Document AFGP-2002-800621—Letters on Al-Qa'ida's Operations in Africa* (West Point, NY: Combating Terrorism Center, U.S. Military Academy, 2007).

27. Combating Terrorism Center, *Al-Qa'ida's (Mis)Adventures in the Horn of Africa,* 40.

28. Ibid., 34.

29. Ibid., 50–54.

30. See the Revolutionary Armed Forces of Colombia's creation of landing strips and roads in the territory it controls in Angel Rabasa and Peter Chalk, *Colombian Labyrinth: The Synergy of Drugs and Insurgency and Its Implications for Regional Stability* (Santa Monica, CA: RAND, 2001). The drug-trafficking insurgent groups of Myanmar have also built roads and even entire towns to facilitate trafficking. See Carl Grundy-Warr and Elaine Wong, "Geopolitics of Drugs and Cross-Border Relations: Burma-Thailand," *Border and Security Bulletin* 9, no. 1 (2001): 108–21 and Sheldon X. Zhang and Ko-lin Chin,

"The Chinese Connection: Cross-Border Drug Trafficking between Myanmar and China" (Washington, DC: U.S. Department of Justice, 2007).

31. Author Interview, Ethnic Conflict Researcher, Jakarta, July 2005.

CHAPTER 3

1. See, for example, Angel Rabasa, *Political Islam in Southeast Asia: Moderates, Radicals and Terrorists* (Adelphi Series) (Oxford: Oxford University Press for the International Institute for Strategic Studies, 2003); Zachary Abuza, *Political Islam and Violence in Indonesia* (New York: Routledge, 2007).

2. Kenneth Conboy, *The Second Front: Inside Asia's Most Dangerous Terrorist Network* (Jakarta: Equinox, 2006).

3. Zachary Abuza, *Militant Islam in Southeast Asia: Crucible of Terror* (Boulder, CO: Lynne Rienner, 2003); Maria A. Ressa, *Seeds of Terror* (New York: Free Press, 2003).

4. Natasha Hamilton-Hart, "Terrorism in Southeast Asia: Expert Analysis, Myopia and Fantasy," *Pacific Review* 18, no. 3 (2005): 303–25; Graham Brown, "The Perils of Terrorism: Chinese Whispers, Kevin Bacon and Al Qaeda in Southeast Asia—A Review Essay," *Intelligence and National Security* 21, no. 1 (2006): 150–82.

5. David Wright-Neville, "Dangerous Dynamics: Activists, Militants and Terrorists in Southeast Asia," *Pacific Review* 17, no. 1 (2004): 27–46.

6. Mike Millard, *Jihad in Paradise: Islam and Politics in Southeast Asia* (Armonk, NY: M.E. Sharpe, 2004).

7. Hamilton-Hart, "Terrorism in Southeast Asia," 316–20.

8. Ibid., 317. See also John Thayer Sidel, *Riots, Pogroms, Jihad: Religious Violence in Indonesia* (Ithaca: Cornell University Press, 2006).

9. With that said, it is conceivable that the uptick in Islamic violence against Christians in the late 1990s might have been in response to frustrated political ambitions. This is one of the main arguments in Sidel, *Riots, Pogroms, Jihad.*

10. See, for example, Duncan McCargo, *Tearing Apart the Land: Islam and Legitimacy in Southern Thailand* (Ithaca: Cornell University Press, 2008) on the local origins of the southern Thai insurgency.

11. International Crisis Group, "Al Qaeda in Southeast Asia: The Case of The 'Ngruki Network' in Indonesia" (Jakarta: International Crisis Group, 8 August 2002), 11.

12. Abuza, *Militant Islam in Southeast Asia,* 127.

13. See Kejaksaan Tinggi DKI Jakarta, "Berita Acara Pendapat Tersangka Muzahar Muhtar Alias Taslim Alias Musa" (Jakarta: Kejaksaan Tinggi DKI Jakarta, 3 August 1987), 6 and Kejaksaan Tinggi DKI Jakarta, "Berita Acara Pemeriksaan Saksi Sarjono Al. Harun Al. Rasyid Al. Muhtar Suroso Al. Salamun" (Jakarta: Kejaksaan Tinggi DKI Jakarta, 2 September 1986), 3. See also Kejaksaan Tinggi DKI Jakarta, "Berita Acara Pemeriksaan Tersangka Muzahar Muhtar Alias Taslim Alias Musa" (Jakarta: Kejaksaan Tinggi DKI Jakarta, 20 September 1986), 2.

14. Kejaksaan Tinggi DKI Jakarta, "Berita Acara Pemeriksaan Tersangka Muzahar Muhtar Alias Taslim Alias Musa" (20 September 1986), 2–3.

15. Ibid., 3.

16. Kejaksaan Tinggi DKI Jakarta, "Berita Acara Pemeriksaan Tersangka Muzahar Muhtar Alias Taslim Alias Musa" (Jakarta: Kejaksaan Tinggi DKI Jakarta, 26 August 1986), 5–6.

17. International Crisis Group, "Al Qaeda in Southeast Asia," 12. See also Kejaksaan Tinggi DKI Jakarta, "Berita Acara Pendapat Tersangka Muzahar Muhtar Alias Taslim Alias Musa" (3 August 1987), 9.

18. Kejaksaan Tinggi DKI Jakarta, "Berita Acara Pemeriksaan Tersangka Muzahar Muhtar Alias Taslim Alias Musa" (20 September 1986), 3–4.

19. Nasir Abas, *Membongkar Jamaah Islamiyah: Pengakuan Mantan Anggota JI* (Jakarta: Grafindo, 2005), 32.

20. Abas, *Membongkar Jamaah Islamiyah,* 32–37. It is unclear to whom or to what they were pledging loyalty.

21. Ibid., 37.

22. Ibid., 38.

23. Ibid., 45–47.

24. International Crisis Group, "Jemaah Islamiyah in Southeast Asia: Damaged but still Dangerous" (Jakarta: International Crisis Group, 26 August 2003), 4.

25. International Crisis Group, "Jemaah Islamiyah in Southeast Asia," 4–10; Abas, *Membongkar Jamaah Islamiyah,* 50.

26. Author Interview, Counterterrorism Official, Indonesian Government, Jakarta, September 2005.

27. International Crisis Group, "Jemaah Islamiyah in Southeast Asia," 6.

28. Ibid., 6; Abas, *Membongkar Jamaah Islamiyah,* 67–68.

29. International Crisis Group, "Jemaah Islamiyah in Southeast Asia," 6; International Crisis Group, "Recycling Militants in Indonesia: Darul Islam and the Australian Embassy Bombing" (Jakarta: International Crisis Group, 22 February 2005), 22.

30. Abas, *Membongkar Jamaah Islamiyah,* 82.

31. Ibid., 84–85.

32. Ibid., 85–86; International Crisis Group, "Jemaah Islamiyah in Southeast Asia," 6.

33. "Ba'asyir Ketua JI Sejak 1999," *Suara Pembaruan,* 4 July 2003.

34. Author Interview, Former Jemaah Islamiyah Regional Leader, Jakarta, December 2005.

35. Specifically, they were the *fatwa* branch, which issued religious decrees, the *hisbah* branch which was in charge of moral, political, and economic anti-corruption policing, and the *syura* branch, which was roughly akin to a consultative council.

36. Abas, *Membongkar Jamaah Islamiyah,* 112–25.

37. Ibid.

38. Ibid., 122; Ministry of Home Affairs, "Singapore Government Press Statement on Further Arrests under the Internal Security Act, 19 Sep 2002" (Singapore: Ministry of Home Affairs, 19 September 2002).

39. Abas, *Membongkar Jamaah Islamiyah,* 122.

40. Ministry of Home Affairs, "Singapore Government Press Statement on Further Arrests under the Internal Security Act, 19 Sep 2002."

41. Author Interview, International NGO Researcher on Terrorism and Insurgency, Singapore, April 2005; Author Interview, Malaysian Counter-Terrorism Official, Kuala Lumpur, December 2005; Author Interview, Counterterrorism Official, Indonesian Government, Jakarta, September 2005.

42. Abas, *Membongkar Jamaah Islamiyah,* 128, 131–32.

43. Ibid., 88–89.

44. Abuza, *Militant Islam in Southeast Asia,* 128–29.

45. Author Interview, Former Jemaah Islamiyah Regional Leader, Jakarta, December 2005. Nasir Abas, for example, was "tracked" into specialization as an instructor.

46. Ibid.

47. Author Interview, Singaporean Internal Security Officials, Singapore, November 2005.

48. Abas, *Membongkar Jamaah Islamiyah,* 126–28.

49. Ibid., 128–30.

50. Author Interview, Former Jemaah Islamiyah Regional Leader, Jakarta, December 2005.

51. Abas, *Membongkar Jamaah Islamiyah,* 141.

52. Ibid., 143.

53. Ibid., 143–47.

54. Ibid., 144–45.

55. Ibid.; Author Interview, Former Jemaah Islamiyah Regional Leader, Jakarta, December 2005.

56. Author Interview, Former Jemaah Islamiyah Regional Leader, Jakarta, December 2005; Abas, *Membongkar Jamaah Islamiyah,* 146–48.

57. Abas, *Membongkar Jamaah Islamiyah,* 153.

58. Ibid., 165.

59. International Crisis Group, "Jemaah Islamiyah in Southeast Asia," 16.

60. Abas, *Membongkar Jamaah Islamiyah,* 155–56.

61. International Crisis Group, "Jemaah Islamiyah in Southeast Asia," 17.

62. Abas, *Membongkar Jamaah Islamiyah,* 156–64.

63. Author Interview, Former Jemaah Islamiyah Regional Leader, Jakarta, December 2005.

64. Kepolisian Negara Republik Indonesia, "Berita Acara Pemeriksaan Faiz Bin Abu Bakar Bafana" (Jakarta: Korps Reserse Polri, Kepolisian Negara Republik Indonesia, 22 October 2002).

65. International Crisis Group, "Jemaah Islamiyah in Southeast Asia," 18–19.

66. Abas, *Membongkar Jamaah Islamiyah,* 90.

67. International Crisis Group, "Jemaah Islamiyah in Southeast Asia," 19.

68. Ibid., 19.

69. Author Interview, Former Jemaah Islamiyah Regional Leader, Jakarta, December 2005.

70. International Crisis Group, "Jemaah Islamiyah in Southeast Asia," 19–21.

71. Author Interview, Counterterrorism Official, Indonesian Government, Jakarta, September 2005.

CHAPTER 4

1. Kepolisian Negara Republik Indonesia, "Berita Acara Pemeriksaan Faiz Bin Abu Bakar Bafana" (Jakarta: Korps Reserse Polri, Kepolisian Negara Republik Indonesia, 22 October 2002).

2. Nasir Abas, *Membongkar Jamaah Islamiyah: Pengakuan Mantan Anggota JI* (Jakarta: Grafindo, 2005), 132.

3. Author Interview, Singaporean External Intelligence Officials, Singapore, October 2005.

4. Author Interview, Former Jemaah Islamiyah Regional Leader, Jakarta, December 2005.

5. Author Interview, Singaporean Internal Security Officials, Singapore, November 2005.

6. Author Interview, International NGO Researcher on Terrorism and Insurgency, Singapore, April 2005.

7. Ministry of Home Affairs, "The Jemaah Islamiyah Arrests and the Threat of Terrorism" (Singapore: Ministry of Home Affairs, 7 January 2003), 7.

8. Author Interview, International NGO Researcher on Terrorism and Insurgency, Singapore, April 2005.

9. Author Interview, Ethnic Conflict Researcher, Jakarta, July 2005.

10. Kepolisian Negara Republik Indonesia, "Surat Pernyataan Ja'afar Bin Mistooki" (Singapore: Kepolisian Negara Republik Indonesia, 4 September 2002), 5.

11. Author Interview, International NGO Researcher on Terrorism and Insurgency, Singapore, April 2005.

12. Author Interview, Philippines Military Intelligence Officer, Manila, December 2005.

13. Zachary Abuza, *Militant Islam in Southeast Asia: Crucible of Terror* (Boulder, CO: Lynne Rienner, 2003), 137–38.

14. Author Interview, International NGO Researcher on Terrorism and Insurgency, Singapore, April 2005.

15. International Crisis Group, "Jemaah Islamiyah in Southeast Asia: Damaged but Still Dangerous" (Jakarta: International Crisis Group, 26 August 2003), 21.

16. Ibid., 20–21.

17. Author Interview, Counterterrorism Police Official, Jakarta, September 2005.

18. Author Interview, Singaporean External Intelligence Officials, Singapore, October 2005.

19. Combating Terrorism Center, *Al-Qa'ida's (Mis)Adventures in the Horn of Africa* (West Point, NY: Combating Terrorism Center, U.S. Military Academy, 2007), 31–32. See also Kenneth Menkhaus, "Quasi-States, Nation-Building and Terrorist Safe Havens," *Journal of Conflict Studies* 23, no. 2 (2003): 7–23.

20. Author Interview, Philippines Government Negotiator with the MILF, Manila, December 2005.

21. Author Interview, Philippines Military Intelligence Officer, Manila, December 2005.

22. Author Interview, Philippines Government Negotiator with the MILF, Manila, December 2005.

23. Ibid.

24. Author Interview, Philippines Police Intelligence Analysts, Manila, December 2005; Author Interview, Philippines National Security Council Official, Manila, December 2005.

25. Author Interview, Philippines National Security Council Official, Manila, December 2005; Author Interview, Philippines Military Intelligence Officer, Manila, December 2005.

26. Author Interview, Philippines Government Negotiator with the MILF, Manila, December 2005.

27. Ibid.

28. Author Interview, Singaporean External Intelligence Officials, Singapore, October 2005.

29. Author Interview, Philippines Military Intelligence Officer, Manila, December 2005.

30. Presentation by senior staff officer, Armed Forces of the Philippines, Manila, December 2005.

31. See, for example, Darwin T. Wee, "New Lead on Zamboanga Blast," *BusinessWorld,* 2 June 2008. And Roel Pareno and James Mananghaya, "Philippine Troops Seize Bomb-Making Camp," *Philippine Star,* 1 May 2008.

32. "Army Arrests Nine Terror Suspects," *Manila Times,* 16 January 2009.

33. Zachary Abuza, *Balik-Terrorism: The Return of the Abu Sayyaf* (Carlisle Barracks, PA: Stategic Studies Institute, Army War College, September 2005). Abuza questions whether there is even a meaningful difference between Abu Sayyaf members, JI members, and certain MILF members.

34. International Crisis Group, "Philippines Terrorism: The Role of Militant Islamic Converts" (Jakarta and Brussels: International Crisis Group, 19 December 2005), 16–18. The report also suggests that the *mantiqi* structure in the Philippines had completely broken down by 2004, which means that the JI members were probably "freelancing."

35. Author Interview, Singaporean External Intelligence Officials, Singapore, October 2005.

36. Abuza, "Balik-Terrorism," 3.

37. See International Crisis Group, "Terrorism in Indonesia: Noordin's Networks" (Jakarta and Brussels: International Crisis Group, 5 May 2006), 13; Author Interview, Counterterrorism Police Official, Jakarta, September 2005.

38. Author Interview, Malaysian Counter-Terrorism Official, Kuala Lumpur, December 2005.

39. Abuza, *Militant Islam in Southeast Asia,* 158.

40. Kepolisian Daerah Bali, "Berita Acara Pemeriksaan Ali Ghufron Als. Mukhlas" (Denpasar: Direktorat Reserse, Kepolisian Daerah Bali, 20 December 2002), 3–4.

41. Kepolisian Negara Republik Indonesia, "Berita Acara Pemeriksaan Wan Min Wan Mat" (Jakarta: Badan Reserse Kriminal, Kepolisian Negara Republik Indonesia, 8 January 2003), 4–5.

42. Kepolisian Daerah Bali, "Berita Acara Pemeriksaan Ali Ghufron Als. Mukhlas" (20 December 2002), 3–4.

43. Abas, *Membongkar Jamaah Islamiyah,* 308.

44. Author Interview, Singaporean Internal Security Officials, Singapore, November 2005.

45. Author Interview, Former Jemaah Islamiyah Regional Leader, Jakarta, December 2005.

46. Badan Reserse Kriminal Polri, "Berita Acara Pemeriksaan Mohammad Nasir Bin Abas Als. Khairudin Als. Sulaeman Als. Leman Als. Maman Als. Nasir Abas Als. Husna Als. Abu Husna Als. Eddy Mulyono Als. Malik" (Jakarta: Direktorat I/Keamanan & Transnasional, Badan Reserse Kriminal Polri, 20 August 2003), 2.

47. "18 Anggota JI Diringkus," *Suara Karya,* 24 April 2003.

48. Author Interview, Singaporean External Intelligence Officials, Singapore, October 2005.

49. Author Interview, Former Jemaah Islamiyah Regional Leader, Jakarta, December 2005.

50. "Malaysian Police Arrest 2 Suspected JI Members," *Jakarta Post,* 13 January 2003.

51. Badan Reserse Kriminal Polri, "Berita Acara Pemeriksaan Mohammad Nasir Bin Abas" (20 August 2003), 3.

52. Badan Reserse Kriminal Polri, "Berita Acara Pemeriksaan Mohammad Nasir Bin Abas Als. Khairudin Als. Sulaeman Als. Leman Als. Maman Als. Nasir Abas Als. Husna Als. Abu Husna Als. Eddy Mulyono Als. Malik" (Jakarta: Direktorat I/Keamanan & Transnasional, Badan Reserse Kriminal Polri, 10 July 2003), 2.

53. Steven Gutkin, "Terrorists in Asia Replace Captured Leaders," *Jakarta Post* (Associated Press), 18 October 2003.

54. Badan Reserse Kriminal Polri, "Berita Acara Pemeriksaan Mohammad Nasir Bin Abas" (20 August 2003), 2.

55. Badan Reserse Kriminal Polri, "Berita Acara Pemeriksaan Mohammad Nasir Bin Abas Als. Khairudin Als. Sulaeman Als. Leman Als. Maman Als. Nasir Abas Als. Husna Als. Abu Husna Als. Eddy Mulyono Als. Malik" (Jakarta: Direktorat I/Keamanan & Transnasional, Badan Reserse Kriminal Polri, 9 May 2003), 4–5.

56. Author Interview, International NGO Researcher on Terrorism and Insurgency, Singapore., April 2005.

57. Author Interview, Former Jemaah Islamiyah Regional Leader, Jakarta, December 2005; International Crisis Group, "Indonesia: Jemaah Islamiyah's Current Status" (Jakarta and Brussels: International Crisis Group, 3 May 2007), 3.

58. Author Interview, International NGO Researcher on Terrorism and Insurgency, Singapore, April 2005.

59. "Hambali's Brother Arrested in Pakistan," Associated Press, 22 September 2003.

60. Author Interview, Singaporean External Intelligence Officials, Singapore, 25 October 2005.

61. Ibid. See also International Crisis Group, "Indonesia: Jemaah Islamiyah's Current Status," 13.

62. "2 Men Helped Mas Selamat," *New Straits Times* (Malaysia), 10 May 2009. See also "The Great Escape—How Mas Selamat Evaded the Dragnet," *Bernama*, 13 May 2009.

63. See a discussion of the Bali bombing investigation in Greg Barton, *Jemaah Islamiyah: Radical Islamism in Indonesia* (Singapore: Singapore University Press, 2005).

64. Tom Allard, "While We're Not Looking …; Bali's Agony," *Sydney Morning Herald*, 8 October 2005. In the same article, Sidney Jones casts doubt on the report of Laskar Jihad in Papua.

65. Lindsay Murdoch, "Bashir Clear on Bali Blasts as Attack Fears Grow," *Age* (Melbourne), 22 December 2006.

66. Seth Mydans, "A Jailhouse Conversion Splits Terrorists, and in-Laws," *New York Times,* 15 March 2008.

67. "Many Indonesians Support JI: Survey," Australian Associated Press, 15 October 2006.

68. Eli Berman and David D. Laitin, "Religion, Terrorism and Public Goods: Testing the Club Model," National Bureau of Economic Research Working Paper no. 13725 (Cambridge, MA, January 2008).

CHAPTER 5

1. See International Crisis Group, "Indonesia Backgrounder: How the Jemaah Islamiyah Terrorist Network Operates" (Jakarta: International Crisis Group, 11 December 2002), 5–17 for an English-language account of how JI operated during this period, and specifically for details on the Christmas Eve 2000 bombings.

2. Kepolisian Negara Republik Indonesia, "Berita Acara Pemeriksaan (Tersangka) Abdul Azis Bin Sihabudin Al. Abu Umar Al. Imam Samudra Al. Fais Yunshar Heri Al. Hendri Al. Kudama" (Batam: Kepolisian Negara Republik Indonesia, Daerah Riau, Kota Besar Barelang, 27 November 2002), 5.

3. Kepolisian Negara Republik Indonesia, "Berita Acara Pemeriksaan Faiz Bin Abu Bakar Bafana" (Jakarta: Korps Reserse Polri, Kepolisian Negara Republik Indonesia, 22 October 2002), n.p.

4. Ibid.

5. Kepolisian Negara Republik Indonesia, "Berita Acara Pemeriksaan (Tersangka) Abdul Azis Bin Sihabudin Al. Abu Umar Al. Imam Samudra Al. Fais Yunshar Heri Al. Hendri Al. Kudama" (27 November 2002), 5.

6. Kepolisan Negara Republik Indonesia, "Berita Acara Pemeriksaan Faiz Bin Abu Bakar Bafana" (22 October 2002).

7. Ibid.

8. It would not be surprising if there were at least two meetings, because JI loved meetings, and it generally had separate meetings to discuss overall planning, and then specific operational details.

9. "JI Biayai Bom Di Malam Natal," *Suara Pembaruan,* 29 October 2002.

10. Sardjono was the fisherman who helped JI smuggle weapons and people between Indonesia and the Philippines. See International Crisis Group, "Jemaah Islamiyah in Southeast Asia: Damaged but Still Dangerous" (Jakarta: International Crisis Group, 26 August 2003), 18–22.

11. Kepolisian Negara Republik Indonesia, "Berita Acara Pemeriksaan (Tersangka) Abdul Azis Bin Sihabudin Al. Abu Umar Al. Imam Samudra Al. Fais Yunshar Heri Al. Hendri Al. Kudama," (27 November 2002), 5.

12. Ibid. See also Kepolisian Negara Republik Indonesia, "Sampul Berkas Perkara, No. Pol.: BP/364/XII/2002/Serse" (Batam: Kepolisian Negara Republik Indonesia Daerah Riau, Kota Besar Barelang, 20 December 2002), 53.

13. Because all the detainees call each other by different aliases, it is extremely difficult to figure out who used what alias when. Imam Samudra referred to a Syamsudin who was at the house with him, but never used the name Abdul Rahim, while both Hashim and Ja'afar used Abdul Rahim only, so it is possible that Abdul Rahim and Syamsudin are one and the same, as there were only five people in the house in Batam.

14. Kepolisian Negara Republik Indonesia, "Surat Pernyataan Ja'afar Bin Mistooki" (Singapore: Kepolisian Negara Republik Indonesia, 4 September 2002), 1, 7.

15. Ibid., 2. The idea was that JI was attacking churches and Christian leaders who involved in supplying Christian forces in the Maluku conflict.

16. Ibid., 2–4.

17. Kepolisian Daerah Bali, "Berita Acara Pemeriksaan Ali Ghufron Als. Mukhlas" (Denpasar: Direktorat Reserse, Kepolisian Daerah Bali, 29 December 2002), 2–3.

18. Kepolisian Negara Republik Indonesia, "Surat Pernyataan Ja'afar Bin Mistooki" (4 September 2002), 3.

19. Kepolisian Negara Republik Indonesia, "Berita Acara Pemeriksaan (Tersangka) Abdul Azis Bin Sihabudin Al. Abu Umar Al. Imam Samudra Al. Fais Yunshar Heri Al. Hendri Al. Kudama" (27 November 2002), 9.

20. Kepolisian Negara Republik Indonesia, "Sampul Berkas Perkara, No. Pol.: BP/364/XII/2002/Serse" (20 December 2002), 64. Imam Samudra claimed that only one person, Tarmizi, came with the supplies from Jakarta. However, Hashim and Ja'afar both say that there were two people, one fat, and one skinny. See Kepolisian Negara Republik Indonesia, "Surat Pernyataan Hashim Bin Abbas" (Singapore: Kepolisian Negara Republik Indonesia, 30 March 2002), 7–8.

21. Kepolisian Negara Republik Indonesia, "Berita Acara Pemeriksaan (Tersangka) Abdul Azis Bin Sihabudin Al. Abu Umar Al. Imam Samudra Al. Fais Yunshar Heri Al. Hendri Al. Kudama" (27 November 2002), 6.

22. Kepolisian Negara Republik Indonesia, "Surat Pernyataan Ja'afar Bin Mistooki" (4 September 2002), 6–7.

23. Kepolisian Negara Republik Indonesia, "Sampul Berkas Perkara, No. Pol.: BP/364/XII/2002/Serse" (20 December 2002), 64.

24. Kepolisian Negara Republik Indonesia, "Surat Pernyataan Ja'afar Bin Mistooki" (4 September 2002), 5–6.

25. Ibid., 7.

26. See, for instance, Kejaksaan Negeri Jakarta Selatan, "Surat Dakwaan Atas Nama Terdakwa Mohd. Rais Al. Edi Indra Al. Iskandar Al. Ryan Arifin Al. Fendi Al. Roni Bin Rusdi Bin Hamid" (Jakarta: Kejaksaan Negeri Jakarta Selatan, 4 January 2004).

27. Author Interview, Singaporean Internal Security Officials, Singapore, November 2005.

28. Ministry of Home Affairs, "The Jemaah Islamiyah Arrests and the Threat of Terrorism" (Singapore: Ministry of Home Affairs, 7 January 2003), 9, 28–29.

29. Author Interview, Singaporean Internal Security Officials, Singapore, November 2005.

30. Ibid.; Author Interview, Malaysian Counter-Terrorism Official, Kuala Lumpur, December 2005.

31. Author Interview, Singaporean Internal Security Officials, Singapore, November 2005.

32. A *fiah* was the standard terrorist cell of JI, consisting of four to eight members.

33. Author Interview, Singaporean Internal Security Officials, Singapore, November 2005.

34. Ministry of Home Affairs, "The Jemaah Islamiyah Arrests and the Threat of Terrorism," 27–29.

35. This initial lack of suicide bombers is an interesting data point for such articles as Scott Atran, "The Moral Logic and Growth of Suicide Terrorism," *Washington Quarterly* 29, no. 2 (2006): 127–47 and Martha Crenshaw, "Explaining Suicide Terrorism: A Review Essay," *Security Studies* 16, no. 1 (2007): 133–62, which reviews most of the recent literature on suicide terrorism.

36. Author Interview, Singaporean Internal Security Officials, Singapore, November 2005; Author Interview, Singaporean External Intelligence Officials, Singapore, October 2005.

37. Author Interview, Singaporean Internal Security Officials, Singapore, November 2005.

38. Author Interview, Singaporean Police Official, Singapore, July 2005.

39. Kepolisian Negara Republik Indonesia, "Surat Pernyataan Hashim Bin Abbas" (30 March 2002), 4–5.

40. Kepolisian Negara Republik Indonesia, "Berita Acara Pemeriksaan Faiz Bin Abu Bakar Bafana" (22 October 2002). Two plans were hatched at the meeting (aside from the Singapore plots). One group, to be composed of people from Mantiqi I, was supposed to kill then-Indonesian president Megawati Soekarnoputri, while the other was supposed to implement a plan to kill Catholic priests who were meeting in Manado. Faiz told Mukhlas about the Megawati assassination plan. Mukhlas responded that there was no way Mantiqi I had the people to plan and carry out such a plot, thus Mantiqi II would have to do it. Because Mantiqi II did not do it, this is apparently why the assassination plan fizzled out.

41. Zachary Abuza, *Militant Islam in Southeast Asia: Crucible of Terror* (Boulder, CO: Lynne Rienner, 2003), 137–38.

42. Author Interview, Singaporean External Intelligence Officials, Singapore, October 2005.

43. Ministry of Home Affairs, "The Jemaah Islamiyah Arrests and the Threat of Terrorism," 27.

44. Author Interview, Singaporean External Intelligence Officials, Singapore, October 2005.

45. International Crisis Group, "Jemaah Islamiyah in Southeast Asia," 18–22.

46. Abuza, *Militant Islam in Southeast Asia,* 137–38; Ministry of Home Affairs, "The Jemaah Islamiyah Arrests and the Threat of Terrorism," 27. The report claims that the ammonium nitrate was shipped to Batam, but in fact it was later found buried in a plantation in Malaysia.

47. Author Interview, Singaporean Internal Security Officials, Singapore, November 2005.

48. Author Interview, Singaporean External Intelligence Officials, Singapore, October 2005.

49. Author Interview, Singaporean Internal Security Officials, Singapore, November 2005.

50. Ministry of Home Affairs, "The Jemaah Islamiyah Arrests and the Threat of Terrorism," 27–28.

51. Author Interview, Singaporean External Intelligence Officials, Singapore, October 2005.

52. Ibid.

53. Ministry of Home Affairs, "The Jemaah Islamiyah Arrests and the Threat of Terrorism," 27–28.

54. Kepolisian Daerah Bali, "Berita Acara Pemeriksaan Ali Ghufron Als. Mukhlas" (Denpasar: Direktorat Reserse, Kepolisian Daerah Bali, 30 December 2002), 5.

55. Kepolisian Daerah Bali, "Berita Acara Pemeriksaan Ali Ghufron Als. Mukhlas" (Denpasar: Direktorat Reserse, Kepolisian Daerah Bali, 20 December 2002), 4.

56. Kepolisian Daerah Bali, "Berita Acara Pemeriksaan Ali Ghufron Als. Mukhlas" (Denpasar: Direktorat Reserse, Kepolisian Daerah Bali, 14 December 2002), 10.

57. Because neither had been caught at the time of Mukhlas's interrogation, it is possible he was trying to cover for them.

58. Kepolisian Daerah Bali, "Berkas Perkara Amrozi Bin H. Nurhasyim (No. Pol. BP/01/I/2003/Dit Serse)" (Denpasar: Direktorat Reskrim, Kepolisian Daerah Bali, 4 January 2003), 146–60.

59. Ibid., 158–60.

60. "Terror Expert Doubts JI Bomber Dulmatin Is Dead," Agence France Presse, 20 February 2008.

61. See "Saksi 3 (Ali Imron)," 11–18 in Kepolisian Daerah Bali, "Berkas Perkara Amrozi Bin H. Nurhasyim (No. Pol. Bp/01/I/2003/Dit Serse)" (4 January 2003).

62. See "Keterangan Tersangka," 146–52 in ibid.

63. Kepolisian Daerah Bali, "Berita Acara Pemeriksaan Ali Ghufron Als. Mukhlas" (14 December 2002), 8; Kepolisian Daerah Bali, "Berita Acara Pemeriksaan Ali Ghufron Als. Mukhlas" (Denpasar: Direktorat Reserse, Kepolisian Daerah Bali, 13 December 2002), 5.

64. Bomb Blast Investigation Task Force, "The Investigation of the Series of Bombing Connected to Jama'ah Islamiyyah Began with the Bali Bombings" (Jakarta: Indonesian National Police, 2003); Kepolisian Daerah Bali, "Berkas Perkara Amrozi Bin H. Nurhasyim (No. Pol. BP/01/I/2003/Dit Serse)" (4 January 2003). See Saksi 3 (Ali Imron), 11–18.

65. "Filipina Selidiki Peran JI," *Kompas,* 13 March 2003.

66. International Crisis Group, "Terrorism in Indonesia: Noordin's Networks" (Jakarta and Brussels: International Crisis Group, 5 May 2006), 2–3; Kejaksaan Negeri Jakarta Selatan, "Surat Dakwaan Atas Nama Terdakwa Mohd. Rais Al. Edi Indra Al. Iskandar Al. Ryan Arifin Al. Fendi Al. Roni Bin Rusdi Bin Hamid" (4 January 2004), 2–3.

67. Kejaksaan Negeri Jakarta Selatan, "Surat Dakwaan Atas Nama Terdakwa Mohd. Rais Al. Edi Indra Al. Iskandar Al. Ryan Arifin Al. Fendi Al. Roni Bin Rusdi Bin Hamid" (4 January 2004), 7.

68. International Crisis Group, "Terrorism in Indonesia," 3–4.

69. Kejaksaan Negeri Jakarta Selatan, "Surat Dakwaan Atas Nama Terdakwa Mohd. Rais Al. Edi Indra Al. Iskandar Al. Ryan Arifin Al. Fendi Al. Roni Bin Rusdi Bin Hamid" (4 January 2004), 4–6.

70. International Crisis Group, "Terrorism in Indonesia," 4–5.

71. Ibid.

CHAPTER 6

1. See E. Edward MacKinnon, "Indian and Indonesian Elements in Early North Sumatra," Peter Riddell, "Aceh in the Sixteenth and Seventeenth Centuries: 'Serambi Mekkah' and Identity," and Anthony Reid, "The Pre-Modern Sultanate's View of Its Place in the World," all in *Verandah of Violence: The Background to the Aceh Problem,* ed. Anthony Reid (Singapore and Seattle: Singapore University Press and the University of Washington Press, 2006), 22–71.

2. Geoffrey Robinson, "Rawan Is as Rawan Does: The Origins of Disorder in New Order Aceh," *Indonesia* 66 (1998): 127–57. This is also true of Tim Kell, *The Roots of Acehnese Rebellion, 1989–1992* (Ithaca: Southeast Asian Program, Cornell University, 1995) to a certain extent.

3. See William Nessen, "Sentiments Made Visible: The Rise and Reason of Aceh's National Liberation Movement," and Ed Aspinall, "Violence and Identity Formation in Aceh under Indonesian Rule," both in Reid, *Verandah of Violence,* 149–98.

4. Edward Aspinall, *Islam and Nation: Separatist Rebellion in Aceh, Indonesia* (Stanford: Stanford University Press, 2009).

5. John F. McCarthy, "The Demonstration Effect: Natural Resources, Ethnonationalism and the Aceh Conflict," *Singapore Journal of Tropical Geography* 28, no. 3 (2007): 314–33; Michael Ross, "Resource and Rebellion in Aceh, Indonesia," in *Understanding Civil War: Evidence and Analysis,* ed. Paul Collier and Nicholas Sambanis (Washington, DC: World Bank, 2005), 35–58.

6. Rizal Sukma, *Security Operations in Aceh: Goals, Consequences, and Lessons* (Washington, DC: East-West Center, 2004); Michael Ross, "Resource and Rebellion in Aceh, Indonesia," in Collier and Sambanis, *Understanding Civil War.*

7. There is already a small literature in English on GAM's activities in Aceh. See, for example, Sukma, *Security Operations in Aceh* and Kirsten Schulze, *The Free Aceh Movement (GAM): Anatomy of a Separatist Organization* (Washington, DC: East-West Center, 2004).

8. Edward Aspinall and Harold Crouch, *The Aceh Peace Process: Why It Failed* (Washington, DC: East-West Center, 2003).

9. McCarthy, "The Demonstration Effect," 314–33.

10. Edward Aspinall, *The Helsinki Agreement: A More Promising Basis for Peace in Aceh?* (Washington, DC: East-West Center, 2005), 9–10.

11. Precisely how many times Di Tiro visited Aceh, and what he did there is disputed. See Aspinall, *Islam and Nation,* 58–60.

12. M. Isa Sulaiman, *Aceh Merdeka: Ideologi, Kepemimpinan Dan Gerakan* (Jakarta: Pustaka al-Kautsar, 2000), 18, 20.

13. Ibid., 25, especially note 1.

14. Moch. Nurhasim et al., *Konflik Aceh: Analisis Atas Sebab-Sebab Konflik, Aktor Konflik, Kepentingan Dan Upaya Penyelesaian* (Jakarta: Lembaga Ilmu Pengetahuan Indonesia, 2003), 40; Sulaiman, *Aceh Merdeka,* 28.

15. Sulaiman, *Aceh Merdeka,* 28–29.

16. Al Chaidar, *Gerakan Aceh Merdeka: Jihad Rakyat Aceh Mewujudkan Negara Islam* (Jakarta: Madani Press, 2000), 169–71.

17. Aspinall, *Islam and Nation,* 66.

18. Al Chaidar, *Gerakan Aceh Merdeka,* 173.

19. Ibid., 171, 173.

20. See Sulaiman, *Aceh Merdeka,* 33.

21. Ibid., 31.

22. Kell, *The Roots of Acehnese Rebellion,* 65–66.

23. Moch. Nurhasim et al., *Konflik Aceh,* 44.

24. Sulaiman, *Aceh Merdeka,* 33.

25. Ibid., 38.

26. Ibid., 39–40.

27. Ibid., 40–41.

28. Al Chaidar, *Gerakan Aceh Merdeka,* 194–95. See also Aspinall, *Islam and Nation,* 104–5.

29. Kell, *The Roots of Acehnese Rebellion,* 66, 71.

30. Sulaiman, *Aceh Merdeka,* 52–53.

31. Author interview with senior GAM negotiator, Banda Aceh. January 2006.

32. Sulaiman, *Aceh Merdeka,* 56.

33. Dandhy Dwilaksono, "Alumni Libya Di Tanah Seulanga," *AcehKita,* August 2005.

34. Ibid.

35. "Serangan Alumni Libya," *AcehKita* August 2005. The number per year must have increased after that, given the total numbers trained over GAM's entire time in Libya.

36. Author Interview, Magazine Reporter, Jakarta, July 2005.

37. Dwilaksono, "Alumni Libya Di Tanah Seulanga."

38. Aspinall, *Islam and Nation,* 107.

39. Dwilaksono, "Alumni Libya Di Tanah Seulanga."

40. Author Interview, Think Tank Researcher on GAM, Jakarta, September 2005.

41. "Libya-Trained Rebel Stands Trial in Aceh," *Jakarta Post* 19 May 1992.

42. "Benang Merah Itu…," *AcehKita* August 2005.

43. Dwilaksono, "Alumni Libya Di Tanah Seulanga."

44. Author Interview, Magazine Reporter, Jakarta, July 2005.

45. "Perjalanan Rahasia Demi Setetes Air Kelapa," *AcehKita,* August 2005; "Benang Merah Itu…"; "Serangan Alumni Libya."

46. Moch. Nurhasim et al., *Konflik Aceh,* 64.

47. Sulaiman, *Aceh Merdeka,* 58.

48. Kell, *The Roots of Acehnese Rebellion,* 67.

49. Ibid., 68.

50. Ibid., 73.

51. Sulaiman, *Aceh Merdeka,* 72–73.

52. Ibid., 83.

53. Kell, *The Roots of Acehnese Rebellion,* 68.

54. Ibid., 73.

55. Sulaiman, *Aceh Merdeka,* 59, 66.

56. Moch. Nurhasim et al., *Konflik Aceh,* 59, 64. See also "GPK Aceh Bagaikan Duri Dalam Daging," *Suara Pembaruan,* 15 August 1994.

57. Sulaiman, *Aceh Merdeka,* 59.

58. Aspinall, *Islam and Nation,* 117–18.

59. Sulaiman, *Aceh Merdeka,* 59.

60. "GPK Aceh Bagaikan Duri Dalam Daging."

61. Kell, *The Roots of Acehnese Rebellion,* 76; "Malaysia Kecam GPK Aceh," *Kompas,* 15 September 1992.

62. Aspinall, *Islam and Nation,* 113–17.

63. Sulaiman, *Aceh Merdeka,* 72.

64. Kell, *The Roots of Acehnese Rebellion,* 76; "Sisa GPK Aceh Ingin Lari Ke Luar Negeri," *Angkatan Bersenjata,* 20 April 1992.

65. "GPK Aceh Bagaikan Duri Dalam Daging."

66. Sulaiman, *Aceh Merdeka,* 74, 82.

67. Ibid., 73.

68. Tuhana Taufiq A., ed., *Aceh Bergolak: Dulu Dan Kini* (Yogyakarta: Gama Global Media, 2000), 103; Al Chaidar, *Gerakan Aceh Merdek,* 211–12. According to Kirsten Schulze, *The Free Aceh Movement (GAM),* 21–22, the split began in 1987, but was not publicized until 1999.

69. Sulaiman, *Aceh Merdeka,* 84–85.

70. Author Interview, Think Tank Researcher on GAM, Jakarta, September 2005.

71. Author Interview, Acehnese Businessman, Kuala Lumpur, January 2006.

72. Ibid.

73. Author Interview, Think Tank Researcher on GAM, Jakarta, September 2005.

74. Author Interview, Magazine Reporter, Jakarta, July 2005.

75. Author Interview, GAM Negotiator, Banda Aceh, January 2006.

76. Aspinall, *Islam and Nation,* 160–61.

77. Schulze, *The Free Aceh Movement (GAM),* 35.

78. Author Interview, GAM Negotiator, Banda Aceh, January 2006.

79. Chart in Sulaiman, *Aceh Merdeka,* 124.

80. Author Interview, GAM Negotiator, Banda Aceh, January 2006.

81. Author Interview, Magazine Reporter, Jakarta, July 2005. See also Aspinall, *Islam and Nation,* 235.

82. Author Interview, GAM Negotiator, Banda Aceh, January 2006; Author Interview, Magazine Reporter, Jakarta, July 2005.

83. Author Interview, Acehnese Businessman, Kuala Lumpur, January 2006.

84. Author Interview, Think Tank Researcher on GAM, Jakarta, September 2005.

85. Aspinall, *Islam and Nation,* 163.

86. Author Interview, Acehnese Businessman, Kuala Lumpur, January 2006.

87. Author Interview, GAM Negotiator, Banda Aceh, January 2006.

88. Author Interview, Acehnese Businessman, Kuala Lumpur, January 2006.

89. Author Interview, Magazine Reporter, Jakarta, July 2005.

90. Author Interview, Think Tank Researcher on Indonesian Politics, Jakarta, September 2005.

91. Author Interview, Acehnese Businessman, Kuala Lumpur, January 2006.

92. Author Interview, Think Tank Researcher on GAM, Jakarta, September 2005.

93. According to Aspinall, *Islam and Nation,* 174–75, GAM's embeddedness in Acehnese villages was similar to the pattern set by Darul Islam in the 1950s.

94. Author Interview, GAM Negotiator, Banda Aceh, January 2006. It seems a bit hyperbolic to claim credit for weakening all of the Indonesian intelligence agency's network, given the turmoil Indonesia in general was experiencing at the time.

95. Author Interview, Think Tank Researcher on GAM, Jakarta, September 2005.

96. Author Interview, Counterterrorism Police Official, Jakarta, September 2005.

97. Abu Jihad, *Gam Hasan Tiro Pembantai Bangsa Aceh* (Jakarta: Titian Ilmu Insani, 2001), 75–76. Although GAM has admitted to killing Don Zulfahri, the source for these stories is quite anti-GAM, and should be treated accordingly.

98. Ibid., 70–75.

99. Ibid., 106–7.

100. That fact that Irwandi was legally arrested rather than just disappeared indicates that some things have indeed changed for the better in Indonesia.

101. Author Interview, GAM Negotiator, Banda Aceh, January 2006.

102. Ibid. In retrospect, this seems counterintuitive. It was the field leaders of GAM, men in their forties, who were the most prone to escape from Aceh via Medan, and then make trouble for the government once outside of Indonesia. In any case, from the evidence, it seems that even young men did not have a problem getting to Medan or Jakarta when carrying out GAM's operation.

103. Ibid. Irwandi's visit to the office was confirmed by *AcehKita* staffers.

104. Ibid.

105. According to the GAM member, the fake passport "didn't work," although it's not clear what the source meant by this.

106. Author Interview, GAM Negotiator, Banda Aceh, January 2006.

107. Ibid.; Author Interview, Counterterrorism Police Official, Jakarta, September 2005.

108. Aspinall, *Islam and Nation,* 188.

109. Author Interview, GAM Negotiator, Banda Aceh, January 2006; Aspinall, *Islam and Nation,* 161 estimates that GAM had 4,000–6,000 weapons at its peak.

110. Author Interview, GAM Negotiator, Banda Aceh, 12 January 2006; Author Interview, Magazine Reporter, Jakarta, July 2005.

111. "Pemasok Senjata GAM Diringkus Polisi," *Media Indonesia,* 13 September 2001.

112. "Sindikat Perdagangan Senjata Api Ke Aceh Tergolong Rapi," *Suara Pembaruan,* 1 September 2001.

113. "Pemasok Senjata GAM Diringkus Polisi," *Media Indonesia,* 13 September 2001.

114. Author Interview, Counterterrorism Police Official, Jakarta, September 2005.

115. Penyidik Tindak Pidana Koneksitas, "Berita Acara Pemeriksaan (Ibrahim Amd. Bin Abdul Wahab)," October 5, 2000 in "Sampul Berkas Perkara (No. Pol.: BP/04/XI/2000/ Koneksitas)" (Jakarta: Penyidik Perkara Pidana Koneksitas, DKI Jakarta dan Sekitarnya, 16 November 2000), 13–18.

116. "Digagalkan, Pengiriman Senjata Ke Aceh," *Republika,* 4 December 1999.

117. Author Interview, Magazine Reporter, Jakarta, July 2005.

118. Author Interview, Buddhist Pandita and Chinese-Indonesian Businessmen, Cipayung, Bogor, Indonesia, July 2005.

119. "Aparat Temukan Amunisi Di Hotel," *Media Indonesia,* 29 April 2003.

120. Author Interview, Buddhist Pandita and Chinese-Indonesian Businessmen, Cipayung, Bogor, Indonesia, July 2005.

121. Author Interview, GAM Negotiator, Banda Aceh, January 2006.

122. Aspinall, *Islam and Nation,* 261.

123. Author Interview, Buddhist Pandita and Chinese-Indonesian Businessmen, Cipayung, Bogor, Indonesia, July 2005.

124. Author Interview, GAM Negotiator, Banda Aceh, January 2006. See also Penyidik Tindak Pidana Koneksitas, "Berita Acara Pemeriksaan (Ibrahim Amd. Bin Abdul Wahab)" (October 5, 2000), 13–18, which lists all the weapons and bullets bought by Ibrahim, and how much they cost.

125. Author Interview, Magazine Reporter, Jakarta, July 2005.

126. Author Interview, Think Tank Researcher on GAM, Jakarta, September 2005.

127. "Diduga Kirim Senjata Ke Aceh 4 Oknum Tni-Au Ditahan," *Suara Karya,* 12 March 2002.

128. Author Interview, Acehnese Businessman, Kuala Lumpur, January 2006.

129. Author Interview, Magazine Reporter, Jakarta, July 2005.

130. "TNI Menemukan Bengkel Senjata Gam," *Koran Tempo,* 6 July 2001.

131. Author Interview, GAM Negotiator, Banda Aceh, January 2006.

132. "Benang Merah Itu…"

133. Author Interview, GAM Negotiator, Banda Aceh, January 2006.

134. "Benang Merah Itu…"; Author Interview, Magazine Reporter, Jakarta, July 2005; Author Interview, Buddhist Pandita and Chinese-Indonesian Businessmen, Cipayung, Bogor, Indonesia, July 2005. According to Aspinall, *Islam and Nation,* 188, Irwandi Yusuf estimates that 80 percent of GAM's weapons came from Thailand. This seems high.

135. Author Interview, GAM Negotiator, Banda Aceh, January 2006.

136. "Senjata Untuk Aceh Dicuri Dari Depot Militer Thailand," *Koran Tempo,* 17 May 2001; "Thailand Gagalkan Pasokan Senkata Untuk Gam," *Koran Tempo,* 12 May 2001.

137. "Polisi Thailand Sita Amunisi Untuk Aceh," *Suara Pembaruan,* 1 May 2001.

138. Author Interview, Acehnese Businessman, Kuala Lumpur, January 2006.

139. "Thailand Waspadai Penyelundupan Senjata Ke Aceh," *Kompas,* 25 May 2003.

140. "Senjata GAM Diduga Hasil Curian Dari Thailand," *Koran Tempo,* 19 February 2004.

141. "Polisi Tangkap Pemasok Senjata Dari Thailand," *Koran Tempo,* 14 February 2004.

142. "Benar, Gerakan Separatis Aceh Membeli Senjata Dari Negara Tetangga," *Kompas,* 3 December 2004.

143. Ibid.

144. Author Interview, GAM Negotiator, Banda Aceh, January 2006.

145. Aspinall, *Islam and Nation,* 163.

146. Author Interview, Think Tank Researcher on Piracy and Smuggling, Kuala Lumpur, July 2005.

147. Author Interview, GAM Negotiator, Banda Aceh, January 2006.

148. Ibid.

149. Author Interview, Think Tank Researcher on GAM, Jakarta, September 2005.

150. Author Interview, GAM Negotiator, Banda Aceh, January 2006.

151. Ibid.; also see Aspinall, *Islam and Nation,* 161.

152. Author Interview, U.S. Government Official, Medan, January 2006.

153. Author Interview, GAM Negotiator, Banda Aceh, January 2006.

154. Ibid.

155. Polisi Daerah Nanggroe Aceh Darussalam, "Perkembangan Situasi" (Banda Aceh: Polisi Daerah Nanggroe Aceh Darussalam, January 2006). This is an unpublished situation report on the Aceh peace process.

CHAPTER 7

1. R. T. Naylor, *Wages of Crime: Black Markets, Illegal Finance, and the Underworld Economy* (Ithaca: Cornell University Press, 2004), 22–23.

2. See, for example, Paul J. Smith, ed. *Terrorism and Violence in Southeast Asia* (Armonk, NY: M.E. Sharpe,2005), which has chapters on individual terrorist groups, but moves in the last section to general trends when discussing the connection between terrorism and transnational crime.

3. See Ko-Lin Chin, *The Golden Triangle: Inside Southeast Asia's Drug Trade* (Ithaca: Cornell University Press, 2009), particularly pp. 99–101, although the entire book is on this topic.

4. Naylor, *Wages of Crime,* 19–22.

5. Vadim Volkov, *Violent Entrepreneurs: The Use of Force in the Making of Russian Capitalism* (Ithaca: Cornell University Press, 2002).

6. Jan Van Dijk, "Mafia Markers: Assessing Organized Crime and Its Impact Upon Societies," *Trends in Organised Crime* 10 (2007): 39–56.

7. Vivienne Walt, "Cocaine Country," *Time,* June 27, 2007.

8. Phil Williams, "Transnational Criminal Organisations and International Security," *Survival* 36, no. 1 (1994): 96–113. See also Phil Williams, "Transnational Criminal Networks," in *Networks and Netwars: The Future of Terror, Crime, and Militancy,* ed. John Arquilla and David Ronfeldt (Santa Monica, CA: RAND, 2001), 61–98. Naylor goes so far as to argue that these networks have always been the predominant form of organization for organized criminals, and that technology is not necessarily making criminals any more powerful. See Naylor, *Wages of Crime,* 4–6, 27–30.

9. Michael Kenney, *From Pablo to Osama: Trafficking and Terrorist Networks, Government Bureaucracies, and Competitive Adaptation* (University Park: Pennsylvania State University Press, 2007), 38–40, 67–69.

10. Susan Strange, *The Retreat of the State: The Diffusion of Power in the World Economy* (New York: Cambridge University Press, 1996); Peter Chalk, *Non-Military Security and Global Order* (New York: St. Martin's Press, 2000).

11. Williams, "Transnational Criminal Networks," 77–78.

12. J. N. Mak, "Unilateralism and Regionalism: Working Together and Alone in the Malacca Straits," in *Piracy, Maritime Terrorism and Securing the Malacca Straits,* ed. Graham Gerard Ong Webb (Singapore: Institute of Southeast Asian Studies, 2006), 134–62.

13. Fort, "Transnational Threats and the Maritime Domain," in ibid., 25–28.

14. Alan Dupont, "Transnational Crime, Drugs, and Security in East Asia," *Asian Survey* 39, no. 3 (May/June 1999): 433–55.

15. Naylor, *Wages of Crime,* 6–7.

16. "Patroli Malindo Gagalkan 46 Kasus Kejahatan Di Laut," *Kompas,* 27 November 2004. The nine daily necessities are rice, sugar, fuel, salt, salted fish, cooking oil, coffee, eggs, and flour.

17. "Banjir Barang Ilegal Di Kalbar," *Kompas,* 24 February 2004.

18. "Penyelundupan Ayam Asal Malaysia Marak," *Kompas,* 24 March 2004.

19. Author Interview, Retired Customs Official, Jakarta, September 2005.

20. Ibid.

21. Author Interview, Foreign Company Executive, Jakarta, September 2005.

22. Ibid.

23. Yelas Kaparino, "Modus Lama Yang Baru Tercium," *Pilars,* 9–15 February 2004.

24. "Elektronik Selundupan Kuasai Pasar Nasional," *Kompas,* 17 September 2001.

25. Author Interview, Buddhist Pandita and Chinese-Indonesian Businessmen, Cipayung, Bogor, Indonesia, July 2005.

26. Author Interview, Maritime Think Tank Researcher, Johor Bahru, Malaysia, May 2005. See also "Perbatasan Sulut-Filipina Rawan Penyelundupan BBM," *Media Indonesia,* 22 March 2004.

27. They were mostly Toyotas, Nissans, and Subarus made between 1995 and 1999.

28. Author Interview, Singaporean Police Official, Singapore, July 2005.

29. Author Interview, Think Tank Researcher on Piracy and Smuggling, Kuala Lumpur, July 2005; Author Interview, Maritime Think Tank Researcher, Johor Bahru, Malaysia, May 2005. Later personal observations on Pulau Ubin confirm the presence of barriers in the water.

30. There are now spikes arrayed out from the pipes to prevent people from walking along them easily.

31. Author Interview, Singaporean Police Official, Singapore, July 2005.

32. Ibid.

33. Author Interview, Buddhist Pandita and Chinese-Indonesian Businessmen, Cipayung, Bogor, Indonesia, July 2005.

34. Author Interview, Singaporean Police Official, Singapore, July 2005.

35. Author Interview, Riau Islands Provincial Police Official, Batam, Indonesia, November 2005.

36. Ibid.

37. Author Interview, Chinese-Indonesian Businessmen, Batam, Indonesia, August 2005.

38. Author Interview, Buddhist Pandita, Jakarta, Indonesia, June 2004.

39. Author Interview, Chinese-Indonesian Businessmen, Batam, Indonesia, August 2005.

40. Author Interview, Retired Customs Official, Jakarta, September 2005.

41. Author Interview, Buddhist Pandita and Chinese-Indonesian Businessmen, Cipayung, Bogor, Indonesia, July 2005.

42. Author Interview, Criminology Professor/National Police Advisor, Jakarta, September 2005.

43. Author Interview, Riau Islands Provincial Police Official, Batam, Indonesia, November 2005.

44. Author Interview, Official, International Maritime Bureau, Kuala Lumpur, Malaysia, May 2005; Author Interview, Capt. Noel Choong, Head, International Maritime Bureau-Kuala Lumpur, Kuala Lumpur, 2005.

45. Author Interview, Capt. Noel Choong, Head, International Maritime Bureau-Kuala Lumpur, Kuala Lumpur, 2005.

46. Author Interview, Official, International Maritime Bureau, Kuala Lumpur, Malaysia, May 2005; Author Interview, Capt. Noel Choong, Head, International Maritime Bureau-Kuala Lumpur, Kuala Lumpur, 2005.

47. Eddi Fernandi, "Suarapublika: Bajak Laut: Penjelasan Komando Armabar TNI AL," *Republika,* 5 February 2004.

48. Author Interview, Official, International Maritime Bureau, Kuala Lumpur, Malaysia, May 2005.

49. Author Interview, Official, International Maritime Bureau, Kuala Lumpur, Malaysia, May 2005.

50. "Catatan Berserak Bajak Laut Modern," *Tempo,* 5 December 1999.

51. Author Interview, Official, International Maritime Bureau, Kuala Lumpur, Malaysia, May 2005.

52. Author Interview, Capt. Noel Choong, Head, International Maritime Bureau-Kuala Lumpur, Kuala Lumpur, 2005.

53. Poedjo Purnomo, "Selat Malaka Di Mata Pelaut," *Kompas,* 18 August 2004.

54. Author Interview, Official, Hong Kong Shipowners' Association, Hong Kong, October 2005.

55. Author Interview, Capt. Noel Choong, Head, International Maritime Bureau-Kuala Lumpur, Kuala Lumpur, 2005.

56. Author Interview, Official, International Maritime Bureau, Kuala Lumpur, Malaysia, May 2005.

57. Author Interview, Official, Hong Kong Shipowners' Association, Hong Kong, October 2005.

58. Author Interview, Official, International Maritime Bureau, Kuala Lumpur, Malaysia, May 2005.

59. Author Interview, Official, Hong Kong Shipowners' Association, Hong Kong, October 2005.

60. Author Interview, Capt. Noel Choong, Head, International Maritime Bureau-Kuala Lumpur, Kuala Lumpur, 2005.

61. Author Interview, Official, Hong Kong Shipowners' Association, Hong Kong, October 2005.

62. See Rumbadi Dalle, "Polisi Kejar Pengupah Bajak Laut," *Koran Tempo,* 27 April 2005, and "Bajak Laut Dibekuk," *Batam Pos,* 27 April 2005.

63. Eduardo Ma R Santos, "Piracy and Armed Robbery against Ships: Philippines Perspective" (Quezon City: Philippines Center for Transnational Crime, n.d.).

64. "Lima Pembajak Kapal Tanker Ditembak," *Kompas,* 13 June 2004.

65. "Perompak Bajak Kapal Bermuatan Batu Bara," *Media Indonesia,* 14 July 2004.

66. "Lantamal Tangkap 9 Bajak Laut Di Teluk Jakarta," *Media Indonesia,* 25 September 2004.

67. "Perompakan Kapal Di Selat Malaka, Tiga Abk Disandera," *Kompas,* 26 November 2004.

68. "Pirates Attack US Cruise Ship," *China Daily,* 7 November 2005.

69. Author Interview, Official, Hong Kong Shipowners' Association, Hong Kong, October 2005.

70. Author Interview, Capt. Noel Choong, Head, International Maritime Bureau-Kuala Lumpur, Kuala Lumpur, 2005.

71. Author Interview, Official, Hong Kong Shipowners' Association, Hong Kong, October 2005.

72. In Somalia, where there is no state to speak of, the situation is different. See Nick Childs, "Somalia's Pirates Are 'Thriving,'" BBC, 16 October 2007; Rob Crilly, "Pirates Help Fund Somali Warlords," *Christian Science Monitor,* August 27, 2008; "Somalia; UN Sanctions Action against Pirates," *Africa News,* 1 July 2008; Sean Kane, "France Raises Stakes with Arrest of Somali Pirates; Legal Issues Complicate Efforts to Try Suspects after Aggressive Pursuit," *Lloyd's List,* 7 May 2008.

73. "TNI AL Selamatkan Tiga Awak Kapal—Setelah Dibajak Di Perairan Pontianak," *Kompas,* 4 February 2003.

74. Santos, "Piracy and Armed Robbery against Ships."

75. "Selat Malaka Rawan Perompakan," *Media Indonesia,* 19 April 2004.

76. "Polisi Tangkap Kawanan Perompak Nelayan Di Laut," *Kompas,* 15 June 2004.

77. According to the International Maritime Organization, from 1998 through 2007, there were 3,289 pirate attacks globally, of which 751 took place in international waters. See www.imo.org.

78. Author Interview, Official, International Maritime Bureau, Kuala Lumpur, Malaysia, May 2005.

79. Ibid.

80. National Geospatial Intelligence Agency, "Anti-Shipping Activity Message 1998–59" (Bethesda, MD: National Geospatial Intelligence Agency, 8 September 1998). In the *Louisa* incident, pirates hijacked the *Louisa* off the southern coast of Taiwan, and held the crew hostage for about a week while they failed to find a buyer. See also Author Interview, Capt. Noel Choong, Head, International Maritime Bureau-Kuala Lumpur, Kuala Lumpur, 2005.

81. Agence France Presse, "Pirate Attack an inside Job: Police," *Jakarta Post,* 17 June 2005.

82. Author Interview, Capt. Noel Choong, Head, International Maritime Bureau-Kuala Lumpur, Kuala Lumpur, 2005; Author Interview, Chinese-Indonesian Businessmen, Batam, Indonesia., August 2005.

83. Edy Budiyarso, Arif Ardiansyah, and Rumbadi Dalle, "Hikayat Kapten Hook Di Selat Malaka," *Tempo,* 4 July 2004.

84. Author Interview, Capt. Noel Choong, Head, International Maritime Bureau-Kuala Lumpur, Kuala Lumpur, 2005; "Kapal Indonesia Dibajak, Lalu Dibawa Ke Malaysia," *Kompas,* 27 April 2005.

85. Author Interview, Official, Hong Kong Shipowners' Association, Hong Kong, October 2005.

86. Author Interview, Maritime Think Tank Researcher, Johor Bahru, Malaysia, May 2005.

87. Ibid.

88. Author Interview, Capt. Noel Choong, Head, International Maritime Bureau-Kuala Lumpur, Kuala Lumpur, 2005.

89. Author Interview, Chinese-Indonesian Businessmen, Batam, Indonesia, August 2005.

90. "Lanal Batam Gagalkan Pencurian Kapal," *Kompas,* 6 June 2005.

91. Rumbadi Dalle, "Polisi Buru Pengupah Bajak Laut," *Koran Tempo,* 27 April 2005.

92. "Bajak Laut Dibekuk"; Dalle, "Polisi Kejar Pengupah Bajak Laut." It is unknown whether Mr. Lee told Doni the exact port in Thailand where they were supposed to go, or whether that information would be forthcoming later.

93. Dalle, "Polisi Kejar Pengupah Bajak Laut."

94. "Bajak Laut Dibekuk."

95. "Polairud Gagalkan Pembajakan Tongkang Di Perairan Natuna," *Kompas,* 26 April 2005; Dalle, "Polisi Kejar Pengupah Bajak Laut."

96. "Bajak Laut Dibekuk."

97. Author Interview, Riau Islands Provincial Maritime Police Official, Batam, Indonesia, November 2005.

98. "Batam Police Arrest Pirates," *Jakarta Post,* 27 April 2005.

99. National Geospatial Intelligence Agency, "Anti-Shipping Activity Message 1998–33" (Bethesda, MD: National Geospatial Intelligence Agency, 17 April 1998).

100. Author Interview, Owner, Shipping Company, Singapore, November 2005.

101. National Geospatial Intelligence Agency, "Anti-Shipping Activity Message 1998–33."

102. Author Interview, Owner, Shipping Company, Singapore, November 2005.

CHAPTER 8

1. The study of how terrorist organizations end is a small but important field. See, for example, Audrey Kurth Cronin, "How Al-Qaida Ends: The Decline and Demise of Terrorist Groups," *International Security* 31, no. 1 (2006): 7–48.

2. See John Arquilla and David Ronfeldt, eds., *Networks and Netwars: The Future of Terror, Crime, and Militancy* (Santa Monica, CA: RAND, 2001).

3. Michael Kenney, *From Pablo to Osama: Trafficking and Terrorist Networks, Government Bureaucracies, and Competitive Adaptation* (University Park: Pennsylvania State University Press, 2007), 25–47.

4. See, for example, Martin C. Libicki, Peter Chalk, and Melanie Sisson, *Exploring Terrorist Targeting Preferences* (Santa Monica, CA: RAND, 2007).

5. Bruce Hoffman, "Terrorism Trends and Prospects," in *Countering the New Terrorism,* ed. Ian O. Lesser et al. (Santa Monica, CA: RAND, 1999), 7–36.

6. A famous case of this was in the 1990s, when al-Qaeda stopped using satellite phones after realizing that the United States could tap them. See also Eli Berman and David Laitin, "Hard Targets: Theory and Evidence on Suicide Attacks," National Bureau of Economic Research Working Paper No. W11740 (Cambridge, MA, November 2005).

7. Brian A. Jackson et al., *Aptitude for Destruction.* Vol. 2: *Case Studies of Organizational Learning in Five Terrorist Groups* (Santa Monica, CA: RAND, 2005), 84–87.

8. Ibid., 87. See also John Thayer Sidel, *Riots, Pogroms, Jihad: Religious Violence in Indonesia* (Ithaca: Cornell University Press, 2006).

9. Brian A. Jackson et al., *Aptitude for Destruction,* 75.

10. Ibid., 64–65.

11. Kejaksaan Tinggi DKI Jakarta, "Berita Acara Pemeriksaan Tersangka Muzahar Muhtar Alias Taslim Alias Musa" (Jakarta: Kejaksaan Tinggi DKI Jakarta, 12 September 1986), 3.

12. Kejaksaan Tinggi DKI Jakarta, "Berita Acara Pemeriksaan Saksi K. Jerunt (?) Adnan Al. Aos Firdaus Al. Haman (?) Syaiful Rahman Bin Mohamad Adnan (Jakarta: Kejaksaan Tinggi DKI Jakarta, 11 September 1986), 4–5.

13. Nasir Abas, *Membongkar Jamaah Islamiyah: Pengakuan Mantan Anggota JI* (Jakarta: Grafindo, 2005), 26–32.

14. Ibid., 40.

15. International Crisis Group, "Recycling Militants in Indonesia: Darul Islam and the Australian Embassy Bombing" (Jakarta: International Crisis Group, 22 February 2005), 21.

16. International Crisis Group, "Jemaah Islamiyah in Southeast Asia: Damaged but Still Dangerous" (Jakarta: International Crisis Group, 26 August 2003), 6.

17. Abas, *Membongkar Jamaah Islamiyah,* 142.

18. Ibid., 40.

19. This is the main mechanism for transition from DI to JI put forward by International Crisis Group. See International Crisis Group, "Jemaah Islamiyah in Southeast Asia," 4–6.

20. Abas, *Membongkar Jamaah Islamiyah,* 84.

21. International Crisis Group, "Jemaah Islamiyah in Southeast Asia," 6.

22. Zachary Abuza, *Militant Islam in Southeast Asia: Crucible of Terror* (Boulder, CO: Lynne Rienner, 2003), 129.

23. Abas, *Membongkar Jamaah Islamiyah,* 84–85.

24. Author Interview, Malaysian Counter-Terrorism Official, Kuala Lumpur, December 2005.

25. Author Interview, Singaporean External Intelligence Officials, Singapore, October 2005.

26. Author Interview, Malaysian Counter-Terrorism Official, Kuala Lumpur, December 2005.

27. Derwin Pereira, "Militants in Region 'Plan to Strike Back,'" *Straits Times* 11 February 2002.

28. See International Crisis Group, "Indonesia: Jemaah Islamiyah's Current Status" (Jakarta and Brussels: International Crisis Group, 3 May 2007).

29. Pereira, "Militants in Region 'Plan to Strike Back.'"

30. Author Interview, Former Jemaah Islamiyah Regional Leader, Jakarta, December 2005.

31. See International Crisis Group, "Recycling Militants in Indonesia," 27.

32. Author Interview, International NGO Researcher on Terrorism and Insurgency, Singapore, April 2005.

33. "Q+A: Noordin Mohammad Top and Islamic Militancy in Indonesia," Reuters, 17 September 2009.

34. Peter Gelling, "Border Security Questioned in Indonesia," *New York Times,* 10 March 2010.

35. This is one of the main arguments of Edward Aspinall, *Islam and Nation: Separatist Rebellion in Aceh, Indonesia* (Stanford: Stanford University Press, 2009).

36. See Tuhana Taufiq A., ed. *Aceh Bergolak: Dulu Dan Kini* (Yogyakarta: Gama Global Media, 2000), 103; Al Chaidar, *Gerakan Aceh Merdeka: Jihad Rakyat Aceh Mewujudkan Negara Islam* (Jakarta: Madani Press, 2000), 211–12.

37. Author Interview, Official, Hong Kong Shipowners' Association, Hong Kong, October 2005.

38. Author Interview, Official, International Maritime Bureau, Kuala Lumpur, Malaysia, May 2005.

39. Author Interview, Official, Hong Kong Shipowners' Association, Hong Kong, October 2005.

40. Ibid.

41. See the reports by the International Maritime Organization at www.imo.org. Although I derived the hijacking numbers from the IMO reports, my definition of hijacking is apparently different from the IMO's, so the numbers do not match exactly. A fuller description of the dataset behind these numbers can be found in Justin V. Hastings, "Geographies of State Failure and Sophistication in Maritime Piracy Hijackings," *Political Geography* 28, no. 4 (2009): 213–23.

42. Author Interview, Capt. Noel Choong, Head, International Maritime Bureau-Kuala Lumpur, Kuala Lumpur, July 2005.

43. Ibid.

44. International Maritime Organization, "AIS transponders" (London: International Maritime Organization, 2002).

45. Author Interview, Official, Hong Kong Shipowners' Association, Hong Kong, October 2005.

46. Author Interview, Capt. Noel Choong, Head, International Maritime Bureau-Kuala Lumpur, Kuala Lumpur, July 2005.

47. Ibid.

48. Justin V. Hastings, "Geographies of State Failure and Sophistication in Maritime Piracy Hijackings," 219.

49. Author Interview, Think Tank Researcher on Piracy and Smuggling, Kuala Lumpur, July 2005.

50. Ibid.

51. Author Interview, Retired Royal Malaysian Navy Admiral, Kuala Lumpur, December 2005.

52. "Missing Cargo Ship Found in Chinese Port," *Korea Times,* 29 December 1998.

53. Glenn Schloss, "Mainland Frees 'Pirates'," *South China Morning Post,* 18 July 1999.

54. Marcus Hand, "International: Piracy: Hijack Links Fuel Syndicate Theory," *Lloyd's List,* 12 May 2000.

55. Jayant Abhyankar, "Piracy and Armed Robbery and Terrorism at Sea," paper presented at the ORF Workshop on Maritime Counter Terrorism, 29 November 2004, Delhi, India.

56. Ibid. A richer description can also be found in Martin N. Murphy, *Small Boats, Weak States, Dirty Money: Piracy & Maritime Terrorism in the Modern World* (London: Hurst, 2008), 141–45.

57. Martin N. Murphy, *Small Boats, Weak States, Dirty Money,* 142.

58. For a more detailed description of the incident, see Indira A. R. Lakshmanan, "After Criticism, China Cracking Down on Pirates," *Boston Globe,* 4 September 2000.

59. Richard Cook, "Smugglers on the Run," *South China Morning Post* 13 September 1998.

60. Ibid.; Stefan Eklöf, *Pirates in Paradise: A Modern History of Southeast Asia's Maritime Marauders* (Copenhagen: Nordic Institute of Asian Studies, 2006), 78.

61. David Hughes, "Piracy Rebuttal by China 'Selective,' Says IMB," *Business Times,* 4 October 1999.

62. Author Interview, Government-Linked Economist, Jakarta, July 2005.

63. Author Interview, Criminology Professor/National Police Advisor, Jakarta, September 2005.

64. Author Interview, Retired Customs Official, Jakarta, September 2005.

65. Author Interview, Riau Islands Provincial Police Official, Batam, Indonesia, November 2005.

66. Author Interview, Buddhist Pandita and Chinese-Indonesian Businessmen, Cipayung, Bogor, Indonesia, July 2005.

67. Video compact discs are popular in Asia for their cheapness relative to DVDs.

68. Author Interview, Chinese-Indonesian Smuggler, Batam, Indonesia, August 2005. It would be unsurprising if since the interview the smuggler has moved on to electronic forms of obtaining movies.

69. See, for example, "More Than One Million Pirated CDs and DVDs, Confiscated by Police in a Major Anti-Piracy Crack Down in Jakarta, Indonesia," *Birmingham Post,* 16 September 2005.

70. Author Interview, Chinese-Indonesian Smuggler, Batam, Indonesia, August 2005.

71. Author Interview, Chinese-Indonesian Businessmen, Batam, Indonesia, August 2005.

72. Author Interview, Chinese-Indonesian Smuggler, Batam, Indonesia, August 2005.

CONCLUSION

1. See, for example, Combating Terrorism Center, *Al-Qa'ida's Structure and Bylaws* (West Point, NY: Combating Terrorism Center, U.S. Military Academy, 2 October 2007); Combating Terrorism Center, *Al-Qa'ida Constitutional Charter* (West Point, NY: Combating Terrorism Center, U.S. Military Academy, 17 March 2006).

2. For discussions of the ideological underpinnings the jihadist movement's territorial ambitions, see Youssef Aboul-Enein, *Three-Part Study of Sheikh Abdallah Azzam,*

Al-Qa'ida's First Ideologue (West Point, NY: Combating Terrorism Center, U.S. Military Academy, 2007) and David Cook, *Paradigmatic Jihadi Movements* (West Point, NY: Combating Terrorism Center, U.S. Military Academy, 2006).

3. Combating Terrorism Center, *Al-Qaida's (Mis)Adventures in the Horn of Africa* (West Point, NY: Combating Terrorism Center, U.S. Military Academy, 2007).

4. See National Commission on Terrorist Attacks upon the United States, "The 9/11 Commission Report" (Washington, DC: National Commission on Terrorist Attacks upon the United States, 2004).

5. Combating Terrorism Center, *Al-Qa'ida's Structure and Bylaws;* Combating Terrorism Center, *Al-Qa'ida Constitutional Charter.*

6. Angel Rabasa et al., *Ungoverned Territories: Understanding and Reducing Terrorism Risks* (Santa Monica, CA: RAND, 2007), 64–65.

7. Ibid., pp. 49–76, goes into great depth about the advantages that various militant groups enjoy on the Afghan-Pakistan border, but is cagey about the extent to which al-Qaeda enjoys the same advantages.

8. On the Salafist Group for Preaching and Combat (GSPC), see Lianne Kennedy Boudali, *The GSPC: Newest Franchise in Al-Qa'ida's Global Jihad* (West Point, NY: Combating Terrorism Center, U.S. Military Academy, 2007).

9. "Al-Qaeda Disowns 'Fake Letter,'" BBC, 13 October 2005.

10. "Iraq: British 'Fleeing' Claims Al-Qaeda," *ADNKronos,* 17 December 2007.

11. Ian O. Lesser et al., *Countering the New Terrorism* (Santa Monica, CA: RAND, 1999) is one of the primary proponents of this idea.

12. Bruce Hoffman, *Combating Al Qaeda and the Militant Islamic Threat (Testimony Presented to the House Armed Services Committee, Subcommittee on Terrorism, Unconventional Threats and Capabilities on February 16, 2006)* (Santa Monica, CA: RAND, 16 February 2006), 5–6. See also Yassin Musharbash, "Interview with Terrorism Expert Bruce Hoffman: 'Al-Qaida Is More Dangerous Than It Was on 9/11,'" *Spiegel Online,* 10 October 2006.

13. "Madrid Bombers Get Long Sentences," BBC 31 October 2007.

14. Sean Boyne, "Uncovering the Irish Republican Army," *Jane's Intelligence Review,* 1 August 1996. The Troubles were the time period of ethnic and political conflict in Northern Ireland that largely coincided with the rise of the Provisional IRA in 1969 to the signing of the Belfast Accords in 1998.

15. See reports on incidents of piracy and armed robbery from the International Maritime Organization; www.imo.org.

16. See Robert Rotberg, "The New Nature of Nation-State Failure," *Washington Quarterly* 25, no. 3 (2002): 85–96 for a discussion of failed and collapsed states.

17. See "Somali Rivals to Seek MPs' Votes," BBC, 29 January 2009. As of January 2009, the Transitional Federal Government was meeting in Djibouti.

18. James A. Piazza, "Incubators of Terror: Do Failed and Failing States Promote Transnational Terrorism?" *International Studies Quarterly* 52, no. 3 (2008): 469–88.

19. Combating Terrorism Center, "Al-Qaida's (Mis)Adventures in the Horn of Africa," 15.

20. These figures are taken from International Maritime Organization (IMO) narrative reports from 2000 through 2007. The IMO has different figures for total hijackings, but because it does not define "hijacking" in its reports, nor does it categorize individual incidents, I attribute the different totals to different definitions of the act.

21. This tendency of pirates in failed states to choose kidnappings for ransom over ship and cargo seizures remains even when one controls for region (and thus region-specific characteristics). See ibid.

22. "Harardhere: The Capital of Somali Piracy," Agence France Presse, 19 November 2008; Xan Rice, "Focus: Ocean Terror: How Savage Pirates Reign on the World's High

Seas," *Observer* (UK), 27 April 2008; Xan Rice and Abdiqani Hassan, "Hostage Ships: The Stronghold: Life Is Sweet in Piracy Capital of the World," *Guardian* (UK), 19 November 2008; "Pirate Attack an inside Job: Police," *Jakarta Post,* 17 June 2005; "Yacht Raid Reveals Hi-Tech Somali Pirate Network; Former Fishermen Armed with Hand-Held Missiles," *Belfast Telegraph,* 10 April 2008; "Not Feeling More Secure," *Lloyd's List,* 29 August 2008.

23. Rob Crilly, "Pirates Help Fund Somali Warlords," *Christian Science Monitor,* August 27, 2008.

24. Ibid.

25. "Somalia; Pirates Hijack UN Food Ship Off Coast," *Africa News* 26 February 2007.

26. Jayshree Bajoria, "The Sri Lankan Conflict" (New York: Council on Foreign Relations, 18 May 2009).

27. Preeti Bhattacharji, "Liberation Tigers of Tamil Eelam (AKA Tamil Tigers) (Sri Lanka, Separatists)" (New York: Council on Foreign Relations, 20 May 2009).

28. Kate Pickert, "The Tamil Tigers," *Time,* 4 January 2009.

29. Preeti Bhattacharji, "Liberation Tigers of Tamil Eelam (AKA Tamil Tigers) (Sri Lanka, Separatists)."

30. Kristian Stokke, "Building the Tamil Eelam State: Emerging State Institutions and Forms of Governance in Ltte-Controlled Areas in Sri Lanka," *Third World Quarterly* 27, no. 6 (2006): 1021–40.

31. N. Manoharan, "Tigers with Fins: Naval Wing of the LTTE" (New Delhi: Institute of Peace & Conflict Studies, 1 June 2005).

32. N. Sathiya Moorthy et al., "The Way Ahead in Sri Lanka" (New Delhi: Observer Research Foundation, November 2006), 10.

33. Ibid., 7. See also John C. Thompson and Joe Turlej, *Other People's Wars: A Review of Overseas Terrorism in Canada* (Toronto, ON: The MacKenzie Institute, June 2003), 93.

34. Manoharan, "Tigers with Fins."

35. Thompson and Turlej, "Other People's Wars," 46.

36. Steve Herman, "Sri Lanka Army Amazed by Size of Captured Rebel Arsenal," *Voice of America News,* 6 May 2009.

37. D. B. S. Jeyaraj, "The Taking of Elephant Pass," *Frontline,* 13–26 May 2000; "The Fall of Elephant Pass," *Sri Lanka Sunday Times,* 22 April 2001.

38. "Key Tamil Tiger Sea Base 'Falls,'" BBC, 5 February 2009.

39. Jeyaraj, "The Taking of Elephant Pass"; "The Fall of Elephant Pass."

Bibliography

A., Tuhana Taufiq, ed. *Aceh Bergolak: Dulu Dan Kini.* Yogyakarta: Gama Global Media, 2000.

Abas, Nasir. *Membongkar Jamaah Islamiyah: Pengakuan Mantan Anggota JI.* Jakarta: Grafindo, 2005.

Abhyankar, Jayant. "Piracy and Armed Robbery and Terrorism at Sea." Delhi: ORF Workshop on Maritime Counter Terrorism, 29 November 2004.

Aboul-Enein, Youssef. *Three-Part Study of Sheikh Abdallah Azzam, Al-Qa'ida's First Ideologue.* West Point, NY: Combating Terrorism Center, U.S. Military Academy, 2007.

Abuza, Zachary. *Political Islam and Violence in Indonesia.* New York: Routledge, 2007.

——. "Balik-Terrorism: The Return of the Abu Sayyaf." Carlisle Barracks, PA: Strategic Studies Institute, Army War College, September 2005.

——. *Militant Islam in Southeast Asia: Crucible of Terror.* Boulder, CO: Lynne Rienner, 2003.

Al Chaidar. *Gerakan Aceh Merdeka: Jihad Rakyat Aceh Mewujudkan Negara Islam.* Jakarta: Madani Press, 2000.

Andreas, Peter. "Redrawing the Line: Borders and Security in the 21st Century." *International Security* 28, no. 2 (2003): 78–112.

Arquilla, John, and David Ronfeldt, eds. *Networks and Netwars: The Future of Terror, Crime, and Militancy.* Santa Monica, CA: RAND, 2001.

Aryasinha, Ravinatha. "Terrorism, the LTTE and the Conflict in Sri Lanka." *Conflict, Security & Development* 1, no. 2 (2001): 25–50.

Aspinall, Edward. *Islam and Nation: Separatist Rebellion in Aceh, Indonesia.* Stanford: Stanford University Press, 2009.

——. *The Helsinki Agreement: A More Promising Basis for Peace in Aceh?* Washington, DC: East-West Center, 2005.

Aspinall, Edward, and Harold Crouch. *The Aceh Peace Process: Why It Failed.* Washington, DC: East-West Center, 2003.

Atran, Scott. "The Moral Logic and Growth of Suicide Terrorism." *Washington Quarterly* 29, no. 2 (2006): 127–47.

Badan Reserse Kriminal Polri. "Berita Acara Pemeriksaan Mohammad Nasir Bin Abas Als. Khairudin Als. Sulaeman Als. Leman Als. Maman Als. Nasir Abas Als. Husna Als. Abu Husna Als. Eddy Mulyono Als. Malik." Jakarta: Direktorat I/Keamanan & Transnasional, Badan Reserse Kriminal Polri, 20 August 2003.

——. "Berita Acara Pemeriksaan Mohammad Nasir Bin Abas Als. Khairudin Als. Sulaeman Als. Leman Als. Maman Als. Nasir Abas Als. Husna Als. Abu Husna Als. Eddy Mulyono Als. Malik." Jakarta: Direktorat I/Keamanan & Transnasional, Badan Reserse Kriminal Polri, 10 July 2003.

——. "Berita Acara Pemeriksaan Mohammad Nasir Bin Abas Als. Khairudin Als. Sulaeman Als. Leman Als. Maman Als. Nasir Abas Als. Husna Als. Abu Husna Als. Eddy Mulyono Als. Malik." Jakarta: Direktorat I/Keamanan & Transnasional, Badan Reserse Kriminal Polri, 9 May 2003.

Bajoria, Jayshree. "The Sri Lankan Conflict." New York: Council on Foreign Relations, 18 May 2009.

Barber, Benjamin. "Plenary Roundtable: The Clash of Cultures and American Hegemony." Paper presented at the American Political Science Association Annual Meeting, Philadelphia, 1 September 2006.

Barton, Greg. *Jemaah Islamiyah: Radical Islamism in Indonesia.* Singapore: Singapore University Press, 2005.

"Benang Merah Itu…" *AcehKita,* August 2005, 24–25.

Bergen, Peter L. *The Osama Bin Laden I Know: An Oral History of Al-Qaeda's Leader.* New York: Free Press, 2006.

———. *Holy War, Inc.: Inside the Secret World of Osama Bin Laden.* New York: Simon and Schuster, 2002.

Berman, Eli, and David D. Laitin. "Religion, Terrorism and Public Goods: Testing the Club Model." National Bureau of Economic Research Working Paper no. 13725, Cambridge, MA, January 2008.

———. "Hard Targets: Theory and Evidence on Suicide Attacks." National Bureau of Economic Research Working Paper No. W11740, Cambridge, MA, November 2005.

Bin Laden, Osama. "Declaration of War against the Americans Occupying the Land of the Two Holy Places." *Al Quds Al Arabiy,* London, August 1996. http://www.pbs.org/newshour/terrorism/international/fatwa_1996.html.

Bhattacharji, Preeti. "Liberation Tigers of Tamil Eelam (AKA Tamil Tigers) (Sri Lanka, Separatists)." New York: Council on Foreign Relations, 20 May 2009.

Black, Donald. "The Geometry of Terrorism." *Sociological Theory* 22, no. 1 (2004): 14–25.

Bomb Blast Investigation Task Force. "The Investigation of the Series of Bombing Connected to Jama'ah Islamiyyah Began with the Bali Bombings." Jakarta: Indonesian National Police, 2003.

Boudali, Lianne Kennedy. *The GSPC: Newest Franchise in Al-Qa'ida's Global Jihad.* West Point, NY: Combating Terrorism Center, U.S. Military Academy, 2007.

Boyne, Sean. "Uncovering the Irish Republican Army." *Jane's Intelligence Review,* 1 August 1996.

Brenner, Neil. "Beyond State-Centrism? Space, Territoriality, and Geographical Scale in Globalization Studies." *Theory and Society* 29, no. 1 (1999): 39–78.

Brown, Christopher. *Sovereignty, Rights and Justice: International Political Theory Today.* Cambridge: Polity Press, 2002.

Brown, Graham. "The Perils of Terrorism: Chinese Whispers, Kevin Bacon and Al Qaeda in Southeast Asia—A Review Essay." *Intelligence and National Security* 21, no. 1 (2006): 150–82.

Byman, Daniel. "Al-Qa'ida as an Adversary: Do We Understand the Enemy?" *World Politics* no. 56 (2003): 139–63.

Camilleri, Joseph, and Jim Falk. *The End of Sovereignty? The Politics of a Shrinking and Fragmenting World.* Brookfield, VT: Edward Elgar, 1992.

Campbell, Kurt M. "Globalization's First War?" *Washington Quarterly* 25, no. 1 (2002): 7–14.

Chalk, Peter. *Non-Military Security and Global Order.* Houndsmills, UK: Macmillan, 2000.

———. "Low Intensity Conflict in Southeast Asia: Piracy, Drug Trafficking, and Political Terrorism." *Conflict Issues* 305/306 (1998).

Chin, Ko-Lin. *The Golden Triangle: Inside Southeast Asia's Drug Trade.* Ithaca: Cornell University Press, 2009.

Collier, Paul, and Nicholas Sambanis, eds. *Understanding Civil War: Evidence and Analysis.* Washington, DC: World Bank, 2005.

Combating Terrorism Center. *Al-Qa'ida Constitutional Charter.* West Point, NY: Combating Terrorism Center, U.S. Military Academy, 17 March 2006.

——. *Al-Qa'ida's (Mis)Adventures in the Horn of Africa.* West Point, NY: Combating Terrorism Center, U.S. Military Academy, 2007.

——. *Al-Qa'ida's Structure and Bylaws.* West Point, NY: Combating Terrorism Center, U.S. Military Academy, 2 October 2007.

——. *Harmony Document AFGP-2002-800621—Letters on Al-Qa'ida's Operations in Africa.* West Point, NY: U.S. Military Academy, 2007.

Conboy, Kenneth. *The Second Front: Inside Asia's Most Dangerous Terrorist Network.* Jakarta: Equinox, 2006.

Cook, David. *Paradigmatic Jihadi Movements.* West Point, NY: Combating Terrorism Center, U.S. Military Academy, 2006.

Cooper, Richard N. *Tariffs and Smuggling in Indonesia.* New Haven: Economic Growth Center, Yale University, 1974.

Crenshaw, Martha. "Explaining Suicide Terrorism: A Review Essay." *Security Studies* 16, no. 1 (2007): 133–62.

Cronin, Audrey Kurth. "How Al-Qaida Ends: The Decline and Demise of Terrorist Groups." *International Security* 31, no. 1 (2006): 7–48.

——. "Behind the Curve: Globalization and International Terrorism." *International Security* 27, no. 3 (2002–2003): 30–58.

Cutter, Susan L., Douglas B. Richardson, and Thomas J. Wilbanks, eds. *The Geographical Dimensions of Terrorism.* New York: Routledge, 2003.

Della Porta, Donatella, ed. *Social Movements and Violence: Participation in Underground Organizations.* Greenwich, CT: JAI Press, 1992.

Della Porta, Donatella, and Sidney G. Tarrow, eds. *Transnational Protest and Global Activism.* Lanham, MD: Rowman & Littlefield, 2005.

Deutsche Bank Research. "Container Shipping: Overcapacity Inevitable Despite Increasing Demand." Frankfurt: Deutsche Bank, 25 April 2006.

Dijk, Jan Van. "Mafia Markers: Assessing Organized Crime and Its Impact Upon Societies." *Trends in Organised Crime* 10 (2007): 39–56.

Dragonette, Charles N. "Lost at Sea." *Foreign Affairs* 82, no. 2 (2005).

Dupont, Alan. "Transnational Crime, Drugs, and Security in East Asia." *Asian Survey* 39, no. 3 (1999): 433–55.

Dwilaksono, Dandhy. "Alumni Libya Di Tanah Seulanga." *AcehKita,* August 2005, 28–29.

Eklöf, Stefan. *Pirates in Paradise: A Modern History of Southeast Asia's Maritime Marauders.* Copenhagen: Nordic Institute of Asian Studies, 2006.

Esty, Daniel C., Jack Goldstone, Ted Robert Gurr, Barbara Harff, Pamela T. Surko, Alan N. Unger, and Robert Chen. "The State Failure Project: Early Warning Research for Us Foreign Policy Planning." In *Preventive Measures: Building Risk Assessment and Crisis Early Warning Systems,* ed. John L. Davies and Ted Robert Gurr, 27–38. Boulder, CO and Totowa, NJ: Rowman and Littlefield, 1998.

Flint, Colin. "Terrorism and Counterterrorism: Geographic Research Questions and Agendas." *Professional Geographer* 55, no. 2 (May 2003): 161–69.

Friedman, Thomas. *The World Is Flat.* New York: Farrar, Straus and Giroux, 2006.

Fund for Peace. "Failed State Index." Washington, DC: Fund for Peace/Foreign Policy, 2008.

GAM/Government of Indonesia. "Memorandum of Understanding between the Government of the Republic of Indonesia and the Free Aceh Movement." Helsinki: GAM/Government of Indonesia, 15 August 2005.

Ganor, Boaz. "Terrorist Organization Typologies and the Probability of a Boomerang Effect." *Studies in Conflict & Terrorism* 31, no. 4 (2008): 269–81.

Ganster, Paul, and David E. Lorey, eds. *Borders and Border Politics in a Globalizing World.* Lanham, MD: SR Books, 2005.

Gilpin, Robert. *Global Political Economy: Understanding the International Economic Order.* Princeton: Princeton University Press, 2001.

Grundy-Warr, Carl, and Elaine Wong. "Geopolitics of Drugs and Cross-Border Relations: Burma-Thailand." *Border and Security Bulletin* 9, no. 1 (2001): 108–21.

Gunaratna, Rohan. *Inside Al Qaeda: Global Network of Terror.* New York: Columbia University Press, 2002.

Haigh, Stephen Paul. "Globalization and the Sovereign State: Authority and Territoriality Reconsidered." Paper presented at First Oceanic International Studies Conference, Australian National University, Canberra, Australia, 14–16 July 2004.

Hamilton-Hart, Natasha. "Terrorism in Southeast Asia: Expert Analysis, Myopia and Fantasy." *Pacific Review* 18, no. 3 (2005): 303–25.

Hastings, Justin V. "Geographies of State Failure and Sophistication in Maritime Piracy Hijackings." *Political Geography* 28, no. 4 (2009): 213–23.

Hazbun, Waleed. "Globalisation, Reterritorialisation, and the Political Economy of Tourism Development in the Middle East." *Geopolitics* 9, no. 2 (2004): 310–44.

Herbst, Jeffrey. *State and Power in Africa: Comparative Lessons in Authority and Control.* Princeton: Princeton University Press, 2000.

Hoffman, Bruce. *Combating Al Qaeda and the Militant Islamic Threat (Testimony Presented to the House Armed Services Committee, Subcommittee on Terrorism, Unconventional Threats and Capabilities on February 16, 2006).* Santa Monica, CA: RAND, 16 February 2006.

——. "The Changing Face of Al Qaeda and the Global War on Terrorism." *Studies in Conflict and Terrorism* 27, no. 6 (2004): 549–60.

Huntington, Samuel P. "Transnational Organizations in World Politics." *World Politics* 25, no. 3 (1973): 333–68.

International Crisis Group. "Indonesia: Jemaah Islamiyah's Current Status." Jakarta and Brussels: International Crisis Group, 3 May 2007.

——. "Terrorism in Indonesia: Noordin's Networks." Jakarta and Brussels: International Crisis Group, 5 May 2006.

——. "Recycling Militants in Indonesia: Darul Islam and the Australian Embassy Bombing." Jakarta: International Crisis Group, 22 February 2005.

——. "Philippines Terrorism: The Role of Militant Islamic Converts." Jakarta and Brussels: International Crisis Group, 19 December 2005.

——. "Jemaah Islamiyah in Southeast Asia: Damaged but Still Dangerous." Jakarta: International Crisis Group, 26 August 2003.

——. "Indonesia Backgrounder: How the Jemaah Islamiyah Terrorist Network Operates." Jakarta: International Crisis Group, 11 August 2002.

——. "Al Qaeda in Southeast Asia: The Case of the 'Ngruki Network' In Indonesia." Jakarta: International Crisis Group, 8 August 2002.

International Maritime Organization. "AIS transponders" London: International Maritime Organization, 2002.

Jackson, Brian. "Groups, Networks, or Movements: A Command-and-Control-Driven Approach to Classifying Terrorist Organizations and Its Application to Al Qaeda." *Studies in Conflict and Terrorism* 29, no. 3 (2006): 241–62.

Jackson, Brian A., John C. Baker, Kim Cragin, John Parachini, Horacio R. Trujillo, and Peter Chalk. *Aptitude for Destruction.* Vol. 2: *Case Studies of Organizational Learning in Five Terrorist Groups.* Santa Monica, CA: RAND, 2005.

Jeyaraj, D. B. S. "The Taking of Elephant Pass." *Frontline,* 13–26 May 2000.

Jihad, Abu. *Gam Hasan Tiro Pembantai Bangsa Aceh.* Jakarta: Titian Ilmu Insani, 2001.

Kaparino, Yelas. "Modus Lama Yang Baru Tercium." *Pilars,* 9–15 February 2004, 8–10.

Kejaksaan Negeri Jakarta Selatan. "Surat Dakwaan Atas Nama Terdakwa Mohd. Rais Al. Edi Indra Al. Iskandar Al. Ryan Arifin Al. Fendi Al. Roni Bin Rusdi Bin Hamid." Jakarta: Kejaksaan Negeri Jakarta Selatan, 4 January 2004.

Kejaksaan Tinggi DKI Jakarta. "Berita Acara Pendapat Tersangka Muzahar Muhtar Alias Taslim Alias Musa." Jakarta: Kejaksaan Tinggi DKI Jakarta, 3 August 1987.

———. "Berita Acara Pemeriksaan Tersangka Muzahar Muhtar Alias Taslim Alias Musa." Jakarta: Kejaksaan Tinggi DKI Jakarta, 20 September 1986.

———. "Berita Acara Pemeriksaan Tersangka Muzahar Muhtar Alias Taslim Alias Musa." Jakarta: Kejaksaan Tinggi DKI Jakarta, 12 September 1986.

———. "Berita Acara Pemeriksaan Saksi K. Jerunt (?) Adnan Al. Aos Firdaus Al. Haman (?) Syaiful Rahman Bin Mohamad Adnan." Jakarta: Kejaksaan Tinggi DKI Jakarta, 11 September 1986.

———. "Berita Acara Pemeriksaan Saksi Sarjono Al. Harun Al. Rasyid Al. Muhtar Suroso Al. Salamun." Jakarta: Kejaksaan Tinggi DKI Jakarta, 2 September 1986.

———. "Berita Acara Pemeriksaan Tersangka Muzahar Muhtar Alias Taslim Alias Musa." Jakarta: Kejaksaan Tinggi DKI Jakarta, 26 August 1986.

Kell, Tim. *The Roots of Acehnese Rebellion, 1989–1992.* Ithaca, New York: Southeast Asian Program, Cornell University, 1995.

Kenney, Michael. *From Pablo to Osama: Trafficking and Terrorist Networks, Government Bureaucracies, and Competitive Adaptation.* University Park: Pennsylvania State University Press, 2007.

Kepolisian Daerah Bali. "Berkas Perkara Amrozi Bin H. Nurhasyim (No. Pol. BP/01/I/2003/Dit Serse)." Denpasar: Direktorat Reskrim, Kepolisian Daerah Bali, 4 January 2003.

———. "Berita Acara Pemeriksaan Ali Ghufron Als. Mukhlas." Denpasar: Direktorat Reserse, Kepolisian Daerah Bali, 30 December 2002.

———. "Berita Acara Pemeriksaan Ali Ghufron Als. Mukhlas." Denpasaar: Direktorat Reserse, Kepolisian Daerah Bali, 29 December 2002.

———. "Berita Acara Pemeriksaan Ali Ghufron Als. Mukhlas." Denpasar: Direktorat Reserse, Kepolisian Daerah Bali, 20 December 2002.

———. "Berita Acara Pemeriksaan Ali Ghufron Als. Mukhlas." Denpasar: Direktorat Reserse, Kepolisian Daerah Bali, 14 December 2002.

———. "Berita Acara Pemeriksaan Ali Ghufron Als. Mukhlas." Direktorat Reserse, Kepolisian Daerah Bali, 13 December 2002.

Kepolisian Negara Republic Indonesia. "Berita Acara Pemeriksaan Wan Min Wan Mat." Jakarta: Badan Reserse Kriminal, Kepolisian Negara Republik Indonesia, 8 January 2003.

———. "Sampul Berkas Perkara, No. Pol.: BP/364/XII/2002/Serse." Batam: Kepolisian Negara Republik Indonesia Daerah Riau, Kota Besar Barelang, 20 December 2002.

———. "Berita Acara Pemeriksaan (Tersangka) Abdul Azis Bin Sihabudin Al. Abu Umar Al. Imam Samudra Al. Fais Yunshar Heri Al. Hendri Al. Kudama." Batam: Kepolisian Negara Republik Indonesia, Daerah Riau, Kota Besar Barelang, 27 November 2002.

———. "Berita Acara Pemeriksaan Faiz Bin Abu Bakar Bafana." Jakarta: Korps Reserse Polri, Kepolisian Negara Republik Indonesia, 22 October 2002.

———. "Surat Pernyataan Ja'afar Bin Mistooki." Singapore: Kepolisian Negara Republik Indonesia, 4 September 2002.

———. "Surat Pernyataan Hashim Bin Abbas." Singapore: Kepolisian Negara Republik Indonesia, 30 March 2002.

King, Gary, and Langche Zang. "Improving Forecasts of State Failure." *World Politics* 53, no. 4 (2001): 623–58.

Kliot, Nurit, and David Newman, eds. *Geopolitics at the End of the Twentieth Century: The Changing World Political Map.* London: Frank Cass, 2000.

Krasner, Stephen D. *Sovereignty: Organized Hypocrisy.* Princeton: Princeton University Press, 1999.

——. "Power Politics, Institutions, and Transnational Relations." In *Bringing Transnational Relations Back In: Non-State Actors, Domestic Structures, and International Institutions,* ed. Thomas Risse-Kappen, 257–79. Cambridge: Cambridge University Press, 1995.

Langewiesche, William. *The Outlaw Sea.* New York: North Point Press, 2004.

Lesser, Ian O., Bruce Hoffman, John Arquilla, David Ronfeldt, Michele Zanini, and Brian Michael Jenkins. *Countering the New Terrorism.* Santa Monica, CA: RAND, 1999.

Lewis, James A. "The Internet and Terrorism." Proceedings of the 99th Annual Meeting of the American Society for International Law, 2005.

Lia, Brynjar. *Globalisation and the Future of Terrorism: Patterns and Predictions.* London: Routledge, 2005.

Libicki, Martin C., Peter Chalk, and Melanie Sisson. *Exploring Terrorist Targeting Preferences.* Santa Monica, CA: RAND, 2007.

Luft, Gal, and Anne Korin. "Terrorism Goes to Sea." *Foreign Affairs* 83 no. 6 (2004).

Makarenko, Tamara. *The Terror-Crime Nexus.* London: C. Hurst, 2007.

Manoharan, N. "Tigers with Fins: Naval Wing of the LTTE." New Delhi: Institute of Peace & Conflict Studies, 1 June 2005.

McAllister, Brad. "Al Qaeda and the Innovative Firm: Demythologizing the Network." *Studies in Conflict and Terrorism* 27, no. 4 (2004): 297–319.

McCargo, Duncan. *Tearing Apart the Land: Islam and Legitimacy in Southern Thailand.* Ithaca: Cornell University Press, 2008.

McCarthy, John F. "The Demonstration Effect: Natural Resources, Ethnonationalism and the Aceh Conflict." *Singapore Journal of Tropical Geography* 28, no. 3 (2007): 314–33.

Menkhaus, Kenneth. *Somalia: State Collapse and the Threat of Terrorism.* Oxford: Oxford University Press, 2004.

——. "Quasi-States, Nation-Building and Terrorist Safe Havens." *Journal of Conflict Studies* 23, no. 2 (2003): 7–23.

Mentan, Tatah. *Dilemmas of Weak States: Africa and Transnational Terrorism in the Twenty-First Century.* Aldershot, UK: Ashgate, 2004.

Merari, Ariel. "A Classification of Terrorist Groups." *Studies in Conflict and Terrorism* 1, no. 3 (1978): 331–46.

Millard, Mike. *Jihad in Paradise: Islam and Politics in Southeast Asia.* Armonk, NY: M.E. Sharpe, 2004.

Ministry of Home Affairs. "The Jemaah Islamiyah Arrests and the Threat of Terrorism." Singapore: Ministry of Home Affairs, 7 January 2003.

——. "Singapore Government Press Statement on Further Arrests under the Internal Security Act, 19 Sep 2002." Singapore: Ministry of Home Affairs, 19 September 2002.

Mishal, Shaul, and Maoz Rosenthal. "Al Qaeda as a Dune Organization: Toward a Typology of Islamic Terrorist Organizations." *Studies in Conflict and Terrorism* 28, no. 4 (2005): 275–93.

Moorthy, N. Sathiya, K. Venkataramanan, Ashik Bonofer, R. Hariharan, R.S.Vasan, and Dr V Suryanarayan. "The Way Ahead in Sri Lanka." New Delhi: Observer Research Foundation, November 2006.

Murphy, Martin N. *Small Boats, Weak States, Dirty Money: Piracy & Maritime Terrorism in the Modern World.* London: Hurst, 2008.

Murray, Dian H. *Pirates of the South China Coast, 1790–1810.* Stanford: Stanford University Press, 1987.

National Commission on Terrorist Attacks upon the United States. *The 9/11 Commission Report.* Washington, DC: National Commission on Terrorist Attacks upon the United States, 2004.

National Geospatial Intelligence Agency. "Anti-Shipping Activity Message 1998–59." Bethesda, MD: National Geospatial Intelligence Agency, 8 September 1998.

——. "Anti-Shipping Activity Message 1998–33." Bethesda, MD: National Geospatial Intelligence Agency, 17 April 1998.

Naylor, R. T. *Wages of Crime: Black Markets, Illegal Finance, and the Underworld Economy.* Ithaca: Cornell University Press, 2004.

Norwitz, Jeffrey H., ed. *Armed Groups: Studies in National Security, Counterterrorism, and Counterinsurgency.* Newport, RI: U.S. Naval War College, 2008.

Nurhasim, Moch., Abdulla Rahman Patji, Fadjri Alihar, and Lamijo. *Konflik Aceh: Analisis Atas Sebab-Sebab Konflik, Aktor Konflik, Kepentingan Dan Upaya Penyelesaian.* Jakarta: Lembaga Ilmu Pengetahuan Indonesia, 2003.

Office of the Coordinator for Counterterrorism. "Country Reports on Terrorism." Washington, DC: U.S. Department of State, 30 April 2008.

Ohmae, Kenichi. *The Invisible Continent.* New York: HarperBusiness, 2000.

Ong, Graham Gerard. "'Ships Can Be Dangerous Too': Coupling Piracy and Maritime Terrorism in Southeast Asia's Maritime Security Framework." Institute of Southeast Asian Studies Working Paper, Singapore, 2004.

Ong-Webb, Graham Gerard, ed. *Piracy, Maritime Terrorism and Securing the Malacca Straits.* Singapore: Institute of Southeast Asian Studies, 2006.

Penyidik Perkara Pidana Koneksitas. "Sampul Berkas Perkara (No. Pol.: BP/04/XI/2000/ Koneksitas)." Jakarta: Penyidik Perkara Pidana Koneksitas, 16 November 2000.

"Perjalanan Rahasia Demi Setetes Air Kelapa." *AcehKita,* August 2005, 10–11.

Piazza, James A. "Incubators of Terror: Do Failed and Failing States Promote Transnational Terrorism?" *International Studies Quarterly* 52, no. 3 (2008): 469–88.

Pickert, Kate. "The Tamil Tigers." *Time,* 4 January 2009.

Polisi Daerah Nanggroe Aceh Darussalam. "Perkembangan Situasi." Banda Aceh: Polisi Daerah Nanggroe Aceh Darussalam, January 2006.

Rabasa, Angel. *Political Islam in Southeast Asia: Moderates, Radicals and Terrorists* (Adelphi Series). Oxford: Oxford University Press for the International Institute for Strategic Studies, 2003.

Rabasa, Angel, Steven Boraz, Peter Chalk, Kim Cragin, Theodore W. Karasik, Jennifer D. P. Moroney, Kevin A. O'Brien, and John E. Peters. *Ungoverned Territories: Understanding and Reducing Terrorism Risks.* Santa Monica, CA: RAND, 2007.

Rabasa, Angel, and Peter Chalk. *Colombian Labyrinth: The Synergy of Drugs and Insurgency and Its Implications for Regional Stability.* Santa Monica, CA: RAND, 2001.

Rapoport, David C., ed. *Inside Terrorist Organizations.* New York: Columbia University Press, 1988.

Reid, Anthony. *Southeast in the Age of Commerce 1450–1680.* Vol. 2: *Expansion and Crisis.* New Haven: Yale University Press, 1993.

——, ed. *Verandah of Violence: The Background to the Aceh Problem.* Singapore and Seattle: Singapore University Press and the University of Washington Press, 2006.

Ressa, Maria A. *Seeds of Terror.* New York: Free Press, 2003.

Robinson, Geoffrey. "Rawan Is as Rawan Does: The Origins of Disorder in New Order Aceh." *Indonesia* 66 (1998): 127–57.

Rotberg, Robert. "The New Nature of Nation-State Failure." *Washington Quarterly* 25, no. 3 (2002): 85–96.

——, ed. *Battling Terrorism in the Horn of Africa.* Washington, DC: Brookings Institution Press, 2005.

——, ed. *State Failure and State Weakness in a Time of Terror.* Cambridge, MA: World Peace Foundation, 2003.

Santos, Eduardo Ma R. "Piracy and Armed Robbery against Ships: Philippines Perspective." Quezon City: Philippines Center for Transnational Crime, n.d.

Schulze, Kirsten. *The Free Aceh Movement (GAM): Anatomy of a Separatist Organization.* Washington, DC: East-West Center, 2004.

Seawright, Jason, and John Gerring. "Case-Selection Techniques in Case Study Research: A Menu of Qualitative and Quantitative Options." *Political Research Quarterly* 61, no. 2 (2008): 294–308.

"Serangan Alumni Libya." *AcehKita,* August 2005, 32–33.

Sidel, John Thayer. *Riots, Pogroms, Jihad: Religious Violence in Indonesia.* Ithaca: Cornell University Press, 2006.

Singh, Daljit, and Chin Kin Wah, eds. *Southeast Asian Affairs 2003.* Singapore: Institute of Southeast Asian Studies, 2003.

Smith, Paul J., ed. *Terrorism and Violence in Southeast Asia.* Armonk, NY: M.E. Sharpe, 2005.

Stohl, Michael, ed. *The Politics of Terrorism.* New York: CRC Press, 1988.

Stokke, Kristian. "Building the Tamil Eelam State: Emerging State Institutions and Forms of Governance in LTTE-Controlled Areas in Sri Lanka." *Third World Quarterly* 27, no. 6 (2006): 1021–40.

Strange, Susan. *The Retreat of the State: The Diffusion of Power in the World Economy.* New York: Cambridge University Press, 1996.

Sukma, Rizal. *Security Operations in Aceh: Goals, Consequences, and Lessons.* Washington, DC: East-West Center, 2004.

Sulaiman, M. Isa. *Aceh Merdeka: Ideologi, Kepemimpinan Dan Gerakan.* Jakarta: Pustaka al-Kautsar, 2000.

Tagliocozzo, Eric. *Secret Trades, Porous Borders.* New Haven: Yale University Press, 2005.

Takeyh, Ray, and Nikolas Gvosdev. "Do Terrorist Networks Need a Home?" *Washington Quarterly* 25, no. 3 (2002): 97–108.

Thompson, John C., and Joe Turlej. "Other People's Wars: A Review of Overseas Terrorism in Canada." Toronto: MacKenzie Institute, June 2003.

Thomson, Janice E. *Mercenaries, Pirates, and Sovereigns: State-Building and Extraterritorial Violence in Early Modern Europe.* Princeton: Princeton University Press, 1994.

Tosini, Domenico. "Sociology of Terrorism and Counterterrorism: A Social Science Understanding of Terrorist Threat." *Sociology Compass* 1, no. 2 (2007): 664–81.

Volkov, Vadim. *Violent Entrepreneurs: The Use of Force in the Making of Russian Capitalism.* Ithaca: Cornell University Press, 2002.

Walt, Vivienne. "Cocaine Country." *Time,* June 27, 2007.

Walter, Barbara, and Andrew Kydd. "Strategies of Terrorism." *International Security* 31, no. 1 (2006): 49–80.

Warren, James. *Pirates, Prostitutes and Pullers: Explorations in the Ethno- and Social History of Southeast Asia.* Crawley, Western Australia: University of Western Australia Press, 2008.

——. *Iranun and Balangingi.* Singapore: Singapore University Press, 2002.

Williams, Phil. "Transnational Criminal Organisations and International Security." *Survival* 36, no. 1 (1994): 96–113.

Wright-Neville, David. "Dangerous Dynamics: Activists, Militants and Terrorists in Southeast Asia." *Pacific Review* 17, no. 1 (2004): 27–46.

Yunanto, S., Sri Nuryanti, R. Farhan Effendi, and Jamaluddin F. Hasyim. *Militant Islamic Movements in Indonesia and South-East Asia.* Jakarta: Friedrich-Ebert-Stiftung, 2003..

Zhang, Sheldon X., and Ko-chin Lin. "The Chinese Connection: Cross-Border Drug Trafficking between Myanmar and China." Washington, DC: U.S. Department of Justice, 2007.

INTERVIEWS

Acehnese Businessman, Kuala Lumpur, January 2006.
Buddhist Pandita, Jakarta, June 2004.
Buddhist Pandita and Chinese-Indonesian Businessmen, Cipayung, Bogor, Indonesia, July 2005.
Capt. Noel Choong, Head, International Maritime Bureau-Kuala Lumpur, Kuala Lumpur, July 2005.
Chinese-Indonesian Businessmen, Batam, Indonesia, August 2005.
Chinese-Indonesian Smuggler, Batam, Indonesia, August 2005.
Counterterrorism Official, Indonesian Government, Jakarta, September 2005.
Counterterrorism Police Official, Jakarta, September 2005.
Criminology Professor/National Police Advisor, Jakarta, September 2005.
Ethnic Conflict Researcher, Jakarta, July 2005.
Foreign Company Executive, Jakarta, September 2005.
Former Jemaah Islamiyah Regional Leader, Jakarta, December 2005.
GAM Negotiator, Banda Aceh, January 2006.
Government-Linked Economist, Jakarta, July 2005.
International NGO Researcher on Terrorism and Insurgency, Singapore, April 2005.
Magazine Reporter, Jakarta, July 2005.
Malaysian Counter-Terrorism Official, Kuala Lumpur, December 2005.
Maritime Think Tank Researcher, Johor Bahru, Malaysia, May 2005.
Official, Hong Kong Shipowners' Association, Hong Kong, October 2005.
Official, International Maritime Bureau, Kuala Lumpur, May 2005.
Owner, Shipping Company, Singapore, November 2005.
Philippines Government Negotiator with the MILF, Manila, December 2005.
Philippines Military Intelligence Officer, Manila, December 2005.
Philippines National Security Council Official, Manila, December 2005.
Philippines Police Intelligence Analysts, Manila, December 2005.
Retired Customs Official, Jakarta, September 2005.
Retired Royal Malaysian Navy Admiral, Kuala Lumpur, December 2005.
Riau Islands Provincial Maritime Police Official, Batam, Indonesia, November 2005.
Riau Islands Provincial Police Official, Batam, Indonesia, November 2005.
Singaporean External Intelligence Officials, Singapore, October 2005.
Singaporean Internal Security Officials, Singapore, November 2005.
Singaporean Police Official, Singapore, July 2005.
Think Tank Researcher on GAM, Jakarta, September 2005.
Think Tank Researcher on Indonesian Politics, Jakarta, September 2005.
Think Tank Researcher on Piracy and Smuggling, Kuala Lumpur, July 2005.
U.S. Government Official, Medan, January 2006.

Index